CULTURAL STRATEGY

CULTURAL STRATEGY
Using Innovative Ideologies to Build Breakthrough Brands

DOUGLAS HOLT AND
DOUGLAS CAMERON

OXFORD
UNIVERSITY PRESS

OXFORD

UNIVERSITY PRESS

Great Clarendon Street, Oxford OX2 6DP

Oxford University Press is a department of the University of Oxford.
It furthers the University's objective of excellence in research, scholarship,
and education by publishing worldwide in

Oxford New York

Auckland Cape Town Dar es Salaam Hong Kong Karachi
Kuala Lumpur Madrid Melbourne Mexico City Nairobi
New Delhi Shanghai Taipei Toronto

With offices in

Argentina Austria Brazil Chile Czech Republic France Greece
Guatemala Hungary Italy Japan Poland Portugal Singapore
South Korea Switzerland Thailand Turkey Ukraine Vietnam

Oxford is a registered trade mark of Oxford University Press
in the UK and in certain other countries

Published in the United States
by Oxford University Press Inc., New York

© Douglas Holt and Douglas Cameron 2010

The moral rights of the authors have been asserted
Database right Oxford University Press (maker)

First published 2010

British Library Cataloguing in Publication Data

Data available

Library of Congress Cataloging in Publication Data

Data available

Typeset by SPI Publisher Services, Pondicherry, India
Printed in Great Britain
on acid-free paper by
Clays Ltd, St Ives plc

ISBN 978–0–19–958740–7

1 3 5 7 9 10 8 6 4 2

For Ali and Kaya

CONTENTS

Part 3: Organizing for Cultural Innovation

PREFACE

We began this book in 2002, as we were finishing up the manuscript for *How Brands Become Icons: The Principles of Cultural Branding.* In that earlier book, we developed a new cultural approach to brand strategy. Our goal then was to transform the practice of brand management, challenging the psychology-driven model that had gained favor in the 1970s. As we used our model to develop brand strategies for a wide range of companies, we soon realized that we had sidestepped the most powerful application of our cultural approach—innovation. Cultural strategy offers a distinctive way to identify major new marketplace opportunities and, then, guides managers on how to craft their offering to take advantage. So it is a particularly valuable tool for starting up new businesses, or for reviving moribund brands. Thus we designed this research project to develop a new socio-cultural model for market innovation, which offers a different emphasis from and significant advancements beyond the cultural branding model that we proposed in the first book.

When we explored the most influential innovation models in the management literature, we found the same restrictive intellectual parameters that we had encountered in the marketing literature—except this time the myopia was a result of the domination of economics rather than psychology. The leading innovation models all assume that markets work only in the way that they are described in basic economics textbooks, where innovation is driven by what we call "better mousetraps." These models ignore that innovation proceeds at the cultural level, not just the nuts-and-bolts level of the physical product or service. Likewise, these models ignore history and societal change. Yet the innovations we have studied in our research and worked on in our consulting projects all take advantage of emergent opportunities caused by such changes. The cultural strategy model that we develop in this book addresses this gap.

Academic innovation models are often criticized for constructing post-hoc explanations of business successes that are of little prescriptive use for real-world innovation efforts. Management books seduce the reader with compelling success stories, but then fail to deliver value-added management tools.[1] We have taken this critique seriously in writing *Cultural Strategy* (which is one reason it took us eight years to complete the project!). We developed cultural innovation theory (Part 1 of the book) using careful academic research. Then we spent another five years improving and refining the model, through a great deal of trial and error in the marketplace, to ensure that it works well as a powerful strategy tool, not just a post-hoc celebration of breakthrough businesses. We took on a variety of consulting projects and co-founded a brand communications firm, Amalgamated, to put our theory to work. In Part 2 of the book, we draw upon four case studies from our work at Amalgamated to detail the cultural strategy framework and cultural research toolkit that we have created through these ongoing applications. These cases illustrate how the cultural strategy model can create success stories, not just explain them.

We were surprised to discover that most of the blue-chip consumer goods companies that we worked with, while excellent at the day-to-day management of existing business, had little capacity for cultural innovation. Managers bemoaned the fact that, despite their huge advantages in resources and market power, tiny start-ups continually beat them to the innovation punch. So a second focus of our research became to explain why this is: what keeps large consumer-marketing companies from innovating? And what sort of alternative organizational approach nurtures cultural innovation? In the last part of the book, we address this crucial organizational question.

A Note on Theory and Method

We developed the ideas in this book over the past eight years using a "laboratory" approach. Our research goal was threefold: first to develop a cultural theory of innovation, then to adapt the theory to serve as a practical framework for strategy development, and finally to prescribe how companies should organize to do cultural innovation. To build cultural innovation theory, we conducted academic research on historic cases of cultural innovation—what we call brand genealogies. Our analyses are informed by socio-cultural theories central to academic disciplines that have had little prior influence on innovation theory, such as history, politics, media studies, cultural sociology, cultural anthropology, and geography. We used a comparative case theory-building methodology, which is a common technique in academic research in management and the social sciences. The details of the brand genealogy method and comparative case theory development are explained in *How Brands Become Icons*. Concurrently, we launched an academic investigation into the organizational structuring of cultural innovation, which required that we push our case research to a much more detailed level, reconstructing organizational details of eleven pioneering innovations.

In our consulting and brand communications work, we adapted these ideas to formulate a cultural strategy model that could be used to build new businesses and revitalize dormant ones. As we applied our ideas in more than forty client projects, we were able to improve our academic theory and transform it into a systematic strategy discipline.

We have written this book in an accessible style so that it can be a useful guide for managers, entrepreneurs, and activists. But this book is also a work of applied academic theory that stems from an intellectually vibrant marketing discipline called Consumer Culture Theory (CCT). While not yet well known outside the academy, the CCT literature has generated some of the most exciting and sophisticated ideas on marketing and consumption in recent years.[2]

For the Nike case, we relied on the extensive documentation of Nike, including oral histories, archived at the Smithsonian Museum in Washington, DC. For the Marlboro case, we analyzed the entire collection of Marlboro advertising held in the Library of Congress archives, as well as the oral history accounts of the campaign offered by Phillip Morris and Leo Burnett executives, also collected by the library. The Brown-Forman Company graciously provided access to its extensive archives for the Jack Daniel's case, as did Patagonia. We became intimately familiar with Ben & Jerry's through our work over the past seven years as the company's agency of record. The Starbucks and Vitaminwater cases relied upon secondary materials in the public domain.

The organization cases that provide the empirical foundation for Part 3 required particularly intensive research. For each of the eleven cases, we requested full access to archival materials and to the key participants involved in the innovation. We conducted intensive interviews with all the key protagonists at both the company and its creative partners, and studied all the meeting minutes, planning documents, and research reports we could gather from their archives. For these cases we engaged in forensic research to reconstruct the sequence of events that led to the cultural innovation.

Notes

1 For example, see "Book Review: Blue Ocean Strategy," *UNITAR E-Journal* (June 2007), http://ejournal.unitar.edu.my/index.php?option=com_content&view=article&id=87: blueocean&catid=40:vol-3-no-2-2007&Itemid=55
2 See Eric J. Arnould and Craig J. Thompson "Consumer Culture Theory (CCT): Twenty Years of Research," *Journal of Consumer Research*, 31 (2005).

ACKNOWLEDGMENTS

We are most grateful to the many executives who participated in the research we report in this book, as well as the many collaborators and clients with whom we have worked as we developed our cultural strategy model. For the case research reported in Parts 1 and 3, we are greatly indebted to: Bob Rockey, Carl Von Buskirk, Derek Robson, John Hegarty, Nigel Bogle, Tim Lindsay, Jim Carroll, Gwyn Jones, Philippa Crane, Tony Davidson, Kim Papworth, Russell Ramsay, Kenny Wilson, and the rest of the team at The Levi Strauss Co. and BBH; Tony Hillyer, Andrew Marsden, Steve Henry, Al Young, Trevor Robinson, Chas Bayfield, Jon Leach, Richard Huntington, David O'Hanlon, and the rest of the team at Tango/Britvic and HHCL; Gordon Harton, Kathy Collins, Rob White, Bruce Tait, Dodie Subler, Greg Hahn, Harvey Marco, Dave Lubars, Bob Moore, and the rest of the Lee team at VF Corporation and Fallon; Jude Hammerle, Richard Kirshenbaum, Rosemary Ryan, Risa Mickenberg, Amy Nicholson, Nick Shore, Maryanne Farrell, and the rest of the team at Snapple and Kirshenbaum & Bond; Neal Tiles, Eric Silver, Colin Mitchell, Jason Gaboriau, Dan Morales, Rosie Bardales, and the rest of the team at FOX Sports and Cliff Freeman & Partners; Walt Freese, Dave Stever, Lee Holden, and the rest of the team at Ben & Jerry's; Charles Stone III, Bob Lackey, Gary Grote, Stevens Jackson, Marty Kohr, Jim Crimmins, John Greening, and the rest of the Bud team at Anheuser-Busch and DDB; Steve Wilhite, Lance Jensen, Ron Lawner, Alan Pafenbach, Bob Silagi, Dave Weist, Fran Kelly, John Castle, and the rest of the team at Volkswagen and Arnold; Jeff Goodby, Steve Dildarian, Jeff Manning, Sue Smith, Leslie Kennedy, and the rest of the Got Milk team at Goodby Silverstein & Partners; Jeff Hicks, Alex Bogusky, Rich Steinberg, Jack Pitney, Kerri Martin, Kevin Phillips, and the rest of the team at MINI

USA and Crispin Porter & Bogusky; Hank Perlman, Allan Broce, Rick McQuiston, Jerry Cronin, and the rest of the team at ESPN and Wieden + Kennedy; and Jochen Zeitz, Antonio Bertone, Jay Piccola, Neil Beeson, Peter Mahrer, Paul Gautier, Malcolm McDowell, and the rest of the team at Puma. We also thank those participants who preferred to remain anonymous.

The four applications that we profile in Part 2 were the collective products of four cultural studios. We use the authorial *we* in reporting on these cases, which applies not only to ourselves, but to all of the studio members whose contributions were crucial. In particular, we want to acknowledge our key cultural studio partner at Amalgamated, Jason Gaboriau, who managed the development of the creative work that we describe in these cases. For their pivotal roles in the Fuse relaunch, we would like to acknowledge Marc Juris, Mary Corigliano, Tommy Noonan, Laura Potsic, Dan Morales, Kim Jacobs, Charles Rosen, and Dave Carson. Dave played a particularly critical role, spanning from consultant to client to creative visionary. For their central roles in Fat Tire's cultural innovation, we wish to acknowledge Kim Jordan, Greg Owsley, Jamie Mastin, Bill Hepp, Austin McKenna, Jake Scott, Chris Soos, and Rick Lawley. For their critical role in developing Clearblue's breakthrough Pee-Ship campaign, we would like to acknowledge Julie Godon, Hanna Salminen, Fedora Leon, Ryan Daly, and Jon Yasgur. Key collaborators in the transformation of Working Today into Freelancers Union included Sharon Slaughter, Dan Morales, and, of course, Sarah Horowitz, the organization's inspiring founder.

We are most grateful for the highly professional and diligent work done behind the scenes by many people at Oxford University Press in steering this book to publication. In particular David Musson, Emma Lambert, Carol Bestley, and Phil Henderson provided crucial and timely guidance and support throughout the process. As well, we would like to thank Susan Rabiner for astute early advice on the best route to publish this book.

Our comrades at Amalgamated were instrumental in allowing us to complete this research. In particular, our partners Jason Gaboriau and Charles Rosen graciously tolerated the many mini-sabbaticals required to complete what often seemed like the project-with-no-end. Other colleagues who created time for our work and helped push our thinking include Karen Evans, Colin Mitchell, Margaret Rimsky, Jonathan Leong, Ed Tracy, Scott Karambis, Faun Chapin, and Fiona McBride. Part of this research was funded by the Harvard Business School, way back in 2002–4. For their ace research assistance on individual cases, we thank Mike Genett (ESPN), Mark Renella (Marlboro), and Ed Tracy (Vitaminwater). And we also thank John Cameron for his help in transcribing hundreds of hours of interviews. The Oxford MBA Class of 2010 provided useful feedback on drafts of many chapters, as did ace designer-thrill jockey Bill Donavan.

Finally, we would like to thank our friends, partners, and family members who have supported us over the eight years it took us to finish this project. Tuba Üstüner, Ian Cameron, and Sarah Cameron provided valuable insights, feedback, and editorial suggestions along with their moral support. Nicole Salm's smiles, sense of humor, and companionship on Rocky Mountain hikes and Brooklyn bicycle rides made writing the book so much more pleasant for Doug C. We started this project when Doug H. was wondering whether he would ever get up the nerve to become a father. *Cultural Strategy's* long-awaited birth follows the arrival of two charming young boys—Ali and Kaya—to whom this book is dedicated.

Douglas Holt
Salida, Colorado
Douglas Cameron
Brooklyn, New York

April 2010

1

Rethinking Blue Oceans

Market innovation has long been dominated by the world view of engineers and economists—build a better mousetrap and the world will take notice. This functional point of view certainly has merit. But, because it is the *only* way that we approach innovation, the better-mousetraps approach has had the effect of eclipsing a very different innovation world view—champion a *better ideology* and the world will take notice as well.

The market power that can be garnered by advancing innovative ideology has long been understood outside the business world. For politicians, artists, and social activists, innovative ideology is the name of the game. Think about Gloria Steinhem or Ann Coulter, Martin Luther King or Nelson Mandela, John Wayne or Bono, Ronald Reagan or Hugo Chavez, Greenpeace or Focus on the Family. In fact, the phrase "build a better mousetrap" would not be so familiar if its author, Ralph Waldo Emerson, had not advanced an immensely influential romantic spin on American individualism.

These individuals and groups became immensely influential by advancing innovative ideology, and thereby developing intensely loyal followers. The same phenomenon is found everywhere in consumer markets. For example, farmer–cookbook–author–television host Hugh Fearnley-Whittingstall, author Michael Pollan, the international Slow Food movement, and the American grocery retailer Whole Foods Market, amongst others, have transformed food consumption for the upper middle class. These cultural innovators have championed an alternative approach to agriculture and food as an ideological challenge to the dominant scientific–industrial food ideology. They have brought to life the value, even necessity, of winding the clock back to some sort of pre-industrial food culture in such a way that it is irresistible for the upper middle class in the United States, the United Kingdom, and other countries. Relying upon what we term *myth* and *cultural codes*, these cultural innovators have massively transformed food preferences. We call this phenomenon *cultural innovation*.

Cultural innovation has been ignored by management strategists, despite its pivotal role in launching and reinvigorating any number of billion-dollar businesses. The Body Shop, Ben & Jerry's, Marlboro, Method, Whole Foods, Dove, Marlboro, Harley-Davidson, the Mini, Starbucks, Coca-Cola, Levi's, and Snapple, to name a few, have all profited from cultural innovations. When these enterprises advanced a more compelling ideology—leapfrogging the staid cultural orthodoxies of their categories—consumers beat a path to their doors. We assert that, in ongoing conversations to improve the management of innovation, the cultural dimension of what we consume deserves a prominent seat at the table.

Blue Oceans as Better Mousetraps

Launching "the next big thing"—the innovative idea that resonates powerfully with consumers and takes off to establish a profitable new business—is the holy grail of managers and entrepreneurs alike. Strategy experts have been offering advice on how to identify and exploit such opportunities for decades. Fifteen years ago, Gary Hamel and C. K. Prahalad offered a pioneering call to arms: to "create the markets of tomorrow," they urged managers to focus on industry foresight and strategic intent. To avoid getting bogged down in an established market's internecine tactical battles, they encouraged managers to stake out new market space—what they famously termed *white space*—in order to create and dominate emerging opportunities.[1] More than a decade later, W. Chan Kim and Renée Mauborgne introduced a new metaphor *blue ocean*—to dramatize a very similar idea.[2] Existing markets are characterized by dog-eat-dog fights to outdo competitors on a conventional set of benefits. Incumbents rely on incremental changes in product and tactical marketing to fight over thin margins. This is a *red ocean*. In order to develop future-leading businesses, companies must reject the conventions of the category to craft "value innovations" that have no direct competition—blue oceans. These marching orders have inspired many managers and entrepreneurs. But what kinds of future opportunities should we be looking for? And how does one actually go about spotting these opportunities and designing new concepts that will take advantage of the blue oceans? Innovation experts have offered us two paths.

Technological Innovation

For most innovation experts, future opportunities mean one thing— the commercialization of new technologies. Technology-driven innov- ations are the stars of business. From historic innovations such as the light bulb, the telephone, the television, the Model T, and the personal computer to recent stars like the iPod, Amazon.com, Blackberry, Viagra, and Facebook, the commercialization of breakthrough tech- nologies has clearly had a huge impact on business and society. In *The Innovator's Dilemma* and subsequent books, Clayton Christensen argues that new technologies allow companies to design "disruptive innovations" that transform their categories. Disruptive innovations are products and services that trump the value delivered by existing category offerings because they are cheaper, more useful, more reliable, or more convenient. Disruptive innovations dramatically alter the conventional value proposition of an existing category, often attracting new or underserved customers, or even inventing a new category.[3]

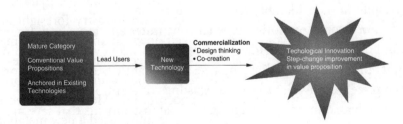

Figure 1. Blue Ocean Type 1: Technological Innovation

Mix-and-Match Innovation

In recent years, a "mix-and-match" approach to innovation has become influential. In the view of Kim and Mauburgne, blue oceans are untapped opportunities that can be exploited through unique value combinations that had not yet been formulated. In order for companies to offer customers a significantly better value proposition, they must methodically break the rules of their existing category: subtracting and enhancing conventional benefits, as well as importing new ones from other categories.

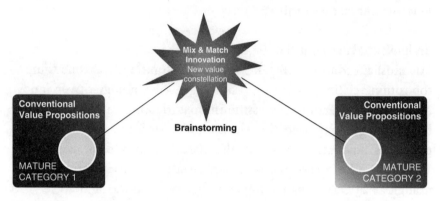

Figure 2. Blue Ocean Type 2: Mix & Match Innovation

For instance, in *Blue Ocean Strategy*'s lead example, the authors describe how Cirque du Soleil created a blue ocean by borrowing from theater and Broadway musicals to reinvent the circus. Andrew Hargadon's *How Breakthroughs Happen* and *The Medici Effect* by Frans Johansson both advocate a similar idea—the unexpected mixing and matching of existing features and technologies across different categories, leading to a unique constellation of benefits for the consumer.[4]

Despite the considerable differences between these two models, they rely upon a common notion of what constitutes an innovation. Innovation boils down to providing a step change in the value proposition (or, if you prefer marketing language, significantly better benefits for a given price). Innovations beat out existing competition on the tangible benefits that count in the category: medical instruments that save more lives, cars that run longer with higher miles per gallon and less carbon emissions, cell phones that have more applications, hard drives that hold more data and are cheaper and smaller and more reliable. In other words, these two better-mousetraps innovation models are based upon the world view of the economist and the engineer—a world in which it is only the material properties of what we buy that is important. Blue oceans exist where there is latent demand for products and services with truly novel whiz-bang features.

Rethinking Blue Oceans

Curiously, this is not how consumers see it. Consumers—the ultimate arbiters of market innovation efforts—often find offerings to be innovative even though they seem quite pedestrian from a product-design standpoint. It turns out that blockbuster new businesses do not necessarily require radically new features that fundamentally alter the value proposition.[5]

Consider beer. From a better-mousetraps perspective, the American beer market has long been a mature category—a notoriously red ocean that resists innovation. Many product innovation efforts have been tried, and the vast majority have failed despite their seeming combinatorial creativity. Brewers have tried to follow blue-ocean strategy for many years. Combining concepts across categories, they have launched beer + energy drinks (Sparks, Be), beer + tequila (Tequiza), beer + soft drinks (Zima), and so on. All these supposed innovations were failures in the mass market.

Now let us look at the beer category from an ideological viewpoint. While the product—the beer itself—has seen only minor changes over the past thirty years, the category has been very dynamic in terms of the cultural expressions that consumers value. Incumbents have been pushed aside by new entrants with better ideology. In the popular price tier, Budweiser took off in the 1980s with branding that showcased men working cheerfully and industriously in artisanal trades, men whom Budweiser beer saluted with a baritone-voiced announcer proclaiming "This Bud's for you!" The results were startling. The beer brand quickly became the go-to choice for working-class American men. By the middle of the decade, Budweiser was unchallenged as the most desirable beer in the country.

By the early 1990s, Bud's ideology had lost resonance and the business sank, to be replaced by its stable mate. Bud Light took off in the 1990s to become by far the dominant American beer brand, speeding by the brand that had pioneered light beer as a product innovation, Miller Lite. Bud Light tastes little different from Miller Lite. Rather what was different was a decade's worth of silly Peter Pan stories of men who engage in all sorts of juvenile high jinks, which conjured up a new kind of rebellious masculinity for adult men.

At the same time, Corona became the leading import brand, rocketing ahead of the long dominant Heineken, by offering a new way of thinking about how to relax with a beer—escaping the American white-collar sweatshop to do absolutely nothing on a Mexican beach. These beers were me-too product offerings, not original at all as mousetraps. But, as brands, they offered very innovative cultural expressions that resonated perfectly with the ideological needs of their target.

Or consider soft drinks—a category that would seem to be one of the most masochistic red oceans around. The two leading soft-drinks marketers in the world, PepsiCo and The Coca-Cola Company, have invested hundreds of millions of dollars to innovate their way out of this mature category. Both companies have aggressively pursued mix-and-match concepts to create new value propositions. For example, The Coca-Cola Company has made big bets on Coke Blak (coca-cola + coffee) and Enviga (a "calorie-burning" green tea). Both of these ambitious efforts—supposedly targeting distinctive consumer "need states"—have failed to break through.

Likewise, many drinks entrepreneurs have tried their hand at mix-and-match strategies, and also with little evidence of success. A basic problem with undertaking blue-ocean-styled product innovation in mature categories is that it forces the innovator to pursue ever smaller niches—aimed at ever narrower "need states"—to carve out a truly new offering. For example, some British entrepreneurs got their food engineers to concoct Alibi—billed as "the world's first pretox drink"—to serve a very focused niche of young partiers who might be interested in downing a prophylactic drink to prepare them for a weekend binge. A blue puddle does not an ocean make.

While the food scientists were struggling to make oddball mix-and-match drinks combinations, cultural entrepreneurs were playing an entirely different game. They pursued radical innovations in culture, not product. We recount in *How Brands Become Icons* the cultural restagings of Snapple and Mountain Dew, two spectacularly successful cultural innovations in the 1990s. In Chapter 7, we analyze Vitaminwater—another startlingly successful drinks brand based upon cultural innovation.

We find this same phenomenon—enormous and durable new businesses created out of what innovation experts deem to be red oceans—to be widespread across many categories around the world. Georgia Coffee—a chilled ready-to-serve canned coffee, one of many on the market in Japan—became The Coca-Cola Company's most profitable business when it offered a pep talk to Japan's salarymen as the economic meltdown of the "forgotten decade" threatened their status in Japanese society. The British soft drink Tango transformed from an also-ran brand to a powerful challenger to Coke and Pepsi—not by inventing some non-traditional flavor or through some new-fangled packaging innovation, but by delivering a potent new cultural viewpoint. The soft drink playfully appropriated "lad culture" to propose a nationalistic rebuttal to the American brands.

More recently, in the United Kingdom, Innocent Drinks did the same thing. The market for alternative natural fruit smoothies had long been established in the USA, pioneered by Odwalla (est. 1980) and Fresh Samantha (est. 1992). The big UK grocers such as Marks & Spencer, Sainsbury's, and Tesco imported the concept and developed their own versions. Innocent grabbed hold of this well-established mousetrap and added a heavy dose of leading-edge ideology that was beginning to resonate widely amongst British middle-class consumers. Innocent asserted through its package design—featuring a childlike anthropo-morphized apple sporting a halo, and a stripped-down transparent listing of ingredients such as "ingredients = 3 apples + 1 banana + 16 raspberries + 43 blueberries"—that their smoothies were the antithesis of the scientific-industrial foods that big corporations marketed. Innocent easily won over consumers worried about health issues by making a cultural assertion—championing the pre-industrial purity of "only fruit" against drinks full of preservatives and synthetic ingredi-ents. Further, Innocent turned the personal act of drinking a smoothie into a broad environmental statement through a diverse range of provocative guerilla communications efforts, all of which suggested that Innocent was an anti-corporate green company wishing to trans-form the drinks marketplace toward sustainability. The Coca-Cola Company, which had paid $180 million to buy out the ideologically innovative Odwalla in 2001, followed suit by paying $50 million for about 15 percent of Innocent in 2009—a $333 million valuation. Failing at its better-mousetraps innovation strategy, Coca-Cola has had no choice but to acquire ideologically innovative brands at very steep prices.

These businesses have been every bit as innovative as the techno-logical and mix-and-match businesses celebrated by innovation experts. But what was radical about them was what the product stands for—its ideology, which, when staged through myth and cultural codes, becomes a distinctive cultural expression. And these examples are anything but idiosyncratic. The list of cultural innovations that have launched or reinvigorated businesses worth billions goes on and on: Marlboro, Coca-Cola, Levi's, Diesel, Dove, Axe/Lynx, American Express, American Apparel, The Body Shop, Target, Virgin, Pepsi-Cola, Polo, Harley-Davidson, Seventh Generation, Method, Burt's Bees, Brita, Whole Foods, Patagonia, Jack Daniel's, Mountain Dew, Absolut, Starbucks, Volkswagen. Just as important, cultural innovation often serves to turbo-charge better-mousetraps innovation: witness Apple, Google, MINI, Red Bull, JetBlue, and Wikipedia.

Conventional Marketing Creates Red Oceans

We might expect that the discipline of marketing would play a leading role in the development of strategy for cultural innovation. Yet, con-ventional marketing—what we term *mindshare marketing* because it is couched in psychology—emphasizes the day-to-day stewardship of existing businesses and, in so doing, slights innovation.[6]

The Functional Benefits Trap

Depending on the company and category, today's mindshare strategies focus either on "functional benefits" (sometimes termed "rational bene-fits"), or on "emotional benefits," or on both. The functional benefits mode of mindshare marketing was introduced by adman Rosser Reeves in the 1950s, with his *unique selling proposition* (USP), a concept made famous through ad campaigns like M&M's "melts in your mouth, not in your hand." This view came to dominate marketing strategy, propelled by the publication of Ries and Trout's incredibly influential book *Posi-tioning: The Battle for your Mind.*[7] Mindshare marketing relies on an easy and intuitively appealing metaphor: brands succeed when they colonize valued "cognitive territory" in consumer minds. The model directs managers to determine the cognitive "gap": which functional benefit in a given category is most valued by consumers and least dominated by other brands? Targeting the gap, the marketing goal is to stake out a claim to the cognitive association in consumers' minds, then hammer home the connection between the trademark and the benefit claim as simply and consistently and frequently as possible. Over time, the theory maintains, consumers would unconsciously associate the brand with the benefit, and as a result the brand would come to "own" (in a cognitive sense) the benefit.

The functional benefits model is most useful when a product really does command a novel functionality that gives the brand a substantial and durable advantage over competitors. In such instances, the mind-share model simply reinforces what economists have been preaching about reputation effects for decades. Such advantages, however, are hard to come by, and, when a new technology with a truly improved performance is introduced, it is summarily copied by competitors. Incumbent firms like to believe that they are innovation-driven organizations industriously pursuing blue oceans. But, in reality, brand competition is usually mired in the red ocean of what we call "benefits slugfests," where companies try to avoid commoditization by claiming that trivial and ephemeral points of difference are crucial to consumers. As a result, the functional benefits model has become a marketing whipping boy in recent years, with leading experts like David Aaker counseling marketers to avoid the "functional benefits trap."[8]

The Commodity Emotions Trap

Unfortunately, the new style of mindshare marketing has proven to be even more problematic. To avoid the functional benefits trap, many marketers now focus on identifying what they term "emotional benefits," the softer values, thoughts, and feelings that consumers associate with the product, brand, or category. Although the intentions may seem noble and sophisticated, "laddering up" to the consumer's "higher order values," or "probing deeper" to unveil the consumer's "fundamental need-states" and the "brand truth" is anything but. In practice, the result is simply to push for vague abstractions that hold a negligible value for consumers. At least functional benefits forced marketers to remain grounded in the product's material performance. There are no constraints at all for emotional benefits: all emotions are fair game. We are witnessing an emotions arms race in which companies vie to own one of the short list of top *emotion words*.

This process encourages companies to pursue generic "emotional territories" that any brand in any category can claim. Coca-Cola becomes the champion of "happiness," Pepsi becomes the champion of "joy," Fanta becomes the champion of "play," Snapple becomes the champion of "fun." The marketers at Oscar Meyer, the lunch meats and bacon brand, have launched a $50 million advertising campaign consisting entirely of slice-of-life vignettes featuring people being happy while eating Oscar Meyer and the tagline "It Doesn't Get Better than This." The company expects that these ads will "recapture the joy and exuberance" of the brand.[9]

These emotion words blur into a fuzzy sameness. Levi's becomes the champion of "confidence" and "freedom." But so do Lee Jeans and Guess Jeans. For that matter, so do Oxford Health Insurance, Volvo Station Wagons, and Verizon Mobile telephone plans. Only through such a process could Procter & Gamble house a pregnancy test, a washing powder, an oral hygiene brand, a feminine hygiene brand, a line of cosmetics, and an antiperspirant, all of which offer "confidence" or "confidence in results." While the pursuit of emotional benefits has helped many a brand manager avoid the functional benefits trap, the unintentional consequence is to land in an even more strategically bereft space—what we term the *commodity emotions trap*. Emotional benefits render the brand even less distinctive from a consumer's perspective. As with the functional approach, emotional branding drives brands to mimic the cultural orthodoxy of the category. Mindshare marketing not only limits innovation; it creates red oceans.

Ultimately, both the functional and emotional benefits tangents of mindshare marketing are severely limited as innovation tools because they are rooted in psychology. Both approaches imply that marketing is about embedding associations between brand and valued benefits in consumers' minds. As a property of mind, the brand and its benefits are both assumed to be durable and contextless. Mindshare marketers' favored terms for a brand's key benefits—brand essence and brand

DNA—reflect this assumption. Because the strategic core of the brand has no connection to society or history, mindshare marketers push the job of making their brands resonate with consumers onto their creative partners. They are charged with injecting some "trends" or "fame" or "cool" into the brand in an effort to make it relevant.

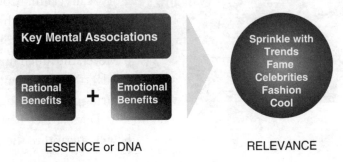

ESSENCE or DNA   RELEVANCE

Figure 3. Mindshare Strategy

Conceiving of brands as a phenomenon of the mind—rather than of society, culture, and politics—means that opportunities for innovation created by historical changes in society are totally ignored. Mindshare marketing can be useful for keeping an existing business in healthy shape in the short run, but it is dysfunctional for pursuing innovation, as well as for ensuring that a brand sustains a leadership position over time. Managers and entrepreneurs are left in the dark as to how to locate and exploit new market opportunities, or revive a failing business that has been made irrelevant by historical changes.

Part 1: Cultural Innovation Theory

How does cultural innovation work? In the first part of this book, we draw upon a decade of academic research to propose a theory of cultural innovation. We have conducted detailed historical analyses of more than two dozen important cultural innovations. We systematic-ally compare our analyses of these different cases to build a theory explaining why these efforts succeeded. In this part, we review seven of these cases: Nike, Jack Daniel's, Ben & Jerry's, Starbucks, Patagonia, Vitaminwater, and Marlboro. Three of these cases—Nike, Starbucks, and Marlboro—are part of the pantheon of breakthrough branding stories that have circulated in management folklore for decades. Our

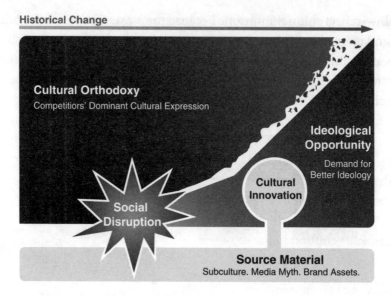

Figure 4. Cultural Innovation Theory

analyses of these cases directly challenge this conventional wisdom. The result is a model that is shown in summary form in Figure 4.

We explain how this model works as we take the reader through these seven analyses, introducing the key concepts along the way. The name of the game in cultural innovation is to deliver an innovative cultural expression. Since cultural expressions consist of an ideology, which is "brought to life" with the right myth and cultural codes, we examine how innovation works across these three core components.

Cultural blue oceans are fundamentally different. From a cultural perspective, blue oceans are defined by latent demand for ideology, not latent demand for functionality. According to technological and mix-and-match models, opportunities are always out there in the world, lying dormant, until the right new technology or creative mix-and-match offering comes along. People always want better functionality. Ideological opportunities, in contrast, are produced by major historical changes that shake up cultural conventions of the category, what we call a social disruption. These shifts unmoor consumers from incumbent brands, and prod them to seek out new alternatives. It is an emergent kind of opportunity that is specific to a historical moment and a particular group of people.

Likewise, the cultural innovations that respond to these opportunities are fundamentally different from better mousetraps. They are composed of specific cultural expressions, which are conveyed by the brand across consumer touchpoints. We demonstrate throughout the book that powerful cultural expressions can be dramatized via product design (Ben & Jerry's, Starbucks, Vitaminwater), print ads (Jack Daniel's), guerrilla stunts (Ben & Jerry's, Fuse), corporate business policies (Ben & Jerry's, Fat Tire, Freelancers Union), retail design (Starbucks), packaging (Starbucks, Vitaminwater), the service encounter (Starbucks), naming (Vitaminwater), outdoor media (Freelancers Union), and television ads (Nike, Marlboro, Clearblue, Fat Tire, Levi's, ESPN). All touchpoints are fair game for cultural innovation.

Ideological opportunities provide one of the most fertile grounds for market innovation. Yet, these opportunities have gone unrecognized because of the extraordinary influence of economics, engineering, and psychology on management thinking. These disciplines, as different as they are, share a common assumption—in order to simplify the world, they purposely ignore cultural context and historical change. These theories remove all the messy bits of human life in order to present a tidy theory that is easy for big companies to work with. We argue that it is in these untidy hard-to-measure parts of social life that some of the greatest innovation opportunities lie.

Part 2: Applying the Cultural Strategy Model

Can cultural innovation become a systematic pursuit? What sort of strategy can guide companies and entrepreneurs to identify and leverage these ideological opportunities? What research methods are most suited to inform this kind of strategy development?

In the past, cultural innovation has been a serendipitous crapshoot—lucky discoveries that are all too rare. Cultural innovation theory opens the door to a novel approach to strategy, which can significantly improve the odds of success. But only if we allow ourselves to rethink what a "strategy" is. Strategy is a blueprint that guides action. But strategy is usually conceived in highly abstract generic terms. In conventional innovation strategies, the more specific and contextual directives are left out because such nuanced details are considered to be outside the domain of strategy. But these abstract strategies are of no use for cultural innovation. Since cultural innovation is about locating a specific historic opportunity and then responding to this opportunity with specific cultural content, cultural strategy must be tailored to these more specific historical and contextual goals. Because cultural strategy directs the details of the brand's cultural expression, it provides considerably more structure and guidance to what has always been the "creative" side of branding—a domain that heretofore has been ruled by the intuition of creative practitioners.

In Part 2, we transpose cultural innovation theory into an actionable six-stage strategic framework—what we call the *cultural strategy model*. Cultural strategy is a detailed blueprint guiding the development of a cultural innovation. We detail a step-by-step approach, which is derived directly from our cultural innovation theory and supported by a systematic toolkit of cultural research methods.

We have used this model to develop cultural strategies for many dozens of clients, including PepsiCo, Brown-Forman, Microsoft, BMW, Bacardi, and The Coca-Cola Company. We have used the cultural strategy model to launch new brands (e.g., Svedka, truTV, Planet Green), to reinvigorate struggling brands (e.g., Coca-Cola, Mike's Hard Lemonade, Big Lots, Qdoba), and to help successful brands sustain their historic cultural leadership (e.g., MINI, Mastercard, Jack Daniel's, Ben & Jerry's, Mountain Dew). In this part, we provide four diverse examples of projects where we have applied cultural strategy to develop brands with innovative cultural expressions: Clearblue pregnancy tests, Fat Tire beer, the Fuse music television network, and the Freelancers Union.

Part 3: Organizing for Cultural Innovation

How should companies and entrepreneurs organize to pursue cultural innovation? How does this form of organizing differ from conventional organization structures? Management experts have long recognized that organizational structures can facilitate or hamper innovation. One of the quandaries that initially motivated this book was the following: why is it that the world's best consumer marketing companies—such as Procter & Gamble, Unilever, and The Coca-Cola Company—routinely fail at cultural innovation? We have found in our research that the innovation processes routinely used by blue-chip companies are actually dysfunctional. Coming up with innovative cultural expressions is a very different task from commercializing a better mousetrap.

In this part, we demonstrate that cultural innovation requires a new mode of organizing. In the first chapter, we develop an organizational critique pinpointing the dysfunctional institutional logic that derails innovation at big companies, which we term the *brand bureaucracy*. In the following two chapters, we use two cases—Levi's 501s in Europe, and ESPN—to detail the alternative organizational structure that facilitates cultural innovation, which we found lurking in all our cultural innovation cases. We term this new organizational form the *cultural studio*.

Social Innovations as Well

Cultural innovation is just as important for social and environmental applications: for example, launching businesses that contribute to environmentally sustainable markets, or for designing new brands that contribute to the economic progress of the global South. While the main focus of the book is commercial applications, much of our current work focuses on developing applications to social innovation. As a precursor to this ongoing work, in this book we include four cases—Ben & Jerry's, Patagonia, Fat Tire, and Freelancers Union—that show how the cultural strategy model can be used by social entrepreneurs and social enterprises working toward social change.

Notes

1. Gary Hamel and C. K. Prahalad, *Competing for the Future* (Boston: Harvard Business School Press, 1994).
2. W. Chan Kim and Renee Mauborgne, *Blue Ocean Strategy* (Boston: Harvard Business School Press, 2005), 4–5.
3. Clayton M. Christensen, *The Innovator's Dilemma* (New York: Collins Business, 2003). Clayton M. Christensen and Michael E. Raynor, *The Innovator's Solution: Creating and Sustaining Successful Growth* (Boston: Harvard Business School Press, 2004).
4. Andrew Hargadon, *How Breakthroughs Happen: The Surprising Truth about How Companies Innovate* (Boston: Harvard Business School Press, 2003); Frans Johansson,

The Medici Effect: What Elephants and Epidemics Can Teach Us about Innovation (Boston: Harvard Business School Press, 2004).

5. Cultural innovation and better-mousetraps innovation are powerful complements. Cultural innovation can lead to extraordinary new business success without significant product innovation, as the examples at the beginning of the chapter illustrate. And, just as important, better mousetraps are much more likely to succeed when combined with cultural innovation. We will argue that new value propositions are far more powerful when harnessed to new ideologies, the two working synergistically to create new businesses and renovate failing ones.

6. We first developed this term in Douglas B. Holt, *How Brands Become Icons: The Principles of Cultural Branding* (Boston: Harvard Business School Press, 2004).

7. Al Ries and Jack Trout, *Positioning: The Battle for your Mind* (New York: Warner Books, 1980).

8. David Aaker, "Beyond Functional Benefits," *Marketing News*, Sept. 30, 2009.

9. Stephanie Clifford, "Oscar Mayer Counts on the Joy, Not the Jingles," *New York Times*, Jan. 14 2010, www.nytimes.com/2010/01/15/business/media/15adco.html?ref=business

Part 1

Cultural Innovation Theory

2

Nike: Reinventing the American Dream

Phil Knight and Bill Bowerman sold their first pair of Nike running shoes in 1971. A decade later, the brand's sales reached $458 million a year. Two decades later, they reached $3 billion. *Business Week* ranked Nike the twenty-sixth most valuable brand in the world in 2009—estimating its worth at more than $13 billion. How did consumers come to value Nike so much compared to its competitors?

Nike is a seminal cultural innovation. Yet, conventional explanations avoid grappling with the cultural aspects of Nike's innovation and, as a result, fail to explain why Nike was so successful. Many experts view Nike as a better-mousetraps poster child: Nike engineered the best shoes and earned a reputation for great performance as a result. But, as we demonstrate, this argument does not align with the historical facts. Nike's famed shoe innovations happened early on and do not coincide with the brand's takeoff. Nike succeeded with innovative cultural expressions, not with innovative products.

Marketing experts give the better-mousetraps explanation a mindshare spin, claiming that Nike succeeded because it colonized a key category benefit—performance—in consumers' minds. But this "explanation" confuses consequence (Nike did indeed become *the* sports performance brand) with cause (a proper explanation must explain how Nike came to dominate this key category benefit). All Nike's competitors also aimed to be the preferred performance brand, but none of them succeeded anything like Nike. So we need to understand what Nike did *differently*: what did Nike do that resonated so powerfully with Americans, and then people around the world, such that they came to perceive that Nike made shoes that performed much better than competitors' shoes? What Nike did was to view "performance" far more expansively than just how well one can dribble down the court, broadly enough to tap into the anxieties and desires of many Americans who were not competitive athletes. Nike proposed that a particular sports myth about performing beyond all expectation provided a powerfully motivating metaphor for the ideological anxieties Americans faced as globalization hit the American job market.

Better-Mousetraps Innovations

Nike did indeed contribute important technical advances to sports-shoe design, but only in the first phase of the company's trajectory. Beginning in the 1960s, a number of entrepreneurial companies subjected athletic shoes for the first time to experimentation with new materials and production techniques, careful testing, and eventually the adaptation of advances in medical science.[1] This was the better-mousetraps phase of innovation in the athletic-shoe category, and it was largely focused on professional and serious amateur athletes—the athlete subcultures that one finds for each sport.

In 1957, Phil Knight joined the University of Oregon track team coached by Bill Bowerman. Bowerman was an innovator who influenced numerous aspects of competitive running, from improving the design of racing tracks to figuring out how to employ film to analyze runners' strides. Most of all, he loved to tinker with shoes. He pulled running shoes apart and put them back together again. Bowerman began his shoe innovations because Wilson and Spaulding, the dominant athletic-shoe companies in the 1940s, had stopped making lightweight spikes when they shifted their emphasis to war production in the Second World War. So, Bowerman took it upon himself to create the perfect high-performance track shoe. In the 1950s, Bowerman started to experiment with materials such as snakeskin and carpskin, eventually settling on more durable materials such as kidskin and nylon mesh that attached to a spiked-shoe sole.

As a young runner on the Oregon team, Phil Knight displayed a work ethic on the track that aligned with Bowerman's approach to running. Although Knight was not the most gifted runner at the university, he despised losing, trained incredibly hard, and so performed well. He moved on to earn an MBA and eventually used this degree to work in the world of running, setting up an American distribution business for Tiger running shoes. Bowerman joined up as inveterate tinkerer, bent upon improving the Tiger designs. Each scraped together $500 as an initial investment to launch Blue Ribbon Sports and placed their first order (for $1,107) in February 1964. Revenues climbed to a modest $83,000 by 1967.

Knight and Bowerman launched the Nike brand in 1971, continuing the flow of innovative Bowerman designs.[2] They developed innovative new fabrics and soles for running shoes at great price points using Japanese manufacturing. In 1966, Bowerman designed the "moon shoe," which eventually became the influential Nike Cortez, launched in 1971. And Bowerman famously poured shoe rubber into his wife's waffle iron, inventing the waffle sole that would become ubiquitous in the 1970s. Importantly, at the same time, several entrepreneurial companies drew upon the emerging discipline of biomechanics to enhance the ergonomics of athletic shoes, something that did not concern Nike, because it was focused on reducing weight for competitive runners. Etonic came up with the dynamic heel cradle, start-up Brooks developed the "kinetic wedge," while Asics (which evolved from the dominant player Onitsuka Tiger) introduced dual density midsoles.

These technical achievements were crucial at this early stage of the market, making quantum leaps in performance and comfort. But soon these advances became more incremental. The only group that paid close attention to the new designs was competitive runners, for whom even subtle functional improvements were crucial to their success. They became big fans of Nike and the other start-ups. For everyone else, casual joggers and people who would begin to use running shoes for everyday uses, these technical differences were largely irrelevant. So incumbents like Tiger—the brand that Bowerman and Knight had originally distributed—continued to dominate the mass market.

Bowerman and Knight believed that their technical expertise would lead Nike to mass-market success. Yet their first big effort to advance a better-mousetraps approach into the mass market was an abject failure. Nike licensed technology, developed by a former NASA engineer, that consisted of durable polyurethane bags filled with pressurized gas that compress under impact, then spring back.[3] The bags, embedded in the heel of the shoe, provided more cushion. Nike launched the first "air" shoe—the Tailwind, a silver, sparkling shoe that looked like a sleek machine—in 1978 for the record-setting running-shoe price of $50 a pair. Despite providing what Nike management viewed as a clear functional advantage, the air sole was scarcely noticed by mass-market consumers and, so, had little impact on revenues. Ten years later, the same technology would be remarketed with vastly increased impact.

Nike's reputation for technological prowess amongst runners did not convert into mass-market success. The functional differences were not dramatic enough for mass-market consumers to notice the difference. For them, "performance" was a cultural construct: it was a marketplace convention that these casual running-shoe consumers believed in, or not. And Nike was marketing "performance" using the same tired formula that all other athletic-shoe companies had used for decades.

Cultural Orthodoxy: Feats of the Star Athletes

Running-shoe companies had long followed the marketing approach used by companies marketing shoes in the biggest selling categories such as basketball, tennis, and football. They copied what had become a well-worn marketing approach to claim performance—what we call the star athletes' feats myth. Following this cultural orthodoxy, companies signed up star athletes as endorsers, placed them in ads to show off their superhuman skills while wearing the product, and then claimed that the company's branded gear made a significant contribution to these feats. Consumers would buy the branded gear, with the faint hope that it would improve their performance as well.

Nike followed this formula throughout its first seven years, using athletes such as Steve Prefontaine and then later, to support its new tennis shoes, John MacEnroe, in formulaic advertising highlighting their athletic prowess, with a rebellious "bad-boy" spin. Nike's more powerful competitors such as Adidas and Tiger, and other entrepreneurial brands, especially Brooks, were doing the same. Nike seemed no different from other sports brands, and the mass market responded with indifference.

The star athletes' feats myth could excite hardcore athletes, especially if it were tied to design improvements, since competitive athletics was the central focus in their lives. But they made up a tiny percentage of the market. This performance discourse had no traction on the mass market: it was not only uninteresting; it was irrelevant, easily ignored.

Nike faced what we will term a *cultural chasm*, a concept that we detail in the Patagonia case in Chapter 6. Nike had established a powerful position in the runner's subculture by designing high-performance shoes for their specific needs—a better-mousetraps strategy. But this strategy did not work with consumers who were not hardcore athletes, and these consumers made up the large majority of sales. How could Nike traverse this divide? What was needed was a cultural innovation to make Nike's performance meaningful to consumers outside the athlete subcultures. To understand why Nike's new marketing resonated so well with non-professional athletes, convincing them that Nikes were *the* high-performance running shoe, we need to understand their ideological desires in this historical moment.

Social Disruption: The Post-War American Dream Unravels

Beginning in the late 1970s, the US economy entered a crucial transformative period that would reverberate through society and culture. The ideology that had undergirded the country for the previous quarter-century collapsed, to be reconstituted by the end of the 1980s. Historically, Americans had embraced the American Dream: the idea that, through hard work and determination, people who came as poor immigrants could create for themselves a prosperous and happy life. The most audacious goals are always achievable, but only if you develop the drive, sheer grit, industry, and optimistic tenacity needed to overcome the hurdles and setbacks you will encounter while pursuing the dream. It was a world view of big life goals and gritty optimistic determination toward work that would make achieving these goals inevitable.

The post-war era, however, was an anomaly. The United States was the last major economy standing after the Second World War, and the country had tremendous political clout and cultural goodwill around the world. Because there was little competition from other countries and seemingly unlimited demand, the American workplace was transformed. The huge economic and political advantages enjoyed by the United States in this period led to a considerable decline in the tenacious push toward self-improvement at the core of American ideology. Life was good, the standard of living skyrocketed upward seemingly without much effort, and so it seemed that one did not have to work so hard after all. The stereotypes of the era exaggerated only slightly: this was the era of the three-martini lunch if you were a businessman, and the cushy job-for-life union contract if you were a skilled laborer. For two decades, the goals of the American Dream—wealth, opportunity, a better life—came easily, without the entailments of hard work, thrift, and tenacity to overcome difficult challenges.

This post-war era of unrivaled prosperity began to unravel in the early 1970s as the OPEC oil cartel pushed up oil prices, and other countries that had been decimated in the war finally caught up and began competing successfully, particularly Japan and West Germany. The economy entered a period of stagflation: pitiful economic growth combined with high inflation. By the late 1970s, the social contract that had created tens of millions of American Dreams during the previous twenty-five years began to fall apart. Fed chief Paul Volker pushed the economy into a deep recession to get rid of inflation. Americans finally came to accept that the era of comfortable secure well-paid jobs was over—the backyard picnic version of the American Dream had ended. These new economic conditions would require a character makeover. This economic and ideological collapse led many Americans to search for alternative ideological moorings that would allow them to realize their American Dreams, a search that would go on for over a decade, until the country had once again securely established its political and economic leadership in the world.

Buffeted by this new world of work, Americans looked anxiously to culture to provide models, motivation, and aspiration. Ideologically speaking, the order of the day was a demand not only to revive the original industrious version of the American Dream, but to push these ideals even harder in the face of the economic challenges of the day. As the economy came to a halt, and along with it the increases in standard of living that had become a birthright, Americans struggled to find out what went wrong and how they should respond. The emerging rough-and-tumble free-agent economy demanded a very different mentality from what they were used to. Rugged individualism was back in vogue. It was no longer aimed at life on the frontier, however. It was now the manifesto for the go-it-alone worker struggling to succeed in the face of the supreme challenge of global competition. Toughness and rigor, both mental and physical, were required.

Sport has long served as a powerful metaphor for work, as a model of the traits required to be successful in life, and as an analogue for masculinity, for what is required to be a powerful man in society.[4] Spend some time with parents and their kids in little league America— baseball, football, basketball, and, as we heard in the 2008 Presidential Election, hockey—and you will learn about the aspects of American ideology that are most important to parents, the aspects that they work mightily to instill in their kids. Nike used its credibility as a competitive sports brand to speak to people during the ideological tumult generated by the new economic situation.

To Get Fit for New Competitive Rigors, Americans Take up Jogging
For spectators during the post-war years, team sports (for example, football, basketball, baseball, hockey) were far more popular than individual sports (for example, golf, tennis, track and field), with American football way out in front. But, in the late 1970s, one of the most individualist sports there is—running—took off, and with participants rather than spectators. This was not a random fad. Americans had come to realize that they needed to rid themselves of the sedentary "soft" ways of the post-war era and rekindle the tough tenacious grit of the country's historic rugged individualism. They needed to condition their bodies and minds for the new competitive world of work. And jogging fitted the bill.

For the previous fifteen years, on television and in books (including the efforts of Bowerman noted above), fitness and health professionals had been prodding Americans to jog, but the regimen took off only in 1978. Despite its lack of athletic charisma compared to Americans' favorite sports, jogging suddenly made sense to tens of millions of Americans. Jogging was the way many Americans chose to challenge their sedentary lives and try to condition their bodies so that they could compete more effectively in the emerging labor market.

Jim Fixx, the once-pudgy editor turned running guru, set off the jogging boom with his *The Complete Book of Running*. The book quickly became the best-selling non-fiction book of all time, and Fixx became a regular on the talk-show circuit, extolling the benefits of running. He presented Americans with a story of personal transformation: how a once-sedentary man, beneficiary of the post-war economy, had used jogging to retool his sluggish body into its opposite—thin, athletic, muscle-toned.

As running became more popular, so did running shoes. Many consumers used them just for day-to-day activities such as shopping or walking. The cover of the book featured Fixx's legs in a pair of Onitsuka Tigers, a leading running brand of the day. Yet somehow Nike became the running shoe for this vanguard of Americans who adopted a daily run as part of their regimen. Why? Unlike its competitors, Nike had turned away from better mousetraps and the star athletes' feats myth. Instead, Nike had begun to use advertising to publicize the runner's ideology—the perfect antidote for Americans looking to revive their competitive spirit.

Nike Innovative Ideology: Combative Solo Willpower

Knight and Bowerman were embedded in the heart of the running subculture, selling their pioneering shoe designs from car trunks at meets. They came to share the view that competitive runners were deviants in the world of sport. American athletics was dominated by team sports with great camaraderie and huge spectator interest. What kind of people would devote their lives to running solo around a track with not a fan in sight? Knight, an overachieving runner who competed successfully because of sheer grit rather than physical gifts, believed that great runners had extraordinary determination and inner drive, the will power to endure a grueling training regimen and frequent injuries, all in a lonely lifestyle that provided little in the way of external gratification. Knight and Bowerman also believed that runners who thrived shared their anti-authoritarian sensibility: going it alone and embracing total responsibility for one's success was more rewarding than joining a team with all sorts of institutional trappings such as were found in football, basketball, and baseball. The intense belief that competitive runners gather around this distinctive ideology, what we call *combative solo willpower*, would become the ideological foundation of the Nike brand.

In the late 1970s, Knight—who for many years had despised marketing and advertising as a deceit that true athletes should never succumb to—finally decided that Nike needed to communicate with prospective customers beyond the small circle of runners and runner-wannabes. While Adidas and Tiger continued to market their brands using the star athletes' feats strategy, and Brooks imitated them, Knight made the fateful move to try something different. For his first foray into non-traditional advertising, Knight and his local ad agency decided to stick to Nike's ideological predilections. They launched what they termed "word of feet" advertising, a clunky phrase introducing a surprisingly innovative campaign. The first ad featured, not a notorious rebel celebrity-athlete winning a race, but rather a very personal story of an unrecognizable competitive runner, using the tagline "no finish line." The narrator tells us that this athlete has "become addicted to what running gives you," and, as we see him train intensively, we are told "beating the competition is relatively easy but beating yourself is a never-ending commitment."

And when one of Nike's little-known sponsored runners—Joan Benoit—became famous as the first American woman to dominate the marathon, Nike produced a powerful ad. The spot studiously avoided the star athletes' feats cliché—for instance, showing Benoit looking triumphant as she crosses the finish line. Instead, the ad featured her getting dressed for a workout in the pre-dawn hours in bad weather, the mundane reality of her daily regime convincingly dramatizing her tenacious dedication to doing whatever it takes to win.

Nike celebrated the mundane trials of individual athletic competition. And, when one of these athletes did break through to the big time, Nike did not change the tune. According to Nike, these athletes succeeded because they shared the same ideology as the rest. Nike even produced a short film to dramatize this runner's ideology—a ten-minute documentary of a group of competitive women runners, runners who were not famous and did not expect to be, but who nonetheless found intense joy in competing against each other in their tight-knit group, sharing intensive training sessions together.

These films were the initial explorations of a novel cultural code—celebrating the backstage drudgery of competitive sport to illuminate the athlete's psyche—that Nike management would continue to evolve as a compelling means to communicate Nike's tenacious solo willpower ideology. Nike offered a simple analogy: runners have a unique, seemingly masochistic urge to train tirelessly regardless of hardships, taking pleasure in the unending fine-tuning of their bodies to tease out maximum performance. Nike used its authority as the brand at the center of this subculture to speak to all Americans, encouraging them to use running as a pathway to life lived according to combative solo willpower.

Nike led the "jogging trend," leapfrogging over well-established competitors to become the jogging shoe of the era. Other brands, such as Tiger and Adidas, were better positioned to dominate the new market, but Nike was far more successful. This is because Nike gave jogging an innovative ideology that drove many Americans into the sport. Most revealingly, running shoes became the casual shoes of Americans across a broad socio-economic spectrum, in the same way that basketball shoes would follow a decade later. While the comfort was enticing, the style had little going for it. Rather, it was what jogging stood for—especially the way Nike told the story—that Americans rallied around in this era. The company passed Adidas in sales in 1979, leaving fellow running-shoe innovators like Brooks in the dust.

Despite this initial success, a central strategic problem remained: almost all Nike's sales were running shoes. Nike sold other kinds of sports shoes, especially tennis, but had yet to establish significant sales. Knight and his management faced a basic business problem: they now dominated running shoes, but the jogging craze had leveled off, so growth opportunities in this segment had shrunk. If Nike were to continue to grow, the company would have to develop the brand in other sports.

Nike Shifts to Better-Mousetraps Innovation and Sales Plummet

Nike management approached this expansion by using a better-mousetraps logic: what market opportunities exist where Nike can bring to market a product with a technological advantage to improve shoe performance? This proved to be a disastrous approach. Nike's aggressive expansion plan bombed. Nike went from Wall Street darling to ugly duckling in a matter of months, as sales went flat and profits fell dramatically. After a five-year, 44 percent annual growth rate culminating in 1984, Nike's profits fell more than 80 percent between 1983 and 1985. Reebok exploited the explosion of interest in aerobics with its Freestyle aerobics shoe featuring soft calf leather, sprinting past Nike in sales ($1.4 billion versus $900 million by 1987).

Knight's most problematic decision was to launch a line of casual shoes. Nike market research, premised upon better-mousetraps thinking and the benefits mentality of mindshare marketing, showed that consumers really liked functional enhancements in their casual shoes, enhancements of the sort that Nike built in their athletic shoes. This is not surprising, since many people had taken to wearing running shoes as everyday walking shoes and had come to like the extra cushioning. But what Knight had not yet learned was that Americans wore running shoes primarily because they liked what they stood for. His customers wanted to wear Nikes to get a piece of the combative solo willpower ideology that the company had instilled in the brand. Customers could then justify their ideological purchase with the rationale that the shoes performed better. Shoes designed expressly for casual use denied this ideological lineage. Even though it delivered a superior product, the new line never caught on. Nike's slump lasted for five years; sales would not get back on track until 1988.

In 1985, at the beginning of this period of mediocre performance, Nike signed Michael Jordan. To leverage Jordan, Nike abandoned its nascent cultural strategy and instead followed the category's cultural orthodoxy, relying on the star athletes' feats myth. Nike assumed that Jordan would become a widely admired athlete, and that basketball fans who admired Jordan would want to emulate him and wear the shoes he wore. Nike built the trickle-down push around a better-mousetraps benefit. The company was having trouble getting consumers to pay attention to its air-cushion technology. Jordan flew through the air in superhuman fashion on the way to his patented dunks. Therefore, Nike management reasoned, he was a natural spokesman for "air" (never mind that the technology was to cushion shocks, not to propel mere mortals toward the rim). Nike went to the trouble of designing a unique Jordan shoe for this purpose—Air Jordans. What set them apart was the flashy red and black design, echoing the team colors of the Chicago Bulls, in contrast to the white shoes everybody else in the league wore.

Chiat/Day created the first Air Jordan ads, featuring Jordan taking off in slow motion from the free throw line and sailing through the air for a dunk. The soundtrack of a jet taking off reinforced the airborne feat. An announcer asks the rhetorical question: "Who says man was not meant to fly?" Jordan was a hugely impressive athlete from the start, and teen athlete wannabes bought Air Jordans to emulate him, just as they did other shoes with athlete sponsors. However, this clichéd marketing effort had little mass-market impact. Jordan's huge influence on the basketball subculture did not carry over to the Nike brand; the prime adult market for casual sports shoes did not respond. While Michael Jordan became the new NBA phenomenon, for the first three years he had a negligible impact on Nike sales.

Knight and others did not realize at the time that they should have couched their strategic question in cultural terms: how could Nike move its highly valued *combative solo willpower* ideology, which it had credibly established for running shoes, to other shoe categories? In 1988, a break-through by the ad agency Wieden + Kennedy allowed Nike not only to migrate its ideology, but even more importantly, to develop a potent new cultural expression that powerfully motivated many Americans, and then the rest of the world.

The Ideological Opportunity Expands

As the 1980s progressed, and the meltdown of the post-war economy traversed most industries, a dramatically different labor market began to take shape. The post-war compact, which allowed the majority of Americans to enjoy well-paid jobs with good benefits and reasonable hours, was becoming a distant memory. Massive layoffs were constantly in the news. American companies were becoming much more efficient and agile, and they were finally able to compete effectively with Japanese and German rivals. But at a price. Competition was global, and corporate goals were mandated by Wall Street. Companies were now working solely for stockholders, with little concern for employees and local communities. Americans would hereafter have to work harder and longer than workers in any other country if they were going to have a shot at the American Dream. While rewards for success had expanded at the very top, the social safety net that had protected Americans for a

OXFORD
UNIVERSITY PRESS

Customer Services Contact

Saxon Way West
Corby, Northants,NN18 9ES
Tel: 01536 454535
Fax: 01536 454519
Returns Tel: 01536 742025 Fax:

Account No	Customer VAT Reg No		Due da
3027091			09.11

Bill-To

Dr Ian Elliott
Queen Margaret University
Business, Enterprise & Management
Queen Margaret University Dri
MUSSELBURGH
EH21 6UU

Ship-To

Dr Ian Elliott
Queen Margaret University
Business, Enterprise & Man
Queen Margaret University
MUSSELBURGH
EH21 6UU

Any damage or shortage must be notified within 14 days of receipt.

Qty	ISBN-13	ISBN-10	Title
			Please accept this FREE examination cop
			would appreciate your comments on the e
			any items you do not want to the Custor
			above. Write R in the decision box.
			Please be sure to write the
			above in the space provi
			card/cards. You can also return
			inspection copy/copies via ou
			service at
			http://www.oup.co.uk/academic/
			Customer PO No: ML_5481707
1	9780199587407	019958740X	CULTURAL STRATEGY C

Totals
Amount Due (GBP):

E. & O. E. All goods are sold subject to our Conditions of Sale in force at the date of this invoice. Copies of the C

Remittance Advice

Invoice Details		OUP Address
Invoice No:	15242308	Oxford University Pr
Account No:	3027091	Great Clarendon Stre
Invoice Date:	09.11.2010	Oxford
		OX2 6DP

Bank Details: Barclays Bank Plc, Account No. 00715654, Sort Code 20-65-18, IBAN: GB5

Gratis Inspection

	Page No	Date & Tax Point	Invoice No.
	1 of 1	09.11.2010	**15242308**
	VAT Reg No	GB195275334	

Delivery: 86807737
Total number of lines supplied: 1
Total quantity supplied: 1
Net weight: 0.732 KG
Shipped via: 2ND CLASS POST

	Author	List Price	Decision A/P/R	Adoption Qty
our compliments. We				
card. Please return				
ices Contact address				
e number printed				
n your comment				
comments on your				
ine comment card				
oncomments				
	HOLT, CAMERON			

0.00

of Sale applicable to your order are available on request.

Total Owed		
Total (if purchased)(GBP):		**0.00**

2065 1800 7156 54, SWIFTBIC: BARCGB22

generation was pulled away. Americans were now free agents, with many of the risks of life (health, poverty, unemployment) pushed upon citizens, rather than socialized by the state and big companies.[5]

This economic shift was accompanied by a powerful ideological justification. The communitarian spirit of the Great Society had been effectively shattered by a conservative counter-movement begun in the 1960s with presidential candidate Barry Goldwater and then astutely "marketed" by a handful of right-wing think tanks including the Cato Institute, the Heritage Foundation, the American Enterprise Institute, and the Scaife Foundation (all funded by wealthy Americans and big companies), which had developed close ties both to conservative media and to Washington political insiders. They stirred a backlash against welfare to the poor, against affirmative action for African-Americans, and against equal economic rights for women, arguing that American society is a meritocracy based on hard work not handouts.[6] This new libertarian ideology naturalized the market as the source of wealth and personal freedom, and it positioned government as a parasitical force that systematically robs Americans of their wallets and their freedom— "we're all on our own, and we're better off for it."

Americans found themselves in a far more risky, difficult, and insecure workplace. They needed new cultural expressions to guide them through this new world and to help them take advantage of it. The incipient demand for new instructions to achieve the American Dream in the late 1970s had blossomed into a massive cultural desire. To respond to this opportunity, Wieden + Kennedy went exploring in a most unexpected place—the African-American ghetto.

The "Just Do It" Myth: Transcending Societal Discrimination

The foundation for Nike's comeback was constructed of seemingly odd materials. On July 1, 1988, Nike aired the first "Just Do It" ad. It featured an octogenarian named Walt Stack who had become something of a legend in the Bay Area for his grueling and scenic daily exercise regime, which involved crossing the Golden Gate Bridge and taking a swim in the bay at the end. He was one of the oldest competitive marathoners in the country. The spot showed him preparing for his daily run, taking out his dentures before hitting the pavement. Other launch spots offered a clue as to what Wieden creatives were up to. One ad featured a paraplegic fiercely competing in racquetball and basketball in a wheelchair; another showcased Priscilla Welch, a formerly plump couch potato, who won the New York City Marathon when she was 42. By showcasing people overcoming huge handicaps to succeed in sport, Wieden had found a way to communicate the combative solo willpower ideology in a new and compelling manner. However, this "overcoming handicaps" myth had serious weaknesses compared to the old runner's myth. The problems that these people faced were quite idiosyncratic and thereby provided an imperfect analogy to the new economy. Also, this type of story could quickly become formulaic and hackneyed, forcing Wieden to pilfer ever more unusual personal handicaps in order to develop original creative ideas. It would take Wieden another year to arrive at the fully realized cultural innovation.

These launch spots were soon followed by one of the most influential ads of all time: Nike's anthemic "Revolution," which used John Lennon's "Revolution #9" as the soundtrack. The screaming power chords introduce a montage of black-and-white photos that roll by the screen at the same energetic pace as the soundtrack. Whatever meanings the song once carried—and Lennon's intentions have never been clear—were effectively erased by the images chosen by Wieden executives, who were repurposing the song with a much more obvious intention: Nike's advocacy of a "revolution of character" for American society. The photo-montage linked the revolutionary song to "pure" athletes, who stood apart from commercialization and celebrity to embrace the combative solo willpower ideology required to succeed at sport. Nothing satisfies more than succeeding in situations where you are not supposed to, which could work for the audience too if they adapted the right mindset.

The meaning of this myth was abundantly clear to Americans, who were inspired beyond all expectations by the ad. Nike was challenging all Americans to up their game, to use the determination of these kinds of athletes only Nike celebrated as a resource in their own lives, not only to persevere but to succeed in joyous triumph, despite the trying new circumstances. The ad called on Americans to rise to the challenges of the new competitive environment, to work their bodies and minds with optimism and tenacity. At the end of the spot, Nike assured Americans (via Lennon's frenzied voice) that "It'll be all right, all right, ALL RIGHT!" The ad made many Americans want to jump off the sofa, fist in the air, and yell "F**k yeah, I can do it too!"

Nike's "Just Do It" Myth.
Nike's cultural innovation was based upon a radical extension of its runner's ideology of the late 1970s. For Nike, sport is the great equalizer. Sport, in its purest form, is a utopian world in which all barriers and handicaps imposed by the "real world" are dissolved, providing a level playing field in which the most determined and conscientious and confident—not necessarily those whom society has favored with the most privileges and support—will win. The soul of sport is about athletes with tenacious determination overcoming adversity to win. What is particularly fascinating about athletes, then, is their mindset: how do they do it? In the guise of selling sports shoes, Nike pinpointed the cultural disruption that many Americans were living with, and provided a resoundingly American answer, filled with optimism earned through determination. "Just Do It" offered an inspirational call to self-empowerment: "No matter who you are, no matter what your physical, economic, or social limitations. Transcendence is not just possible, it is waiting to be called forth. Take control of your life and don't submit to the mundane forces that can so easily weigh us down in daily life. No more rationalizations and justifications, it's time to act."[7]

"Just Do It" was ostensibly a launch campaign for the Air Max technology. Nike had installed cushioning air bladders in its shoes since 1978 with little to show for it. But now, Nike's advertising imbued its air soles with a powerful myth—one that provided consumers with a great deal of cultural and social value—and sales took off. On the one hand, consumers wanted to buy the shoes so that they could tap into Nike's potent ideology. On the other hand, they could now rationalize their purchase with the Air Max technology: the cool plastic "window" in the heel provided them with all the justification that they needed.

The launch spots and "Revolution" nailed Nike's myth. But the generic use of hero shots of Nike athletes in "Revolution" left considerable room for improvement—they blurred with the conventional visuals of star athletes' feats. With better cultural codes, Nike's cultural expression could be even more powerful. But how? Wieden + Kennedy creatives made their most important breakthrough: expanding beyond the world of sport, they began to reference different types of societal discrimination that athletes must overcome. Nike ads would henceforth be littered with cultural codes referencing racism, sexism, and global poverty. This was a fortuitous choice, since these devastating institutional barriers served as a convincing metaphor for the extreme challenges of the new global economy that Nike consumers faced.

Subculture: African-American Athletes in the Ghetto

In the United States of the 1980s, urban ghettos were the country's most troubled and stigmatized places. These poor neighborhoods could be found in nearly every big city: New York, Chicago, Detroit, Los Angeles, St Louis, Washington, and Philadelphia all had well-known ghettos. These pockets consisted mostly of African-Americans, many of whom had left the rural South, pushed by the loss of sharecropper jobs with the mechanization of agriculture and pulled by the promise of industrial jobs. Ghettos emerged through a combination of racism and failed urban policies. The populations were herded into small sections of the big cities by "red lining": tacit racist zoning and real-estate practices that led to extremely overcrowded conditions in dilapidated housing with poor sanitation, barely attended to by white landlords. The city's poorest residents were crowded together and starved of public resources, including access to basic education, health services, and even grocery stores.

Utopian urban planning schemes of the 1950s and 1960s sought to resolve this "blight" with public housing projects consisting of densely packed high-rise buildings. For instance, Chicago's Robert Taylor Homes, the largest such project in the country, consisted of twenty-eight sixteen-story buildings lining the expressway, with 28,000 people packed inside. While these buildings were originally mixed with respect to both race and social class, they soon evolved into "warehouses" for the poorest and most discriminated segment of society. This concentration of poverty led to the breakdown of families and the rise of an informal economy dominated by gangs, which sold drugs and controlled territory, and to the violence and criminality that comes with such concentrated social problems. The ghetto was the sort of place where people struggled to get by, to survive with modest comforts. Other than joining the gangs that ran drugs, striving for success, economic or otherwise, was out of the question.

In the 1980s, the media took to sensationalizing the goings-on in "the 'hood," frequently reporting on spectacularly violent events, such as Wild West showdowns between gangs and police. Young African-American men who lived in the ghetto were sensationally stigmatized as "super predators"—out to pillage with little concern for human life. Young women, often single mothers, were berated by conservative pundits as "welfare queens," abusing the country's welfare benefits for the poor. Rap music and hip-hop culture emerged as a subcultural response to this situation, often presenting African-American men as hypersexual and bombastically masculine. It is not surprising, then, that the adult middle class deeply feared the ghetto, and particularly its young men. The threat to the middle class was, of course, very appealing to white suburban boys, who became wannabe gangsters practicing their hip-hop swagger and dress, a further affront to adult middle-class America.

It is this racialized discourse that made the ghetto an extremely surprising and provocative subculture for Nike to draw from as cultural source material. The ghetto offered the most provocative analogy one could imagine for America's new labor market. The 'hood was perceived as far and away the toughest place in the country: a Mad-Max world in which broken families, gang-infested housing projects, racist cops, and penitentiary-like schools made life a constant struggle just to sustain a meager subsistence. It was a dog-eat-dog world with no institutions to fall back on. The only way to get by was with individual tenacity and street smarts.

Except—at least as the media reported it—for sport. In a myth that resonated powerfully with Americans (the low budget documentary *Hoop Dreams* would become a blockbuster a few years later), the idea that sport offered the level playing field that allowed even the most underprivileged to compete their way out of a terrible situation appealed powerfully to people who wanted to believe that the social Darwinian world could offer a silver lining after all. The African-American men who miraculously find their way out of the 'hood to sports success embodied in a most profound way the new American

Dream: despite the extraordinary hardships of the new economy, one can still will one's way to the top if only one pushes hard enough.

Michael Jordan: Dramatizing Combative Solo Willpower

To tap into these potent cultural codes required dramatizing the "Just Do It" myth in the ghetto: Nike athletes needed to rely upon the combative solo willpower ideology to fight their way out of the inner city. Unfortunately, Michael Jordan, Nike's star "property," grew up in a middle-class family and had none of the charismatic jive-talking swagger that had become associated with both musical and athletic break-outs from the 'hood. Jim Riswold, a Wieden + Kennedy creative, solved the problem by bringing in Spike Lee to develop a campaign called "Spike and Mike," which paired Jordan with Spike Lee's character Mars Blackmon. The campaign intertwined Blackmon's identity as the wise-cracking jabbermouth in Lee's film *She's Gotta Have It* with the Air Jordans he was wearing.

Lee had ultimate credibility as an impresario of the 'hood. His Mars Blackmon routine, the huckster in the 'hood celebrating basketball as the way to fame and fortune, was the perfect metaphor for the new economy. By incorporating Jordan, the ads implied that he had worked his way out of Spike's world. It mattered little that he did not actually come from the 'hood. The media had spun the story so many times that, in the cultural imagination of America, the 'hood was where all black athletes came from and relentless determination was how they got out. Once Jordan received his ghetto makeover, Nike advertising would communicate the inner workings of Jordan's psyche in ad after ad for the next decade, so that Americans could find motivation in his combative solo willpower.

At this point, Nike and Wieden had no idea about the power of the ghetto as source material to dramatize the brand's ideology. "Spike and Mike" was a one-off Spike Lee feature in their minds. They placed their bet on a sequel featuring David Robinson—the quintessential American role model, a brainy mathematics major from a military family who deferred basketball riches so he could serve in the Navy. But such standard American Dream stories had little purchase in the new American econ-omy; the Robinson campaign was a dud. A third celebrity effort starring the thuggish Charles Barkley gave them another clue. He grunted at the

NIKE

audience in his "Role Model" ads, protesting against the widely held belief that famous athletes should set an example for the kids who idolize them. "I'm paid," Barkley proclaimed, embracing the superpredator stereotype, "to wreak havoc on the basketball court. Just because I can dunk a basketball doesn't mean I should raise your kids." The ideological message was clear: in the dog-eat-dog world from which Barkley comes, ideals about etiquette and good sportsmanship were antiquated. Rather, to thrive in a world of brute competition, one did whatever one could to win, which often included intimidation and aggression. Through these serendipitous encounters with the cultural codes of the ghetto, Wieden creatives discovered its rhetorical power and would then systematically exploit its cultural codes in subsequent advertising.

Competitive Solo Willpower in the 'Hood

For the next half-decade, Weiden creatives would refine their storytelling around this foundational concept, becoming increasingly aggressive in their use of the cultural codes of the ghetto—what sociologists Robert Goldman and Stephan Papson have called "street vernacular"—and then expanding the idea to other contexts where similar claims could be made. Consider a typical ad from this era, "Hardrock Miner," which aired in 1993.[8] The ad is composed as a "day in the life" in the ghetto, with shots of black teens playing basketball amidst the chain-link fences and high-rise buildings of a public housing project. The players are shown in slow motion, which turns their athletic moves into workman-like exertion, back and forth, across the court.

The ad's meaning is powerfully framed by its soundtrack "Mining for Gold," a working man's ballad of plaintive resistance sung in the style of a gospel spiritual, "We are miners, hardrock miners, to the shaft house we must go..."[9] It would be hard to imagine a more unorthodox soundtrack for a sports shoe, which is one reason why Wieden's choice had such an impact. This wasn't the 'hood as the media portrayed it. Nike's poor black teens working on their basketball technique are no different from minorities of the past trudging on to their grueling manual labor. The song encourages us to appreciate the extraordinary resilience of such young men, who summon the will to achieve despite the grim realities of the ghetto wasteland in which they live.

While Nike took on the most important social inequalities of the day—wildly transgressive for any marketer, much less a sports-shoes company—its implicit politics were hardly progressive. Nike's world was social Darwinist. These problems were treated as natural structural features of society. Hence, overcoming these barriers was inevitably a personal challenge, which only people with nearly superhuman fortitude would be able to achieve. Nike myth was to create a revolution of the mind that would allow for personal transcendence, despite the seeming bleakness of the situation.

Wieden would go on to make dozens of ads that drew imaginatively from street vernacular to recount a myth of the most oppressed African-Americans overcoming their horrid situation through combative solo willpower. And, once Wieden's creatives had mastered placing Nike's "Just Do It" myth in the 'hood with provocative and nuanced cultural codes, they began experimenting with extending this cultural expression in a variety of ways. They moved from American basketball shoes for men, to other sports, other demographics, and other countries, adapting the same cultural expression everywhere the brand was expanded.

Nike Women: Taking on Patriarchy and Title IX

Nike had tried a number of times to expand their appeal to women, with little success, because the efforts relied upon formulaic sports marketing. It was only when Weiden creatives began to think about women in the same sociological terms as the ghetto basketball communications that they cracked the code. The breakout campaign used the tagline "If you let me play." In their most overtly political campaign ever, Nike took on America's historic barriers keeping girls out of many of the more physical sports in high school and college. A law called "Title IX" had passed in the woman's rights era of the early 1970s barring discrimination against women. But the law did not mention sports explicitly, and most high schools and colleges devoted massive resources to men's teams while starving women's sports and often refusing even to sanction a team. Nike's campaign framed this imbalance as a massive form of the discrimination, faced by all women, that handicapped them in life. The lead spot used young girls on a playground facing the camera with a collage of voiceovers offering a litany of extraordinary statistics on the benefits of sport to women: "If you let me play sports . . . I will like myself more, I will have more self-esteem, I will be 60 percent less likely to get breast cancer, I will suffer less depression, I will be more likely to leave a man who beats me, I'll be less likely to get pregnant before I want to," ending with "I will learn what it means to be strong . . . If you let me play sports." Wieden then expanded the concept, first combining it with the original 'hood concept by dramatizing how poor black women athletes are discriminated against, and then moving into issues regarding women's body image, and finally more playful and reflexive feminist expressions. For instance, one of these feminist "Just Do It" spots featured a tongue-in-cheek punk rock reworking of Helen Reddy's women's lib anthem "I Am Woman" ("I am woman | hear me roar | I am strong | I am invincible | I am woman.").

Tiger Woods: Taking on Middle-Class Racism

Emboldened by its success in basketball, Nike became more ambitious, aiming to conquer every major sport. The social discrimination tactic worked well for racism and patriarchy in basketball, but what about upper-middle-class sports, especially golf? The point of entry became clear when wunderkind Tiger Woods won his first major in 1997, running away with the Masters, and overnight becoming a sensation in the sport. Tiger was a perfect cultural fit for Nike's combative solo willpower. He was famous for his meticulous perfectionism, his incredible concentration, and his will to win, groomed over decades of dedicated practice.

As with Jordan, there was a slight problem of accuracy: Tiger had a middle-class upbringing, a doting father who had served in the military, and a Stanford education. By the age of 2, he was a celebrity, performing miraculous golf shots on national television. Perhaps a bigger problem was that, despite the color of his skin, Woods is predominantly Asian in ethnicity and is only 25 percent African-American. Not much discrimination in sight, much less the mean streets of the 'hood. Nonetheless, mythology works with ideological prejudices; it is never purely factual. Tiger's skin color was enough to provide Wieden creatives with the sociological material they needed to work with.

Golf was a sport associated with the upper classes, carousing at private country clubs. And some of these clubs had long histories of discrimination based upon race. Likewise, professional golf was always dominated by white players. So, working with these cultural assumptions, it was easy for Wieden to propose that Tiger was breaking a huge discrimination barrier—the Jackie Robinson or Arthur Ashe of his era—in his rise to become one of the greatest golfers of all-time. (No matter that Charlie Sifford had broken the color barrier more than thirty years earlier, and that Lee Elder had faced continual racial harassment while becoming the first African-American to play in the Masters in 1975, and that he had famously broken the race barrier for golf in South Africa.)

The launch spot "I am Tiger Woods" begins with television coverage of Tiger competing in a high-pressure tournament. The spot cuts abruptly to a montage of children and teens, mostly ethnic and racial minorities, stating matter-of-factly to camera "I am Tiger Woods." We see many of them carrying golf clubs, on their way to practice, following Tiger in breaking golf's discriminatory barrier. Despite the suburban green-grass nature of the sport, many of the shots show kids coming from a gritty urban context, and one of the shots shows an old dilapidated building marked "Golf Exchange," its paint peeling from the red brick—an obvious street vernacular cultural code. The "I am Tiger Woods" mantra appropriates a scene from Spike Lee's film *Malcolm X*, in which a schoolteacher tells his African-American students in celebration of Malcolm X's birthday: "We celebrate Malcolm X's birthday because he was a great, great African-American. Malcolm X is you. All of you. You are Malcolm X,"[10] at which point student after student stands up in the classroom to declare "I am Malcolm X." Nike provocatively associates the revolution of the oppressed to inspire a moment of transcendence in all who would identify with Tiger's triumph.[11]

A follow-up spot, "Hello World," takes the audience through the litany of Tiger's early achievements. Over each image in the segment demonstrating his amazing early successes, we read large superimposed type, which declares the various firsts Woods achieved in his teen years (for example, "I won the US Amateur when I was 18"). The sequence of images depicts his ferociously competitive character;

then, as the images show Tiger getting older and more accomplished, winning tournament after tournament, the audience reads:

"There are still courses in the US I am not allowed to play…"

"…because of the color of my skin."

"Hello World."

"I've heard I'm not ready for you."

"Are you ready for me?"

"Just Do It."

Following the cultural recipe of its earlier campaigns, Nike positioned Tiger as yet another minority athlete who overcame seemingly insurmountable barriers of discrimination to make it to the top. Having positioned him in this manner, Nike then represented Woods as the poster child for combative solo willpower, just as it had done with Jordan. One of the company's most influential ads, "Never," makes much of the fact that Tiger spent his entire lifetime, from the time he could walk, being pushed by his father's constant instruction and scrutiny to improve his golf game. Tiger's dad himself does the voice-over, describing how he was continually playing with Tiger's mind—dropping a bag of golf clubs in the middle of Tiger's swing—to develop his mental toughness. "I promise you you'll never meet another person as mentally tough as you in your entire life," he says to Tiger. Then, to us, "And he hasn't. And he never will."

Globalizing Nike's New American Dream

Wieden's creatives repurposed the overcoming societal discrimination myth for the Latin-American market to powerful effect. Nike's first Spanish-language ad, "La Tierra de Mediocampistas" (The Land of Shortstops), told Nike's version of why it is that so many professional shortstops come from the tiny and poor island of the Dominican Republic. Rather than summoning the African-American ghetto, the spot borrows from the vernacular of the impoverished Dominican Republic streets. The visuals work hard to emphasize that this is a "Third World" setting: we see shirtless men, bare feet, burros, a shanty town, outdoor cooking amongst roosters, homemade bats, and make-shift ball fields. The spot then focuses on boys who work in a determined fashion with their improvised equipment, hoping to transcend their situation and make it in the American major leagues.

The setting provided a powerful metaphor for the labor market that many Latino/as faced at that time in the United States. For Latin American immigrants, the situation was particularly daunting: they often entered the country illegally to get any work, much of the work was the most grueling manual labor and migrant agricultural work, and because of their status at the bottom of the labor market these workers faced horrid workplace conditions. So the story of Dominican youth competing their way out of their impoverished condition and into the Major Leagues offered a poignant myth, a glimmer of hope.

Against this grim reality, the spot's voiceover offered the possibility of transcendence: "Seventy shortstops in organized baseball are from the Dominican Republic. So when you see a great Dominican shortstop go for the ball, and you hear, 'Boy, he had to go far in the hole to get that one,' you'll know how far is far." With its tagline, the spot threw the ball into the hands of the viewers and urged them to find the same determination to overcome the social barriers in their own lives: like the aspiring baseball players in places like Dominican Republic, Puerto Rico, and Mexico, viewers should "Just Do It."

Wieden's creatives further extended the myth to win over consumers in other countries and finally take on the one sport that the American company had yet to crack—football (or soccer, for Americans). Once again they adapted the "Just Do It" myth (overcoming societal discrimination with combative solo willpower) by using the cultural codes of the particular kinds of societal discrimination all too familiar to this new audience.

In the mid-1990s Nike management made an aggressive push into South America as part of its decision to pursue in earnest the enormous global market for football shoes. In Brazil, South America's largest market, the stakes were particularly high. In 1996, Nike inked a ten-year $200 million sponsorship contract with the Brazilian national team, and journalists in Brazil and around the world cried foul, accusing the company of trying to buy its way into the sport. At that time, football shoes made up less than 1 percent of Nike's footwear sales, and football enthusiasts accused the brand of being an interloper that lacked credibility, an American company trying to make a quick buck, with no real understanding of, or passion for, the game.

Then, Nike began to advertise. Wieden's first Portuguese language spot featured Brazil's most renowned footballer, Ronaldo Luis Nazario de Lima, who was known throughout the country, and now the world, simply as Ronaldo. Rather than focus on Ronaldo's brilliant accomplishments using the star athletes' feats orthodoxy, Wieden instead cast him as a child playing soccer in a dilapidated urban street. Although Ronaldo's childhood was not particularly underprivileged—his father was an engineer for the Rio Telephone Company—he did grow up in a relatively poor suburb on the outskirts of Rio. This was enough for Wieden's creatives to consign him to a scene that suggested a *favela* (a Brazilian slum): crumbling buildings, high urban density, large numbers of shirtless kids, most of them Afro-Brazilian, playing soccer in the street. The final kick dramatically shatters the window of a parked car.

The imagery of shirtless children playing on an inner-city street had a particular resonance with Brazilian audiences. The Brazilian media had long portrayed *favelas* as vicious dog-eat-dog worlds, in which seemingly innocent landscapes of children playing could instantly turn into violent scenes of youth gangs wielding shotguns, pistols, and even submachine guns. In the mid-1990s, the coverage became even more lurid, as the media sensationalized a series of police shoot-outs with drug gangs, including one instance of the police gunning down eight children all at once. And the journalistic sensationalism was not too far-fetched: Rio alone had over 800 *favelas*, an estimated half of the city's drug gang members were aged 17 and under, and the city's rates of gunshot death were similar to those in conflict zones such as Kosovo, Sierra Leone, Uganda, and Angola. Brazilians understood their poorer inner-city districts to be harsh environments with endemic poverty, constant fear of violence, and few work opportunities to allow individuals to climb out of their dismal economic situation.

Toward the end of the spot, the scene cuts from the shirtless children on the inner-city street to reveal that Ronaldo has been the narrator. We see Ronaldo as the star of the Brazilian national team in a visual that suggests that he, like the Major League Dominican shortstops, has come a long way and succeeded despite the odds.

A year later, Wieden's copywriters pushed this cultural expression even further, and even more successfully, in a global campaign that they created to play on the 1998 FIFA World Cup broadcasts. The breakthrough spot, "Steak," was wordless. The spot opens on a Latin American boy carrying a soccer ball, entering his home from a back alley. A makeshift tire swing, an unkept yard, a clothes line, and a dilapidated car all signal that this is not a middle-class neighborhood. The boy places the ball on an old kitchen table, pulls a bloody steak from a rundown fridge, and proceeds to squeeze large quantities of blood onto his football. The camera focuses on all the gory details: his hands getting bloodied, the ball turning red, blood dropping onto the kitchen floor. When he is finally satisfied, he runs back into the alley, places the bloodied ball on the ground, and waits. The camera cuts to a rabid dog letting out a vicious snarl. Then another vicious-looking dog rears its head from an abandoned tire. We then hear a cacophony of ferocious barking as stray dog after stray dog come from under and over alleyway fences, and begin to race toward the boy in a threatening, predatory manner. The boy waits calmly and determinedly as the ravenous pack of dogs speed violently toward him until, at the last moment, he takes off at breakneck speed, skillfully dribbling as he strives to outpace them. The spot ends with the word Nike and the title, "What are you getting ready for?" This ad became a favorite of audiences, not only in Brazil, but around the world. Entirely void of celebrity athletes, the spot expressed Nike's myth that any individual, with enough willful determination, can overcome grim social realities in a supremely provocative and memorable way.

Conclusion

Nike is one of America's most impressive market innovations. Explaining how Nike rose to such prominence should yield important clues as to how innovation works. Innovation experts explain Nike's success in terms of better mousetraps: Nike was a technology-driven company that led the way in engineering excellent athletic shoes; its success was driven by the likes of its waffle soles and its air cushions. But this explanation is problematic. While Knight and Bowerman were pouring shoe rubber into waffle irons and embedding polyurethane air bags into

Nike shoe heels, their competitors were using the emerging discipline of biomechanics to develop technologies that were at least as powerful. Moreover, the air sole—Nike's most significant technological innovation—failed to have significant impact on revenues until a decade after it had been launched, when it was restaged with an innovative advertising campaign. By the late 1970s, at the beginning of Nike's ascent, most athletic shoe companies had become quite competent in designing and manufacturing high-performance shoes, often reverse engineering each other's designs, such that the shoes looked and performed more and more alike. From a product perspective, rather than a better mousetrap, Nike seemed to be marketing barely differentiated shoes in a red ocean.

What Nike did differently was to be found in its advertising, not its shoes. Marketing models should be of some help in understanding how Nike communications led its innovation. But, instead of delving into the empirical details to make sense of what Nike did that was so distinctive, marketing experts instead offer up industry clichés. For instance, Kevin Lane Keller, an academic branding expert who is author of the best-selling brand-management textbook and co-author on Phillip Kotler's marketing textbooks, claims that the Nike brand is based upon the "mantra of authentic athletic performance," which exists as a knowledge structure in customers' minds.[12] Proponents of this "performance benefit" story, such as Keller, stress that Nike's use of celebrity athletes was integral to the brand's rise: how better to convey the performance benefit than to show professional athletes pulling off superhuman feats while wearing Nikes?

This explanation is even more unsatisfying than the technological innovation explanation, since it not only gets the story wrong, but actually inverts the correct explanation. All Nike's competitors—Adidas, Converse, Puma, Reebok—were doing exactly this: using atheletic feats of celebrity athletes to convey "authentic athletic performance." Nike's success was premised upon breaking away from this cultural orthodoxy—the star athletes' feats myth. In fact, what is so distinctive about Nike's communication is that it downplays demonstrations of athletic high-performance prowess in favor of a different athlete's story. Rather than conventional battles on the playing fields, Nike offered a much more expansive vision of competition that took us to the ghettos and the *barrios*, so that we could appreciate that the seemingly insurmountable challenges in our own lives have nothing on the barriers of racism, sexism, and global poverty.

While the objective functionality of Nike's shoes differed only marginally from its competitors, the perceived functionality became huge precisely because Nike's motivational myth to succeed in tough times with a new psyche that is up for the challenge—what we call combative solo willpower—was so novel and highly valued. Nike made Adidas and Reebok and Converse irrelevant by proposing a particularly apt ideology for the times, packaged in a rhetorically powerful and unexpected myth. Nike earned its position as one of the most powerful new brands of the twentieth century by providing Americans, and then the rest of the world, with the inspirational coaching they required to pursue the American Dream in a historical moment when this quest seemed otherwise impossible. Nike mythologized this new ideology using highly provocative cultural codes—drawing upon the American ghetto and other peoples facing severe social barriers—to dramatize how this ideology allowed one to overcome even the most severe forms of social discrimination. Nike became *the* sports performance brand only when the brand delivered cultural expressions so compelling that consumers *wanted* to believe that Nike performed better.

Notes

1. This narrative synthesizes the early history of Nike reported in two books: Donald Katz, *Just Do It: The Nike Spirit in the Corporate World* (New York: Adams Media, 1994); and J. B. Strasser, *Swoosh: The Unauthorized History of Nike and the Men Who Played There* (New York: Harper, 1991).
2. In this period, Bowerman was an early advocate of jogging, proselytizing on the topic beginning in the early 1960s. In 1966 he co-authored a book, *Jogging*, which advocated jogging as a fitness regime. Unfortunately, the book did not translate into BRS sales.
3. "Nikebiz.com: The Inside Story (1978)," www.nike.com/nikebiz/nikebiz.jhtml?page=50 (accessed Nov. 13, 2003).
4. The sports ideology of the post-war mimicked the country's new embrace of big organizations and institutions. The media celebrated dynastic teams and the coaches who finessed the optimum team effort out of the players. The media celebrated sports dynasties—UCLA Bruins and Indiana Hoosiers in NCAA basketball; USC Trojans, Ohio State Buckeyes, and Penn State Nittany Lions in NCAA

football; the Green Bay Packers, Pittsburgh Steelers, and Miami Dolphins in professional football. With all of these teams, the coaches who managed the dynasties were even more celebrated than the players: John Wooden, Bobby Knight, Woody Hayes, Joe Paterno, Vince Lombardi, and Don Shula. Publicity for the teams featured their aggressive strength. The Steelers had their intimidating "Iron Curtain," while the Minnesota Vikings countered with the "Purple People Eaters." The brainwork of the coaches and the collective strength of the teams made an effective motivating metaphor for work in this era.

5. Jacob Hacker, *The Great Risk Shift: The New Economic Insecurity and the Decline of the American Dream* (Oxford: Oxford University Press, 2006).

6. For a history of the conservative social movement in the United States, see Kim Phillips-Fein, *Invisible Hands: The Making of the Conservative Movement from the New Deal to Reagan* (New York: W.W. Norton, 2009)

7. Robert Goldman and Stephan Papson, *Nike Culture: The Sign of the Swoosh* (Thousand Oaks, CA: Sage, 1999), 19–20. This academic book, while a difficult read with a sometimes scattered analysis, is far and away the best treatment of Nike's cultural innovation of the many published works on the brand. It is telling that two critical sociologists have delivered such an analysis while the many dozens of "case studies" of Nike in the management literature do not even touch on the obvious cultural foundations of Nike's success.

8. See Goldman and Papson's more detailed analysis (*Nike Culture*, 94–6) of this ad, from which part of this interpretation is adapted.

9. The song was originally arranged by Canadian folksinger James Gordon, based upon a traditional worker's song. The Nike ad uses the popular version performed by Margo Timmons of the Cowboy Junkies, from their famous *Trinity Sessions* album, which was recorded with a single microphone in a Toronto church.

10. Which in turn nods to the famous "I am Spartacus" scene from the 1960 film *Spartacus*.

11. Goldman and Papson, *Nike Culture*, 115.

12. Kevin Lane Keller, *Strategic Brand Management* (2nd edn.; Upper Saddle River, NJ, Prentice-Hall, 2002).

3

Jack Daniel's: Mythologizing the Company to Revive Frontier Masculinity

Jack Daniel's Tennessee Whiskey—while an award-winning liquor dating back a century—was nonetheless in the early 1950s a tiny and unprofitable brand, one of many dozens of nondescript regional whiskeys in the United States.[1] In 1955, a Saint Louis ad agency concocted a new print advertising campaign and insider relationship strategy based upon homespun parables from the rural Tennessee distillery. A decade later, Jack Daniel's was *the* premium whiskey in the United States, an American icon. In short order, Jack Daniel's became a billion-dollar business, expanding around the world.

The brand took advantage of an ideological opportunity that had spread like wildfire amongst many American men in the 1950s—the fracturing of the new "organization man" and the pent-up desires for rekindling the masculine ideology of the American frontier. While Hollywood was serving up reams of cowboy films and television programs to feed this desire (which was key source material for Marlboro, as we explain in Chapter 8), Jack Daniel's celebrated a different and considerably more distinctive subculture that also evoked the frontier—what we shall call the hillbilly subculture of the rural South and Appalachia. The ad agency adapted photojournalist stories in the most popular magazines of the day as source material for this brand innovation, and artfully extended this material to create one of the most impactful cultural innovations in American business history.

Whiskey's Cultural Orthodoxy: The Good Life of the Organization Man

Ideological competition in the whiskey category centered on two cultural categories: masculinity and status. Alcoholic beverages can engage other cultural categories, including sociality, sex, and relaxation. However, in the United States, because of historic reasons that we unfold below, whiskey competition has focused on which brand can offer better ideology with respect to masculine ideals and social class.

In mid-century America, men drank whiskey and middle-class men drank premium whiskey. The shift to white spirits was still decades off. All the major whiskey brands jumped on the same masculinity-status bandwagon, championing the comfortable and luxurious middle-class life of what came to be stereotyped as "the organization man." Men's work had shifted massively from agriculture and small business to white-collar jobs in big organizations and professional service occupations. Cookie-cutter suburbs sprouted on the outskirts of all America's big cities to create the proper lifestyle for these men and their families. The organization-man ideology was decidedly corporate, centered on acting as a team player in large bureaucracies and steadily climbing the organizational ladder in the quest for ever greater respect and income. He collaborates well, takes orders, carefully manages others impressions of himself, and does not ruffle feathers. Sociologists of the era famously captured this new ideology: David Reisman coined the term the "other directed" personality in his best-selling book *The Lonely Crowd*, and Erving Goffman observed their "impression management" strategies in *The Presentation of Self in Everyday Life*.

The mass media promoted a homogeneous mass-culture-centered lifestyle, bringing this ideology to life as the 1950s portrait of the American Dream—stereotyped as the modern grey-suited businessman living in the suburbs with his nuclear family enjoying all the accoutrements of "modern living." This lifestyle quickly became dominant in magazines and the new television medium. As the news media and popular culture celebrated the well-to-do lifestyle of the organization man, marketers across many categories followed suit, which they perceived as a hot and profitable trend.

The big brand-name whiskeys, dominated by Seagram with its 7-Crown, VO, Lord Calvert, and Chivas Regal brands, sought to claim the mantle as the luxury status symbol that conveyed that the drinker has "made it," using the new organization-man cultural codes to convey success. The VO tagline was "known by the company it keeps." Advertising showed confident successful well-dressed men, often with beautiful women admiring them surrounded by the new consumer props of modern living.

In the early 1950s, Jack Daniel's was no different. The company's print ads sought to associate the brand with the upscale organization-man lifestyle, using line drawings of well-dressed professional men. This orthodox symbolism was combined with a benefits campaign built around the whiskey's distinctive charcoal mellowing process. Ads and promotions used the tagline "drop by drop"—which referenced how the raw liquor dripped through 10 feet of pulverized hardwood maple charcoal before being barreled. This process was promoted as an "extra blessing" that made the whiskey smoother than its competitors. Another newspaper campaign used cartoons that equated Jack Daniel's with a work of art. The header read "You Ought to TASTE Jack Daniel's" and followed with "if you can ever get it."

The media strategy emphasized "prestige magazines" including *True, Wall Street Journal, Holiday, Esquire, New Yorker, Time, Fortune,* and *Gourmet.* Likewise, sales and promotion efforts followed the same strategy. The company's newssheet to distributors advocated that Jack be positioned as a "luxury whiskey, a natural for clubs, hotels, and bars with an exclusive atmosphere and discriminating clientele, any place with customers who really appreciate the finer things in life." Displays that dramatized the filtering process were developed for high-end men's clothiers, a creative retail strategy for liquor, which sought to embed the brand in an upper-middle-class milieu. A display unit incorporated the statue of Jack Daniel and the cave spring, with a demonstration of the "drop-by-drop" process. The company produced a silver-plated server for the bottle, which was packaged in a fancy blue box, as a retail promotion.

This masculinity-status strategy did not work, which was not surprising, given that all the major brands in the category sought to convey the same ideology using similar myths and cultural codes. And they had much larger marketing budgets. The fight to establish the Tennessee charcoal-filtering process as a distinctive benefit that refined professional men would appreciate did not catch on. Unless accompanied by valuable ideology, such appeals to better benefits typically fall on deaf ears. Barrels of mature whiskey were piling up in Jack Daniel's storehouses, and the company needed to move product. The brand was in desperate need of an innovative strategy, but what to do? To abandon the category orthodoxy was a risky move. To do so for a concept centered on pudgy disheveled men in overalls doing simple manual labor in rural Tennessee? No doubt executives at the House of Seagram viewed this as a naive move by a backwoods Tennessee company and their equally backwoods ad agency.

Ideological Opportunity: Reviving Frontier Masculinity

Despite the fact that many American men were enjoying higher salaries and the economic status derived from these new jobs, the organization-man ideology rubbed many the wrong way. For them, the organization man seemed to violate historic American ideals of masculinity.[2] Since before the founding of the nation, American men had been acculturated in the ideology of rugged individualism. America's masculine ideals originated in the country's story of development, in which poor European immigrants and religious outcasts industriously built a new nation by pioneering land carved out from a vast wilderness, facing up to extraordinary challenges to pursue their material ambition and personal freedom. The pioneer's life on the frontier came to be viewed as the fountainhead of America's strength as a nation. Stories accumulated dramatizing how men attained virtuous traits—toughness, individualism, self-reliance, cantankerous honesty, pragmatism—through the struggles of life on the frontier. The frontier produced the type of men that America relies on when the going gets tough, men of action who can single-handedly change the course of events. This myth became dominant in the mid-nineteenth century, spread through immensely popular novels such as Cooper's Leatherstocking tales, and iconic characters such as Daniel Boone and Davey Crockett. When the frontier closed toward the end of the nineteenth century, sustaining this ideal became paramount in the culture. East Coast aristocrat Owen

Wister's Wild West novels became best-sellers. His friend Teddy Roosevelt extracted bits of Wister's vocabulary and imagery to paint his vision of a country in need of frontier ideals to combat the soft emasculating taint of city life. He reinforced this myth through his reputation as a big-game hunter, by writing memoirs of his times with fellow cowboy Rough Riders fighting in the Spanish–American war, and by setting aside vast areas of the West to remain as wilderness in the form of National Parks, so that Americans could continue to seek out something like the frontier experience.

Since the closing of the frontier, whenever the country has experienced social disruptions that threaten to undermine this frontier masculinity, there is inevitably a conservative backlash seeking to revitalize this ideology in American life by altering its cultural codes so that it resonates with contemporary masculinity issues. Such was the case in the post-war period, as giant bureaucracies encouraged a softer more agreeable more urbane form of masculinity while at the same time American political elites were stirring the hearts and minds of American men with images of nuclear annihilation.

The American build-up for the war left behind a giant military complex. And the economic boom that followed led to the exponential growth of huge corporations, while the newfound wealth allowed the United States to build a welfare state with its attendant civil-service bureaucracies. As the American economy took off, so did a range of massive new institutions—multinational corporations, government services, armed forces spread around the world, and a fleet of new professionals (psychologists, social workers, human-relations departments) whose job it was to guide Americans on how to think, feel, and behave. At the same time, American political elites and the national media whipped the public into a frenzy over a possible nuclear Armageddon—perhaps the Soviets would put Americans in state-run collective farms if Americans did not rise to the occasion. How could Americans protect their way of life now that men were being groomed as soft sedentary organization men instead of hardened men of the frontier? In the cold-war discourse, the organization man took a pounding. American whiskey brands were in a particularly good position to take advantage of this ideological opportunity, if only they could break away from the category orthodoxy.

Whiskey and the Resurgent Cold-War Western
This cultural rebuttal took shape in subcultures and social
movements, and then was quickly picked up by the mass media,
which provided large doses of frontier ideology tailored for cold-war
anxieties. Cultural producers turned to the obvious vehicle to respond
to this demand—the Western film—shifting characters and plots to
make the stories speak to the particular anxieties of the post-war era.
In hugely popular films like *The Gunfighter, High Noon,* and *Shane,* as
well as various John Wayne vehicles, gunfighters were portrayed as
professional killers for hire on the Western frontier. Gunfighters are a
special breed of men whose character is forged in rough-and-tumble
land that is not yet ruled by social institutions and that lacks the basic
accoutrements of modern life. So these films celebrated gunfighters
as self-reliant, vigorous, plain-spoken men who live by a personal code
of honor hewn from living in lawless and dangerous places. Their
violent proclivities must be tolerated because gunfighters, ultimately,
are the only people with the character and strength to uphold
America's values. Gunfighters are reactionary populists who stand up
for self-reliance and use their semi-barbaric aptitude to take on
"totalitarian" modern institutions and ever more vigorous barbarian
enemies.

Brands can champion only those ideologies that are credibly linked
to the product, usage context, or its customers. Whiskey has been a key
accessory of the gunfighter since the early days of the frontier.[3] Prior to
prohibition, Jack Daniel's was one of many dozens of regional whiskeys
made in the Kentucky–Tennessee "whiskey belt." The earliest recorded
Tennessee distillery was opened by Evan Shelby in 1771. By 1810, over
14,000 whiskey distilleries were registered in the USA, which together
produced over 25 million gallons of whiskey. Tennessee was becoming a
major producer—because of a combination of good soil to produce the
grain, ample hardwood for barrel-making, abundant limestone water,
and effective river transport links—but production was equally strong
in New York, Ohio, and Pennsylvania. During the Civil War, whiskey
production became illegal, so that grain could be used to feed the
troops. After the war, commercial whiskey production centered in
Kentucky and Tennessee, and this poor rural region became known
for its fine whiskeys.

In Western novels and films, whiskey was usually found wherever there were gunfighters. Whiskey was conceived as one of the gunfighter's dearest possessions, along with his horse and his gun. Novels, films, and television programs have routinely depicted gunfighters in saloons of the Wild West, with whiskey generously flowing from bottle after bottle that the bartender would plunk on the counter. From these clear unlabeled bottles, gunfighters poured generously into their glasses and knocked back the whiskey with abandon, round after round. When things got out of hand, we would often see gunfighters gulping their whiskey straight from the bottle, occasionally using the bottles as weapons.

For men looking to express their reignited embrace of the frontier, drinking whiskey was an obvious choice. However, at the brand level there was a problem. All the major whiskeys were championing the antithesis of the frontier—status-climbing in the world of the organization man—in their marketing. Since none of the major marketers recognized this extraordinary ideological opportunity, it was inevitable that whiskey drinkers and the media would seek out marginal brands that better exemplified the frontier ethos.

The most obvious path would have been directly to appropriate the popular Westerns, as Marlboro would do a decade later. Instead, Jack Daniel's offered a more creative spin on the frontier. Of the hundreds of minor brands on the market, Jack Daniel's Tennessee Whiskey emerged as the iconic whiskey of the frontier because of fortuitous magazine coverage and adept repurposing of this coverage by a culturally astute ad agency.

Source Material: Lynchburg as Hillbilly Frontier

As the revitalization of the frontier ideology got traction, the media went in search of other more intriguing subcultures where the frontier ideology was still alive and well. The undeveloped rural pockets of the South proved to be fertile cultural territory. In particular, the media became fascinated with that holdover from colonial days that could still be found in the Appalachian hinterlands if you hunted for it—the backyard distillery. Colonial settlers made whiskey in backyard distilleries from the corn, rye, and barley they grew on their farms. Whiskey was the common cheap liquor on the frontier, often used as a barter currency. And whiskey was the favored drink of the early American soldiers, who were largely volunteers and conscripts drawn from farmers and frontiersmen. This tradition lived on in the South, providing cultural fodder for television shows like *The Beverly Hillbillies* and *The Dukes of Hazzard*, and the subcultural source material for Mountain Dew.

While the company was trying to cover up its backwoods roots and instead present Jack Daniel's with a slick citified veneer, the media—searching for stories where pockets of the frontier had somehow escaped the forces of modern development—found the real story of the making of Jack Daniel's whiskey far more interesting. Photojournalists working for two of the leading upscale magazines of the day, *Fortune* and *True*, discovered in this small-time distillery located in Lynchburg Tennessee the makings of a potent frontier parable. The first article, titled "Rare Jack Daniel's," appeared in *Fortune* in July 1951. The lead played off the headline, telling of Jack's word-of-mouth reputation amongst whiskey aficionados as one of the best-made, if least-known, whiskeys in the country. The whiskey's quality was attributed to the small rural distillery, which had not changed its methods since the mid-nineteenth century, located in a picture-perfect "sylvan" setting as if reliving nineteenth-century pioneer life. Photos featured Lem's sons, who now ran the distillery, as old-time pioneer types doing business the old-fashioned way, gossiping on the porch of their one-room office in suspenders and hats, having a chat in a cluttered old office, a panoramic shot of the stacks of maple ricks set against the hollow, and an employee checking the huge oak leaching tanks, the primitive construction and hand-written signs again evoking life a century past.

The *True* story, which appeared in November 1954, largely followed the framing of the brand developed by *Fortune* three years earlier. The feature-length article was embellished with photos of the Lynchburg distillery, the hollow, and its old-time whiskey-makers, similar to the *Fortune* photos. The cover promoted the feature title "Sippin Whiskey and the Shirtsleeve Brothers," which told in loving detail about the pre-modern frontier values and processes that have distinguished Jack Daniel's from the days of the founder through the Motlow family in the post-prohibition era. The story introduced the reader to the kind of place that was quickly disappearing: Lynchburg, a tiny dry Southern town that retains its pre-industrial charm and values. The story and images showcase savvy old-timers who take a leisurely approach to their business but have the know-how and stubbornness not to mess it up, the old-fashioned distillation process done in huge wood vats, and the great burning ricks of maple charcoal fore-grounded against the wooded hollow. The story proved very popular, and the distillery used the article aggressively in subsequent promotions.

These articles relied on a romantic storytelling format to reveal the back story of the old-world artisanal processes that yielded such a good-quality whiskey. The oddball characters and evocative details of making whiskey by stubbornly holding on to pre-industrial techniques painted an original portrait of frontier life compared to the onslaught of Westerns. These details imbued in the whiskey a story that resonated powerfully with men looking for a frontier rebuttal to the organization man.

While the major whiskey brands were trying to modernize their symbolism by taking American men's historic favorite drink out of the backwoods and into middle-class suburban life, these magazine articles pushed Jack Daniel's in exactly the opposite direction, as a real-world exemplar of the tenacity of frontier ideology. By emphasizing the stubbornly traditional ways of frontier whiskey making, these stories promoted Jack Daniel's as the reactionary champion of the old whiskey values of the frontier, reasserting the ideology of the nearly extinct gunfighter who threw back glassfuls of whiskey in saloons. Crucially, they did so by "discovering" a real place—a seemingly lost anachronistic throwback to the pioneer days when men lived in the backwoods making whiskey.

Cultural Innovation: Mythologizing the Lynchburg Distillery

That American whiskey-drinkers resonated with these magazine articles was hard to ignore as letters poured into Lynchburg from all over the country inquiring about the whiskey. So, when the company's new St Louis ad agency, Gardner, took on the account, it is not surprising that it immediately began tinkering with the photojournalist images and folksy narratives of Lynchburg that had appeared in *Fortune* and *True*. The diffusion of the Lynchburg narrative from journalism to advertising was helped along by a well-regarded photojournalist from *Life* magazine whom the agency hired to work with them on the project. The journalist had created a photo-essay on Jack Daniel's for *Life* magazine, but he couldn't get it published, perhaps because two articles had already run in competitor publications. Like his fellow scribes at *Fortune* and *True*, he was enamored by Lynchburg as a powerful metonym for historic America as the country rapidly suburbanized its way out of its past. The Gardner concept drew directly on his photojournalism and added a complementary folksy narrative.

The first ads of the campaign experimented with inserting into the existing drop-by-drop benefits campaign the cultural codes that the *Fortune and True* articles had established. Instead of the men in suits who had previously populated Jack Daniel's ads, we suddenly find ourselves in the heart of Lynchburg, portrayed as Norman Rockwell's small town USA, where men in overalls made "sippin whiskey." As the agency creatives grew more knowledgeable in their appropriation and confident in their work, they evolved the whiskey's attributes and benefits to fit more organically with the Lynchburg narrative. They celebrated everyday life in Lynchburg and work at the distillery, which naturally led to an artisanal product personally made with pride. The ads were dominated by work life at the distillery and town shots of Lynchburg—men overseeing the charcoal burning, barrelmen pushing barrels to be aged, old men whittling outside the general store. We see grizzled men dressed in overalls, portrayed as people whom time forgot, men who cared little about what was happening in the world outside Lynchburg.

The innovation concept came to be called "Postcards." Gardner invented a folksy voice for the brand by narrating the ads as if they were postcards from the proprietors in Lynchburg to the rest of the country, alerting them to the local goings-on in a personal homespun style. The main innovation beyond the prior magazine stories was to develop this plain spoken "tell it like it is" populist voice that nicely expressed frontier masculinity—conveying the folk wisdom that comes only through hard experience, not professional expertise. Long body copy gently boasted about the value of the Lynchburg's pre-industrial world while poking a gentle finger at Fifties obsessions with modern "organization man" life. The campaign's mode of communication was also critical in building the brand's authenticity as a relatively "unmarketed" product. The ads presented the owners of the distillery talking to customers in simple, straight-talking discussion about the product, the distillery, and the town, which made the advertising feel like everyday talk rather than brand communication. The images and art design reinforced this celebration of the rustic, antique qualities that Americans associated with the frontier. As opposed to competitive brands, which tried to create an upscale image by showcasing well-to-do patrons, Jack Daniel's came across as the real deal—not a marketing company but a real distillery.

The print campaign was an immediate hit. And so the company and agency extended the concept to every consumer touchpoint: from retail and promotions to the development of a secret society for mass-market fans and celebrities who drank Jack Daniel's. Many drinkers wanted to visit the distillery to see if it was as portrayed in the ads, and so the tour was developed to convey exactly the pre-industrial frontier ethos promised in "Postcards." Whiskey pilgrims could come and meet the characters they first encountered in the pages of their favorite magazines.

Insider Tactics: Tennessee Squire Secret Society

Jack Daniel's pioneered the pairing of an insider cultural strategy with the mass-market strategy we have discussed so far. An insider strategy anoints those in the subculture from which the company borrows source material as more authentic and original compared to the mass market. This is a crucial counterbalance to the mass-market strategy. If the brand is not recognized as an authentic and credible participant in the subculture, insiders are likely to label the mass-market effort as a kind of cultural pillaging done by imposters that are just out to make money off the culture of others.

In this case, insiders were contrarian American men; whiskey-drinkers had always held onto America's historic frontier ideals, men who had been repulsed by the organization man from the beginning. The company launched a spoof "secret society" called the Tennessee Squires, to give special recognition to, and to create an intimate relationship with, these whiskey-lovers who were similarly enamored by frontier masculinity. The distillery corresponded with handwritten letters to these special friends of the whiskey, providing homespun stories of Lynchburg life along with an invitation to visit the distillery. Many of them did, and they were given VIP treatment, including sipping some special vattings of the whiskey in the "Squire's Room." Each squire member was given a certificate granting him (usually) one square foot of property at the distillery.

By far the most important insiders were celebrities and journalists, with whom the society established a tight and beloved relationship. They served as the brand's advocates, drinking Jack Daniel's in public and singing its praises in print. These unpaid advocates provided powerful credibility upholding the whiskey's gunfighter bone fides, a vastly more impactful mode of branding than hiring paid spokespeople. The brand's ideological posturing attracted Squire members in two elite circles: macho male artists and hawkish political elites. Jack Daniel's was the tipple of choice in the State Department and the media reported on how cold-war warrior Richard Nixon enjoyed the drink. William Faulkner, famous for his alcoholic binges almost as much as for his writing, loved Jack Daniel's, and this was occasionally reported in the media. Journalist Lucius Beebe was a flamboyant high-society gourmand, educated at Yale, who became a writer for upscale publications while also pursuing his deep interests in the American West. He wrote dozens of books on trains, and moved to the middle of the dessert in Nevada to start a newsweekly. In his magazine and newspaper columns he trumpeted his affection for Jack Daniel's alongside travelogue accounts of the West.

John Huston drank Jack Daniel's with Humphrey Bogart, Lauren Bacall, and their crowd, representing what might be called the Hemingway school of Hollywood actors, writers, and directors. They unabashedly championed an old-school view of manhood, aligned with the Western frontier, which directly challenged the new organization man. John Huston was a major celebrity in his day, and the media closely reported his film-making and lifestyle. During the making of his film adaptation of *Moby Dick*, magazines such as *Newsweek* and *Harper's Bazaar* reported on the director's finicky tastes: he likes tweed caps, cigarillos, Jack Daniel's, and hunting in Ireland. Huston was a quintessential gunfighter character: he both lived the life as well as sought to capture the existential tensions that such men face in his films, particularly the quartet of films he made with Bogart. The cigar-chomping womanizing Huston bought a castle in rural Ireland, where he went on sabbatical to hunt, drink, and be merry. And, when he tired of his castle (and his wife at the time), he sold it, bought a strip of Mexican jungle on the Pacific Ocean accessible only by boat, married a young Mexican woman, and lived in a compound he built there.

Frank Sinatra hung out with this crowd as a young acolyte and adopted their drinking habits. As his career took off in 1957, his drinking exploits and love for Jack Daniel's formed one of the media's favorite Sinatra stories. His debauched escapades with his "rat-pack" tribe of fellow men were constantly reported in the media, frequently with Jack Daniel's as a central prop. When out on their adventures, they were even known to wear blazers with a Jack Daniel's insignia on the pocket. Sinatra was the company's most prized catch as a Tennessee Squire member.

Mass Media Cements the Brand's Ideology

Mass-culture producers soon picked up on Jack Daniel's symbolism, cementing the brand as a powerful cultural symbol in American society. The drink's position as the iconic whiskey of the frontier was etched in stone in 1962 by the film *HUD*, Paul Newman's most memorable early film. Hud is a hard-drinking womanizer working on his father's Texas ranch, a self-described frontier luddite who will not tolerate modern incursions into his cowboy way of life. He drinks Jack Daniel's from the bottle throughout the film—whether chasing women, getting into bar fights, or wrestling with pigs.

He is a reactionary cowboy, fighting to retain his libertarian ideology of personal freedom from big modernizing institutions, while expressing his manly virility through women, whiskey, and fighting. Jack Daniel's is Hud's comrade and truth serum. It consoles him when other men fail to uphold his ideology, and it allows him to assert his frontier ideals in the most aggressive and even violent way.

HUD's popularity, and Paul Newman's rise to fame in cowboy roles, affirmed Jack Daniel's iconicity as the drink for those American men, typically of a more conservative political bent, who identified with this ideology. In subsequent years, Jack Daniel's would become a famous prop in many popular films—such as *Platoon, Scent of a Woman, Lethal Weapon, Get Carter, Basic Instinct, A Few Good Men, Man on Fire, Gone in 60 Seconds, Heat, Pearl Harbor, Monster's Ball,* and *Mystic River*—always drawing upon and reinforcing the same gunfighter myth.

Conclusion

Jack Daniel's whiskey is one of the most successful cultural innovations in American business history, ranking consistently as one of world's 100 most valuable brands. The emergent demand for a new frontier ideology was an extraordinary opportunity for any whiskey brand in the 1950s. But the major whiskey marketers were deaf to this opportunity, because they were wedded to the cultural orthodoxy of the day—embracing the trendy new organization-man ideology to respond to the status aspirations of middle-class men. Jack Daniel's followed suit for a time with little success until its ad agency came up with a radically different approach. Jack Daniel's rode the coat-tails of the exploding demand for culture promoting the revival of frontier masculinity and defiantly rejected the keep-up-with-the-Joneses snobbery that whiskey had previously stood for.

Film-makers were most adept in perceiving the growing demand for a frontier revival to respond to cold-war anxieties, and began delivering Westerns that did just that. But soon enough the market had become saturated with cold-war Westerns, and, so, the search was on for a fresh subculture that could convey the same frontier ideology that was in such demand. Journalists beat whiskey marketers to the punch as they opportunistically scanned American culture for intriguing stories. The old-world production of charcoal-filtered whiskey in a dry rural county in Tennessee fit the bill perfectly. To its credit, the Gardner Agency picked up on these magazine stories and usefully embellished the cultural codes established by the journalists. In particular, the agency created a folksy straight-talking "anti-marketing" style of communication that pre-dated by five years Bill Bernbach's famous Volkswagen campaign, which has previously been widely recognized as this style's originator. Its innovation exemplifies two cultural tactics that remain particularly consequential today.

Resuscitating Reactionary Ideology

Jack Daniel's revitalized frontier masculinity during what might seem to have been a most improbable moment—a time when America was shedding its agricultural roots for good for a world of big companies, science and technology, and massive projects such as the Marshall Plan and the Apollo space program. Rather than following trends, Jack Daniel's turned back the clock to reassert the value of historic ideology—a reactionary cultural strategy. In *How Brands Become Icons*, we documented how Mountain Dew and Harley-Davidson exploited exactly the same tactic, and in Chapter 8 we will demonstrate how Marlboro used the same reactionary strategy.

Subcultures often harbor residual ideologies, once-dominant ideologies that have been pushed aside. Sometimes these subcultures spawn conservative social movements, in the parlance of sociology and politics, since they seek to revitalize a traditional ideology. In the United States, the most influential conservative subcultures and movements have leveraged the American frontier as the prime source material. We find such movements at the beginning of the twentieth century as the frontier closed, in the 1950s and early 1960s at the height of the cold war; in the 1980s as the core of the so-called Reagan Revolution, and in the "war on terrorism" that has served as the ideological basis to support the remilitarization of the country in the 2000s.

Mythologizing the Company

The Lynchburg "Postcards" concept also pioneered a tactic that we call *mythologizing the company*. The branding relied on realistic portrayals of the company's backstage business practices. This is the most significant early example of a strategy that has become increasingly important in recent years. Rather than rely on participants of the subculture to express the brand's ideology, the company itself becomes the stage for the branding. By demonstrating that the company—its locale, workers, managers, and production processes—had forever lived the frontier ideology and never gave a thought to moving on to modern life, the Jack Daniel's myth established enormous credibility and authenticity.

Mythologizing the company has become a particularly powerful tactic now that many people are quite cynical about corporate motives and business practices.[4] As consumers have become increasingly skeptical about the "truth" behind brands that spout ideologies, they are increasingly responsive to brands that are much more transparent about such claims. Companies that walk the walk, living their ideology every day in their business, have much more credibility with today's consumers than do companies that promote brands as champions of an ideology that is unrelated to the company's business practices. While not all companies can express their brand ideology through the company, those that can do so earn a considerable premium in the market of the early twenty-first century.

Notes

1. This chapter adapts some of the cultural analysis found in Douglas B. Holt, "Jack Daniel's America: Iconic Brands as Ideological Parasites and Proselytizers," *Journal of Consumer Culture*, 6/3 (2006), 355–77.
2. This synthesis relies on Richard Slotkin's trilogy analyzing the evolution of the frontier myth in American mass culture, especially the last volume *Gunfighter Nation* (Norman, OK: University of Oklahoma Press, 1998). We have analyzed American masculinity in Douglas B. Holt and J. Craig Thompson, "Man-of-Action Heroes," *Journal of Consumer Research*, 31 (Sept. 2004), 424–40.
3. This summary of the history of the whiskey category in the USA relies heavily on Kay Baker Gaston, "Tennessee Distilleries: Their Rise, Fall, and Reemergence," *Border States: Journal of the Kentucky-Tennessee American Studies Association*, 12 (1999), http://spider.georgetowncollege.edu/htallant/border/ bs12/fr-gasto.htm (accessed July 12, 2006).
4. For the academic argument on this point, see Douglas B. Holt, "Why Do Brands Cause Trouble? A Dialectical Theory of Consumer Culture and Branding," *Journal of Consumer Research*, 29 (2002), 70–90.

4

Ben & Jerry's: Provoking Ideological Flashpoints to Launch a Sustainable Business Myth

In less than a decade, Ben & Jerry's Ice Cream grew from a scoop shop in a converted gas station in Burlington, Vermont, into the second largest super-premium ice-cream brand in the USA. The business grew from about $180,000 in sales in 1979 to $58 million in 1989, and then to $237 million by 1999. Unilever purchased the company for $326 million in 2000 and now touts Ben & Jerry's as one of its premier brands and has successfully expanded the business around the globe.

Ben & Jerry's accomplished this feat without an original product. Haagen-Dazs pioneered super-premium ice cream back in 1961, selling rich dense ice cream with high-quality ingredients in pint-sized containers for a price more than double the category norm. Jerry and Ben learned how to make their ice cream from a $5 extension course taught by the Penn State University creamery. Their business did not seem that different from the thousands of local ice-cream parlors found throughout the country. In fact, the original Ben & Jerry's scoop shop and its ice-cream flavors bore a striking resemblance to Steve's Ice Cream. Since 1973, Steve Herrell had been serving rich super-premium ice cream with "smoosh-ins" and "mix-ins" such as broken Oreo cookies, Heath bars, and Reese's peanut butter cups. His ice-cream brand was popular in the Boston area, but never took off nationally, despite a well-financed push to do so.

Moreover, Ben and Jerry set out to run a business grounded in the bohemian ideals of the counter-culture of the 1960s and 1970s. But they were beaten to the punch by many hundreds of ex-hippies (including Steve) who had been opening such businesses since the early 1970s. The vast majority of these start-ups flopped. Some became successful small businesses within the subculture but never grew to an appreciable size. Ben & Jerry's was one of a handful of counter-cultural business start-ups that broke out of the subculture—accomplishing what in later chapters we will call *crossing the cultural chasm*—and became wildly appealing to a segment of Americans dominated by the liberal upper middle class.[1] How is it that Ben & Jerry's entered a mature category with no money, no new technologies, and no product innovation, and yet became one of the most important brands of one of the biggest multinational food companies fifteen years later? According to better-mousetraps innovation models, this should never have happened.

Ben & Jerry's succeeded through cultural innovation: by designing a provocative cultural expression that served as the perfect ideological counterpoint to the rise of Reaganism. Ben & Jerry's targeted an ideological opportunity that took shape in reaction to Ronald Reagan's radical, turn-back-the-clock, remaking of American society in the 1980s. The small company's marketing adapted the ideology, myth, and cultural codes of the back-to-the-land agrarian communes, a utopian subculture that had flourished in the 1970s. The ice-cream maker championed the myth that businesses could be humanitarian and sustainable and still make a profit, using creative adaptations of eco-agrarian ideas about food culture and their playful prankster style of communiqués.

In so doing, Ben & Jerry's pioneered a cultural innovation tactic that we term *provoking ideological flashpoints*. Ben Cohen became increasingly astute at identifying issues of the day that particularly stuck in the craw of the middle-class liberals who were the core of the Ben & Jerry's franchise. Then the company designed products and communiqués as provocative cultural expressions that asserted the company's ideological counterpoint.

Ideological Opportunity: Resistance to Reaganism

Beginning in the mid-1960s, sharp differences erupted between American liberal and conservative political views on issues spanning beyond conventional politics, initiating what became known as the "culture wars."[2] In the 1960s, the federal government had pushed through a wide range of liberal laws and national programs at breathtaking speed, including civil rights, the war on poverty, environmental protection, and the near passage of the Equal Rights Amendment. Civil-rights initiatives such as open housing and desegregating local schools were particularly contentious, setting off a conservative backlash, especially amongst less educated whites.[3] The conservative movement gained momentum throughout the 1970s, culminating in the election of Reagan in 1980 and his landslide victory in 1984. While many Americans were enthralled with Reagan's masterful rhetoric reinvigorating the country's frontier ideology, his sweeping policy changes were an alienating affront to liberals. Reagan dramatically cut taxes for the wealthy and uncritically supported big business, deregulating industries, and creating a lax antitrust enforcement environment. Reagan made sure that the strict pollution laws passed in the liberal regulatory wave were not enforced, and he appointed a Secretary of Interior from the energy sector who viewed his role as opening up public lands for mineral extraction on the cheap. Reagan famously challenged unions by firing en masse all air-traffic controllers working at airports throughout the country. He berated welfare as producing lazy parasites, cut back on spending on poverty, and returned to his role as a McCarthy era cold warrior, reigniting fear in the Soviet Union as the evil empire, even though the USSR was in the midst of a rapid economic deterioration at the time. He fluffed up the threat of small guerrilla movements in Central America as the next Vietnam, and funded "freedom fighters" to undermine these movements.[4]

By Reagan's re-election in 1984, many liberals felt politically alienated, and questioned whether they belonged in the same country as Reagan's supporters. The American population was divided, with fully half of the population identifying strongly with either the conservative or the liberal pole. This political polarization created enormous ideological opportunities. Harley-Davidson motorcycles and Jack Daniel's whiskey took advantage of conservative desires for the return of frontier ideology. Ben & Jerry's leveraged the other side of the spectrum. Reaganism created a massive latent demand for a credible counterpoint. Environmental NGOs that had crashed in the late 1970s, when many people believed their task was done, suddenly found a flood of new members. These same liberals also looked to business to respond, using their choices as consumers to reflect their political desires. It was an ice-cream company that provided the most incisive business rebuttal.

Source Material: The Back-to-the-land Business Utopia Movement

The founders relied heavily on a social movement that we will term the *back-to-the-land business utopia* as cultural source material for branding Ben & Jerry's. Ben Cohen had been immersed in the movement prior to starting Ben & Jerry's and became increasingly adept at making use of its ideology, myth, and cultural codes to advance a view that persuasively challenged Reaganism. The movement began in the late 1960s as an alternative "personal is political" strategy for taking on the growing irrationality of big business, especially in the food industry.

The pre-history of this movement began with the Diggers, a group of guerrilla street actors operating in San Francisco's Haight district. The Diggers opened a radical, "free-food" cooperative to feed hippie youth with food grown at a nearby communal farm. They promoted the store using prankster stunts while driving around in a bus called the yellow submarine. The Diggers circulated manifestos that railed against modern industry, portraying it in terms of a suicidal war against the earth. Only by returning to the land could people straighten their heads and become physically and mentally healthy again.[5] Through their antics, the Diggers became nationally famous.

In April 1969, a group of student radicals calling themselves the Robin Hood's Park Commission took over a Berkeley lot owned by the University of California, named it The People's Park, and, using the slogan "Power to the People," declared it public property for the purpose of producing free speech and free food. Visitors were encouraged to help plant vegetable seeds, share food and drugs, listen to performing bands, and enjoy a space that existed outside American governmental rule. Ronald Reagan, in his inaugural address as governor of California, warned Berkeley students to "obey the rules or get out," worrying that "a small minority of beatniks, radicals and filthy speech advocates have brought such shame to...such a great university."[6] Reagan placed the entire city under martial law, called in the National Guard, had a helicopter drop a tear-gas bomb, and sent in riot police, who shot and killed one man, wounded others, and arrested hundreds.

The confrontation brought national media attention to both the park and the new movement.

The idea of pursuing a back-to-the-land business utopia was inspired by the counter-culture's critique of the American economic system, what Theodore Rozak famously termed the technocracy.[7] Inspired by intellectuals like Jacques Ellul and Herbert Marcuse, youth damned the techno-industrial systems that, in their size and power, dominated all facets of society. They challenged the recklessness and inhumanity of technocracy—the unintended irrationality of businesses that competed to produce goods in an ever-more rationalized manner. It built stuff faster and better without any concern for the consequences to society and planet. The counter-culture found it absurd that companies could act in an orderly and efficient way to produce bombs and Agent Orange and DDT.

They called for the reinvention of society on a much smaller, less technology-obsessed, more humane scale, in which expert knowledge was democratized.[8] While the emphasis was on the military industries, the critique was also extended to food and education. Other influential thinkers, such as E. F. Schumacher (the author of eco-agrarian bible *Small is Beautiful*), Wendell Berry, and Kirkpatrick Sale, gave the critique an ecological spin. Ecological thinkers, writers, and activists such as Rachel Carson, Aldo Leopold, J. I. Rodale, David Brower, Edward Abbey, Barry Commoner, and Buckminster Fuller, many of whom had been writing on sustainability issues for many years, suddenly became celebrity intellectuals and thought-leaders.

The movement first took on technocracy with the conventional tools of non-violent protest: sit-ins, marches, and other forms of spectacle.[9] When these efforts to overturn "the system" came to an inglorious end with the splintering of the peace movement, inner-city riots, and the assassinations of Martin Luther King and Robert Kennedy, a significant segment adopted a new strategy. Instead of using the social-movement strategies of Gandhi and King to overturn the system directly, they went off in the woods to reinvent society in microcosm—a pastoral utopia that would be truly sustainable. Taking their cue from the long American tradition of utopian communities, they moved to the hinterlands, predominantly to the counties north of San Francisco and in the mountainous areas of Vermont, Massachusetts, and upstate New York.

Eleanor Agnew, in her book *Back from the Land*, estimates that more than one million young people joined the rural migration.[10]

If the communards were to reinvent society in miniature, this meant that they had to reinvent business as well. While certain technologies— cars, electronics, and such—were out of the question, the rudimentary basics of everyday life became fodder for a do-it-yourself lifestyle that sought inspiration from pre-industrial societies. Participants learned how to make tools, build houses, and grow, store, and prepare their own foods. To assist them, Stewart Brand launched *The Whole Earth Catalog*—a folksy catalogue and guide for do-it-yourself living. Many of its items could have been in a nineteenth-century Sears Roebucks catalogue sent to families on the frontier. It became the how-to bible of the movement, providing wherewithal for a scaled-down and sustainable life in nature. It gave instructions about building deep-well pumps, using solar cookers, and setting up potter's wheels. It showed how agrarian living lent itself to a wide range of craft businesses. For instance, a typical item promoted in the catalogue was called *The ABC and XYZ of Bee Culture*, a book that taught not only how to make honey, but how to market it and make money from it. For middle-class youth with no experience in do-it-yourself living, the catalogue made the transformation of civilization to a pre-modern agrarian paradise a tangible pragmatic goal. As they experimented with this new lifestyle, a potent ideology grew, imagining a nation of small businesses, family farmers, village stores, craft production, personalized interaction, political involvement, and community ties.

The back-to-the-land business ideology transformed production and consumption in everything from fashion (faded cotton and wool, peasant skirts, worn and torn denim) to music (softer country rock, outdoor festivals), to home decor (houseplants, clay, woodcraft). But food was the core, the most tangible domain for exercising the movement's principles. Responsible back-to-the-landers could effectively challenge the technocracy of agribusiness three times a day by eating foods that were natural, unprocessed, and sustainably grown by small-scale producers. Vegetarianism became a political act in support of sustainable living, thanks largely to Frances Moore Lappe's *Diet for a Small Planet*. Foods free of chemicals, additives, and preservatives were to be cherished; anything that you could not pronounce was to be avoided. The demand for these alternative foods led to the explosive growth of food cooperatives, which sought to reinvent capitalism along ecological lines. Between 5,000 and 10,000 coops, emphasizing organics and minimal processing and packaging, came onto the scene between 1969 and 1979.[11] The pre-modern cuisines favored by the communards were well represented. Most used bulk bins to reduce the environmental impact of packaging. All of them stocked books and periodicals proselytizing the ideology of the back-to-the-land movement.

A bourgeoning scene of subcultural restaurateurs also emerged, with Alice Waters's Berkeley restaurant Chez Panisse leading the way. Waters forged relationships with nearby organic farms and celebrated the use of seasonal local ingredients in her restaurant. Similarly, Mollie Katzen and her Moosewood Collective in upstate New York started an employee-owned restaurant that soon spun off into an enormously successful series of cookbooks that championed vegetarian cuisine. As with the food cooperatives, thousands of new restaurants appeared around the country following their lead.

The back-to-the-land business utopia—and especially its precepts about food—became a source for many cultural innovations in the coming decades. Ben & Jerry's was one of the first businesses to commercialize the ideological precepts of this movement successfully for the mass market.

Designing the Cultural Innovation

Early Concept: Ben & Jerry's as Subcultural Brand
In the early years of the business, Ben & Jerry's operated as a subcultural business, successfully targeting fellow eco-agrarians in Burlington, Vermont, and surrounding areas.[12] Ben Cohen and Jerry Greenfield graduated from a Long Island high school in 1969, just as the hippies were moving to the rural communes and the back-to-the-land ideology was taking off. Cohen dropped out of college to learn pottery, and then moved to the East Village to try to make money using his newfound hobby as a form of therapy. Soon enough, he found his "dream job" in the help-wanted section of the *New York Times*, as a crafts teacher at an experimental school called Highland Community, situated on a 600-acre working farm in rural New York.

Highland Community was an exemplary rural commune, where the staff and students could grow their own produce and milk their own cows. The buildings were an assortment of geodesic domes, A-frame houses, and wood cabins, all hand-made by staff and students. The scene was straight out of the *Whole Earth Catalogue*. The school had an informal, anti-authoritarian ethos, and staff had loosely defined roles. Ben became interested in food, working as a school cook and even experimenting with home-made ice cream.

Three years later, when the commune was shut down for building-code violations, Ben talked his friend Jerry into moving upstate with him. Since both were unemployed, they began brainstorming over businesses they could start to support themselves. Scheming over a number of community-oriented food businesses, they settled on the idea of an ice-cream parlor. They wanted to open their parlor in Saratoga Springs, in New York's Adirondack mountains, but, after another home-made ice cream parlor opened up there, they started looking at other rural college towns with sizable counter-cultural communities. They chose Burlington, Vermont. With combined assets of $12,000, they leased an abandoned gas station and started making ice cream.

Ben enlisted his friends from Highland Community to help with the start-up, including the design of the logo. In return for their services, Jerry and Ben offered them "ice cream for life" for as long as the business remained open, since they could not afford a fee. The Highland Community group infused the entire enterprise with cultural codes from the back-to-the-land movement. They hand-painted the store, hand-sawed the tables, and gave the space a rustic feel. Ben picked out a funky burnt orange paint for the walls. The logo was hand-drawn and the menus hand-written. To make the ice cream, Jerry used a small, old-fashioned, 4½-gallon hand-cranked bucket, rock salt, and ice freezer. Only natural, unprocessed, simple ingredients such as cream, milk, honey, cane sugar, and egg yolks went into it. They improvised flavors, using the likes of granola, hand-broken peanut brittle, and local Vermont maple syrup. The name, Ben & Jerry's Homemade, conveyed a small-scale, personalized, and pre-modern ethos. Even the clunky tagline—"Ice Cream for the People"—recalled the naming of People's Park in Berkeley and the populist sentiment of the movement. When they began wholesaling pints of ice cream, a friend designed a hand-drawn package with a low-fidelity photo of Jerry and Ben. In all, Ben & Jerry's used a wide variety of cultural codes that aligned the company ideologically with the back-to-the-land movement and stamped them as the antithesis of a big, industrial agribusiness.

Ben & Jerry's began to earn a reputation through a series of stunts reminiscent of the Robin Hood Park Commission and the Diggers. Just as the Diggers had used their Free Food Store to promote their ideology, Jerry and Ben decided to celebrate the end of their first year in business with Free Cone Day. For Free Cone Day, they gave out a free cone for a day—and other free food—to anybody who came to their store, and they handed out a flyer that declared: "Business has a responsibility to give back to the community from which it draws its support."

By its fifth year, Ben & Jerry's had become a real business, with lots of employees and a budding hierarchy. Ben began to worry that his own business was becoming part of the industrial technocracy that he believed was intrinsically exploitative, and he came close to selling the business. He was ultimately talked out of it by his close confidants, who were just as embedded in the back-to-the-land movement as he was.[13] What Ben soon discovered was that his business could serve as political bully pulpit for poking fun at the qualities of corporate capitalism he disliked. In 1984, Ben & Jerry's began to expand distribution beyond Vermont. As the company grew, Cohen discovered that his most powerful marketing tool was to use the brand as a credible challenge to the politics and business ideology of Reaganism. In so doing, he adapted the same sort of media tactics that the 1960s counter-culturalists had used to challenge technocracy. This conversion of Ben & Jerry's—from a successful business within the subculture, to a platform for leveraging the subcultural ideology to challenge Reaganism in an arresting manner—attracted continual national press attention, resonated powerfully with liberal middle-class consumers outside the subculture, and brought the company undreamed-of success.

Agrarian Utopia's Stock Offering
The first rhetorical arrow came from an unlikely place. When the company needed to raise money in 1984, Cohen decided to forgo the usual Wall Street investment banks. Instead, he created an imaginative financing

vehicle that reflected back-to-the-land ideals. Instead of offering the stock to large investors, he wanted it to be available to local farmers, families, and community members, and he set the minimum investment at as little as $125. In the end, nearly 1,800 households purchased stock—roughly one in every hundred Vermonters. About a third of the investors purchased the minimum amount.[14] This creative subversion of Wall Street made Ben & Jerry's immensely popular in Vermont and surrounding states, giving Ben the confidence to pursue more sharply barbed pranks, and on the national rather than regional stage.

What's the Doughboy Afraid Of?

In March 1984, Cohen learned that the Pillsbury Company, owner of Haagen-Dazs, was threatening to pull its account from grocery retailers if they continued to sell Ben & Jerry's. Because Haagen-Dazs dominated the segment with more than a 70 percent market share, the grocers felt that they had to buckle to this predatory move.[15] Ben & Jerry's lawyers told Cohen that this restrictive distribution arrangement was in direct violation of anti-trust law, but Reagan's administration was not enforcing the law, so it was unclear how a legal fight would come out, and the costs and time of the suit would bankrupt a company as small as theirs. All this, Pillsbury knew. It was using its corporate might to push the upstart out of its new markets.

Cohen intuitively understood that Pillsbury's move could work in Ben & Jerry's favor. Here was a big techno-industrial company, of the type Reagan favored, all set to squash a tiny company trying to advance a populist alternative based upon back-to-the-land principles. Cohen brainstormed over protest ideas with his senior executives. In the midst of the session his CEO, Fred "Chico" Lager, blurted out "What's the Doughboy Afraid Of?"—a playful jab at Pillsbury's famous icon—and Cohen knew he had a winner. Ben & Jerry's used the slogan to headline a press release and a hand-out flyer that pitted little Ben & Jerry's against "the Doughboy, a huge conglomerate with sales of $3,948,100,100." The copy described Ben & Jerry's as a start-up run according to the best back-to-the-land ideals, trying to fend off Pillsbury's predatory attempt to keep it out of the marketplace. On the back of the flyer, Ben included instructions on how to take direct personal action. People could call the "Doughboy Hotline" for a kit with protest letters addressed to the

Federal Trade Commission and Pillsbury's Chairman of the Board. The flyer urged consumers to boycott Pillsbury's various subsidiaries such as Burger King and Green Giant. The kit included "What's the Doughboy Afraid Of?" bumper stickers and an offer for T-shirts that read "Ben & Jerry's Legal Defense Fund—Major Contributor."

Next, Jerry Greenfield showed up alone at Pillsbury headquarters with a "What's the Doughboy Afraid Of?" protest placard and started handing out flyers. Cohen called up the local media, and the media bit. First, Minneapolis Public Radio showed up to interview Greenfield. Then came articles in the Minneapolis and Saint Paul dailies. Cohen then sent out a press release to seed this story into the media. When a photo of Jerry wearing a Doughboy T-shirt and holding a protest sign went out on the AP press wire, papers around the country picked up the story, including the *New York Times*, the *Wall Street Journal*, the *San Francisco Chronicle*, and the *Boston Globe*. The *Globe*'s cover story was headlined "New England's Own Cold War." The guerrilla campaign was then extended to include print, outdoor, on-package, and other non-traditional media. The print ad in *Rolling Stone* read: "What's the Doughboy Afraid Of? Help two Vermont hippies fight the giant Pillsbury Corporation. Send $1.00 for the facts and a bumper sticker."

A billboard on Route 128, the main arterial road around Boston, read, "Don't Let Pillsbury Put the Squeeze on Ben & Jerry's!" An airplane flew over Boston's Foxboro Stadium during a football game trailing "What's the Doughboy Afraid Of" and a 1-800 number to call. Every pint container now had a sticker with that headline and the Doughboy Hotline number. Four months into the campaign, Pillsbury agreed to settle out of court and drop all restrictive distribution arrangements.

The Doughboy campaign established Ben & Jerry's as a comedic hippie underdog in business to counter Reaganite business ideology with the humane ideals of the back-to-the-land movement. The Doughboy campaign generated such strong demand for Ben & Jerry's ice cream that the company easily accessed distribution points in grocery freezers up and down the East Coast that would otherwise have been impossible to win. The company raced to increase its manufacturing capacity as revenue grew 250 percent in 1985, and sales doubled again in 1986.

Emboldened by the success of the Doughboy campaign, Cohen set about specifying how Ben & Jerry's would advance a brand of capitalism that flew in the face of Reaganism. The company established the Ben & Jerry's Foundation to wed the business to social activism, and the company wrote into its bylaws that 7.5 percent of annual profits would be distributed to the foundation. The foundation funded projects that "worked toward eliminating the underlying causes of environmental and societal problems."[16] Furthermore, to respond to Reagan's trickle-down economics that had increased social inequality with huge tax cuts for the wealthy, the company established an innovative corporate pay policy: no employee could earn more than five times what was paid to the employee who was earning the lowest salary. Ben & Jerry's business policies proved that they "walked the walk" of their quixotic back-to-the-land business model, providing the credibility for the company's increasingly sophisticated provocations, most of which took the form of new product launches.

Cherry Garcia

Much of Ben & Jerry's appeal came from flouting the Reaganite mantra that the hippie counter-culture and successful enterprise did not mix. The conservative pro-business character Alex P. Keaton (played by Michael J. Fox) on the hit show *Family Ties* thrived on teasing his ex-hippie baby-boomer parents about their lack of business savvy. The Reagan narrative was that hippies were lazy, zonked out on drugs, and a parasitic drain on the economy. Reagan was famous for his anti-hippie quips like "a hippie is someone who looks like Tarzan, walks like Jane, and smells like Cheetah."

It must have been a particular shock, then, when a successful business enterprise so firmly embraced the "zonked-out drug culture" that it named one of its products "Cherry Garcia." Cherry Garcia was a homage to Jerry Garcia, the lead guitarist of the Grateful Dead. No other band in the history of music has been so closely identified with the use of marijuana, LSD, and other hallucinogens. Their concerts were notorious for the band of "deadheads" who followed them around the country in VW buses in a swirl of drugs, patchouli, and free love. And there was no denying that drugs, particularly marijuana, were prevalent in the back-to-the-land movement.[17] Prior to Cherry Garcia, drug use had remained an insider subtext for the Ben & Jerry's brand, with customers sharing stories about eating pints of Ben & Jerry's when they get the munchies from smoking pot. Now Ben & Jerry's was flaunting the connection. The inspiration for the new product came from two deadheads who wrote in, pleading that Ben & Jerry's make a Grateful Dead flavor. Cohen appropriated the idea, coming up with the Cherry Garcia name and using psychedelic writing in the packaging.

Cherry Garcia was launched in 1987, after Reagan had ratcheted up his anti-drug rhetoric in the national media. In 1986, Reagan had delivered a series of speeches calling for a "nationwide crusade against drugs, a sustained, relentless effort to rid America of this scourge."[18] Just before Cherry Garcia's launch, he had signed into law a $1.7 billion anti-drug bill that mandated much tougher prison terms for drug offenders, including a death-penalty provision for drug kingpins. Reagan's stumping helped create a full-scale moral panic across the country. According to a *New York Times*/CBS poll, the number of Americans ranking drug abuse as the nation's worst problem increased more than sixfold during the five months that Reagan was making his speeches.

Cherry Garcia served as a finger-poking prank aimed at Reagan's moralism. Print ads in magazines such as *Rolling Stone*, signage in the scoop shops, and tie-dyed T-shirts all made use of Grateful Dead acid-trip references such as "Euphoria again" and "What a long, strange dip." The flavor became an instant hit.

Peace Pops
A key plank of Reaganism was its bellicose global posture, calling out the Soviet Union as the "evil empire" and threatening any national leader who challenged American dominance. Reagan backed this rhetoric with a massive military build-up, pushing American nuclear weapons into Europe, promoting a "Star Wars" defense system, and spending vast sums on new weaponry. When George H. W. Bush took over in 1989, these policies continued, most famously with the invasion of Panama to take out dictator Manuel Noriega, who had been on the CIA payroll for years but had made the mistake of rebuffing American demands. Ben formed a non-profit organization called "1% for Peace" inspired by a white paper written by a peace activist, "The One Percent

Plan: A People-to-People Step toward Durable Peace."[19] The idea was to take 1 percent of the total military budget of the United States and the Soviet Union and devote it to cultural and economic exchanges to help the people of each country overcome their misapprehensions and suspicions of one another. To promote the cause, Cohen wanted to tie it into a new product. Once again appropriating the Diggers' idea of using food as a medium for agitprop, Ben came up with the idea for Peace Pops. Ben & Jerry's set about manufacturing 12.5 million chocolate-covered ice cream popsicles, packaged in boxes covered with peace copy challenging the Reagan administration to devote 1 percent of its military budget to peace. The Peace Pops launch was picked up by the AP newswire and was promoted by newspapers across the country.

Rain Forest Crunch
In December 1988, the killing of environmental activist Chico Mendes sparked an international outcry about the destruction of the Brazilian rainforest. Industrial conglomerates were hacking down large swathes of the rainforest for cattle ranches that would supply America and Europe with beef. Mendes advocated an alternative sustainable model of business, and founded a union of rubber-tappers in an attempt to preserve the rainforest. When he was murdered by slash-and-burn loggers, his cause made headlines around the world, including the front page of the *New York Times*. Environmental organizations had been concerned about rainforest destruction for some time, but with Mendes's murder the issue hit a tipping point and exploded in the American discourse.

Activist Jason Clay, who was heavily involved in the rainforest-protection movement, suggested to Cohen that the company use sustainably harvested rainforest nuts as an ingredient in the ice cream. Ben recognized that the publicity surrounding the Mendes murder could help fuel interest in a product of this kind. So the company formed a collaborative venture aimed at creating demand for sustainably harvested rainforest nuts. It would purchase nuts from the Xapuri cooperative in Brazil, the birthplace of Chico Mendes's rubber-tapper movement, and sell them to Ben & Jerry's. Its charter mandated that 60 percent of its profits would be directed to environmental activism.[20] Meanwhile, Ben & Jerry's invented Rainforest Crunch, a new flavor combining vanilla ice cream and a cashew and brazil-nut brittle. The package used a striking rainforest theme along with instructions of how to get involved in the rainforest-protection movement. The product hit the shelves on the twentieth anniversary of Earth Day in 1989 and received an enormous outburst of media attention. Rainforest Crunch became a top-selling flavor, and entered into the national discourse. When *Time* magazine did its New Year's edition in December 1990, to describe significant social changes as the country moved into a new decade, it cited Rainforest Crunch as leading the new zeitgeist: "The ostentation of the 1980s vanished; hello, '90s humility. Good intentions became fashionable once more—even marketable. Ben & Jerry's Rainforest Crunch ice cream was a best seller."[21]

Media coverage always amplified Ben & Jerry's provocative efforts to advance its utopian back-to-the land sustainable business concept. This coverage accomplished much more persuasive branding than advertising and required only minimal expenditures. For example, a 1992 *USA Today* affectionately asks:

What other company could market Peace Pops with a straight face? Or funnel money toward Amazon rain forest preservation through sales of Rainforest Crunch? And quick—name another business that donates 7.5% of its pretax income to charity? Ben & Jerry's has a unique take on the free-enterprise system, in keeping with the views of its 41-year-old co-founder. "Somehow, business has set itself up to be valueless, to be completely unspiritual," Cohen says, vestiges of Brooklyn flavoring his speech. "It's very possible for business to make a profit and integrate a concern for the community into its day-to-day activity. If most businesses operated in that fashion, we wouldn't have all these social and environmental problems that we have."[22]

Milk, Family Farms, and rBGH

Throughout the 1980s, farming became increasingly politicized in the USA. Activists drew attention to how agriculture had become dominated by huge agribusiness firms like Cargill, Archer-Daniels-Midland, and Monsanto. They had transformed farming into a rationalized enterprise based upon economies of scale, which was driving family farms out of business. Willie Nelson organized the first Farm Aid benefit concert in 1985 to increase awareness of the problems faced by family farms. By 1991 small-scale dairy farmers from around the country were trying to organize how to survive a devastating drop in wholesale milk prices. In the past, federal price supports had helped farmers through hard times. Now, industrial farming lobbyists pushed governments to let market forces ease the less efficient producers out of the picture. They argued that their computerized 10,000-head operations were the future, because they could produce milk more cheaply.[23]

Cohen had responded early to this issue. In 1985, even as Ben & Jerry's expanded distribution across the country, the company committed to purchasing its milk and cream from a local Vermont farming cooperative, the St Alban's Coop. So far, the company had not done much to publicize the effort. But now, following the success of Rainforest Crunch, Cohen decided to use Ben & Jerry's supply chain as the foundation for his next branding effort. Ben resolved to make up for that year's 25 percent drop in dairy prices by paying farmers significantly *more* than the market price. Rather than accept the downward spiral of rationalized production, which lowered quality as it pushed down price, Ben & Jerry's set prices according to what would keep local family farmers in business.

In 1991, Ben & Jerry's joined up with Farm Aid to launch a campaign to help save family farms. Resuscitating his Doughboy tactics, Cohen tried once again to turn the ice cream into a medium, and printed a "Support Farm Aid" message on all Ben & Jerry's pint containers. He created a 1-800 number so that people could call in to support the cause of the family farm. But this was a conventional me-too sponsorship effort that did not garner much attention.

Dairy burned brighter in 1993, however, when the FDA, caving in to intensive lobbying by the industrial food science conglomerate Monsanto, approved the use of the company's product, recombinant bovine growth hormone (rBGH), for dairy farming. The decision was one of the most controversial the FDA has ever made. Activists attacked the FDA for concealing information about the hormone's negative effects upon cows and possibly its negative effects upon human health. One FDA veterinarian, Richard Burroughs, was fired after accusing both Monsanto and the FDA of "suppressing and manipulating data to hide the effects of rBGH injections on the health of dairy cows."[24]

In 1994, the year that rBGH came into widespread use on large industrial farms, Cohen agreed to pay the farmers of the St Alban's Coop a premium for guaranteeing that their milk and cream was rBGH-free. To the press, Ben declared that the growth hormone is detrimental to the health of cows, threatens family farms by increasing the milk supply, and has unknown long-term human health effects.[25] Again using the pint containers as a medium of protest, Ben sought to label all Ben & Jerry's containers with a statement against rBGH and assurances that the milk and cream used in Ben & Jerry's was rBGH-free. But, because the FDA left individual states to regulate labeling claims, Monsanto began to lobby heavily at the state level and filed numerous lawsuits. As a result, several states banned companies from labeling products as rBGH-free. The efforts of Ben & Jerry's and a handful of family dairies to stop rBGH became a cause célèbre amongst liberal political activists, who took up the campaign for the next decade.[26]

Conclusion

Ben & Jerry's became an iconic brand, massively resonant amongst liberal middle-class Americans, because the company championed an ideology that responded to their collective desires for a commercial counterpoint to Reaganism. The brand effectively mined the ideology, myth, and cultural codes of the back-to-the-land movement, which had already developed the key ideas and practices to counter techno-industrial business. As a result of these efforts, Ben & Jerry's delivered extraordinary social and cultural value to its target: customers indulged in both ice cream and idealism, rallying around the dream that a humane sustainable business ethos can win out over the predatory version of capitalism they associated with Reaganism. Likewise, this powerful symbolism had a pronounced impact on consumers' perceptions of the ice cream. Customers swayed by Ben & Jerry's ideology perceived, as a result, that Ben & Jerry's ice cream was higher quality, tastier, and more natural than any other ice cream on the market.

If Ben & Jerry's had just spouted its back-to-the-land ideology in the declarative terms of a social mission statement, the company would never have succeeded. Thousands of movement activists preceded

Ben and Jerry in failed attempts to launch sustainable businesses using back-to-the-land principles. What set Ben & Jerry's apart is that Cohen was able to formulate provocative cultural expressions that dramatized the back-to-the-land ideology, expressions that powerfully resonated with the mass market yet cost little to execute. He learned to play his provocative cultural cards at just the right ideological moment—when Pillsbury arrogantly moved to eliminate its competition, echoing the Reaganites' subservience before big business; when loggers murdered Chico Mendes, echoing the Reaganites' buccaneering in Latin America as well as their disdain for environmentalism; when the FDA approved the use of rBGH, echoing the Reaganites' contempt for regulation.

Ben Cohen pioneered a cultural innovation tactic we term *provoking ideological flashpoints.* He put his finger on the controversial and newsworthy issues of the day that most dramatically exemplified the ideological divide between Ben & Jerry's and Reaganism. Then he designed new products, business practices, and guerrilla campaigns to place Ben & Jerry's at the center of the controversy, championing the back-to-the-land alternative. These provocations won people over because they relied upon the sensibility of a playful prankster, poking fun at the omnipotent business and political elites of the country. And they were always centered on how the company did business, so the provocations were always very credible and persuasive, quite the opposite of conventional cause-related marketing campaigns and CSR publicity.

In our work, we have found this strategy to be extremely powerful. Marketers view media attention and consequent word of mouth—"buzz," "viral," "memes," "talk value"—as the holy grail. But they continually struggle to cut through in the oversaturated environment of the national media. And, even when they succeed, the buzz they create is usually superficial and does little to advance the brand's point of view. Ben & Jerry's attracted media coverage and generated word of mouth better than any brand in recent American business history, and the media coverage always amplified the brand's ideological position. Cohen's provoking ideological flashpoints strategy is much more effective than conventional viral marketing efforts for two reasons. First, he intervened in a contentious national issue, leveraging the public's attention and interest, rather than trying to start a media sensation from square one.

Second, he did so with funny ideologically charged forays that powerfully expressed Ben & Jerry's point of view, rather than media tricks that attract attention empty of meaning.

Notes

1. Others include Patagonia, Stonyfield Yogurt, Tom's of Maine, Burt's Bees, Snapple, Cascadian Farm, Kashi, Muir Glen, White Wave, and Odwalla, all of which have been purchased by major consumer goods companies. A few of the original counter-cultural businesses remain independent, including the Whole Foods Market and Seventh Generation.
2. Nolan McCarty, Keith T. Pool, and Howard Rosenthal, *Polarized America: The Dance of Ideology and Unequal Riches* (Cambridge, MA: MIT Press, 2006) provide detailed quantitative data charting this divide.
3. Rick Perlstein, *Nixonland: The Rise of a President and the Fracturing of America* (New York: Scribner, 2008).
4. Sean Wilentz, *The Age of Reagan: A History, 1974–2008* (New York: HarperCollins, 2008).
5. For our historical overview of the back-to-the-land food movement, we draw extensively from Warren Belasco's *Appetite for Change: How the Counterculture Took on the Food Industry* (New York: Cornell University Press, 2006).
6. Seth Rosenfeld, "The Governor's Race," *San Francisco Chronicle*, June 9, 2002, a Chronicle Special Report, www.sfgate.com/cgi-bin/article.cgi?f=/c/a/2002/06/09/MNCF3.DTL (accessed Jan. 9, 2010)
7. Theodore Roszak, *The Making of a Counterculture: Reflections on a Technocratic Society and its Youthful Opposition* (Berkeley and Los Angeles: University of California Press, 1995). See also Jacques Ellul's *The Technological Society* (New York: Vintage Books, 1967), which was also a highly influential analysis of the period.
8. Belasco, *Appetite for Change*, 25–6.
9. See Todd Gitlin, *The Whole World is Watching: Mass Media in the Making and Unmaking of the New Left* (Berkeley and Los Angeles: University of California Press, 1980).
10. See Frances Fitzgerald, *Cities on a Hill: A Journey through Contemporary American Cultures* (New York: Simon & Schuster, 1987).
11. Belasco, *Appetite for Change*, 90–1.
12. For our account of Ben & Jerry's pre-history, founding, and first decade and a half of growth, we rely heavily on Fred "Chico" Lager, *Ben & Jerry's: The Inside Scoop* (New York: Crown Books, 1994). Drawing from Lager's historical record, we add our own cultural analysis to the marketing, publicity, and new product efforts that Lager details.
13. Lager, *Ben & Jerry's*, 57.
14. Ibid. 103.

15. Ibid. 106–14.
16. Ben & Jerry's Foundation Homepage, "Ben & Jerry's: Greening the Grassroots since 1985," www.benjerry.com/company/foundation (accessed Jan 10, 2010).
17. For example, see Timothy Miller's discourse analysis of the counterculture's 'zines in *The Hippies and American Values* (Knoxville, TN: University of Tennessee Press, 1991).
18. Erich Goode and Nachman Ben-Yehuda, "The American Drug Panic of the 1980s," in *Moral Panics: The Social Construction of Deviance* (Oxford: Blackwell, 1994).
19. Lager, *Ben & Jerry's*, 173–4.
20. Ibid. 205.
21. 'Best of '90s: Well, Hello to '90s Humility,' *Time*, Dec. 31, 1990, www.time.com/time/magazine/article/0,9171,972087,00.html
22. *USA Today*, Dec. 8, 1992.
23. 'Milked Dry on the Dairy Farm,' *Business Week*, Sept. 9, 1991, www.businessweek.com/archives/1991/b323057.arc.html
24. Brian Tokar, "Monsanto: A Checkered History," *Ecologist* (Sept./Oct. 1998), theecologist.org
25. 1999 Ceres Report, Section 7, 'Supplier Relations,' www.benjerry.com/company/sear/1999-ceres/page7.cfm (accessed Jan. 9, 2010).
26. www.benjerry.com/company/sear/1999-ceres/page7.cfm

5

Starbucks: Trickling down New Cultural Capital Codes

In 1987, Howard Schultz acquired Starbucks for $3.8 million, intent upon redesigning the sixteen-year-old company around a new coffee concept. In two decades, Starbucks expanded to over 16,000 stores worldwide, with revenues of well over $9 billion and a market cap of nearly $18 billion. How did Schultz do it?

According to Schultz, he succeeded by delivering simply the best coffee, and, in particular, by introducing Americans to an authentic high-end Italian espresso bar experience. The marketing pundit Seth Godin echos Schultz's claim, anointing Starbucks as a "purple cow" for its "remarkably" superior product. In other management treatments, Starbucks succeeded because it offered a "mass luxury" (giving mass-market consumers a taste of luxury at an affordable price) and a "third space" (a place for people to hang out and socialize). Our analysis suggests that these explanations entirely miss the core of Starbucks' innovation. Torrefazione, a Seattle-based chain, also launched in the 1980s, offered gourmet lattes and provided a space for its customers to loiter, but it never took off nationally, despite a well-financed push to do so. The same goes for New Orleans' Café du Monde, Denver's Peabury Coffee, and Orlando's Barnie's. In fact, the conventional management book explanation of Starbucks' success fails to account for the thousands of other coffee houses, cafés, and pastry shops in existence in the USA at the time that also offered upscale products at affordable prices and provided a place for people to hang out and socialize. Why did Starbucks succeed so spectacularly while no other mass-luxury third-space offering even came close?

Starbucks inadvertently took advantage of an ideological opportunity born of a massive demographic shift, in which a new cohort emerged—what we term the *cultural capital cohort*—that demanded more sophisticated lifestyle goods and services than those that existed at the time in the American marketplace. Howard Schultz and his team designed a pioneering retail offering that imbued coffee with a highly accessible form of cultural sophistication that was adapted from the artisanal-cosmopolitan codes of elite coffee subculture. This tactic, what we term *cultural capital trickle-down*, is a particularly important variation of the cultural innovation model.

This chapter also examines the dynamics of cultural innovation after a business succeeds with a breakthrough innovation. What strategies enable an innovation to sustain its pioneering position? Initially, Starbucks adeptly sustained its cultural leadership by appropriating new cultural codes. However, as time progressed, Schultz and his team significantly eroded Starbucks' customer value through actions that abandoned the company's position as a fast follower of new cultural codes for sophistication. First, let us consider Starbucks' initial innovation.

Cultural Orthodoxy: Coffee as Middle-Class Staple

In the early 1990s, Americans from a particular social class background came to perceive Starbucks coffee and espresso drinks as superior to any other offerings on the market and well worth a much higher price tag. Prior to Starbucks, the idea that a takeout coffee could be worth more than a dollar and change seemed bizarre. But notions of consumer value are always culturally constructed, as marketplace participants come to share a common way of thinking about the category, and it becomes taken for granted. We need to examine how Starbucks was able to shift these perceptions.

While colonial-era Americans preferred booze to coffee, events that challenged men's endurance—particularly the Civil War and the Gold Rush—increased the national demand for the new stimulant. The firms that grew to dominate the national market followed the better-mousetraps innovation model: they used industrial techniques to rationalize the production of coffee, standardize its quality, and lower costs. Beans were sourced globally to obtain the lowest possible commodity price and to assure a consistent supply. To push down the price and maximize profit, the industry moved increasingly toward cheaper robusta beans. By the post-war era, coffee was a cheap and widely accessible industrial staple—an easy-to-drink beverage that had become woven into households and the workplace as an everyday ritual. Coffee was sold in uniform vacuum-packed tins, and quality was virtually indistinguishable across brands: all offered lightly roasted blends that delivered a very smooth and predictable cup of coffee. New-fangled technology made coffee even more convenient and ubiquitous: instant coffee, led by Nestlé (Taster's Choice brand in the USA, Nescafé in the rest of the world), grew to 17 percent of all coffee purchased, while the Sanka brand pioneered the market for decaffeinated coffee.

Americans viewed coffee as a food staple, similar to bread, eggs, and a hamburger.[1] Drinking coffee was an everyday communal act, a taken-for-granted social ritual that took place at home and at work. The beans themselves mattered little: coffee was coffee. Consumers were not interested in where the beans came from, how they were grown, or how they were roasted. Most people made coffee in the same way, scooping the grounds into percolators or automatic drip machines. Coffee was retailed everywhere: from McDonald's and Dunkin' Donuts to national convenience store chains like 7–11, Stop-and-Go, and White Hen Pantry, from many thousands of mom-and-pop stores to gas stations, and sandwich carts. A freshly brewed cup of coffee could be purchased just about anywhere, and all cups contained roughly the same nondescript taste profile.

The industry was dominated by vacuum-packed tins sold primarily through grocery stores. Major brands in the pre-Starbucks era included Folgers (Procter & Gamble), Maxwell House (General Foods), and Hills Brothers, complemented by a handful of medium-sized regional brands such as MJB, Chase & Sanborn, and Chock Full o' Nuts. These brands competed to convince Americans that they should pay slightly more for a brand that enjoyed the seal of approval of middle-class society.

In the 1950s and 1960s, the major coffee brands took advantage of a cultural shift that occurred in the aftermath of the Second World War, when the American economy was transformed with the rise of major industrial corporations, a vital public sector, and a host of new professions, creating a massive middle class. As millions of erstwhile laborers and renters moved into white-collar jobs and middle-class suburban homes, demand piled up for cultural products that promised middle-class respectability. Magazines, television sitcoms, and brands appeared on the scene to resolve the arrivistes' new social status anxieties, offering them advice on how to be good middle-class citizens.

From the mid-1950s through the 1970s, Folgers created ad after ad that conjured the suburban social situations that were likely to produce the highest levels of social anxiety: a couple meeting neighbors for the first time at a welcoming party; a woman preparing to host other school parents at a PTA meeting; a couple inviting in a wealthier neighbor when her tail-finned car breaks down in front of the house. In each spot, a husband causes his wife to worry that her coffee is not good enough, and then a vaguely Scandinavian, pearl-wearing, character named Mrs Olson saves the wife from embarrassment by introducing her to Folgers. Each spot begins with a title that sets up Mrs Olson as social sage and savior: "Mrs Olson Saves a Hostess"; "Mrs Olson Fixes a Fuss"; "Mrs Olson Bails out a Barbecue". In the barbecue spot, a man with a checkered short-sleeved shirt suggests to his wife that her coffee is not up to snuff for the guests, and complains to her about having to serve "your awful coffee with my steaks." "You make me feel very unwifely," the wife responds. When she heads back to the kitchen, she confides to Mrs Olson, "Oh, I'm a washout at making coffee." Mrs. Olson offers, "This will help, Folgers coffee." The ad then cuts to the husband enjoying the coffee, as guests do the same. "Honey, you surprise me," says the husband, "your coffee's terrific."

Over the decades, Folgers spots changed in order to oblige new suburban, middle-class ideals. In the 1984, P&G's advertising began to accommodate the new economic aspirations of the Reagan era: the suburban houses became larger and more colonial; the filmic style and copy became more like Hal Riney's "Morning in America" ads for Reagan; the situations became less about socializing with neighbors and more about family values. One ad, "Peter Comes Home for Christmas," features a son arriving home from college, early in the morning, at the door of his parents' brick colonial home. His 4-year-old sister is the first to wake, and after she has run to greet him, they decide to wake up their parents by brewing a pot of Folgers coffee. Peter's teenage sister, his father, and his mother descend the central hall's staircase. His mom runs toward him and gives him a hug: excitedly "Oh, you're *home!*" The spot ends with the whole family enjoying coffee, and the jingle culminates with Folgers' new Riney-esque themeline, "The Best Part of Wakin' up is Folgers in Your Cup," and a title appears: "Best wishes for this and all your mornings!"

Locked in the cultural orthodoxy, for forty years coffee marketers had dramatized a social class ideology born in the 1950s, which asserted that all Americans could live the "good life." From the mid-1980s onward, this kind of social class expression became increasingly obsolete. The mass media had latched onto the escalating social inequality created by Reagan's economic policies and had "upscaled" the good life to such an extent that Americans perceived that they had to be rich and famous to feel that they had succeeded in life. Despite efforts by admen to place the category's orthodox cultural expressions—the middle-class coffee lessons—in a more upscale setting, this sort of social class expression soon became antiquated and quaint.[2]

Columbian Coffee as Artisanal–Cosmopolitan Precursor

The most successful exception to this cultural orthodoxy came from the Columbian coffee producers' cooperative. They launched an "ingredient-branding" effort to differentiate their Columbian beans in the otherwise anonymous global commodity market. Their ad campaign starred Juan Valdez, a humble, straight-talking coffee farmer dressed in peasant clothing, who hauled burlap bags of beans on his mule, against the backdrop of a coffee plantation. Juan spoke with humility and sincerity about the quality of his coffee. He conveyed the dignity of his craft. This early cultural innovation directly violated the category's cultural codes in its romancing of coffee as a pre-industrial artisanal product, prefiguring the ideology that Starbucks would champion decades later. The cooperative's extremely successful campaign convinced many Americans that Colombian beans were superior, and it forced all the major coffee brands to launch "100% Colombian" line extensions. This effort, however, was ultimately only an incremental innovation. Juan's claim was no different from Mrs Olsen's—that his Columbian coffee was the smoothest in the world. And coffee marketers readily co-opted this intrusion by introducing Colombian coffee as a particularly smooth-tasting, light-roasted blend—packed in vacuum tins and barely distinguishable from their regular blends. While the Juan Valdez campaign was extremely successful from the point of view of Columbian coffee-growers, the impact on consumers was not transformative, and probably could not have been, since there was simply not a large enough market for aestheticized coffee at this time, as we explain below.

Juxtaposing this successful Columbian branding effort with the mass marketer's most significant effort to push coffee upscale in the pre-Starbucks era is revealing. General Foods, a blue-chip marketer of the era that later merged into Kraft, sought to develop an up-market coffee brand that would appeal to a wealthier demographic than its Maxwell House brand. The company introduced International Coffees, tins of sweetened instant coffee with artificial flavors such as "Café au Lait," "Suisse Mocha," "Dutch Chocolate," and "Café Vienna." The coffees were heavily promoted as representing Europeans' sophisticated tastes, yet their sales never amounted to much. The concept was fundamentally flawed: a marketing fabrication that claimed that Euro sophistication could be achieved by drinking manufactured flavors of sugary instant coffee with powdered milk. As we shall see, International Coffees conveyed an ideology that was completely antithetical to the emerging demand for sophisticated coffee.

The coffee category's middle-class staple orthodoxy held sway into the 1980s. But category ideologies are fragile constructs that will inevitably be disrupted. Time moves forward; social changes inevitably crack the ideological edifice and spur demand for brands that present different ideologies. In the late 1980s just such a shift—the rise of the cultural capital cohort—swiftly made this orthodoxy obsolete. But what would rise in its place? Starbucks transformed the coffee category by responding to this ideological opportunity with a deft adaptation of cultural codes developed by an elite subculture to convey cultural sophistication. To understand the significance of this ideological opportunity, it is useful to consider the bigger picture of how social class influences consumption.

Bourdieu's Theory of Cultural Capital

Most managers view status consumption according to the classical economic trickle-down model pioneered by Thorsten Veblen and Georg Simmel over a century ago:

- The social class hierarchy is based upon economic differences, with the rich at the top, tiering down to the poorest at the bottom.
- Wealthy people at the top define status symbols based upon luxury, exclusivity, and celebrity.
- People in classes below them aspire to be wealthy and famous, and so they desire and emulate the consumption of those who are wealthier, creating demand for status symbols.
- So the market opportunity is to design "aspirational" offerings that tap into the cultural codes of luxury, exclusivity, and celebrity that convey perceptions of wealth.

This logic is often used to explain Starbucks' success. According to the conventional wisdom, middle-class Americans sought to emulate the wealthy upper class by consuming what are often termed "mass luxuries"—symbols of wealth and luxury that do not cost too much. The $4 latte (which has led to the mocking name "Fourbucks") served as a luxurious indulgence, a brief encounter with the world of the well-to-do. But this is a superficial and inaccurate account of Starbucks. It focuses only on price and fails to explain the crucial aspects of Starbucks' offering that distinguished it from other coffee retailers. The eminent sociologist Pierre Bourdieu long ago demonstrated that status consumption consists not only of the emulation of economic elites in the pursuit of luxury and fame (what he calls *economic capital*), but also of the emulation of cultural elites in the pursuit of distinctive and sophisticated tastes (what he calls *cultural capital*).

In the late 1980s, the United States began to experience a major demographic shift, which we explain in greater detail below. This shift transformed the status consumption of the upper middle class (we estimate close to 10 percent of the US population). The pursuit of

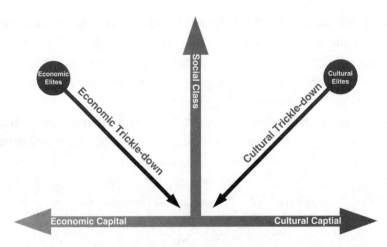

Figure 5. Bourdieu's Two Dimensions of Social Class

cultural capital became far more important to this group than it had been for prior generations of upper-middle-class Americans. New cultural codes became immensely desirable amongst the upper middle class as a means to convey cultural sophistication, including cosmopolitanism and artisanal craft.[3] These codes of cultural sophistication were pioneered by elite movements and subcultures. Just as with our other cases, these subcultures provide the raw cultural material for cultural innovations that "trickle down" the cultural class hierarchy, in the same way that the desire for luxury goods does, according to the conventional social class model. We call this innovating dynamic the *cultural trickle-down model.*

Ideological Opportunity: The Cultural Capital Cohort

The pursuit of material abundance has long been a central feature of American ideology. The United States has attracted massive waves of immigrants from peasant and working-class backgrounds, lured by the country's promise of fluid class mobility. For most of American history, improving one's lot in life was defined by climbing the class ladder to arrive at the "good life"—thought of in terms of conventional consumer goods, such as (in the late twentieth century) a nice big house, two late-model cars, the latest appliances and electronic gear, and so on—in Bourdieu's terms, amassing economic capital.[4] The pursuit of cultural sophistication (Bourdieu's cultural capital) was until recently a niche phenomenon in America. It existed mainly in "old-money" families, which dominated elite breeding grounds (prep schools, Ivy League universities, elite liberal-arts colleges), and in the small Bohemian circles in the country's biggest cities.

The transformation of the American class dynamic from a single-minded striving for economic abundance to a multi-dimensional striving for sophistication in addition to abundance—a mixture of status pursuits more typical of Europe—was seeded in the 1960s. The federal government instituted The Higher Education Act in 1965 as part of Lyndon Johnson's "Great Society" programs, at the same time as elite universities were adopting meritocratic admissions policies in place of their old nepotistic approach. As a result, the percentage of youth attending college expanded massively to roughly a third of the American population. From 1965 to 1975, the percentage of Americans graduating with four-year college degrees doubled, increasing to more than 20 percent of the population. This generation still shared the American dream of material abundance, like their parents, which Bourdieu would predict, since cultural capital is inculcated largely in childhood. (After dabbling in the world of critique, art, and cultural experiences in college, baby boomers went on to be a highly acquisitive generation.) However, when this cohort eventually became parents, they raised their children to appreciate culture at least as much as expensive stuff. So when these children came of age, beginning in the late 1980s, the United States experienced a tectonic shift in its status markets. These young adults were not raised as cultural elites, so they were not socialized in the most rarified tastes; but their status compass was pointed much more toward cultural sophistication compared to earlier generations. They looked to emulate cultural elites, in addition to the wealthy and powerful.[5] They strove to create a lifestyle that was more aestheticized, more sophisticated, and more creative than that of their parents' generation. We shall call this demographic phenomenon the *cultural capital cohort*.

As this cohort looked for ways to express its sophistication, it faced a moribund marketplace, especially when it came to cuisine. The United States was still the land of meatloaf, mashed potatoes, McCormick's spices, and green-bean casseroles made from recipes on the backs of cans of Campbell's mushroom soup. Mainstream grocery stores had yet

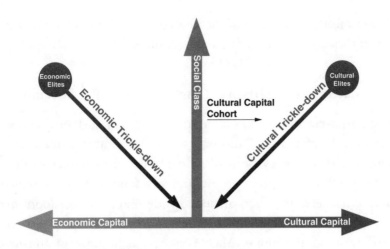

Figure 6. The Cultural Capital Cohort

to start stocking the likes of arugula, heirloom tomatoes, edamame, and free-range chicken. Few Americans knew of espresso or how to pronounce the word *latte*. Until the cultural capital cohort arrived, the United States did not have enough people interested in a more aestheticized food culture to develop a significant cuisine of its own (outside of a few subcultural pockets, which we shall get to below). In the 1990s, entrepreneurs rushed in to fill this gap, thereby launching the tremendous growth of businesses that offered new expressions of sophisticated consumption. From hotels (Ian Schrager's boutique hotels, W Hotels) to autos (Mini Cooper, the restaged Volkswagen) to fashion (Zara, H&M, Target) to food and drink (Whole Foods Market, Trader Joe's, Sam Adams, Ben & Jerry's) to home furnishings (Williams-Sonoma, West Elm, Design within Reach) to consumer electronics (Apple), a generation of new businesses took advantage of this ideological opportunity. To meet the emergent demand for goods and services laden with cultural capital, these entrepreneurs were exploiting raw material supplied by subcultures at the top of the cultural capital hierarchy and "trickling it down."

Coffee was no different. The cultural capital cohort demanded that its coffee provide more cultural sophistication. An elite artisanal–cosmopolitan subculture had formed two decades earlier, pioneering a new highly aestheticized approach to marketing and consuming coffee. This subculture served as potent raw material for companies

CULTURAL INNOVATION THEORY

looking to feed the demand of the new cohort. Schultz's reinvention of Starbucks took advantage of this opportunity.

Source Material: The Artisanal–Cosmopolitan Coffee Subculture

The artisanal–cosmopolitan subculture emerged in northern California as an upscale offshoot of the back-to-the-land sustainable business utopia that Ben & Jerry's mined so fruitfully (see Chapter 4). In the late 1960s, a Bay Area group of restaurateurs, food-and-drinks retailers, boutique farmers, and food aficionados developed a new food ideology, borrowing heavily from European food culture and pre-modern cuisines around the globe. Alice Waters, the founder of the iconic Berkeley restaurant Chez Panisse, was at the forefront of the movement. Wine proprietors from Napa and Sonoma valleys upped their game, developing an American style of winemaking that challenged the best French wines. Anchor Steam, New Albion, and Sierra Nevada became subculturally famous for promoting American styles of ale and "steam" beer. It is not a coincidence that the movement's epicenter emerged in north Berkeley, a locale swarming with cultural elites. Around Chez Panisse in north Berkeley formed what eventually became known as the Gourmet Ghetto, with a cheese cooperative, a charcuterie with homemade sausages, an artisanal bakery ironically named Acme, and—second only to Chez Panisse in renown and influence—a coffee retailer called Peet's.

The subculture consecrated seasonal and local agricultural products for their distinctive flavors and freshness. The subculture's proponents took great pleasure in finding a heritage breed of duck raised on an organic farm in Petaluma, or sourcing abalone hand-gathered by divers in Mendocino, or cultivating a native herb found only in the Santa Cruz hills. They cooked with considerable care to bring out nuanced flavors, not deigning to disguise them in sauces. The subculture progressed from mastering the old-world craft skills to reworking these ingredients and techniques with an eclectic mixing and matching style—what would later be called "fusion cuisine." The subculturalists applied the same highly aestheticized artisanal approach to a wide range of food and drinks: meats and cheeses, beer and wine, bread and tapenades, creams and ice creams, pastries and chocolate, and coffee.

Together, their efforts coalesced into a coherent ideology that directly challenged what the 1960s critics had damned as technocracy (recounted in Chapter 4 on Ben & Jerry's homemade ice cream). They used their disgust with the industrial food culture that the multinational food and agriculture companies, modern science, and government had together instituted as impetus to drive a new kind of food culture. Highlighting the artisanal and cosmopolitan qualities of food and drink, this ideology would prove to be the perfect source material for new expressions of cultural capital in the 1990s.

At the center of the subculture, hitting all the right artisanal–cosmopolitan notes, was Alfred Peet.[6] The son of a Dutch coffee roaster, Peet had traveled to Indonesia and developed a great appreciation for its rich and distinctive coffees. Disappointed with the cheap coffee degraded with robusta beans so commonly found in the United States at the time, Peet set out on a mission to change the coffee culture. He was a coffee connoisseur. As one journalist put it, "He developed an extremely fine palate, a vocabulary of taste, and he could translate it and make it come alive. His philosophy was, there should be the shortest distance possible between the roaster and the customer."[7] Peet was obsessed with sourcing the best beans from countries around the world, accentuating the different taste and aromatic profiles of coffees from different countries and regions. At Peet's you could find coffee from Java and Sumatra, Kenya and Ethiopia, Guatamala and Costa Rica. And Peet was fastidious about roasting—he advocated a dark roast that to this day has many detractors. He insisted that his coffee should be freshly roasted, purchased whole bean, and then ground just before brewing. Of course Mr Peet would be happy to tell you exactly how to brew your coffee to bring out the distinctive flavors and aromatics. In a world of vacuum-packed Folgers brewed in a Mr Coffee machine, Peet's artisanal–cosmopolitan approach to coffee was heretical.

Peet's, along with fellow artisanal–cosmopolitan start-ups, offered a provocative ideological rebuttal to the domination of the industrial agro-food business. The latter had insistently rationalized food production in the United States since the Second World War, optimizing profits and lowering consumer prices with little regard to taste or health. Each plank of Peet's ideology, which we have inferred from their marketing efforts and list below, directly challenged mass-market coffee:

Industrial Staple Ideology	Peet's Artisanal–Cosmopolitan Ideology
Standardized Taste/Offend No one	Culinary Pleasure
Anonymous global beans	Terroir beans
Machine made	Skilled hand crafted
Mass scale	Small lots, special batches
Homogeneous	Idiosyncratic, exotic
Modern Scientific	Pre-modern traditions
Cheap	Whatever the best costs
Ubiquitous	Rare, requires seeking out
Convenience, speed	Savoring the experience

In so doing, Peet powerfully reframed the "middle-class staple" coffee offered by Folgers and Maxwell House, which the majority of Americans were still drinking, as overly processed and homogenized industrial dreck. Years later, Peet's ideology, and the range of cultural codes he developed to express this ideology, would serve as the foundational raw materials from which Howard Schultz would create the Starbucks brand.

Experimentation through Failed Efforts

Starbucks was originally launched by three coffee aficionados who were seduced by the Bay Area's artisanal–cosmopolitan coffee subculture and wanted to import it to Seattle. And, ten years later, Howard Schultz was in turn seduced by their successful Seattle incarnation. Upon drinking a cup, he insisted that the founders hire him as marketing manager because he projected a huge opportunity to take Starbucks coffee to the mass market. But this original Starbucks concept never was able to expand beyond the artisanal–cosmopolitan subculture. Likewise, Schultz was unable to penetrate the mass market when he left Starbucks to open a new coffee concept—Il Giornale—that was an exacting imitation of Italian coffee culture. It was only on his third try, when Schultz bought out his former partners at Starbucks and radically reconfigured the offering, that Starbucks caught on, tapping into the huge pent-up demand for coffee infused with cultural capital.[8]

Original Starbucks

Jerry Baldwin, Zev Siegl, and Gordon Bowker opened the first Starbucks on March 29, 1971, near the Pike Place market in downtown Seattle. Bowker, a writer, and Siegl, whose father was a symphony conductor, went to college together in San Francisco. So, when Bowker—the first to catch the specialty coffee bug—invited the other two to start up a coffee retail business with him, it is not surprising that they looked to the Bay Area, the epicenter of the artisanal–cosmopolitan coffee subculture, for inspiration. (And not surprisingly, given their arts background, they chose a literary brand name, picking a character, Starbuck, from a Melville novel.) In the Bay Area, they discovered Alfred Peet, the most influential pioneer of the new artisanal–cosmopolitan coffee, and they convinced him to teach them the ropes and help them set up shop. The original Starbucks concept was a Seattle-based clone of Peet's; in fact, Starbucks bought its coffee from Peet's until the orders became too large for Peet to fill.

Starbucks offered the same range of dark-roasted terroir coffees and blends as Peet did. And, like Peet, they focused on educating consumers to buy the best beans, and grind them and brew them at home, offering only sample cups in the store. For a population raised on industrial coffee, Starbucks was very challenging to drink, requiring that consumers re-educate their palates. Learning to love Starbucks coffee soon became a potent sign of cultural sophistication in Seattle. Starbucks earned the reputation as the food snob's coffee, and its patrons believed themselves to be part of the enlightened tribe who appreciated good coffee.

Ten years later, New York marketer Howard Schultz paid a visit to Seattle to see what Starbucks was all about. Upon drinking his first cup of Starbucks and witnessing the fanaticism of the artisanal–cosmopolitan insiders who patronized the store, he immediately concluded that the concept had far more potential than the partners had the ambition to pursue. He pestered them for a year until they made him the company's marketing manager in 1982.

Schultz realized early on that the original Starbucks offering—selling superb beans to customers who like to grind and brew at home—served only a small niche market of coffee aficionados, with no chance of expanding to the mass market. So he came up with a different business model. The idea was inspired by a business trip to Italy, where he fell in love with the Italian espresso bar. He decided that installing an authentic Italian espresso bar would be the breakthrough concept that could take Starbucks to the next level. He badgered the owners, again and again, to set up a bar. Finally, they set up an espresso counter in the corner of one store, but they took the concept no further. Frustrated, Schultz left to set up his own venture.

Il Giornale: Artisanal–Cosmopolitan Purism does not Work

Schultz teamed up with two local coffee experts, Dave Olsen and Dawn Pinaud, to launch Il Giornale. The concept was a clone of the cafés he admired in Italy: a sleek modern espresso drinks-only café with the hard-to-pronounce Italian name outside, a massive gleaming European espresso machine filling the front stage inside, counter staff in bowties, and Italian opera arias wafting through the air.

Though the cultural raw material was different, Schultz pursued the same cultural-capital strategy at Il Giornale as at the original Starbucks: he was trying to pull mass-market consumers up the cultural capital ladder, educating them in the ways of the elite coffee aficionado. The retailer took on a proselytizing role, teaching Seattle coffee-drinkers how to enjoy the most authentic artisanal espresso, one that matched the best Italian standard. The business did well enough for the ever-aggressive Schultz to open several new outlets, but it did not drive the kind of sales that Schultz needed for a national chain. He learned, once again, that highly aestheticized coffee is primarily of interest only to a niche of culturally elite customers. Peet's and the original Starbucks that mimicked Peet's were both wildly appealing to the cultural elite but to few others, because the tastes were too strange, the obsession with terroir and cultivars and agricultural methods was too academic and arcane, and the insistence on precise preparation was too fussy. Similarly mass-market coffee-drinkers never bought into the espresso-based Italian coffee culture that Schultz was trying to disseminate. Seattle patrons vastly preferred lattes, steamed milk with a splash of coffee flavor, to a straight espresso, by far the most popular coffee style in Italy.

Schultz's first two efforts to develop an innovative mass-market coffee business failed because they were simply too elitist: they presented artisanal–cosmopolitan coffee in its most authentic form, which is precisely how cultural elites like it, but most others do not. If Starbucks had run with this hyper-accurate translation of the Italian café experience, the concept would never have appealed to the mass market.[9] Schultz and his collaborators failed at the mass market because they had not yet learned how cultural trickle-down works. These outings were learning experiences that provided the clues they needed to get it right the third time. Instead of stubbornly insisting upon indoctrination into highbrow tastes, à la Alfred Peet, Schultz designed the new concept based upon cultural accessibility.

Accessible Sophistication: Democratizing Artisanal–Cosmopolitan Codes

In 1986, Peet's Coffee came up for sale, and Baldwin and his pals, ever the groupies, jumped at the chance. They needed to sell Starbucks to free up capital, and so they sold the business to Schultz. Schultz combined the Starbucks and Il Giornale outlets, keeping the Starbucks name. He abandoned his quest to fill America with thousands of authentic Italian cafés and instead used the occasion to launch a third concept. Schultz and his team finally discovered how to finesse the mechanics of cultural capital. Instead of delivering a pure and rarified artisanal–cosmopolitan experience, the new Starbucks would trickle the elite coffee subculture's codes down to deliver a much more accessible version. Starbucks now tailored its drinks to the American palate, but packaged them with just enough artisanal–cosmopolitan sophistication to give the new cohort the cultural capital it demanded.

Accessible Coffee Drinks
The center of artisanal–cosmopolitan coffee is the taste experience. For drip coffee, the coffee should be selected, roasted, and brewed to accentuate the exotic flavor notes and aromatics of the terroir—Eastern African cups should offer citrus and winey notes, while Indonesian coffees should be quite earthy and nutty. For espresso, it is the "art of the shot" that is central. The emphasis is on the perfect grind, packing

pressure, water temperature, and length of the extraction in order to deliver an ounce or two of syrupy, crema-laden espresso, which must be drunk in less than a minute or else it deteriorates.

The original Starbucks could not penetrate the mass market with its purist's focus on terroir. Similarly, at Il Giornale, the celebration of espresso did not catch on beyond a niche cultural elite clientele. Shultz and his team learned that most customers appreciated the Italianized naming system—words like *grande, doppio,* and *barista*—a lot more than they appreciated the authentic Italian tang of espressos. Lattes were very popular, thanks to a milky make-up that masked the espresso's bitter notes. These discoveries gave Schultz and his team important clues for how to proceed: offer highly palatable beverages surrounded by a sea of marketing elements that convey rarified cultural sophistication. Schultz and his team soon became masters at imbuing these palatable drinks with accessible versions of the artisanal–cosmopolitan codes of the elite coffee subculture.

Dramatizing Artisanal–Cosmopolitan Retail Props

Schultz's retail merchandizing decisions were crucial, as he converted the original Starbucks concept, which focused on selling whole beans, into a café emphasizing takeout drinks. Schultz had to sustain Starbucks' terroir bean business, along with espressos and cappuccinos, in order to sustain credibility as a serious aficionado's café, with ties to the coffee subculture. What he soon discovered, though, was that retailing terroir beans added considerably to the brand's cultural value for the new patrons he wanted to pull in, even if these customers wanted to drink only milky lattes or a simple cup of Joe. In his merchandizing decisions, Schultz romanticized the beans to envelop these cultural capital cohort customers, as they ordered up lattes and drip coffee, with a very accessible version of the cultural codes favored by the coffee aficionados of the elite subculture.

For subcultural purists, drinks should be prepared by fellow aficionados who romanced the coffee by talking up the taste profiles of different varietals and chatting with customers about the coffee's back story. These customers delighted in discussing everything from the merits of particular cultivars, to growing and harvesting techniques, to why a particular roast brought out all the right notes, to sharing delight in tasting a particularly intriguing new shipment. Few members of the cultural capital cohort had the taste, time, or patience for such subtle artisanal–cosmopolitan details. They got no satisfaction out of sitting at a counter for ten minutes, nattering away with a barista about an upcoming shipment of Sulawesi. Furthermore, there was no way Schultz could attract or afford an army of real coffee connoisseurs to serve as coffee gurus in every outlet. He needed his stores to do the storytelling, rather than baristas. So, over the next decade, Starbucks strove to perfect its use of all the consumer touchpoints in the store—packaging, signs, service encounters, collateral materials, educational displays, cups, music—to deliver artisanal–cosmopolitan codes in a simple, educational, and visually compelling manner. Starbucks used the terroir coffees prized by cultural elites, not as revenue drivers, but as marketing material to create an in-store artisanal–cosmopolitan experience for its customers. African coffee labels featured riffs on wild animals and local textiles to convey the exotic nature of the product. Starbucks romanticized coffee appellations in simple visually appealing stories in store in collateral materials. For example, Starbucks used three leading Ethiopian appellations—*Sidamo, Harrar,* and *Yirga Cheffe*—to tell stories about thousand-year-old cultivars and harvesting techniques, relying on pictures of peasants gathering beans in the field to imbue the stores with the aura of traditional local craft. Regardless of one's drink order, Starbucks' effective store designs made all patrons feel as if they were imbibing in exotic artisanal coffees produced by peoples far removed from modern life in the North.

Sanitizing the Bohemian Café
Just as Starbucks offered up an accessible version of the cultural codes of the artisanal–cosmopolitan foods subculture, the company's designers concocted the same simplified treatment of another haunt of cultural elites—the bohemian café—to compose its retail spaces. Historically, these cafes were social hubs for the artists, writers, musicians, and other members of the cultural elite. The unkempt beards, the facial piercings, the tattoos, the angry protest leaflets, the incense-burning, and the cynical blackboard scribblings combined to create an atmosphere that was just as offputting to the mass-market coffee-drinker as a double shot of espresso. By the time Starbucks began its aggressive

expansion in the 1990s, this café genre had largely evolved into what are sometimes called indie cafes (indie for independent), which is essentially a bohemian café that has embraced the artisanal–cosmopolitan foods ideology, producing superb artisanal espresso and terroir coffees with the same care as the original subculture.

Starbucks developed a sanitized version of such places. Instead of furniture from the Salvation Army, Starbucks relied on a clean color-coordinated look that reminded many commentators of the likes of IKEA, Crate and Barrel, Pottery Barn, and other furniture retailers that catered directly to the cultural capital cohort. Starbucks' designers studiously avoided the bohemian café's messy stacks of alternative newspapers and chaotic walls of flyers that advertised yoga classes and recruited drummers for indie rock bands. Rather than host poetry readings, activist meetings, and intellectual debates, Starbucks simply put quotes of celebrated social activists and members of the intelligentsia on each and every paper cup. Starbucks replaced the junk-shop tapestries and confounding paintings by local artists with neatly framed posters featuring bohemian stereotypes such as a Vespa scooter in an Italian streetscape. Background music alluded to bohemian roots, but was always much more accessible than what one was likely to hear at an indie café. Typical indie café music selections were a tacit demonstration of esoteric bohemian tastes: Albert Ayler, TV on the Radio, Coco Rosie, Skip Spence, or The Mekons. Instead, Starbucks played accessible jazz (Norah Jones), accessible indie rock (Natalie Merchant), and lots of "global music" as a very digestible nod to cosmopolitan tastes (Buena Vista Social Club, Gipsy Kings).

Explanations that focus on Starbucks as a "third space"—propagated by Schultz and amplified by the media—fail to explain what distinguished Starbucks in a sea of other coffee houses, cafés, and casual restaurants that also provided the same basic "hanging-out" function. Starbucks' particular third space appealed to the cultural capital cohort because it offered them a "lite" accessible version of the avant-garde hang-outs frequented by cultural elites.

Starbucks' cultural innovation was to perform a commercial alchemy, what we call accessible sophistication. It transformed the coffee subculture's drinks into a much more palatable form, while imbuing them with a simplified and sanitized version of the subculture's artisanal–cosmopolitan codes. This cultural capital trickle-down strategy imbued Starbuck's offerings with an aura of sophistication that was in great demand, but in a manner that was far more accessible than the elite subculture's offerings.

Sustaining an Innovation through Cultural Leadership

The seven case studies in this part of the book together develop a theory that explains how a cultural innovation initially takes root. But what happens after the concept succeeds and expands, after it becomes a successful and established incumbent? Here we use Starbucks' evolution to consider the strategic issues that need to be addressed in order to sustain a cultural innovation. Cultural competition unfolds in four overlapping stages:

1. Competitors mimic the innovative ideology, leading to commodification.
2. New entrepreneurial efforts seek to leapfrog the successful innovation with a better ideology.
3. Existing competitors reposition to adjust for the altered market dynamics created by the successful innovation.
4. Meanwhile, consumer demand for ideology does not sit still. Responding to new social disruptions, consumer demand for ideology in the product category also evolves.

Given these four intersecting dynamics, how can companies sustain their cultural innovations? Starbucks faced this four-dimensional challenge as the company sought to expand its established business from the late 1990s onward. Innovations require ongoing management to sustain cultural leadership. After the pioneering innovation, brands must continue to break new ground, albeit in a more incremental fashion. Initially, Starbucks was successful in using incremental innovation to sustain cultural leadership, but since then the company has made a number of strategic mistakes that have seriously damaged the brand.

Appropriating Ethical Consumerism to Sustain Cultural Leadership

Starbucks had uncovered the key ideological components necessary for marketing accessible sophistication: trickled-down artisanal craft, cosmopolitanism, and elite aesthetic codes. Ideologies, however, are not static. The cultural capital cohort's tastes continued to develop throughout the 1990s, spurred on by media that promoted culturally sophisticated consumption (for example, magazines such as *Dwell* and *Real Simple*), and stimulated by the intense competition amongst entrepreneurs to develop new businesses to take advantage of this opportunity. To avoid being outflanked, Starbucks needed to synchronize its branding with the evolution of cultural capital ideology.

The first important evolution was the transformation of cosmopolitan codes.[10] During Starbucks' first twenty-five years in business, cosmopolitanism was expressed through travel, as well as knowledge of and appreciation for cultural products from faraway, little-known places. Enjoying a cup of java sourced from Sulawesi functioned well as a cosmopolitan expression. However, as social-movement efforts to politicize goods made by poor, disempowered workers of the Global South got traction (the anti-sweatshop campaigns targeting Nike and other shoe and garment marketers was an early and particularly poignant example), the concept of cosmopolitanism started to seem shallow and myopic. Cultural elites adopted the view that it was not sufficient to appreciate the coffee sourced from a specific countries; one should also care about the coffee's production methods as well as its economic and political impact. The established understanding of cosmopolitanism merged with progressive politics to champion what is now often called ethical consumerism—the idea that consumers, properly politicized, could influence the actions of multinational companies and advance social justice. Beginning in the late 1990s, innumerable new brands espousing an ethical-consumerism ideology were launched. And older brands were retooled to evoke this new cultural code, Starbucks included.

Starbucks had never before demonstrated interest in the livelihood of coffee farmers. Take, for example, Schultz's best-selling corporate autobiography *Pour your Heart into It* (1999), which pays no attention to these issues. And, alternative trade organizations like Equal Exchange had pestered Starbucks for years to embrace fair-trade coffee to no avail. Like other multinational companies, Starbucks viewed its supply chains in purely economic terms. But in the late 1990s, Starbucks finally gave in to pressure from Transfair USA, and purchased a small amount of fair-trade coffee—perhaps because the company's aggressive retail expansion had increasingly exposed it to attacks, and this philanthropic act might offer its reputation some protection. To the company's surprise, customers responded enthusiastically. Promises of ethical sourcing made them feel included in a club of enlightened consumers who were fully engaged in the improvement of the world's most intractable social problems. Starbucks had stumbled upon ethical consumerism, a powerful new cultural code expressive of the evolving artisanal–cosmopolitan ideology of the cultural elite.

With the strong early response from its customers, Starbucks enthusiastically embraced this code, using the same accessible sophistication formula. The company used a variety of marketing-mix elements to surround consumers with an ethical halo. Starbucks appropriated the work of fair-trade activists to stake a claim as a pioneer of sustainable coffee production, improving conditions for the world's poorest coffee farmers. In 2002, the company launched a "Commitment to Origins" campaign—making much use of in-store signage—to support a specialty line of coffees that were fair trade, organic, or shade grown (that is, more ecological). Starbucks publicized its CAFE standards—its own set of guidelines that guaranteed its coffees were sustainably sourced. The company's marketers developed brand names that connoted ethical-consumerism promises (Estima™ fair-trade coffee, Ethos™ bottled water), which they promoted heavily with prominent in-store displays. In 2007, the company launched a major in-store promotion called "Coffee that Cares" that celebrates the company's ethical practices. And, in 2009, Starbucks launched an even more ambitious feel-good ethical-consumerism campaign called "Shared Planet," once again touting the company's progressive policies.

Throughout the decade, Starbucks was the multinational company that most aggressively appropriated the value of ethical consumerism as a new form of cultural capital. The appropriation was very successful, allowing Starbucks to sustain an aura of cultural sophistication at a time when its drinks and food policies were creating a very different impression. While the brand's initial evolution was a big success, Starbucks then misfired badly. The company made three mistakes that significantly compromised the sophistication that the Starbucks brand had once conveyed.

Compromising Starbucks' Role in the Cultural Hierarchy

Starbucks' innovation was premised upon its mediating role: serving up the ideology of the cultural elites' artisanal–cosmopolitan subculture in accessible form to the cultural capital cohort. To sustain this fast-follower position, Starbucks needed to stay one step ahead of its customers, providing them with easy access to new cultural capital codes that would allow their tastes to evolve. But, instead, Starbucks made numerous changes to its product offerings with an eye to maximizing revenue that unwittingly pushed the brand too far down the cultural capital hierarchy. Missing out on the second major shift in artisanal–cosmopolitan codes, Starbucks became a cultural laggard; its offerings were consistently several steps behind the tastes of its key clientele.

Imitating Fast Food

With McDonalds-sized retail ambitions and anointed a growth-stock darling by Wall Street analysts, Starbucks was not satisfied by its success in corralling the cultural capital cohort. Starbucks had reached a saturation point with this target, and limiting the company's ambitions to the cultural capital cohort meant missing around 90 percent of the American population. Surely these other Americans would like to buy Starbucks products as well! So Starbucks pushed hard to make its drinks accessible to a much bigger demographic, comprised of people situated in the social classes below its initial target. It also sought to attract younger customers who spent much of their discretionary income on food and drink. To make this super-ambitious growth strategy work, Starbucks was obliged to play the fast-food game. These prospective customers had been acculturated on fast food, and such tastes are hard to break once established. To draw in this demographic, the company would have to lure potential clients away from McDonalds, Dunkin' Donuts, 7–11, and Subway.

To attract these customers, Starbucks modified the latte range, changing the focus from milky coffee that was sometimes flavored to sugary, dessert-like drinks. Syrupy chocolate and caramel drinks soon became customer favorites, delivering what was in essence a hot caffeinated analogue to the milk shakes found at McDonalds and Burger King. Starbucks pushed this evolution further with the introduction of the frappucino line of frozen drinks, concoctions that could just as easily be offered by Dairy Queen. The company pushed drip coffee offerings in the same direction. In the early 1990s, it was not uncommon to find a different terroir coffee brewed each day—a bright and citrusy Kenyan coffee one day, an earthy robust Papua New Guinea coffee the next. These coffees were often too challenging for the cultural capital cohort, so Starbucks turned to more palatable blends—Gold Coast and Yukon—to offer an alternative to the rotating terroir coffee choice. This rotating portfolio gently challenged customers' palates while remaining accessible.

In order to pursue a broader demographic, Starbucks abandoned this long-standing drip-coffee strategy. Instead of gently challenging consumers' palates, Starbucks began catering to the existing palate of an increasingly downscale, "average" consumer. Drip coffees were standardized and blended to appeal to mass-market tastes by ensuring that no one would dislike the coffee. And so management decided to make House Blend—Starbucks' mildest, lowest-common-denominator coffee—the standard offering for its drip business. Just as cultural capital cohort tastes were becoming more adventurous, Starbucks pushed its primary coffee offering down the hierarchy to approximate the industrial staple coffee that it had once supplanted.

Deskilling the Coffee Experience

Starbucks had once trained its staffers to provide a trickle-down version of the aficionado's service encounter. In the subculture, such as at Peet's and the original Starbucks, customers could always expect to be served by an *avocational worker*—someone who shared similar aficionado tastes and who was particularly enthusiastic and knowledgeable about the foodstuffs he was vending. Employees were amateur enthusiasts who worked not only for the money, but also to promote a product they felt passionate about; they engaged in artisanal labor, a labor of love. Starbucks effectively trickled down this experience by romanticizing its "baristas," making sure they had better coffee knowledge than most of their customers and could handle an espresso machine with authority.

As Starbucks focused on driving down costs in order to please Wall Street, the company rationalized the coffee offering, regardless of the impact on its brand. Coffee grinders gave way to monstrous plastic bags of pre-ground coffee. Starbucks had once garnered respect for using the best espresso machines on the market—La Marzocco machines from Italy—which required some skill to operate. In 2002, in order to increase its line speed, Starbucks switched over to totally automatic machines. Today, a barista needs only to push a computerized button, a skill worthy of a 2-year-old. With the incorporation of the infamous plastic-sheathed frappuccino blenders, Schultz had transformed his barista's duties into the kind of work a teen would expect to perform at a McDonalds. The barista was now just another fast-food worker; the title once worn with pride had become an inside joke.

Starbucks also denigrated the service encounter through aggressive human resources policies. The company provided strong incentives for store managers to squeeze every last drop of profit from its front-line staff. Baristas were paid only slightly more than a minimum wage, roughly the same as their fast-food worker counterparts.[11] For years, Starbucks had boasted about its worker-friendly policies, yet a higher percentage of Wal-Mart employees held company-provided health insurance.[12] In its quest to rationalize its workforce, the company instituted an "Optimal Scheduling" policy that required workers to make themselves available twice as many hours as they were actually required to work. A full-time employee was required to be available for 80 hours a week even though he or she would spend only 40 of these hours on the job. As of 2009, Starbucks' employee turnover rate hovered around 80 percent, while Whole Foods Market, a peer retailer servicing the cultural capital cohort, experienced turnover of about 28 percent. Employees were pushed to work at such a furious and unpredictable pace, for such little money and few benefits, that they had little energy or motivation to become coffee aficionados. The barista's key role in transforming coffee into an accessible artisanal–cosmopolitan experience has been tossed aside.

Starbucks Misses the Eco-Epicurean Take-off

In the Ben & Jerry's case, we recounted the growth of the *back-to-the-land business utopia* of the 1970s. For several decades, these more politicized back-to-the-landers had largely pursued a different agenda—such as launching grocery cooperatives and pushing organic agriculture—than the more epicurean artisanal–cosmopolitan subculture (with a few bridging figures like Alice Waters providing leadership to both). From the late-1990s onward, these splinter movements effectively recombined into the eco-epicurean movement, which dramatically transformed the foods market for upper-middle-class Americans, particularly the cultural capital cohort that Starbucks originally targeted.

Driving this new formation was an onslaught of media discourse—including Fast Food Nation, Supersize Me, and The Omnivore's Dilemma (see the analysis of Vitaminwater in Chapter 7 for an analysis of this mass-media discourse)—which critiqued the flaws of industrial agriculture using many of the same arguments as the back-to-the-land movement in the 1960s and 1970s. Cultural elites embraced these back-to-the-land politics, yielding a movement built around a newly politicized aesthetics of food. Participants advocated a return to pre-industrial modes of agricultural production and consumption: local foods (locavores, food shed), direct purchase from farmers (farmers' markets, community-supported agriculture), ridding agriculture of synthetic chemicals (organics), and treating food once again as the center of convivial social ritual (the Slow Food movement). The cultural capital cohort, seeking to emulate these cultural elites, yearned for trickle-down versions of this movement as a new form of cultural sophistication. This ideological opportunity was masterfully cultivated by Whole Foods Market, among other cultural capital cohort brands.

To sustain its position of cultural leadership, Starbucks needed to act as a fast follower of the major advances in the artisanal–cosmopolitan foods subculture. The eco-epicurean movement was far and away the most important such opportunity of the decade, providing ideal source material for Starbucks to appropriate. Starbucks was pushing heavily into food sales at the time, with the goal of increasing the average check and drawing a lunchtime crowd. The company could easily have built its entire foods business around this ideological platform. Instead, it served conventional deli sandwiches with ingredients sourced from industrial agriculture, and breakfast sandwiches that rivaled McDonalds' Egg McMuffin. While competitors were appropriating this movement as aggressively as possible, Starbucks completely ignored it. No longer guiding the cultural capital cohort's tastes, Starbucks had become a cultural laggard.

As management pushed the brand down-market, it threw away the company's most important strategic asset: its role as fast follower of cultural codes that expressed coffee (and foods) sophistication. In 2002,

78 percent of Starbucks customers held college degrees, and their incomes averaged $81,000 a year. Five years later, these socioeconomic indicators had plummeted to 55 percent and $55,000.[13] The cultural capital cohort had fled from Starbucks in droves, with lower social classes substituting as Starbucks' core customers. No longer a mediator of cultural sophistication, Starbucks became a purveyor of just plain coffee for the mass market; and, without the patina of sophistication, it was a frightfully expensive cup.

To make matters worse, the company attracted the attention of the businesses against whom it was now openly competing. As Starbucks sought inroads into fast food, both McDonalds and Dunkin' Donuts responded vigorously. These fast-food doyens spotted the opportunity to mount a strategy that we call a cultural jujitsu (see our cultural strategy work for Fuse in Chapter 12). They leveraged Starbucks' original branding as a culturally sophisticated drink to assert their own class populism. They satirized Starbucks as a pretentious brand for snobs, and undercut its price points.

Starbucks' run as a Wall Street growth stock had come to an abrupt end. Same store sales stalled. In 2006, the stock crashed, suffering a 40 percent decline in value long before the global recession hit sales and stock prices. Now that Starbucks had tarnished its cultural cache, customers found the store too pricy.

Schultz's Revitalization Efforts Push Starbucks Further down the Hierarchy

In a 2007 corporate memo leaked to the national media, Schultz seemed to grasp at least part of the brand's problem. He described how management had carelessly commoditized the Starbucks brand, offering as examples its automatic espresso machines, coffee in plastic bags, and cookie-cutter store designs. Schultz called for a return to Starbucks' roots while taking back the CEO reins in order to resuscitate the brand. Schultz's key initiatives, however, exacerbated Starbucks' branding problems:

- *Pike Place Roast.*™ House Blend coffee is replaced by a new blend of drip coffee named after the famed original Pike Place Market location in Seattle. This replacement was used as the foundation for a major media campaign.

- *VIA™ instant coffee.* Starbucks simultaneously launched its first instant coffee, claiming (no doubt correctly) that theirs is significantly better than the other instants on the market.

Advertised as "the smoothest yet," the Pike Place blend was the first Starbucks coffee to feature a lighter roast that resembled fast-food brews. This move was tantamount to waving the white flag; a lowest-common-denominator effort that pushed Starbucks drip coffee to be more palatable to a larger percentage of the population. The blend was designed to fight against Dunkin' Donuts and McDonalds, not to resuscitate the cultural sophistication of the Starbucks brand. And launching an instant coffee was an even more problematic move. This was quintessentially scientific-industrial territory: a heavily processed, anonymous, heavily packaged product of mysterious origins that is as far removed from artisanal craft as is possible. The company competed with Nestle to see which company could manufacture the best industrialized coffee powder. The blunt contradictions with Starbucks trickle-down strategy as a fast follower of artisanal–cosmopolitan codes could not be more obvious.

Instead of acting decisively and convincingly to regain its artisanal–cosmopolitan cache—perhaps by scrapping its fast-food fare in favor of a locavore line, scrapping its robot espresso machines for machines that require some skill, and reintroducing a terroir drip coffee that is always available—Starbucks did the opposite. It pushed even further down the cultural capital hierarchy. Curiously, Starbucks aimed its offering at consumers who were more likely to resonate with the populist rhetoric of Dunkin' Donuts and McDonalds, and who could not afford Starbucks anyway. Starbucks seemed destined to become just another coffee brand, a modestly upscale chain with atrocious prices.

Conclusion

Starbucks is the pre-eminent recent American example of a cultural innovation that focuses on social class. We introduce an important variation of cultural innovation theory, what we term cultural capital trickle-down, to explain how such innovations work. Typical analyses of fast-follower brands—usually focusing on fashion brands such as Zara and H&M, so often termed *fast fashion*—adopt an economic trickle-down model.[14] They examine how new business models allow such firms speedily to bring to market popularly priced knock-offs of what is in fashion amongst the rich and famous.

We use cultural innovation theory to advance beyond this sort of analysis. We show that Starbucks employs a trickle-down model, but one that is structured by the quest for cultural capital, not just emulating the rich and famous. And we go on to demonstrate that to innovate with cultural capital requires a deep understanding of the ideology, myth, and cultural codes of the elite subculture that one is appropriating, and then a careful "democratization" of these codes to create a sophisticated experience that is accessible.

Starbucks also provides fruitful case material for understanding what it takes to sustain cultural leadership once an innovation has taken flight. Four historical forces—the innovative cultural expression gets copied, entrepreneurial efforts evolve the codes, competitors position against the innovation, and consumers' ideological tastes evolve—combine to structure the cultural competition that the brand must manage. To sustain cultural leadership, brands must continue to bring incremental cultural innovations to market to stay one step ahead of these otherwise threatening changes in the cultural marketplace. Starbucks succeeded in doing just this in the 1990s, by appropriating the codes of ethical consumerism, but has struggled ever since.

Notes

1. We draw extensively from Mark Pendergrast, *Uncommon Grounds: The History of Coffee and How It Transformed the World* (New York: Basic Books, 1999) for the historical overview, adding our own cultural analysis of particular marketing efforts he describes.

2. See Juliet Schor, *The Overspent American: Why We Want What We Don't Need* (New York: Harper, 1999).

3. Douglas B. Holt, "Does Cultural Capital Structure American Consumption?" *Journal of Consumer Research*, 25 (June 1998), 1–25.

4. For example, see David Potter's classic cultural history *People of Plenty: Economic Abundance and the American Character* (Chicago: University of Chicago Press, 1954).

5. This explanation challenges two very popular accounts of this generation: geographer Richard Florida's account of what he calls "the creative class" and *New York Times* columnist David Brooks's thesis about what he calls Bourgeois-Bohemians. Florida's description is directionally correct, but it is quite limited because he focuses solely on people's occupations rather than upbringing. The two are correlated but imprecisely, and, as Bourdieu demonstrates, it is the early parenting, peer interactions, and education that account for most cultural capital acculturation. In David Brooks's satire *BoBos in Paradise*, he argues that this cohort's tastes were heavily influenced by their parents' bohemian-hippie values. In so doing, he overly politicizes what is really a social shift. True hippies constituted a small minority of the cohort, and many who once counted themselves as hippies did not live anything like a bohemian life years later when raising their kids. So his explanation could not possibly account for the shift toward cultural status in the 1990s.

6. This paragraph summarizes Mark Pendergrast's rendering of Peet and his influence.

7. Carolyn Marshall, "Alfred H. Peet, 87, Dies; Leader of Coffee Revolution," *New York Times*, Sept. 3, 2007.

8. In addition to Pendergrast, this narrative relies on Taylor Clark, *Starbucked: A Double Tall Tale of Caffeine, Commerce, and Culture* (New York: Little, Brown, 2007) and Bryant Simon, *Everything but the Coffee: Learning about America from Starbucks* (Berkeley and Los Angeles: University of California Press 2009). We also borrow selectively from the account of the early development of brand expressions offered by Heckler Associates, the design firm that did much of the early design work for the company (www.hecklerassociates.com/client-studies/starbucks).

9. Schultz often claims in the media that Starbucks is his inspired rendition of the Italian café. His pronouncements are effective brand spin, adding a dose of cosmopolitanism to what is clearly a watered-down and Americanized offering. Marketing pundits such as Seth Godin often parrot this and other claims rather than conduct a legitimate analysis of the brand. See Seth Godin, *Purple Cow: Transform your Business by Being Remarkable* (New York: Portfolio, 2003), 99. He argues that we have moved from an era of brands built via mass communications to an era of "purple cows"—his synonym for better mousetraps. Since the rise of the Internet in the mid-1990s, he claims that the only way to innovate is to develop a "remarkable" product. Companies that develop purple cows will be rewarded by the market, because the product's greatness will be easily recognized by early adopters and, then, will spread like wildfire through word-of-mouth on the Internet. His argument is entirely consonant with the economists and engineers who have argued for better mousetraps for decades, combined with a smattering of Everett Rodgers's diffusion of innovation model from the 1950s. Godin's thesis is very popular, no doubt because it makes marketing a lot simpler. But, as we show here, his lack of attention to the details of Starbucks' innovation means that his purple-cow thesis gets Starbucks exactly wrong. Rather than offer great authentic coffee, Starbucks succeeded because it made "less great" coffee (at least by artisanal–cosmopolitan standards) in order to appeal to the cultural capital cohort.

10. This section of the analysis is an extension of two white papers that Holt circulated in the media to critique Starbucks' reaction to the Ethiopian coffee sector's effort to trademark its regional appellations: Douglas B. Holt, "Brand Hypocrisy at Starbucks" (Nov. 2006), and Douglas B. Holt, "Is Starbucks 'Coffee That Cares?' " (Feb. 2007).

11. www.thebigmoney.com/articles/saga/2008/10/29/starbucks-blues

12. www.seattlepi.com/business/308336_starbucks21.html

13. Simon, *Everything but the Coffee*, 8.

14. For example, see Pankaj Ghemawat and Jose Luis Nueno, *ZARA: Fast Fashion*, Case 9-703-497 (Boston: Harvard Business School Press, 2003).

6

Patagonia: How Social Enterprises Cross the Cultural Chasm

The world is awash with social entrepreneurs who seek to solve social and environmental problems through businesses that are designed to stimulate social change—an approach often termed *social enterprise*. As social enterprise and its allied fields of social innovation, social entrepreneurship, and venture philanthropy have exploded since the turn of the century, so too has an increasingly sophisticated and well-funded infrastructure to nurture social enterprises, to train social entrepreneurs, and to provide venture capital for the strongest social innovation concepts. In the early years of this bourgeoning field's development, its promoters sought to facilitate a massive number of start-ups.[1] The assumption was that, if enough social entrepreneurs launched enough enterprises, surely a significant percentage of them would inevitably break through. But, although this new infrastructure has helped to launch many thousands of innovative small businesses with impressive social-change missions, few have scaled to the size needed to have an appreciable societal impact. Thought leaders in social enterprise are increasingly asking, why are social enterprises not scaling?[2]

Why do a handful of social enterprises take off and have a broad social impact, while the vast majority never grow beyond serving a niche of fellow activists? We argue that, for those social enterprises aimed at consumer markets, the primary impediment today is branding. Social enterprises fail to scale because they use inappropriate brand strategies and, thus, run into what we term *the cultural chasm*. Cultural innovation is required to overcome this chasm.

Cultural innovation is particularly important for social enterprise. The core of a social enterprise is its ideology of social change—using business as a means to address particular social or environmental problems. Marketing this ideology in a way that appeals to the mass market is key to achieving sufficient scale to effect social change. Social enterprises usually brand in a very explicit and literal fashion—they trumpet their ideology as a declarative mission statement. But enterprises that follow this approach typically run into what we term a cultural chasm, shutting down the potential to scale. Through cultural innovation, social enterprises can cross this chasm by transforming their social-change ideology into a cultural expression that creates identity value for mass-market consumers. In this chapter, we analyze one of the earliest and most successful American social enterprises—Patagonia.

The Cultural Chasm

Social enterprises fail to scale because mass-market consumers do not identify with their ideology—they hit a *cultural chasm*. This strategic problem is the cultural analogue to that faced by many start-up technology companies when they take their technological innovations into the mass market. Working with Everett Rodgers's seminal model for the diffusion of innovations, Geoffrey Moore noticed that many tech companies thrive in the niche market comprised of early adopters of the innovation, but fail to make the leap into the mass market. For Silicon Valley industries, this chasm has to do with an aversion to unproven technologies in applications that are critical to the customer company's mission. Start-ups often fail to comprehend these differences in demand. So they launch into the mass market with the same strategy that was successful for them early on, and they fail. Without evolving their strategies, they will not, in Moore's terms, "cross the chasm."[3]

The same principle holds for social enterprises, except that the chasm is cultural rather than technological. Many social enterprises stall because the company is born out of passion around a social issue, nurtured within a world of fellow activists, from which it attracts its early adopter customer base. The business proposition seems obvious—"buy a quality product that will help make the world become a better place if enough people join in." This is the sort of straightforward call to arms that appeals to fellow issue activists. The problem is that the community of activists around any particular issue is tiny, not nearly enough to have an appreciable social impact. And this declarative, literal, lecturing mode of conveying the social-change ideology often alienates the mass market rather than seduces them. So, by focusing the branding on getting the word out that the business advocates a particular cause, the social enterprise ends up just "preaching to the choir" of fellow activists. This approach defeats the transformative goals of the enterprise, which requires pulling in customers who were not previously committed to the social-change ideal. Hence, social enterprises face a cultural chasm: how can they convert a business that is meaningful to activists into a brand that is valuable to the mass market?

What makes a social enterprise distinctive is its business model, which is structured to promote social and environmental change as well as deliver profit to stockholders. This ideological core is potentially the company's biggest asset: it sets the company apart from commercial competitors with much greater resources. Yet, existing strategic models ignore the very feature that distinguishes social-enterprise companies from conventional commerce. Recently, two of the most influential strategy gurus—Clayton Christensen and Jim Collins—have imported their commercial strategy models into social enterprise. Both models rely upon a better-mousetraps logic.

Clayton Christensen's disruptive innovation model focuses on products and services that trump existing category competition because they are cheaper, more useful, more reliable, or more convenient. Innovation is centered on a product or service with features that dramatically alter the conventional value proposition of an existing category.[4] Christensen and his colleagues adapted this model for social enterprise in an influential *Harvard Business Review* article, "Disruptive Innovation for Social Change."[5] They argue that "catalytic innovations" drive how social enterprises can solve social problems:

Like disruptive innovations, which challenge industry incumbents by offering simpler, good-enough alternatives to an underserved group of customers, catalytic innovations can surpass the status quo by providing good-enough solutions to inadequately addressed social problems.

Likewise, Jim Collins applies the recommendations he made in his best-selling book *Good to Great* to the social sector to provide guidance on the strategies required for social enterprises to take off (and become "great").[6] To scale a strong social-enterprise concept (what he calls "the hedgehog concept") into a social enterprise with broad and sustainable social impact, Collins recommends building a brand through "turning the flywheel." Turning the flywheel is none other than a simplified version of the conventional model of branding, in which a company executes so consistently on its better-mousetrap concept over time that it earns a reputation for performance, quality, and reliability.[7]

While developing a better mousetrap, and then earning for the brand a reputation for doing so, is a laudable goal for any business, it is a generic business recipe that ignores the particular strategic opportunities and challenges that social enterprises face. Social enterprises approach business in a distinctive manner. They hope that consumers, through their purchases, will buy into their ideology of social change. When branded properly, social enterprises can engender a more enthusiastic response from mass-market consumers than brands that are structured around a conventional commercial approach. Social enterprises that follow advice to pursue a better-mousetraps strategy necessarily walk away from their ideology, in so doing sidelining what is potentially their most valuable asset.

Crossing the cultural chasm requires cultural innovation to transform an ideology of social change into a brand that is meaningful to the mass market. We analyze Patagonia's breakthrough to specify how the cultural innovation model works for social enterprise.

Why Do Republicans Wear Patagonia?

Beginning in the late 1980s, the outdoor-gear company Patagonia, one of the oldest and most influential social enterprises in the United States, used cultural innovation to break through to mass-market success and widespread market influence. Patagonia is organized around environmental activism: its mission statement declares that Patagonia exists "to inspire solutions to the environmental crisis." The company has not only pioneered sustainable textiles such as organic cotton T-shirts and polar fleece jackets made from recycled PET bottles, but has also used its revenues to fund hundreds of environmental groups, many of which would be considered on the far left of the American political spectrum. Company founder Yvon Chouinard sought to institutionalize this approach by launching "1% for the Planet"—a program in which participating companies give 1% of their sales revenues to approved environmental organizations.

Because of this aggressive and explicit environmental mission, one might expect that Patagonia would attract only liberal environmental activists as customers. Yet, beginning in the late 1980s, the company became hugely resonant with mass-market consumers who were not particularly engaged with environmental problems. In fact, in our research, we discovered that Patagonia appealed to many registered Republicans! This widespread popularity has allowed Patagonia to impact environmental sustainability in the marketplace and in politics. Patagonia did so by following the logic of cultural innovation. Rather than trumpet its environmental mission in the literal declarative mode typical of social enterprises, Patagonia instead championed a mythical world of sophisticated adventure, which resonated powerfully with upper-middle-class Americans of all political stripes.

Source Material: Dirtbag Subculture

Patagonia's mass-market branding is sourced from the dirtbag subculture, which the company's founder helped to pioneer. Long before starting Patagonia, Yvon Chouinard was an impressive American mountain climber, renowned for inspired first assents as well as the revolutionary mountaineering hardware he forged in the blacksmith shop in his garage. Chouinard was unsatisfied with the clunky European products that American climbers used and, even more, was disturbed by the fact that climbers were destroying the pristine "vertical nature" of Yosemite and other spectacular mountain ranges by carelessly driving pitons into the granite and leaving them behind. Chouinard designed and hand-forged the removable "lost arrow" piton in the late 1950s, the first of many innovative climbing hardware designs he introduced over the next decade. While the hardware business would struggle financially and eventually get sold off, it was Chouinard's ideology, which emerged organically from his leadership position at the epicenter of America's mountain-climbing subculture, which would eventually serve as the foundation for his mass-market breakthrough.

He issued the company's first catalogue in 1973, a 36" × 32" broadsheet that folded up like a map (it would take another two years to get around to making another one). Laced between his geeky descriptions of technically advanced gear, Chouinard offered sermons on his climbing ideology:

There is a word for it, and the word is clean. Climbing with only nuts and runners for protection is clean climbing. Clean because the rock is left un-altered by the passing climber. Clean because nothing is hammered into the rock and then hammered back out, leaving the rock scarred and the next climber's experience less natural. Clean because the climber's protection leaves little trace of his ascension. Clean is climbing the rock without changing it; a step closer to organic climbing for the natural man.

In subsequent catalogues, Chouinard would continue to prod his customer-readers on topics he felt were critical to the proper way to do wilderness adventure, from technique, to dress, to aesthetic rumin-ations. And Chouinard continued to walk the walk, whether surfing, mountain climbing, or running death-defying rapids, always exuding the Hemingway-esque adventurer: "He's a man who has made it a point to drink from every stream he has ever fished, no matter how germ-ridden, having decided early on that 'I'd be outside the rest of my life, so I had to adapt. I've gotten sick a lot, but each time I got stronger and less sick.' "[8]

As a result, Chouinard soon became a moral authority for what participants came to call the "dirtbag" subculture. Chouinard and his compatriots combined an aggressively masculine take on wilderness adventure as a risky competitive avocation with a profoundly aesthetic appreciation for nature. Chouinard's early ideological efforts as a widely respected leader of this subculture would later grant him immense credibility in advancing this ideology as the cultural core of his new outdoor clothing company. But this breakthrough would have to wait for the right historical moment. The dirtbag subculture had little traction in the American mass market during the 1960s and 1970s, when Chouinard was at his mountain-climbing prime. However, significant shifts in American society beginning in the mid-1980s would make the dirtbaggers' ideology irresistible to many upper-middle-class consumers.

Ideological Opportunity

Social enterprises break though by developing cultural expressions that respond to an ideological opportunity—a historical moment when a social disruption creates demand for the ideology championed by the social enterprise. Patagonia's breakthrough was made possible by two intersecting shifts in American society: Reagan's revival of the American frontier myth (which we review in the Nike case in Chapter 2) and the vast demographic expansion of a cohort that sent the demand for sophisticated consumption skyrocketing (which we review in the Starbucks case in Chapter 5). Patagonia was a pitch-perfect champion and guide to feed these intersecting desires.

Americans gained the toughness and tenacity required to realize the American Dream on the frontier, where poor European immigrants and religious outcasts built a new nation by pioneering land carved out from a vast wilderness, facing up to extraordinary challenges and countless dangers. This myth produced America's original and still most influential mode of environmentalism—the conservation of wilderness. When the frontier closed toward the end of the nineteenth century, Teddy Roosevelt painted a vision of a country in need of wilderness to combat the soft emasculating taint of city life, and set aside vast tracts of the most rugged terrain in the Western United States as national parks. John Muir pioneered the flip side of American's infatuation with wilderness—the idea, developed by the Romanticism of Emerson and Thoreau in the nineteenth century, that individual freedom, quickly depleting in the modern urban world, could be regained by immersion in nature. He ignited the modern environmental movement with this spiritually inflected plea to preserve wilderness as an aesthetic, in his ill-fated effort to save the Hetch Hetchy valley in Yosemite from a dam. Rekindling American character by rekindling Americans' identification with the wilderness experience has been a central thread of American political discourse ever since.[9]

As we recount in our analysis of Nike, the economic restructuring of the 1980s instigated the most recent frontier revival. These new economic conditions required that Americans pursue a character makeover. Ideologically speaking, the emerging rough-and-tumble free-agent economy demanded a very different mentality. Ronald Reagan led the way—brandishing the revival of the frontier as the antidote to America's troubles.

Upper-middle-class Americans had to come to grips with this newly Darwinist labor market, along with a cultural discourse that put them down. Just as the frontier revivalists of the 1950s heaped scorn on the soft and sedentary "organization man," so too did Reagan and his brethren propose that the American upper middle class—to be found in big bureaucracies, conglomerates, professions, and universities—were dragging down the country. They were scorned as quiche-eating "yuppies"—pampered, materialistic, lacking the masculine vigor to survive in the new economy. Reagan's resuscitation of the frontier myth, equating the character needed to succeed economically with the world-conquering ethos of the gunfighter in the wilderness, had a profound impact on them. The upper middle class felt compelled to adopt a vigorous frontier-styled ideology to demonstrate that they were anything but sedentary bureaucratic yuppies.

At the same time, the upper middle class was caught up in a demographic riptide, as we recount in the Starbucks case. American norms for status consumption were rapidly shifting: from acquiring expensive stuff to engaging in culturally sophisticated experiences. A large demographic cohort that, for the first time in American history, had been raised by college-educated parents had come of age. This cultural capital cohort was at least as interested in the pursuit of a sophisticated and creative lifestyle as in the materialistic ideals of the traditional American Dream.

So upper-middle-class consumers were pulled simultaneously in two directions: toward wilderness adventure and toward new modes of cultural sophistication. These two consumption-shaping forces were usually in conflict. Snowmobiling in Yellowstone or hunting elk in Canada were great expressions of wilderness adventure but were anything but sophisticated, while becoming a connoisseur of indie films or boutique wines potently conveyed one's discriminating tastes, but proclaimed that one was a sedentary urbanite. Thus, activities that solved this cultural puzzle—combining cultivation and wilderness adventure—were highly prized. Patagonia was ideally placed to provide an instruction manual of sorts for how to take on wilderness adventure in a sophisticated cosmopolitan form.

Patagonia's Cultural Innovation

In 1979, Chouinard and his wife Malinda launched Patagonia as a functional adventure clothing line. They were joined in this push to develop technical adventure gear by a slew of other companies, including Marmot, North Face, Sierra Designs, Outdoor Research, Kelty, and Columbia. Patagonia was the only company to do so as a social enterprise, and, through its cultural strategy, became the premium brand, commanding some of the highest price points in the industry.

Patagonia's primary branding vehicle for many years was a large-format catalogue, designed as a magazine with stories, essays, and photojournalism interspersed with the gear. Beginning in the late 1980s, Patagonia catalogues followed an exacting formula, repeated in catalogue after catalogue, that predictably seduced upper-middle-class prospects in search of a dose of sophisticated wilderness adventure. Many customers we talked to looked forward to receiving the catalogues and read them as they would a magazine.

Patagonia catalogues feigned as if its only customers were the original dirtbaggers. Fellow dirtbags were encouraged to send in photos and essays documenting their harrowing adventures, and the catalogue took on the role of the favored insider convening ground. The editorial choices consistently celebrated dirtbag places, techniques, and pleasures, inviting mass-market consumers to peek into this rarified world, where participants live to pursue another unimaginably challenging conquest. Through cultural analysis of two decades of catalogues, supplemented by interviews with Patagonia managers and customers, we isolated the four key components of Patagonia's ideology and their most compelling cultural expressions.

Extreme Adventure

The center of Patagonia's cultural innovation was the romancing of extreme adventure. From the beginning, Patagonia has published "field reports": first-hand accounts of the perils and thrills of risky wilderness adventures, what the company terms "intense glimpses of nature's front lines through travelers and adventurers." Patagonia invites mass-market consumers to peer through the looking glass to see what hardcore adventure is all about, tag along with this subculture, and fantasize about embarking on such intense wilderness challenges.

Hell in Paradise
by Chloë Lanthier

I'm nine hours into a 24-hour mountain bike race. The rain is pounding the course into the night, the temperature is dropping, my body aches, but I know I have to keep the pace. The technical single track has become a dark vein of roots, rocks and slurry mud. At 3 a.m. fog settles down on forested sections and makes visibility impossible, amplifying the dreamlike solitude. My core temperature has dropped and I'm borderline hypothermic: I quicken my pace to stay ahead of the cold night.

By daybreak, voices emerge as I pass the transition area and wake me from a distant dream to face the reality of the moment. I'm being pulled by my focus to maintain a lead I should never take for granted.

I finish with a victory but the joy of winning is bittersweet. I feel a huge void. It's over. The physical effort, the mental drive to battle the elements, the power to keep on climbing . . . the drive that keeps me going. It is all part of a deep passion that enables me to express a part of who I am: the only person I face when I'm crouched over my handlebars.

I could have easily skipped the finish line and kept on going.

What's Next?
by Mark Wilford

My stomach was in my throat. My mind was racing, trying to pinpoint the exact sequence I needed to follow. In thirty years of climbing, I had never rappelled inside a waterfall. I couldn't hear my partner anymore, nor see him through the blinding water. The icy liquid worked its way into every nook and cranny of mine, seeped down my back and finally filled up my boots. I was getting numb. As I looked down into the black pool below, I saw myself trapped, locked to the rappel line, my pack weighing me down, a slow drowning in the bottomless water.

At first, the gorge was benign. We'd just spent five days getting up an unclimbed 21,000 foot peak in the Indian Karakoram and had chosen the gorge as our descent route. But then it got tight, the drops vertical, the rocks polished smooth. A coating of algae added the viscosity of high grade motor oil to the rock. Cracks for gear placements were almost nonexistent.

At one point, we stacked a bunch of rocks on top of a sling and crossed our fingers.

I dropped my pack and unscrewed my locking carabiner from my rappel device. I slid down on my knees as the water bashed me. When I finally hit the pool I instantly unclipped from the rope and waded to the shallows. My pack was there bobbing like a cork. Whoaa! I thought, it doesn't get any better than this.

These visceral accounts of extreme wilderness outings dramatized precisely the kind of super-competitive wilderness adventure ideology that upper-middle-class Americans yearned for.

Adventure Cosmopolitanism

Patagonia catalogues evinced an obsessive fascination with particular places. Dirtbaggers never go on a generic climb. Rather, they hike the Anaktuvuk Valley in the Brooks Range of Alaska, or the Cook Straight in New Zealand, or Pumirini in Peru. These places are well off the beaten track; many are distant and exotic places. So this adventure name-dropping served as a powerful form of cultural capital, conveying the sophistication of participants.[10]

The photo-essays present dirtbaggers as playful cosmopolitan bohemians. One catalogue featured the following: a photo of guys with goofy hats and eyeglasses kicking around a hacky sack on the top of Denali in Alaska with the caption "14,000 feet: when we weren't hacking up a storm, we were hackin' up a storm." A few pages later, we find a waist-down shot of a guy pulling on his pants in the back of a beat-up camper—"Brian Crowder pants after a hard day of bouldering, Camp 4 parking lot, Yosemite Valley." And then we encounter a woman standing up in the passenger seat of an old Cadillac convertible, the rear seat packed to the hilt with climbing gear and skis, with a caption reading "Open road, open air, open to the possibilities of the Toyabe Mountains, Nevada." A few pages later we learn about "Brietta Sjostrom hoopin it up in La Paz, Bolivia." Brietta is wearing an Andean hand-knit alpaca sweater and hat, holding a siku (Andean pan flute) in her hand, and working her hips in an impromptu dance to hold up in the air a handmade hula hoop wrapped in brightly colored local fabrics.

And finally the catalogue's epilogue, a field report by Douglas Peacock, seals the deal. Peacock describes himself as the real-deal dirtbagger, tracking grizzlies in the wild for a decade while living on military C-rations. But then he lets on that he is also fond of Bordeaux and foie gras, which the photo documents. He is shown in a Yellowstone Park hot springs working on a bottle of 1974 Petrus (a bottle that would have cost around $200 at the time of the photo, from one of the most renowned chateaux in Bordeaux!).

Peacock was a good friend of the seminal environmentalist writer Edward Abbey and the basis for a character, Hayduke, in Abbey's most famous book, *The Monkey Wrench Gang*. Patagonia's catalogues routinely featured the most famous of the literate side of environmentalism, from beat poet-turned-environmentalist Gary Snyder to naturalist-author Terry Tempest Williams. Advocating Abbey's (and Peacock's) environmental politics explicitly would have turned off all but the most radical activists. Instead, through the alchemy of cultural innovation, the catalogue transforms their political radicalism into a chic form of adventure sophistication.

The consistent presentation of dirtbaggers as cosmopolitan bohemians, supremely comfortable traveling the globe in search of the next thrilling wilderness experience, fit precisely the emerging upper-middle-class demand for wilderness experience that oozed cultural sophistication.

Wilderness Sublime

Accentuating this nod to sophistication in wilderness tastes, Patagonia catalogues always featured stunning nature photography with an artist's attention to composition: a close-up of a monstrous wave, a panorama of a rock face in Zion National Park, a monumental shot looking up through the center of a frozen waterfall in Banff. This devotion to the aesthetics of nature, alongside the adventure conquest, flows through the photography of every catalogue and often in the essays as well. Nature is portrayed in its most pure and unadulterated form as a source of awe and profound aesthetic experience. In so doing, Patagonia conjures up the Romantic ideal of Thoreau and Muir, in which wilderness is the most potent source of sublime experience.[11]

Paging through a Patagonia catalogue is like paging through a coffee-table book of Ansel Adams's nature photography, except that the adventurer is interposed into the setting. The only sign of human life is the dirtbagger, often alone. Dirtbaggers are presented as tiny props in nature, often taking up only 1/20 of the frame. They are focused on their adventure challenge, never looking at the camera. Sometimes we see just their arms, or a rope, to remind us that we are not just looking at nature but have become enveloped by it in the midst of a risky adventure. This invocation of the romantic celebration of wilderness lets the reader know that dirtbaggers are wilderness aesthetes—stunned by the beauty of nature as they are immersed in their travails.

Wilderness Politics

Patagonia did not establish its formal social mission until the mid-1980s, at which time the company began devoting 1 percent of its revenues to environmental causes. Since then, the company has continually ramped up its commitment and focus on environmental activism as its *raison d'être*. But most of these fundamental changes in Patagonia business philosophy remained in the fine print, invisible to all but the most involved dirtbaggers and environmentalists. Rather than pronounce its environmental mission to prospective customers, Patagonia seamlessly incorporated its environmentalism into its cultural expressions. After early misfires, Patagonia figured out how to integrate its social-change ideology in a way that would appeal immensely to the mass market.

Beginning in 1990, with a lead essay titled "Help Bring the Wolf Back to Yellowstone," Patagonia began its decades-long run of campaigning for remaking modern industrial landscapes into wilderness. The campaigns were communicated in informative and romantic photojournalist essays, in the style of *National Geographic*. In 1993, the company took up the cause of salmon and began campaigning for knocking down dams that interrupted spawning runs. These early campaigning essays would serve as the foundation for Patagonia politics over the next two decades. Much of the campaigning has focused on establishing migration routes for animals such as wolves, bears, and bison that used to roam freely in the American West (using the headline "Freedom to Roam" in the 2000s). Another campaign, "The Ocean as Wilderness," encouraged customers to think of the ocean as the last great wilderness, worth protecting for the same reason as land wilderness. These campaigns promoted the recuperation of pristine wilderness and the species that thrive in such environs.

Patagonia's focus on wilderness politics echoed the original Rooseveltian mode of conservationist environmentalism. Patagonia's professed environmental politics were little different from that of the old-school American conservationist organizations, such as the Audubon Society, the National Wildlife Federation, the Wilderness Society, and the early Sierra Club (before it became radicalized by David Brower in the 1960s).

It is noteworthy that the most important environmental issues of the day—such as climate change, groundwater contamination and depletion, infiltration of chemicals into the food supply, and the impact of Western consumerism on the environment of the developing world— were sidelined. Likewise, Patagonia's focal environmental mission as a company—reducing the ecological footprint of its clothing through detailed lifecycle analysis, innovating supply chains, and encouraging its customers to wear its clothing until threadbare and then recycle it— was barely visible. Environmental problems that have an industrial origin—that have no relation to wilderness—were downplayed. If you did not read the fine print, you might have concluded that Patagonia's environmental politics were focused solely on preserving wilderness. This is precisely what we found when we interviewed mass-market fans of Patagonia: they viewed Patagonia as an advocate for wilderness conservation—a very popular and palatable kind of environmentalism across a broad political spectrum—and had little idea that Patagonia's environmentalism is squarely focused on the ills of industrialization and consumer society.

Summary

Patagonia's tremendously influential catalogues placed the company at the center of the dirtbag subculture, and invited all who happened upon the catalogue to eavesdrop, to become seduced by a life dedicated to harrowing cosmopolitan adventures in the wild. Beginning in the late 1980s, the American upper middle class was taken by the idea of joining a tribe of hardy cosmopolitan adventurers who scraped by with whatever meager way of making a living that allowed them to spend as much time as possible mountain climbing and chasing after other risky wilderness endeavors. It made them feel good that their fellow adventurers shared their concern for the protection of wilderness.

This cultural innovation allowed Patagonia to break through the cultural chasm to become wildly popular amongst upper-middle-class Americans who yearned to participate in sophisticated wilderness adventure. Patagonia quickly grew to pull in over $200 million in annual revenues. With the economic support of these mass-market customers, Patagonia had the economic clout to invest in crucial sustainable supply-chain innovations, as well as the financial resources to donate tens of millions to grass-roots environmental organizations. Ironically, these influential environmentalist efforts were of little interest to the company's mass-market customers. In fact, many mass-market customers who loved Patagonia, and have been largely responsible for allowing Patagonia to push forward its environmental agenda, hold environmental ideologies that conflict directly with the company's activist stance.

Conclusion

Social enterprises use commerce to spark social change. Consumers buy into a social-change ideology when they make a purchase: the more successful the business, the more the new ideology permeates society. So these businesses succeed to the extent that consumers identify with and value this ideology enough to become loyal consumers.

The enterprise's social-change ideology can be a powerful asset, leveraged to outflank commercial enterprises that hold otherwise impenetrable resources and market power. Consumers find the cultural expressions of social change delivered by social enterprises to be much more authentic and persuasive than the corporate social-responsibility initiatives and cause-related marketing corporations offered by many conventional companies when they dabble in social change.[12] But, if marketed poorly, the enterprise's social-change ideology can stunt growth. When start-ups broadcast their ideology in the sort of literal mission statement format that fellow activists find so appealing in hopes of winning mass-market converts, they often find that these prospects turn their back on such overtly political rhetoric. This is what we call the cultural chasm.

Better-mousetraps models cannot solve this problem. They ignore the distinctive character of social enterprise entirely and advocate mimicking conventional businesses. By disguising a company's activism, better-mousetraps models throw away the most powerful asset that a social enterprise can leverage. Few social enterprises can sustain their mission while competing with existing commercial enterprises purely on product and service value.

Patagonia crossed the cultural chasm to enjoy tremendous mass-market success and widespread societal impact because the company rejected these orthodox approaches to branding social enterprise. The same is true of Ben & Jerry's, which we analyze in Chapter 4. Rather than broadcasting their social missions or ascribing to better-mousetraps models, these two companies developed compelling cultural innovations.

Mass-market consumers greatly value ideologically charged goods and services. But, unlike activists, they consume ideology in an implicit "disguised" form, embedded in brand symbolism. Rather than try to convince non-activists of the importance of the enterprise's activist cause, cultural innovation requires a demand-driven approach: the social enterprise responds to the emerging ideological desires of a target segment of mass-market consumers. Patagonia targeted the demand amongst upper-middle-class Americans for a new ideology of sophisticated wilderness adventure that emerged in the late 1980s. Patagonia selectively culled from its environmentalist ideology to tailor cultural expressions that responded to this demand.

And, like their commercial brethren, social enterprises do not break through by pronouncing their ideology, however innovative and in-demand. Rather, they must convert ideology to cultural expression. The most resonant and credible cultural expressions of social-change ideologies are to be found in subcultures and social movements. So, social enterprises must become immersed in an appropriate subculture or movement, one that embodies the social-change ideology, in order to become skilled at the most resonant expressions, and to be perceived as a credible advocate of this ideology by the mass market. Yvon Chouinard drew from the subculture of dirtbaggers, which he had helped to pioneer. Similarly, Ben Cohen and Jerry Greenfield liberally borrowed from the back-to-the-land movement, in which they were active participants.

Subcultures and movements dramatize their social-change ideologies through the particulars of their lifestyles and political actions. Dirtbaggers demonstrated their environmentalism through how they climbed, the gear they chose, and their deep aesthetic appreciation for pristine wilderness. Back-to-the-landers demonstrated their sustainable business ideology through their practice of alternative agriculture, their use of pre-modern provisioning techniques, and their creation and support for cooperatives that treated workers humanely. These ideology-embedded cultural expressions, which implicitly dramatize a social-change ideal, are much more compelling for mass-market consumers than declarative statements of ideology.

Both companies tapped into these expressions and repurposed them in their branding. Social enterprises break through the cultural chasm by viewing customers, not as potential activists, but as consumers with identity projects. Patagonia broke through when Yvon Chouinard used the Patagonia catalogue as a canvas to romanticize the lives of cosmopolitan wilderness adventurers. Ben & Jerry's broke through when it used provocative new-product launches and creative public-relations stunts to stump for a utopian world of do-gooder sustainable business that challenged Reaganism. In each case, the enterprise repackaged the expressions borrowed from the subculture or movement in a manner that responded directly to massive pent-up demand for a particular ideology.

To cross the cultural chasm, social entrepreneurs must give up the notion that, if they stay true to their social mission, and repeat this sermon enough times, they will eventually succeed. Rather—if Patagonia and Ben & Jerry's are any guide—social enterprises are much more likely to succeed if they focus first on developing the ideologically charged cultural expressions that are demanded by the mass-market prospects whose patronage is critical for their diffusion. In each case, the company broke through because they figured out how to create resonant cultural expressions from its social-change ideology to create identity value for the mass market. Only then did Patagonia and Ben & Jerry's develop a formal social mission. Launching a social enterprise in a more "professional" manner—with an explicit and well-conceived social mission that is communicated consistently to consumers—may in fact be precisely the wrong approach to pursuing a business that will scale enough to lead to widespread social impact.

Notes

1. Major promoting organizations include Ashoka, the Skoll Foundation, the Schwab Foundation for Social Entrepreneurship, the School for Social Entrepreneurs, and many elite business schools around the world.
2. Gregory Dees, Beth Battle Anderson, and Jane Wei-Skillern, "Scaling Social Impact: Strategies for Spreading Social Innovation," *Stanford Social Innovation Review* (Spring 2004), 24–32; Paul N. Bloom and Aaron K. Chatterji, "Scaling Social Entrepreneurial Impact," *California Management Review*, 51/3 (Spring 2009), 114–33; Charles Leadbeater, "Social Enterprise and Social Innovation: Strategies for the Next Ten Years," *Report to the Office of the Third Sector*, London: November 2007.
3. Geoffrey A. Moore, *Crossing the Chasm: Marketing and Selling Disruptive Products to Mainstream Customers* (New York: Harper, 1995).
4. Clayton M. Christensen, *The Innovator's Dilemma* (Boston: Harvard Business School Press); Clayton M. Christensen and Michael E. Raynor, *The Innovator's Solution: Creating and Sustaining Successful Growth* (Boston: Harvard Business School Press, 2003).
5. Clayton M. Christensen, Heiner Baumann, Rudy Ruggles, and Thomas M. Sadtler, "Disruptive Innovation for Social Change," *Harvard Business Review* (Dec. 2006), 94–101.
6. Jim Collins, *Good to Great: Why Some Companies Make the Leap…And Others Don't* (New York: HarperBusiness, 2001). Jim Collins, *Good to Great and the Social Sectors: A Monograph to Accompany Good to Great* (New York: HarperCollins, 2005).
7. See, e.g., Tülin Erdem and Joffre Swait, "Brand Equity as a Signaling Phenomenon," *Journal of Consumer Psychology*, 7/2 (1998), 131–57.
8. Patricia Leigh Brown, "The Maverick Who Sent America Outdoors," *New York Times*, Mar. 11, 1998.
9. A full rendition of the frontier myth can be found in Chapter 3 on Jack Daniel's and Chapter 8 on Marlboro.
10. This finding reiterates two of the dimensions of cultural capital we describe in Douglas B. Holt, "Does Cultural Capital Structure American Consumption?" *Journal of Consumer Research* (1998), 1–25.
11. Roderick Nash, *Wilderness and the American Mind* (New Haven: Yale University Press, 2001); William Cronon (ed.), *Uncommon Ground: Rethinking the Human Place in Nature* (New York: Norton, 1996).
12. Douglas B. Holt, "Why Do Brands Cause Trouble? A Dialectical Theory of Consumer Culture and Branding," *Journal of Consumer Research*, 29 (June 2002), 70–90.

7

Vitaminwater: Creating a "Better Mousetrap" with Myth

On May 25, 2007, The Coca-Cola Company purchased Glaceau for $4.1 billion, a stunning sum to pay for an 11-year-old company selling a facile beverage that the founder Darius Bikoff had concocted in his kitchen. Coca-Cola paid this steep price for Vitaminwater, a rainbow-colored line of non-carbonated fruit-flavored drinks sold in 20-ounce plastic bottles. Vitaminwater had been launched in 2000 and sales had taken off in 2004, so that by 2007 the brand turned over $700 million a year at retail.

Vitaminwater exploited a powerful social disruption that emerged in 2000 and continued to grow until 2006. The disruption was created by the media—magazines, newspapers, television shows, and films that attacked American dietary practices and brought attention to the health consequences of sugary soft drinks in particular. As Americans began to rethink entirely what they drank, beverage-makers scrambled to seize the opportunity. Amongst the dozens of new brands, some launched by multinational companies, Bikoff's tiny start-up won out.

Bikoff did not win the race by building a better mousetrap. Vitamin-water's product formulation was far from innovative. Essentially, it was a diluted non-carbonated drink, whose taste, serving size, and sugar content were very similar to Gatorade. And for a drink to offer vitamins was certainly nothing new at the time. In prior decades, many dozens of drinks had touted both their vitamin content and their promise to hydrate. As a mousetrap, Vitaminwater should not have succeeded: it was a me-too proposition that was very late to the game. But consumers did, indeed, perceive that Vitaminwater was a better mousetrap—because it offered a better myth.

Cultural Orthodoxy: Magic Bullet Solutions

The American diet is structured around a ying and yang that, until very recently, was distinctive in the world.[1] On the one hand, most Americans born after 1970 have been acculturated in a food culture centered on fast food and other highly processed and nutritionally bereft convenience foods. In 1970, Americans spent $6 billion on fast food, but by 2000 fast-food consumption had skyrocketed to $110 billion. Americans were spending more on fast food than on cars.[2] These foods, exemplified by the McDonald's menu of hamburgers, fries, and soft drinks, were labeled "junk food" because they were highly processed, full of fat and salt, contained chemical additives, and lacked the whole fruits, vegetables, and grains central to a healthy diet. The massive increase in soft-drinks consumption was a central feature of this new junk-food culture. Americans collectively shifted from drinking milk, juices, and water to drinking instead an average of 600 12-ounce cans of soda per person each year. For teenage boys, over 10 percent of their caloric intake came from the sugar in soft drinks.

Once alerted to the problem, Americans addressed the health hazards of their hedonistic food and drink, not by cutting back, but by countering the "bads" with the "goods" promised by a stream of scientific breakthroughs celebrated in the media. Americans became increasingly interested in and dependent on various "miracle foods" and newly isolated nutrients that promised a quick fix to their poor diets. The news media loved to report on the latest scientific health discoveries, and marketers were quick to follow suit, seeking to beat competitors to the newest scientific discovery in power foods, micronutrients, and anti-oxidants. New products moved from the first wave of additives, like ginseng and ginko, to more trendy and esoteric ones like acai and rooibos. The original miracle foods such as oatbran, fish, and red wine were supplemented by the likes of green tea, walnuts, and pomegranate. When food additives proved too difficult, Americans increasingly looked to over-the-counter supplements to do the same work, popping pills loaded up with beta-carotene, anti-oxidants, and omega 3.

Marketers raced to add the latest and greatest health additive to their offerings, the scientific discovery that had received the most media traction. The problem with this approach, though, was that most consumers could not keep up with what additive was the most credible. And they became jaded, because contradictory reports would often follow that reversed the previously lauded health benefits. In a confusing world of magic-bullet foods, additives, and pills, with too many promises to keep track of, and claims whose credibility was usually transient, Americans by the 2000s had become increasingly frustrated with trying to stay healthy using this neutralization strategy.

Social Disruption: Soda Becomes a Health Hazard

Nutritionists first sounded the alarm about soft drinks in the 1980s, focusing particularly on the preservatives and artificial sweeteners in diet sodas. A number of new soft-drink entrants addressed this earlier social disruption, creating what came to be called the "new-age" drink segment. These non-carbonated teas and fruit drinks from brands like Snapple and Arizona became popularly understood as a more natural and healthful alternative to soft drinks. These drinks boasted that they were "100% natural," lacking the strange chemicals often found listed on a soda can. They did in fact get rid of the artificial additives, but the sugar content remained just as high, and the package sizes were larger, so sugar consumption increased. Along with the concurrent race amongst fast-food chains to supersize drinks to portions that were a challenge to hold in one hand, younger Americans were gulping down more sugar than ever. Despite continual low-level buzz in the media that soft drinks had too much sugar, Americans kept on drinking. They turned a deaf ear until this discursive dam broke once and for all at the turn of the century.

Beginning around 2000, a second and much bigger wave of media reporting on the health crisis in American food finally forced America's sugary-drink enthusiasts to reconsider their habit. The lead story was the obesity crisis: Americans were getting much fatter, and it had become an epic social problem. Between 1980 and 2002, the prevalence of obesity among adults doubled in the USA, while the prevalence of being overweight tripled for children and teens. Following an initial study from the Centers for Disease Control and Prevention in 1995, more triangulating evidence accumulated and the story gathered momentum, so that by 2000 the media began regularly to use the term "epidemic," and the fatness of the population was treated with alarm as a national emergency.[3]

A *Newsweek* cover story in 2000 showed an obese boy holding up a large sugary ice cream cone and asked "Fat for Life? Six Million Kids Seriously Overweight." While previous articles had mentioned the role of "junk food" along with declining exercise, the *Newsweek* article was the first in a string of influential critiques that specifically blamed the obesity spike on soft drinks and fast food. Eric Schlosser's book *Fast Food Nation*, a best-seller for fifteen weeks upon release in early 2001 that then returned to the bestseller charts when launched as a paperback at the end of 2002, made a pariah out of the fast-food business, McDonalds in particular. NYU nutrition professor Marion Nestle's *Food Politics* was published in 2002, lambasting the food industry for damaging the nation's health, including an exposé on how soft-drink marketers pushed their empty calories into American food culture.

Greg Critser published *Fat Land* in 2003 following an influential *Harper's Magazine* cover story in 2002. He framed obesity as a national embarrassment—the book was subtitled "How Americans Became the Fattest People in the World." Critzer chronicled the way in which industry had "taught" Americans to eat an additional 200 calories per day over the course of two decades, what Michael Pollan in his review of the book called the "nutritional contradictions of capitalism." All these books were highly influential amongst the chattering class and trickled down to the primary soft-drinks consumer demographic indirectly through the news media, legitimizing the problem in public opinion. This social problem was dramatized by the 2004 documentary *Super Size Me*, a critique of soft-drinks consumption that had a visceral impact on loyal soda-guzzlers. The film chronicles Morgan Spurlock's disturbing experiment—eating only McDonald's for thirty days. Day by day we watch Morgan growing fatter and sicker. In the end he gained over 24 pounds and began to suffer symptoms of liver dysfunction. The film gained a wide viewership and even wider notoriety in popular culture.

Sugar on Crack: High Fructose Corn Syrup Implicated
The obesity crisis discourse singled out a particularly culpable foodstuff: the high fructose corn syrup (HFCS) sweetener used in soft

drinks. A prominent study on soda consumption in 2001 had pointed specifically at HFCS as a culprit in obesity, and this connection between HFCS and the obesity crisis was routinely reported by the mass media by the end of 2003.[4] *Fatland* pinpointed how supersizing tricked consumers into eating more, and described the rise of HFCS as a cheap substitute for cane sugar, highly suitable for industrial food production. HFCS had been snuck into the American diet with no regulatory oversight in the 1970s and soon became a favored ingredient of food manufacturers, a cheap way to sell calories. Repeated newspaper articles referred to research connecting HFCS to the "expanding waistline" of Americans.[5] HFCS, the studies reported, was stored easily by the body as fat, and also was less filling than sucrose.[6] As a result, the media began to refer to HFCS as "sugar on crack."[7] *Time* magazine ran a special issue devoted to the obesity crisis in June 2004, including among their "ideas for cleaning up our fattening environment" an elimination of fast food and soft drinks from schools and a defiance of the sugar- and corn-processing industries with a public campaign for lowered consumption of sweets.[8] The final blow came in 2006, when Michael Pollan published his hugely influential *The Omnivore's Dilemma*, which charted the rise of HFCS in the American diet.

Lower-Class Couch Potatoes: Sugary Drinks Acquire a Social Stigma
The media supplied Americans not only with a health rationale for abandoning sugary drinks, but also with an identity problem related to social class. Increasingly, the media characterized soft-drink consumers as obese couch potatoes, people who do not care about their bodies and are not smart enough to eat properly. Newspaper reports provided statistics about how the lowest socio-economic strata of Americans consumed the most soft drinks and were also considerably more likely to be obese. Films and news segments made the association unavoidable. In *Supersize Me*, for instance, we see Spurlock visit a morbidly obese man, clearly from a poor economic background, who is at the hospital preparing to get his stomach stapled. He shows us some of his 2-liter bottles of Coke, and explains that on many days he consumes three or four bottles, and that he recently went blind for a couple weeks and did not get his sight back until he temporarily switched to diet drinks.

Once as American as baseball and apple pie, drinking Coke and Pepsi now became stigmatized and started to have a negative impact on perceptions of social status. When combined with the exploding health concerns, this social class stigma finally drove many Americans, particularly those from the middle and upper middle class, to reconsider their drinks habits. Many who had previously been willing to trade off health consequences became less willing to do so when they suspected that, by giving into the sugar rush and taste sensation of soft drinks, they might be compromising their social class status. Sales of soft drinks plummeted. For America's soft-drink consumers who were compelled to give up their old habit, the question was: what should I drink now?

The impact of this media-generated disruption was so overwhelming and obvious that the big beverage marketers and many entrepreneurs took notice. Even those who were deaf to the media clatter could see the sales data that clearly indicated that consumers had begun to abandon carbonated soft drinks (CSDs) en masse. Everyone saw a great opportunity for alternatives that did not rely on 40 grams of HFCS in each bottle. But what?

Vitaminwater was one of many new entrants that crowded the market to exploit this ideological opportunity. Yet, despite the massive resources of The Coca-Cola Company and PepsiCo, not to mention Cadbury-Schweppes, Arizona, and other major drinks marketers, as well as a slew of entrepreneurial efforts, none except Bikoff solved this puzzle. The others pursued better mousetraps, designing new drinks that contained what their market intelligence companies told them were the hottest "magic-bullet" ingredients, with endless flavor and functional combinations. Only Bikoff pursued a cultural strategy.

Vitaminwater's Cultural Innovation

How is it that Vitaminwater vaulted to iconic status, despite being severely handicapped in terms of both marketing resources and distribution clout compared to other entrants? To understand why a seemingly naive marketing proposition—with no obvious innovation from a product or technical perspective—would quickly become the favorite drink of those Americans abandoning CSDs, we need to understand the ideological power of the brand's central promise. Instead of following trends in beverage innovation, Vitaminwater seemingly did just the opposite, offering a throwback drink with simple flavors and a promise of vitamins and water. The Vitaminwater cultural innovation was two-pronged, responding to both dimensions of the media-constructed stigma—health and social class.

To address the health concerns of sugary soft-drink consumers, Vitaminwater promised clearly and redundantly that it is a very healthy drink, while at the same time the drink provided a hedonic experience that approximated the satisfactions of CSDs and New Age beverages. The most important factor in Vitaminwater's success was its name, which conveyed the core proposition in utterly simple terms: vitamins + water. This simple framing device implied to consumers that they were buying a bottle of water with some vitamins tossed in. Nothing else. The ideological power of this claim was derived from two powerful media myths in American society—the vitamin-a-day myth, and the bottled-water hydration myth—both of which we review below.

Vitaminwater addressed not only the health anxieties of Americans who were rethinking their sugary drink habits, but their social anxieties as well. Through avant-garde design and clever copy, Vitaminwater asserted that is was a much more sophisticated drink compared to its sugary competitors. Vitaminwater's logo, label, bottle design, advertising, and point of sales communications all suggested that the beverage was for a more urbane and stylish class of people than those who drank the likes of Coke, Pepsi, or Snapple.

Source Material: Vitamin-a-Day Myth

Unlike the food cultures of Europe, Asia, and Latin America, where food has remained heavily influenced by pre-modern food traditions, in the United States the dominant ideology of food has long centered on the instrumental role of food to provide energy and promote health. Aggressive marketing by pharmaceutical and food companies beginning in the 1920s created what we will call the *techno-medical food ideology*. This marketing used the rhetoric of technological innovation and scientific rigor to promote foods and drinks as magical potions that would either dramatically enhance human performance or act as a defensive shield protecting against illness and death. Scientists applied the modern scientific method to food just as they did to other problems of the natural world and human body: they sought to isolate within foods their elementary components and then they conducted experiments to understand the causal relationships between these elements and human health.

Scientists studying the relationship between nutritional deficiencies and disease began isolating different vitamins in the 1910s and had discovered most of them by the 1930s.[9] These scientific breakthroughs were promoted in the media, and soon vitamins entered the public discourse as essential to good health. Marketers soon exploited this ideological opportunity, promoting their products as healthier because they were supplemented with vitamins. In magazines such as *Good Housekeeping, Hygeia,* and *Parents Magazine,* one could find ads for Ovaltine, dog treats, and handcream all promoting the health advantages of their vitamins.[10] The profound influence of this vitamin myth was captured by two critics of the pharmaceutical industry in 1937, who complained:

Not so long ago the word [vitamins] was unknown to all but the learned. Today, any serious mother is ashamed if she can't discuss vitamins with the greatest of ease. Probably more than one new mother has startled her husband by mumbling in her sleep: "Milk for vitamin A...vegetables for vitamin B...oranges for vitamin C...and for rare vitamin D baby must have cod-liver oil."[11]

The original science on vitamins was focused on diseases caused by extreme vitamin deficiencies—an acute problem to be sure, but one faced by only a small fraction of Americans. These dietary deficiencies lacked commercial potential, but that was a small obstacle for creative marketers of the day. They reframed the nutritional problem to focus on sub-clinical disorders such as nervousness and lack of energy and they blamed the modern diet for causing the problem, since the scientific research had shown that food processing stripped vitamins from foods. As one vitamin manufacturer warned, "Perhaps your diet is too modern."[12] Vitamins were posed as the scientific solution to the hazards of the modern industrial diet.

During the Second World War, some military recruits were rejected as unfit because of poor nutrition. So the US Department of Agriculture strongly promoted the vitamin enrichment of particular foods to make sure all recruits were fit enough to enlist. Vitamins were commonly added to flour, milk, and margarine by 1946. Factories involved in the war effort gave their employees cod liver oil and vitamin supplements to encourage productivity. The government's patriotic vitamin promotion as a wartime tool convinced Americans of the magical value of vitamins not only for health but also for general vigor. The market exploded: sales of vitamin pills grew from $12 million in 1931 to over $130.8 million in 1942.[13]

By the late 1940s, America's modern vitamin myth had begun to take hold. Vitamins had become so embedded in the culture that the popular media could reference these conventional meanings and assume that their audience easily understood them. In the 1943 film *The Gang's All Here*, when a husband complains that his wife has become overly flirtatious, he concludes, "It's that vitamin B_1. I told you that you were taking too much. You're overdoing it."[14] Similarly, in the 1959 film *Operation Petticoat*, the captain is taken aback by a nurse's apparent innuendo in saying, "I hope you won't mind a little professional advice. But when a person is nervous and irritable, you can be sure there is something he is not getting enough of." Of course, the nurse turns out to be talking about vitamins, and she goes on to describe her own increased pep since she started taking vitamin supplements.[15]

One-A-Day Vitamins: Vitamins as Daily Health Insurance
An ambitious company invented the last key component of the modern vitamin myth—the ritual swallowing of a daily vitamin as a key aspect of preventative health. Prior to the efforts of Miles Laboratories, Americans took vitamins sporadically, more as a curative if they were feeling run down or sick. Miles, the makers of One-A-Day, turned vitamins into a prophylactic, a form of health insurance, that vastly increased per capita consumption. Miles's strategy for the brand was to take advantage of Americans' anxiety that they might not be getting enough vitamins to convince them that the remedy was to take a vitamin each and every day. The company built this ritual into the

brand name and used scientific rhetoric to convince Americans to adopt the new habit. Rather than use magazine ads to repeat the quackish hyperbole used by competitors, Miles instead assumed a quasi-governmental persona, claiming to work in the interest of public health.[16] The company blanketed virtually every American household with "educational" materials teaching Americans about the benefits of a daily vitamin as health insurance. These brochures warned Americans that they still needed vitamins despite the fact that they seemed healthy and had no vitamin-deficiency symptoms. The campaign was a huge success: One-A-Day vitamins cemented the public perception that a daily vitamin provided nutritional insurance. Miles then expanded the franchise to focus on kids, playing on parents' deep concern for their children's health. Their Flintstones Vitamins brand, along with other cartoon-anchored vitamins for kids, worked to indoctrinate kids into the ritual. In 2009, 50 percent of Americans still swallowed a vitamin every day.[17]

Over a period of forty years, savvy marketers had leveraged science and the government to institutionalize America's vitamin-a-day myth, which went something like this:

- Vitamins are a basic fuel that the body needs to function; to provide health and energy.
- Vitamins are insurance to ward off colds, to overcome lethargy, and to top up when you do not eat right.
- Vitamins are a metonym for what is good in food. You do not need to know the specifics, you just have to "take your vitamins."
- One gets enough vitamins "naturally" only if one eats all the fruits and vegetables and whole grains that the government's nutrition- ists tell us we must eat—a gold standard that few Americans achieve. So there is a constant risk of "running low" on vitamins.
- Luckily, with daily vitamins, you can eat whatever you want and the vitamin will protect you.

The public's belief in the protective and invigorating properties of daily vitamins was extremely durable, easily withstanding ongoing criticism and skepticism from nutritionists and health agencies, as well as many studies that refuted the alleged effects of vitamins.[18] When *Consumer Reports* published a resolute declaration to avoid vitamins in a 1986 article, its readers responded with angry letters accusing the authors of ignoring scientific research and succumbing to pressure from the American Medical Association (AMA) against the best interests of the public, and countered with personal narratives testifying to the value of the supplements.

Branding with Vitamins

Bikoff's most profound insight was that, while Americans were increasingly confused by and cynical about the latest and greatest scientific health discoveries, their faith in the vitamin myth remained strong. So he sidestepped the functional supplements arms race to rely on a much simpler and irrefutable health claim: a vitamin a day is good for you. In the confusing world of instrumental foods, with a swelter of health promises that were both overwhelming and often ephemeral, Americans took comfort in that one bit of solid faith from their childhood.

To talk about vitamins in the twenty-first century, after two decades of increasingly heated nutritional "innovations" that claimed to surpass vitamins in their functional health benefits, seemed like a naive mistake by an amateur marketer. But, as our genealogy of the vitamin myth reveals, Bikoff had made a culturally brilliant move. In the sea of confusing claims that only the most health obsessed could track, the daily vitamin stood out as the one trustworthy unquestioned health benefit that everyday Americans could believe in. With vitamins in every swallow, Americans giving up their soft-drink fix for a daily Vitaminwater could believe they were practicing the health equivalent of eating an apple a day.

With this overarching "vitamins in a bottle" promise, Bikoff then loaded each flavor with different variations of popular "magic-bullet" ingredients, along with the promised vitamins. The effect was to frame all of the confusing mish-mash of anti-oxidants, power foods, and anti-carcinogens as something that was easy to understand and instantly believable: these were all "vitamins" now. Each flavor was chock-full of innocuous add-ins that were unassailably good for you. All the media ferment on whether these ingredients (not to mention the vitamins) were actually good for you magically disappeared. Just remember to drink your Vitaminwater every day, and you do not have to worry.

Source Material: Bottled Water-for-Hydration Myth

The other component of Vitaminwater's health platform was "water." Just as for vitamins, calling a new brand "water" is seemingly a promise for a has-been commodity until you understand the myth that Glaceau leveraged with this choice. In the late 1980s, influential *New York Times* health columnist Jane Brody wrote about scientific studies indicating that people should drink eight glasses of water a day to stay properly hydrated. The idea caught on like wildfire, even though Brody got the facts wrong—the body needs the equivalent of eight glasses, most of which is gained through eating foods that have water content rather than pounding glass after glass. Americans soon became fastidious water drinkers, carrying bottles wherever they went, continually sneaking a guzzle so as not to allow their bodies to shrivel up.

Pre-packaged bottled water took off in the United States, beginning in the mid-1990s on the back of a massive social disruption. Previously, Americans had faith in the safety of the public water supply. They trusted that modern technologies provided them with water that was safe to drink. But a series of highly publicized studies challenged this notion, claiming that much tap water was tainted with carcinogens well above government-approved levels. These widely disseminated stories piled atop many other media reports on bacteria outbreaks and carcinogenic chemicals in the food supply. In response, Americans reduced their tap-water drinking and looked for alternatives. Bombarded with media reports that their bodies were accumulating imperceptible pollutants that contaminated their food and tap water, many Americans looked to bottled water (perceived at least initially as natural spring water) as an unassailably contaminant-free choice, some even hoping that this pure water would act as a cleanser that would flush the body of these contaminants. PepsiCo entered the market with Aquafina and The Coca-Cola Company with Dasani, using their massive distribution power to put bottles of water within an arm's reach of every possible usage occasion. Bottled water became the gold standard for healthy beverages: a drink that has nothing dangerous in it—the lack of possible bad things being the most important new criterion for a healthy drink—and no sugar so no calories.

Branding with "Water"

Consumers who were abandoning sugary CSDs knew very well that water was the healthiest substitute. By calling Vitaminwater a water, Bikoff claimed all the healthful connotations that came with that term: the drink could not have chemical additives and so would be safe, the drink was a good source of hydration, and, most importantly, the drink could not have much sugar or it could not be "water."

Soft-drinks consumers are not vigilant label readers, and so few paid close attention to the amount of sugar in a Vitaminwater. But, given the damning condemnation of HFCS, they were careful to avoid it. So it was critical for Vitaminwater to use a different sweetener as a proof point for its healthiness claim. Vitaminwater used crystalline fructose, which it claimed was the same sweetener as that found in fruit, so accentuating the implied naturalness of the product. While a review of a range of articles and websites suggests that crystalline fructose is not appreciably different than HFCS, the vast majority of consumers did not know this and were happy to believe that Vitaminwater's sweetener was healthier. Since these scientific findings have not yet found their way into the mass discourse, the use of crystalline fructose readily reinforced drinkers' wishful thinking that the sweetener in Vitaminwater was a vast improvement, even healthful.

Bikoff reinforced the dual "vitamin" and "water" health claims in a variety of savvy and consistent ways. He developed a tagline—*responsible hydration*—that accentuated the health claims, giving recovering CSD drinkers permission to indulge in Vitaminwater because it was much more "responsible" than drinking a Coke. His go-to-market strategy emphasized early distribution in health clubs and gyms to promote sampling in an environment where people would assume that Vitaminwater must be a healthy drink. At retail, Bikoff and his sales team insisted that Vitaminwater be placed on a shelf near the bottled waters, not the CSDs, reinforcing the frame that Vitaminwater was like a bottled water but more tasty, not like a Snapple but watered down.

Source Material: The Artworld's Take on the Apothecary

Vitaminwater claimed to be a much more sophisticated drink relative to existing sugary drinks through a deft appropriation of cultural codes from a design movement that art historians now refer to as *New Design*.

New Design, which gained prominence in America and Europe during the late 1990s, sought to revive the main tenets of high modernist design of the post-war era. The movement emphasized "form follows function," with streamlined, radically simplified forms that eliminated all unnecessary details. Like their mid-century forebears, New Designers embraced mass production, believed that everyone should have access to beautifully designed objects, and sought to inject sophisticated aesthetics into mundane consumer products. The movement's impresarios and entrepreneurs often focused on synthetic materials, pushing new plastic technologies into unorthodox applications such as flexible rubber vases, fluid toothbrushes, streamlined staplers, and translucent chairs.

Designer Karim Rashid, the self-proclaimed "poet of plastic," was celebrated in a March 20, 2000, *Time* magazine cover story for designing colorful, beautifully curved, plastic waste paper baskets for the housewares' company Umbra. Jonathan Ives rose to international prominence with his design for the 1999 iMac, which brought candy colors, beautifully streamlined curves, and translucent surfaces that revealed glimpses into the computer's inner wirings, to the otherwise bland, beige, and boxy world of computer aesthetics. Perhaps the most famous practitioner of New Design was Philippe Starck. Starck designed molded mass-produced plastic in a series of fluid-form designs ranging from ergonomic toothbrushes to plastic chairs. He attained celebrity status when he teamed up with Ian Schrager and extended his streamlined, neo-space age aesthetic to the interior design of a series of seminal designer boutique hotels, including New York's The Paramount, Miami's Delano, and London's St Martin's Lane.

Apothecary Bottle as New Design Fetish
The New Design movement often intersected with the avant-garde art world, especially the so-called Young British Artists, who were similarly committed to advancing a pop-synthetic aesthetic. Of particular importance for Vitaminwater was that one of the most famous artists of the era, Damien Hirst, became renowned for raiding the treasure trove of old pharmaceutical design codes in his work. He fetishized overtly clinical objects such as pill capsules, chemistry beakers, and periodical charts, and made famous use of formaldehyde to preserve

dead animals in vitrines. He launched a Notting Hill restaurant named Pharmacy, which celebrated drug-store aesthetics.

Bikoff hired Philippe Starck to design Glaceau's package design. Starck appears to have taken design cues straight from Hirst's pharmaceutical art. The label layouts, with stark black fonts on white backgrounds, referenced old apothecary design codes. This choice not only brought a striking new aesthetic to the soft-drinks category, but also subtly reinforced Vitaminwater's health claims—an association that consumers readily picked up on. The pale purples, translucent pinks, medicinal reds, and glowing yellows echoed the synthetic monochromatic look of the iMac color palate.

To this design, Bikoff and his team added label copy that reinforced this culturally sophisticated world view. Rather than speak to consumers in bland technical marketing-speak, the labels use the playful voice of an urbane, culturally savvy, peer. For example, Vitaminwater's Power-C, a dark pink dragonfruit flavor spiked with vitamin C and taurine, confessed to label readers:

legally, we are prohibited from making exaggerated claims about the potency of the nutrients in this bottle. therefore, legally we wouldn't tell you that after drinking this, eugene from kansas started using horseshoes as a thighmaster or that this drink gave agnes from delaware enough strength to bench press llamas. Heck, we can't even tell you this drink gives you the power to do a thousand pinkie push-ups ... just ask mike in queens. legally, we can't say stuff like that— cause that would be wrong, you know? vitamins + water = all you need

Cultural Capital Trickle-down with Design Codes

With the New Design-meets-apothecary design codes and the unorthodox copy, Vitaminwater stood out as a relatively sophisticated drink compared not only to Coke and Pepsi, but also to the purposefully amateurish New Age brands such as Snapple and Arizona. Bikoff's adept borrowing of art-world design codes allowed him not only to fend off the sugary drink social stigma, but to transform a sweet, Kool-Aid-like, drink into a beverage that adults perceived as the more sophisticated choice. In other words, Vitaminwater applied the cultural capital trickle-down tactic that we detail in the Starbucks case in Chapter 5: the brand made artworld design codes, usually found in art galleries and expensive hotels, accessible to the masses. While this strategy had become commonplace in fashion (H&M and Puma) and even in housewares (Target), it had not been used at the time in fast-moving consumer goods found in the grocery and the convenience store. This astute move gave Vitaminwater the cultural panache to appeal to consumers who sought a drink that reversed the downmarket stigma of CSDs. With Vitaminwater's cultural expressions of health and social class dialed in, Bikoff went about formulating his new adult Kool-Aid.

Semi-Sugary Kool-Aid

If Vitaminwater had been formulated in literal fashion according to the trademark's promise—as water fortified with some vitamins—the concept would have bombed. CSD consumers gave up their habit only grudgingly, because they greatly enjoyed the hedonics of their favorite drinks: the burst of flavor and sugary buzz. They found water to be too boring. Vitaminwater's framing as a "water" would have been unremarkable had not Bikoff violated Americans' perceptions of what a "water" should contain—or, more precisely, what it should not contain. Bikoff formulated Vitaminwater with a sugar content about half that of the popular soft drinks like Coke and Pepsi.

Drinkers readily perceived that Vitaminwater was much less sugary than CSDs and New Age drinks, allowing them to believe that it was a "water-like" drink. And Bikoff could claim, somewhat disingenuously, that Vitaminwater was much healthier on a per serving basis. But Vitaminwater's sugar content was virtually identical to Gatorade. Like Gatorade, its weaker flavors and diluted sugar content made the drink more chuggable, refreshing, and hydrating compared to soft drinks. This 50 percent sugar ratio proved just enough to satisfy the sweet tooth of ex-soft drink consumers. But they were drinking more too: a 20-ounce Vitaminwater has almost as much total sugar as a 12-ounce Coke. This sugar content was central to why drinkers used to soft drinks and New Age drinks found Vitaminwater so satisfying. Vitaminwater gave them the sugary buzz that they liked while allowing them to believe that they were partaking in a healthy regimen. Bikoff accentuated the hedonics by developing a range of Vitaminwater flavors that taste like nothing so much as watered-down Kool-Aid. The flavors are mostly familiar childhood concoctions: orange, grape, lemonade, and so on. By offering a broad range of very palatable flavors, he insured that there would be a flavor or two that everyone would like.

Conclusion

What made Vitaminwater resonate so powerfully was that it was a sweet-enough drink wrapped in the health promises of America's vitamin and bottled-water myths. Bikoff repurposed these potent myths, delivering them consistently across the marketing mix, along with the aura of sophistication conveyed by New Design codes. Vitaminwater's cultural expression easily trumped the vastly more expensive efforts to exploit the fallout of the CSD stigma by some of the world's most lauded marketers. While competitors sought to devise a better mousetrap in a literal fashion, Bickoff instead devised what consumers perceived as a better mousetrap by repurposing the right myths with all the right cultural codes.

The Vitaminwater case provides a powerful rebuttal to a key axiom of the better-mousetraps model. In the economists' and engineers' world view, category benefits are treated as objective facts, defining the competitive playing field. So the race is to improve upon performance across key dimensions of functionality. Innovation happens when these improvements are a step change rather than incremental, as Clay Christensen has so often argued.

Applying this better-mousetraps logic, all the big soft drinks companies chased the newly health-conscious ex-CSD consumers by seeking out leading-edge science on healthy additives and building these ingredients into their innovation concepts. This approach assumes that consumer products such as soft drinks are similar to technical products like airplanes: healthiness is an objective fact that behaves according to the predictable laws of science, and engineering allows us to improve performance against this fixed target.

Bikoff's approach to innovation was entirely different. He creatively repurposed two conventional understandings of health—the vitamin myth and the bottled-water-for-hydration myth—to propose a new kind of "health" drink. Rather than improving performance upon an accepted construct, he instead proposed a new way to conceive of a healthy drink. He embellished this health proposition, making it even more enticing, by using trickle-down design codes from cultural elites to erase the class stigma associated with drinking CSDs. In consumer markets, perceptions of functionality are rarely determined by cut-and-dried product "truths." Instead, they are usually cultural constructs. Innovators can use cultural expression to transform how functionality is perceived by customers, end-running red-ocean competition to build better mousetraps.

Notes

1. There is mounting evidence that other countries are following down the American path, particularly Commonwealth countries and the middle class of middle-income countries in the developing world.
2. Eric Schlosser, *Fast Food Nation* (New York: Houghton Mifflin, 2001), 3.
3. For example, see Sally Squires, "A Global Quest for Health: Dietary Guidelines, including the US Food Pyramid, Offer a Simple Message about Nutrition to Help Consumers Stay Healthy," *Washington Post*, July 13, 2000, p. H1; Paul Campos, "The Fat Become the Latest Pariahs," *Denver Rocky Mountain News*, July 11, 2000, p. 29A.
4. Greg Critser, *Fat Land: How Americans Became the Fattest People in the World* (New York: Mariner, 2003), 138–40.
5. Sally Squires, "Sweet but Not So Innocent? High-Fructose Corn Syrup, Ubiquitous in the American Diet, May Act More Like Fat Than Sugar in the Body. Some Researchers Are Starting to Suspect It's Feeding the Obesity Epidemic," *Washington Post*, Mar. 11, 2003, p. F01. Colette Bancroft, "The United States of obesity," *St Petersburg Times*, Feb. 11, 2003, p. 1D. Patricia King, "Blaming it on Corn Syrup: Its Increased Use as a Cheap Sweetener is Seen by Some as Responsible for Soaring Obesity," *Los Angeles Times*, Mar. 24, 2003, p. 1. Sally Squires, "Corn Syrup is Linked to Problems of Obesity," *Sun-Sentinel*, Mar. 30, 2003. Sally Squires, "High-Fructose Corn Syrup Concerns Health Experts," *Detroit News*, Apr. 2, 2003, p. 6H.
6. Charles Stuart Platkin, "The Sweet Truth about Sugar can be Hard to Determine," *Miami Herald*, May 22, 2003, p. 3SE.
7. Phil Lempert, "High-Fructose Corn Syrup: Sugar on Crack?" *Today*, Mar. 30, 2006, www.msnbc.msn.com/id/12058364/from/RSS
8. Claudia Wallace, "The Obesity Warriors," *Time*, June 4, 2004.
9. Ron Kennedy, "A Short History of Vitamins," www.med-library.net/content/view/185/41
10. Rima D. Apple, *Vitamania: Vitamins in American Culture* (New Brunswick, NJ: Rutgers University Press, 1996), 14–18.

11. Rachel Lynn Palmer and Isidore M. Alpher (1937), cited in Rima D. Apple, *Vitamania: Vitamins in American Culture* (New Brunswick, NJ: Rutgers University Press, 1996), 14.
12. Ad for Vitroetts in 1939, cited in Apple, *Vitamania*, 6.
13. Ibid. 7–11.
14. Cited in ibid. 10.
15. Cited in ibid. 183–4.
16. Ibid. 103–6.
17. Leslie Alderman, "Knowing What's Worth Paying for in Vitamins," *New York Times*, Dec. 5, 2009.
18. This vitamin ideology has prevailed despite frequent skepticism voiced by researchers, the government, and health organizations. The AMA called the emerging vitamin supplement industry "a gigantic fraud" in 1922. Widely reported studies as early as the 1940s questioned the efficacy of vitamin supplements for anyone who was well nourished. The FDA maintained that the supplements did not provide vitality and were not necessary to meet nutritional requirements. Yet, the public wanted to believe in vitamins, and no scientific reports were going to sway them. When the FDA renewed its effort to limit manufacturers' claims in 1990, it encountered enormous consumer criticism. After four years, Congress responded by approving the bipartisan Dietary Supplement Health and Education Act to strip away much of the FDA's ability to restrict dietary supplements.

8

Marlboro: The Power of Cultural Codes

Two breakthrough cultural innovations transformed Marlboro into one of America's most potent symbols of masculinity, a symbol that would soon extend around the world. Marlboro, a brand that held less than 1 percent of the cigarette market, was relaunched in 1955. By 1972, sales had increased over 1,000 percent, and Marlboro had become the best-selling brand of cigarettes in the world. Marlboro's success was not premised on any sort of technological breakthrough or mix-and-match value recombination. Filter cigarettes were relatively new when Marlboro was restaged, but the technology was hardly novel; Marlboro was one of many filter entrants. Personal opinions about tobacco aside, and for a moment ignoring the insidious corporate cover-up of the links between cigarettes and cancer, Marlboro's startling growth must be accounted for if we are to understand the intricacies of cultural innovation. Like other case studies in this book, Marlboro provides an example that current innovation theories cannot explain.

Marlboro's climb from a tiny, dormant brand to a powerhouse consumer franchise is a story central to management folklore. It is a story that is used time and again to exemplify the strategy necessary for building a powerful brand. The tale claims that Marlboro adopted the cowboy archetype, a powerful American symbol, for its "Marlboro Country" campaign. It assumes that Americans—and later smokers from around the globe—identified with the cowboy, and that this identification carried through to Marlboro. End of story. This bit of industry folklore creeps up everywhere: in trade journals, in textbooks by marketing academics, and in management books by consulting pundits.

This interpretation is seductive in its simplicity: cultural innovation requires only choosing the right cultural symbol or archetype and patching it onto the brand. If only innovation were so simple! But, as with other brands in the pantheon of management folklore, which we have analyzed in this book as well as in *How Brands Become Icons*— Nike, Harley-Davidson, Starbucks, Coca-Cola, Snapple, Volkswagen, Budweiser—the conventional interpretation is significantly flawed.[1] Marlboro has been reduced to an amusing cocktail-party story that is empirically inaccurate and lacking in any sort of rigorous analytic specification. Even the briefest glimpse at the brand's historical record reveals problems with this explanation: Marlboro's initial restaging in 1955 focused on cowboys, but failed to boost market share. Two subsequent attempts to launch "Marlboro Country," again with cowboys, also failed. The iconic "Marlboro Country" advertising began to click only in 1965. If cultural innovation could be reduced to the adoption of an archetype, then Marlboro would have succeeded much earlier. Marlboro's ad agency, Leo Burnett, would have been spared a decade of trial-and-error efforts.

The core idea of "Marlboro Country" did not involve cowboys at all. Burnett first concocted the brand's ideology—what we call *reactionary working-class frontier masculinity*—not for "Marlboro Country," but for the phenomenally successful campaign that first launched Marlboro, a little appreciated cultural innovation that we have termed "Tattooed Throwbacks." "Marlboro Country" would eventually come to champion this same ideology, using a distinctive variant of the frontier myth. In the United States, the cowboy has never been a static archetype. Rather, as historian Richard Slotkin has influentially demonstrated, he has been a character in a dynamic myth central to American culture, the Frontier Myth, which has been routinely reinvented throughout the nation's history. In the 1960s, a particular cowboy figure—the cold-war gunfighter—held sway. But Leo Burnett did not simply imitate this incarnation. Rather, it very selectively borrowed certain aspects of the myth and deleted others in order to advance a particular story about hard-working cowboys thriving on difficult manual labor. "Tattooed Throwbacks" built a powerful ideological platform for Marlboro, and then the second cultural expression of this ideology—"Marlboro Country"—catapulted the brand to become a global icon.

1955: The First Cowboy Restaging Effort Fails

In the 1920s, tobacco marketer Phillip Morris launched Marlboro as a women's cigarette. With the tagline "mild as May," the branding touted Marlboro as a smooth cigarette for classy, upscale women. This branding, however, never broke through. As the first wave of concern about the deadly dangers of smoking pulsed through the media in the 1950s, all of the cigarette marketers responded by launching filter cigarettes, which they hoped would be perceived as less dangerous. Rather than launch a new brand, Phillip Morris decided to restage its stagnant woman's brand Marlboro as a filter cigarette for the mass market. Given the prior woman's positioning and the perception that filters were feminine, Phillip Morris marketers decided that the branding needed to be as masculine as possible.

At the time the Freudian psychoanalyst-turned-marketing consultant Ernst Dichter was leading a revolution in branding, under the rubric "motivation research," convincing America's biggest corporations that they needed to embrace archetypes to power their brands into the consumers' psyche. Leo Burnett, no doubt influenced by this thinking, searched for an archetype that would ooze masculinity. It selected the most popular and overtly masculine symbol of the day: the cowboy.

The launch spot, "Cowboy Introduces Cigarette," features a cowboy on a stage set—seated, stiff, serious, dressed in a white shirt, dark bandana, and tan hat. A rope and saddle complete the decor. He takes long draws on his Marlboro and speaks to the camera:

Light up one of these new Marlboros and be glad you've changed to a filter. Marlboro—the easy-drawing, long-size filter cigarette that delivers the goods on flavor. Marlboro is made in Richmond, Virginia, from a new Philip Morris recipe—easy-drawing, too. Because of Marlboros new flavor-saving filter that gives you all the real tobacco taste you like.

The camera zooms in on the pack of Marlboros.

Comes in this new flip-top box: a firm pocket-size box to keep cigarettes from crushing. Closes tight. No tobacco gets into pocket or purse. All this you get at the popular filter price. Light up a Marlboro and be glad you've changed to a filter. Marlboro, the new long-size filter cigarette from Philip Morris.

The cowboy is patched into the film, uncomfortably so, since cowboys do not belong on indoor soundstages decorated with cowboy props.

A second launch spot reveals a ranch setting where two cowboys in clean hats and shirts are seated upon their horses, facing the camera, talking about cigarettes. One cowboy, handing a cigarette to his buddy, recommends Marlboro. His buddy smokes the cigarette, expressing his approval with an appreciative nod. They exchange positive comments about the box before the second cowboy asserts that Marlboro "delivers the goods on flavor." The last launch ad makes use of Tex Ritter, a country-and-western music star dressed in cowboy garb who had sung the theme song of the famous Western *High Noon*. He too offers similar product benefit arguments by talking to the camera, then finishes with a quick country riff, singing "you can't say no to a Marlboro."

These launch ads borrow the cowboy as a symbol in order to engage in hard-sell benefits branding. Because the spot is devoid of all contextual detail, the cowboy can be understood by viewers only as an archetype, intended to represent a particularly American, rough-hewn, and independent masculinity. The launch of the restaged Marlboro filters stalled at a 1.5 percent market share in 1955. As a result, Phillip Morris dumped the cowboy campaign midway through 1955, and Leo Burnett creatives experimented by taking the branding in several different directions. Along the way, they stumbled upon one of the most powerful cultural innovations of the post-war era.

Marlboro's "Tattooed Throwbacks"

Leo Burnett's new concept took advantage of the same ideological opportunity that launched Jack Daniel's—the reactionary backlash against the new "organization-man" ideology—which we describe in our analysis of Jack Daniel's in Chapter 3. Burnett constructed a fictitious group of middle-aged, mostly working-class men, joined by a telltale tattoo on their wrists. The campaign offered a series of character studies that powerfully conveyed Marlboro's reactionary working-class frontier masculinity—an ideology that championed a seemingly anachronistic idea of self-reliant, inner-directed, and physical manhood over America's new middle-class role model, the other-directed man poised to succeed at his sedentary desk job in a big organization, enjoying a comfortable and modern domestic life in the suburbs. Rather than rely on the Western frontier, hillbillies, or outlaw bikers to convey this ideology, the campaign locates its reactionary masculine figures at the margins of everyday life in the city and suburbs.

In "Man and Car" we find a grizzled man in his fifties, sporting a crew cut, and wearing dirty overalls. He is working intently on an old car that seems to date from the 1930s. He is completely focused, and never looks at the camera. The man works alone, entirely engrossed in rebuilding his car, happy to be by himself. The viewer eavesdrops on a private discussion: the man answers an interviewer's questions about his avocation.

INTERVIEWER.   This is a man who smokes Marlboro cigarettes. What kind of man is he?

MARLBORO MAN.   I'm a guy who likes to work on my car. I like to take it apart and put it back together. I get to working on it and forget where I am. What time it is. I even forget to eat.

The Marlboro man's ideology unfolds as viewers are introduced to different men who enjoy disparate hobbies, but nevertheless share the same ideology, as is signified by a telltale tattoo on their wrist:

- A man cleaning his gun tells us: "I guess I like anything connected with guns. Stripping and cleaning 'em. I like the workmanship and performance of a good gun."
- A man cutting down a tree ruminates: "I guess I'm a weekend farmer. I like to get out and fix up around my place. On a day like this I could work for hours on end."
- A high-diver declares: "I like to get out early and practice diving. I work on hitting the water clean and sharp. A good dive depends strictly on me."
- A mountain climber divulges: "Nothing I'd like to do more than climb a mountain. When you get up here, the world's a million miles away."
- An older man gets out of his canoe to find a spot to camp. He relaxes at a campfire in a forest and smokes. "The only alarm clock is the sun."

- A man negotiates some dangerous rapids in a kayak. After he is done, he reflects: "You look back and wonder how you made it."
- A man and his companion hunt boars with bows and arrows at the edge of the forest. "You have to have a steady hand. Missing a shot is dangerous because wild boars are mean." Next we see a wild boar cornered by two barking dogs on the side of a small hill. The man draws an arrow from his quiver, loads, and fires.

The list of outdoor physical activities continues: a middle-aged man surfing, another sailing a big boat on the ocean, another landing a plane, another fishing on a lake. All reinforce the image of inner-directed, self-assured, self-reliant manhood.

These character studies invite viewers to enter into the mindset of the man portrayed. Each man pursues his favored avocation: he is totally focused, engrossed by the activity, and totally content. He is driven by his love for the hobby, not by status or any other instrumental other-directed goal. The avocations are physical activities, usually outdoors, often the kind that gets hands dirty. An element of adventure is often present as well.

The Working-Class Frontier Rebel Lurks in Everyday Life

In one of the era's most influential books, *The Lonely Crowd* (1950), David Riesman describes the rise of a historically distinctive character in the new media-saturated society: the other-directed man is intensely concerned with what others think of him, searches for their approval, and goes to great lengths to present himself in the best of lights. Riesman's observation pinpoints another key dimension of the "organization-man" ideology. This other-directed ideology was espoused by much of the media and mass marketing of the 1950s, presenting a bubbly, enthusiastic man whose desires are shaped by the consensus about whatever is the newest, best, or classiest lifestyle item ("keeping up with the Joneses").

The Marlboro man rejects all this. His social life does not revolve around refined entertainment with friends and family, nor does he rely on industry for convenient or time-saving gadgets that will save his hands from work. Leo Burnett's moody campaign was entirely out of step with contemporaneous marketing trends that emphasized aspiring social class rhetoric portraying an idealized suburban lifestyle. Marlboro's smokers were explicitly reactionary, seeking to revive the masculinity of America's gritty hard-working past.

Source Materials

Rather than rely on an existing subculture as source material, Leo Burnett made a more audacious move. It patched together a semifictional "subculture": a fraternal order of men who belonged together thanks to a shared ideology. The shared Marlboro tattoo depicting an anchor and stars alluded to hardened Second World War veterans and the working-class subcultures that much-tattooed ex-GIs had rallied around during the 1950s. These men wore denim, flannel, and other working-class garb.

While the type of man the advertising depicted still existed in large numbers in the United States, it was entirely ignored by the mass media, which were infatuated with the new other-directed organization man. Burnett's Marlboro man was a reactionary rebuttal to the widespread celebration of the new masculine ideology. It is no coincidence that Marlboro retooled its launch campaign on the heels of the release of James Dean's *Rebel without a Cause* and Marlon Brando's *The Wild Ones*. These wildly popular films played off the social disruption brought on by the rapid rise of industrial–bureaucratic society during the cold war, demonstrating the huge cultural market for a reactionary masculinity backlash.

Instead of young men in leather jackets and jeans getting into trouble, grizzled older guys, curmudgeons whom we can readily imagine as throwbacks to an earlier America, are the stars. They are the same kinds of characters we find in Jack Daniel's Lynchburg, except, according to Marlboro, they could be found in every nook and cranny of American life. Marlboro men embrace activities that were considered to be antiquated and déclassé in the 1950s. They prefer the outdoors, and engage in activities that hearken back to the previous century (hunting, fishing, tree felling, gun cleaning), adventurous outdoor sports (high diving, kayaking, mountain climbing), or outdated transport (a dingy with a sail, an old car). These are laconic, self-contained men who would rather embrace their hobby than answer an interviewer's questions. They are self-reliant men, entirely content when pursuing their solitary activities. Like America's historic frontier gunfighters, these men favor action over words and emotions. These John Wayne-like characters tell it like it is; they show no interest in smoothing out their rough edges.

This cultural innovation sent Marlboro market share skyrocketing to 5 percent by 1957. In fact, the campaign was so successful that it seeded a fad amongst teenage males to get tattoos, a fad that America's cold-war government, anxious to uphold middle-class decency over teenage delinquency, wished it could extinguish. Feeling the pressure, Phillip Morris voluntarily pulled the campaign, no doubt in part because, in the wake of the first major cancer scare, the company understood that diplomacy would be key to its long-term survival. Replacing the campaign, however, proved vastly more difficult than anyone could have guessed.

Four Years of Creative Experiments Fail

The brand's phenomenal growth immediately stalled when the "Tattooed Throwbacks" campaign was pulled. From 1958 until 1962, client and agency experimented with at least six different branding ideas, none of which worked. The ads blended generic celebrity and comedy with overly literal attempts to make a men's brand appeal to women:

- *Ralph and Bertha.* A comedy team that relies on humor reminiscent of the popular sitcoms of the day such as *I Love Lucy* and *The Jackie Gleason Show,* and performs skits that make fun of Marlboro man masculinity.
- *The Marlboro Woman.* A wealthy, beautiful, and shapely woman shoots skeet. "The Marlboro Woman: What's she like? She's at home in a man's world but she's all woman. And she knows a good thing when she sees it. Her cigarette, for example. Marlboros. The cigarette designed for men that women like." The woman morphs into a beautiful white silky dress while her gun transforms into a dressy umbrella.
- *Max Shulman.* Max was an urban writer and humorist, most famous for his Dobie Gillis character. This very modern "organization-man" campaign places Max in an upscale urban

setting, and has him address the audience in a very literate and ironic voice. This is a reflexive campaign in which Max makes fun of his role as Marlboro spokesman, the benefits of the brand, and the tattooed Marlboro Man. This seven-spot campaign was Marlboro's sole creative broadcast in 1959.

- *Settle Back with Julie London.* A series of vignettes feature the sexy chanteuse Julie London with various male companions. She sings a jingle that tells the audience to "Settle Back" and smoke a Marlboro.
- *Retired Athletes.* Famous athletes such as ex-Bears quarterback Johnnie Lujack reminisce about great feats on the field. With next to no segue, they proceed to hawk Marlboro's product benefits to the camera.
- *Jackie Gleason.* The famous comedian fools around on a golf course interspersed with several generic sell lines for Marlboro, then belts out his trademark line "How Sweet it is!"

None of these efforts worked, despite the wide range of creative ideas and the presence of popular celebrities. The reason is clear enough: the brand had moved from a powerful cultural expression championing a highly desired ideology to frivolously borrowing celebrity endorsements with conventional marketing claims that, to the extent that they offered any ideological view, contradicted the prior branding. The brand now celebrated modern middle-class life.

Source Material: John Wayne and the 1960s Western

With obvious references like cowboys, the soundtrack from *The Magnificent Seven*, and the West Texas ranch landscape, "Marlboro Country" was an overt appropriation of the Western, by far the most popular film and television genre of the post-war era. Any reference to the 1960s Western was also an overt nod to one of America's most influential and revered cultural icons—John Wayne—whose career and cultural influence reached its apex during the same period that Marlboro conquered the cigarettes category.

The Western was centered not on "cowboys" but rather on "gunfighters," as Richard Slotkin and others have exhaustively documented.[2] The Western is a narrative about America's "Manifest Destiny," about the quest to spread the nation's ideology around the world through necessary violence. It is a warrior tale in which various gunfighters take on "barbarians"—a role originally held by Native Americans and outlaws, and then later by indigenous peoples of other countries and communists. The Western is a myth about gritty, self-reliant, and violent men-of-action who are required to remake the world in the image of America's "city on a hill" ideal.

During the 1960s, at the height of the American escalation of the Vietnam War, the gunfighter myth was applied quite literally to the country's self-proclaimed war on Communism. John Wayne was not only *the* iconic gunfighter of the era; he was also extremely outspoken about applying his gunfighter philosophy as a solution to the country's political problems. Wayne fit perfectly with the Marlboro image: he was, famously, a chain smoker—reportedly consuming five to six packs a day—as well as a heavy drinker. In his films, Wayne matter-of-factly gunned down bad guys, disparaged people who were all talk and no action, and threw beautiful women across his lap so he could spank them. A very vocal conservative Republican, Wayne saw the masculine values of the frontier as central to the country. He pursued every opportunity to articulate his views: he nearly went broke funding an independent production of a film on the Alamo so that he could dramatize his views without Hollywood interference. Wayne directed and produced *The Green Berets* in 1967 to advocate for the Vietnam War—for him a quintessential frontier battle—at a time when the war was becoming unpopular.

When brands repurpose source materials for their cultural expressions, they borrow some elements and avoid others, a process called articulation.[3] "Marlboro Country" drew upon certain key aspects of Wayne's cowboy character and edited out others. The violence, misogyny, and conservative politics of John Wayne and other gunfighters of the day did not find their way into "Marlboro Country." Rather, building on "Tattooed Throwbacks," "Marlboro Country" borrowed gunfighter qualities such as thriving in the rugged outdoors, avoiding the city and its slick middle-class lifestyle, engaging in manly physical activities, and taking pride in self-reliant action. At the same time, the branding studiously avoided the other cultural codes that defined the genre. First, however, came a rather embarrassing sequence of cowboy misfires.

Four Early Iterations of "Marlboro Country" Fail

By 1963, Burnett creatives had returned to the cowboy—eight years after its first cowboy effort had been ditched and six failed experiments later—perhaps out of pure desperation. The iconic "Marlboro Country" campaign would eventually pick up where "Tattooed Throwbacks" had left off, paving the way to Marlboro's astounding sales results. For the first three years, however, "Marlboro Country" floundered. The campaign failed despite ads that featured cowboys, often in their native setting, with a Wild West soundtrack borrowed from *The Magnificent Seven* (a movie depicting seven gunmen who reject farm- and town-life—not to mention jobs at big corporations—in order to defend a group of hapless Mexican villagers from a violent gang of *banditos*). The ads included the tagline that would eventually become famous: "Come to Where the Flavor Is. Come to Marlboro Country." But the initial cowboy appropriation was even more generic and goofy than the agency's first effort in 1955. For the next three years, the agency dug deeper and deeper into the cowboy world, making a number of major mistakes along the way. At first Burnett creatives treated the cowboy as a symbol, in accordance with conventional marketing. Later, they began to dig into source materials—like the Western film genre—misfiring on ideology and cultural codes. The creatives finally stumbled upon the right combination of ideology and cultural codes to craft "Marlboro Country" as one of the most compelling myths of the 1960s.

Geographic "Marlboro Country" Fails
The tagline "Come to Where the Flavor Is. Come to Marlboro Country" originally aimed to make a claim about the cigarette's broad popularity, not to stake out an imagined land filled with cowboys. Print ads showed a map of the United States with the "Marlboro Country" banner across the top. The body copy proclaimed that Marlboro was a favorite throughout the fifty states and could be found readily in retail outlets. Other oddly composed print ads showed an enormous cowboy standing on a hill towering over a cityscape in the distance. The television spot proclaimed:

The news came out of the West and spread throughout the land—of a cigarette whose flavor's the best: the Marlboro brand. This is the one that showed up the rest . . . in Cheyenne; New York; Malibu. This is the flavor that won the West, and the rest of the country, too. Come to where the flavor is. Come to Marlboro Country."

Television spots also mapped out the geographical spread of the cigarettes' popularity: "City after city, the move is to filter smoking." As the narrator speaks, the viewer sees Miami Beach and San Francisco, then a giant cowboy pictured in front of the New York skyline; the cowboy is monstrous in scale, not unlike Godzilla.

The Cowboy Archetype "Marlboro Country" Fails

Leo Burnett creatives soon discovered that "Marlboro Country" worked much better as a device to reference the cowboy's world rather than the geographic spread of Marlboro consumers. As a result, they moved the cowboy back to his natural habitat. In "Cowboy and Girl," a lone cowboy in a deserted plain improbably comes across a beautiful young blonde co-ed riding in a convertible Cadillac. The girl takes advantage of this strange coincidence: she asks for a cigarette by suggestively twitching her second and third fingers. After the cowboy has complied, she drives happily away, leaving him alone with his thoughts: "That's my kind o' gal. She goes for my kind of smoke—Marlboro. Got a filter yet it's got some flavor to it." The cowboy in this ad was borrowed to insert into a man-meets-woman story that could have involved virtually any character. Similarly, "San Francisco" follows a cowboy who drives his Jeep down a highway to the edge of a rocky beach, where he lights a cigarette. A beatnik or beach bum, however, would hardly be out of place in this setting. In both cases, Leo Burnett simply pasted the image of a cowboy onto a scenario that could have involved any set of characters.

According to conventional marketing models, with the cowboy symbol in place, the branding should have been a success. As in 1955, the results were less than stellar. Crafting a myth to convey an ideology requires the careful development of character, plot, dialogue, narration, and music—in other words, the careful application of the appropriate cultural codes. Because the cultural codes were mangled in these ads, so too was the ideology. Hence the ads failed to resonate with American consumers.

The Patrician Cowboy Fails

A spot called "Train" presents a spectacular Western landscape, and features a train cutting through a mountainous pine forest. We are introduced to a well-to-do man dressed in formal cowboy attire, white shirt and bolo tie crisp and straightened. He walks through the train's passenger compartments to find his horse in the stable car. He sees his horse among two or three others, and approaches it tenderly while reaching for his pack of Marlboros. He strokes the horse, then looks out to mountains passing in the distance. He smokes while admiring the view.

The spot failed because, instead of a working cowboy living off the land and tending industriously to his cattle, Leo Burnett gave us a patrician cowboy who rides in modern transportation while passively looking out upon the wilderness, as if he were a tourist. Evidently, both client and agency were worried about breaking with the conventional branding game, and its assumption that high-status characters were required if a brand was to be aspirational. Any depiction of working-class cowboys would directly violate these conventional codes, so client and agency preferred to dress an upper-class guy in a cowboy costume.

The Gunfighter Myth "Marlboro Country" Fails

Burnett creatives then began to pay closer attention to the conventional narrative of Western films, rather than simply to appropriate the cowboy as symbol. They tried to re-create this frontier myth, allowing the frontier cowboy (gunfighter) to serve as a symbol for the violent appropriation of nature and its "savages" in the development of the United States and the American character. In "Remington" the creative uses the cowboy as a reference to the violent gunslinger. The ad begins by panning across old photos of pioneers in a style later made famous by documentarian Ken Burns, and accompanied by the *Magnificent Seven* theme. The camera then shifts to a more recent photo that depicts cowboy-soldiers from the Union army preparing for battle against an "Indian" tribe. As the camera pans to the Indians, the music shifts abruptly to Indian drum circle chanting. The camera moves back and forth with increasing speed from army to warriors, the soundtrack simultaneously shifting, with increasing volume. A bugle calls to sound the "charge," and photos now show cowboys and Indians fighting with guns and bows and arrows. As the clash comes to an end, only Indians have fallen from their horses.

The camera pulls back to reveal the hand of a well-dressed older man that turns the pages of an oversized picture book. The book is on a desk in a well-appointed study and a lit Marlboro cigarette is resting on an ashtray. The narrator tells us: "There's nothing that goes with the Old West like the taste of today's Marlboros." The camera pulls back again to reveal a replica of a Remington statue on a desk that features a cowboy riding a bucking bronco. "For the flavor that won the West and the rest of the country, too." When the man opens the blinds that cover a massive window, the New York skyline is revealed. He walks onto a balcony surrounded by the skyline. "Come to Marlboro Country."

This ad failed on several counts. First, the frontier myth was not an ideology that men were demanding. Second, the creatives' efforts to include conventional nods to an aspiring high-status character resulted in an ad that proposed that Marlboro was a nostalgic smoke for a bourgeois urbane man, like the patrician cowboy described above. The ad was the polar opposite of the reactionary masculinity that worked so well in the "Tattooed Throwbacks" campaign, and would work again in the mature "Marlboro Country."

Modern "Marlboro Country" Fails

Several transitional ads developed cowboy characters in rural working ranch settings (similar to the mature ads), but their ideology crumbled because the scenarios contained conflicting cultural codes. "Helicopter" features a ranch boss landing in a helicopter early in the morning to check on his cowboys and exchange cigarettes. While attempting to celebrate working life on a ranch, the spot inadvertently reminded viewers that even the range was controlled by corporations and their managers, and that even cowboys were constrained by bureaucracy— the exact opposite of the mature Marlboro ideology. Likewise, the use of modern technology shattered the image of a self-reliant cowboy who relied solely on his stallions, his own two legs, and his wits to survive.

Despite dozens of ads filled with cowboys, ranch scenery, and the oft-used tagline "Come to Where the Flavor Is. Come to Marlboro Country," the creatives behind the first three years of "Marlboro Country" were culturally blind to the ideology behind the cowboy, and they were oblivious to the cultural codes that would best dramatize this ideology. The composition of the ads continually fought against the reactionary working-class masculine ideology that Marlboro had pioneered nearly ten years earlier. It is not surprising that Marlboro's market share actually dipped lower during this period.

Reinventing "Marlboro Country" as Reactionary Work Myth

In 1966, Leo Burnett finally discovered the right package of cultural codes to convey, in the "Marlboro Country" myth, the ideology that Americans craved. Thereafter, the agency fired off ad after ad—all adhering to the same codes—until 1971, when television advertising for cigarettes was effectively banned. Agency creatives had discovered—after eight years of misfires!—how to reinvent the Western in order to convey an ideology that built directly upon their pioneering "Tattooed Throwbacks" branding of a decade earlier. Despite drawing upon the well-traveled Western genre, "Marlboro Country" in the mid-1960s was received as a provocative myth precisely because its work-focused depiction of the cowboy was so different from what was depicted in the movies and on television.

Consider "Evening Forest." From a vantage point high above a quiet forest at dusk, we spy movement in the trees. As the camera zooms in, we see a lone cowboy riding slowly over the rocky forest floor, pulling another horse behind him. A single guitar plays a slow romantic version of *The Magnificent Seven*, while flutes and violins join in as the spot builds. The cowboy searches for a suitable place to spend the night, stops for a moment to retrieve some cigarettes from his saddlebag, and lights up. The screen splits: to the left, the cowboy is moving slowly and deliberately while riding his horse; to the right, the cowboy's face is portrayed in close-up, with grit, determination, and dignity oozing from his pores. The cowboy finally finds a suitable campsite, and, as the last rays of the sun disappear, he lights a fire and smokes another cigarette. He peacefully surveys his surroundings in a knowing, appreciative way. He appears to have spent his life in this forest; he is one with nature. The camera pans, following the cowboy's gaze to a beautiful pond in which we see the reflection of the pine trees. Not a word is spoken until a narrator finally breaks in: "Come to where the flavor is. Come to Marlboro Country."

"Marlboro Country" is a world where physically challenging work takes place in nature, where cowboys must be self-reliant and determined.

There are no "savages," no guns, no violence. There are no women to rescue. And this cowboy is his own boss. "Marlboro Country" is not, in fact, a Western; rather it presents a myth about an idealized version of pre-industrial men's work on the Western Frontier.

Life in Nature

"Marlboro Country" celebrated America's pioneer past, when risky encounters in nature, hunting, working the land, and raising livestock predominated. Like fish in water, cowboys are most comfortable in the rugged outdoors, not in the big cities. Nature can be dangerous and threatening, but the cowboy is at ease. In "Bedroll," the sun peaks over the horizon, revealing a cowboy who stirs under his blanket before reaching for his hat. He gets up from the ground to keep warm on this chilly morning. The camera follows the cowboy's gaze and settles on the land and horses in his care. He makes coffee alone on an open fire, handling the coffee pot gingerly because it is so hot. He rolls up the bedroll. Finally, the cowboy lights a cigarette with a burning stick—no lighter or match. The narrator plays up the nature codes:

Out here, the sun wakes you up. Your day starts the same time the sun does. You stoke up a fire; light up a Marlboro. Cigarette flavor that's big and broad. Flavor you find whenever you light up in Marlboro Country, where the flavor has always been. Come to where the flavor is. Come to Marlboro Country.

Marlboro living is "rough," situated on improvised campsites in a wide open, rugged landscape, where civilization is nowhere in sight. This celebration of nature stood in direct opposition to the takeover of American work life by big bureaucracies—companies, the public sector, and the military.

Autonomous Work

In "Marlboro Country," cowboys work hard, but they choose their own schedule and organize their lives as they see fit. In "Corral" two cowboys chew the fat while they try to break a wild horse. The narrator tells us: "A working day out here stretches from sunup 'til sundown. But there's always time for a Marlboro." Work in "Marlboro Country" is antithetical to the new corporate world that had emerged in the United

States. Free from the hierarchical bureaucracies where bosses, rules, and time clocks subjugate employees, "Marlboro Country" men choose their work, proceed as they see fit, and answer to no one. These men work really hard because they want to, not because some boss has told them to or because they will be paid more. "Marlboro Country" idealized pre-industrial work as a foil to the post-war "organization man," who was slotted into a bureaucracy, given directed tasks, and had bosses oversee his work.

Pre-Industrial Self-Reliance

Cowboys work solo or with a small group of cowboys. They have no need for advanced technology. The cultural code gaffs of the early campaign—the inclusion of helicopters, Jeeps, trains, and trucks—were corrected. There are no houses, no women, no kids, no civilization. Marlboro cowboys are on their own and prefer this self-reliant life to a life of dependence in the city.

Physical Work

Cowboys are manual laborers. They have acquired practical physical skills from years of herding cattle. They are the opposite of the new "organization man," who sits at a desk and relies on his college degree to provide him with the skills necessary for the mental tasks at hand. In "Marlboro Country," work is physically demanding. Camera shots and sound effects emphasize the physicality of this labor; we see cowboys struggling with calves, roping wayward steers, breaking a wild mare.

Men of Action

Cowboys are in charge of their herd, an arduous and challenging job in the middle of nature. Their work requires a vigorous response to difficult and unpredictable conditions. Marlboro cowboys rise to these challenges and take pride in their ability to react quickly when devising an improvised solution. "Lost Colt" opens with a scene of cowboys rounding up horses. The men emit high-pitched "yee-haws" over the sound of horses' hooves rumbling in the background. A single cowboy stands on the sideline, taking five. He watches calmly, waiting for his turn. He lights up a cigarette, watching the horses he is helping to corral. The narrator breaks the silence: "It gets so you know every mare, every new colt. You know when one's missing ... Without counting, you know. And you know you better find it before dark." The *Magnificent Seven* soundtrack begins emphatically with trumpets and violins, while the camera follows the cowboy's quest to retrieve the lost colt. The cowboy scours the rugged dessert brush, finds the colt, then leads it back to camp. The narrator tells us, "This is Marlboro Country, where a good colt is just as important today as 100 years ago."

Reinventing the Western

"Marlboro Country" was quite different from frontier life as depicted in post-war Westerns. In the Westerns of the 1950s and 1960s, the hero is a gunfighter who is more than casually acquainted with savagery (Indians, outlaws). He usually lives within the confines of "civilization" (in town, around womenfolk). Because the gun-slinging Western movie hero navigates the realm of the savage with such ease, when the savages threaten to disrupt the peace, he comes to the rescue, typically resorting to violence to save the day. Despite his heroism, he remains ambivalent about his place in society. Gunfighters are usually marshals, sheriffs, or even fugitives. They are rarely real cowboys. Ranches and cattle belong on the frontier. Cattle-related events like cattle rustling do as well. But this sort of cowboy work is rarely focal to the plot.[4] Gunfighters live with and protect townspeople, whereas Marlboro Cowboys live on the range with other cowboys as companions and get on with their work managing the herd.

Leo Burnett creatives appropriated some basic cultural codes from the Western—the scene, a stock character, and a famous soundtrack—codes that were plenty familiar to Americans, thanks to the onslaught of Westerns during the 1950s. But the agency took considerable creative license with the Western, and told a very different tale; they spun a reactionary working-class myth about American masculinity. The campaign was a call to turn time back to revive the historic masculine ideal, similar to the ideology that Jack Daniel's championed, but with different cultural codes drawn from different source material.

Marlboro challenged the new masculine ideal of the sedentary "organization man," who works his way up the corporate bureaucracy within the safe confines of the city. The brand proposed that Americans wind the clock back to a masculinity that is earned through autonomous, physical work on difficult and dangerous terrain, a kind of masculinity that challenges men's perseverance and can-do spirit. This myth was the perfect response to the richest ideological opportunity of the era—it was a reactionary rebuttal to the new modern middle-class masculinity embodied by the "other-directed" organization man.

Conclusion

Marlboro is one of the most impressive cultural innovations in American corporate history. Leo Burnett created two new cultural expressions that addressed an ideological opportunity created by the dramatic transformation of the American economy and society following the Second World War. Both expressions—"Tattooed Throwbacks" and "Marlboro Country"—advanced a potent ideology that pushed back on the modern other-directed organization man. Each expression significantly edited and reworked source material found in media myths and subcultures of the day, a process called articulation.

Challenging a raft of popular accounts of Marlboro, we demonstrate that "Marlboro Country" was anything but a simple appropriation of a prominent American symbol or archetype. Leo Burnett made a number of attempts to use the cowboy as the central symbol of Marlboro for over a decade. Each failed because the cultural codes used to craft expressions with the cowboy were wrong. "Marlboro Country" came together only when all the right cultural codes were in place, and the wrong ones edited out.

Beyond Archetypes and Symbols
Mindshare marketing treats the most generic and simple aspects of a brand's expression—the brand's "archetype," "deep metaphor," or "symbol"—as the only thing that counts. Archetypes were first theorized by Carl Jung and later popularized by Joseph Campbell. The concept was used to explain the universal foundations of culture—the commonalities in characters and stories that permeate all societies across space and time. Archetypes, in other words, are durable universal characters that follow equally universal plots. As such, archetype theory is an effort to explain cultural phenomena with theories that are analogous to the natural-sciences such as biology, chemistry, and physics.

In the 1950s, Ernst Dichter and other "motivation researchers" convinced many big companies to seek out their archetypes. Recently, consultants such as Jerry Zaltman, Clotaire Rapaille, and Margaret Mark have had considerable success in renovating these 1950s ideas, selling big companies on archetypes and "deep metaphors."[5]

While the intellectual lineage of archetypes is different from the usual psychological roots of mindshare marketing, the resulting analyses are similarly abstract and reductive and, so, fail to stimulate cultural innovation for the same reasons. Both the psychological and archetypal versions of mindshare marketing reduce cultural expressions to generic decontextualized concepts, stripped bare of all the crucial cultural content that makes such expressions innovative. Big marketing companies make the mistake of reducing culture to archetypes for the same reason that they prefer mindshare benefits and generic emotion words—archetypes reduce a complex reality into something simple and easy to grasp and, thus, to manage. But this reduction necessarily throws out the most important elements from which cultural innovations are constructed.

Advocates of both versions of mindshare marketing have for decades used "Marlboro Country" as a prominent example that buttressed their models. For example, in his brand management textbook, psychologist Kevin Lane Keller attributes Marlboro's success to the creation of "the Marlboro man, a cowboy who is almost always depicted somewhere in the western United States amongst magnificent scenery deemed Marlboro Country."[6]

Our analysis of Marlboro illustrates the insufficiency of this approach. Keller, along with the archetype strategists who construct similar explanations, overlooked just about everything that made the Marlboro branding so successful. Marlboro ads that depicted "cowboys in the Western United States" failed many times over. The first three years of "Marlboro Country" ads failed because Burnett creatives chose the wrong cultural codes, which led to communicating the wrong myth, which embodied the wrong ideology. Details not only count; they are strategically crucial aspects of the innovation.

Mindshare marketing reduces culture to its most crude and primal components, and so necessarily remains ignorant of the critical details that make or break an innovation. Choose the wrong cultural codes, and the ideology is distorted. Or it does not come across at all. The generic use of the cowboy as symbol was never successful. What mattered was getting the cultural codes just right in order to convey a particular ideology—reactionary working-class frontier masculinity—which appealed to smokers because it addressed historically specific anxieties created by a social disruption. Ignoring or misinterpreting cultural codes fatally deforms the brand's cultural expression because, if the cultural codes are not right, then neither is the ideology.

The problem with reductionist models that rely upon archetypes, symbols, and deep metaphors is not that they are wrong; they are simply irrelevant. To take advantage of historical shifts in society and culture—ideological opportunities—historically specific cultural innovations are required. Archetypes are, by definition, incapable of such specification because they are universals; they are terribly imprecise. At best, archetypes are a first baby step toward a cultural solution. "Marlboro Country" relied upon the archetype of a hero. But so did Nike. And so did FedEx. And so did a half-dozen failed American automotive brands.[7] So what?

Notes

1. Douglas B. Holt, *How Brands Become Icons: The Principles of Cultural Branding* (Boston: Harvard Business School Press, 2004).
2. Richard Slotkin, *Gunfighter Nation* (Norman, OK: University of Oklahoma Press, 1998).
3. See the Harley-Davidson analysis in Holt, *How Brands Become Icons*.
4. Paul Newman's *HUD*, recounted in Chapter 3 on Jack Daniel's, is one exception.
5. Gerald Zaltman, *How Customers Think: Essential Insights into the Mind of the Market* (Boston: Harvard Business School Press, 2003). Margaret Mark and Carol S. Pearson, *The Hero and the Outlaw: Building Extraordinary Brands Through the Power of Archetypes* (New York: McGraw-Hill, 2001). And then there is Clotaire Rapaille, who claims, despite all scientific evidence to the contrary, that culture exists in the "reptilian brain" that gets imprinted in early childhood. And so he reduces the cultural content of a brand to a single "code" word, which can only be discovered by leading managers in the equivalent of a New Age regression session, channeling them in dark rooms to extract these primitive meanings. See Clotaire Rapaille, *The Culture Code* (New York: Broadway, 2007).
6. Kevin Lane Keller, *Strategic Brand Management* (2nd edn.; Upper Saddle River, NJ: Prentice Hall, 2003), 718.
7. Mark and Pearson, *The Hero and the Outlaw*.

9

Cultural Innovation Theory

To understand how cultural innovation works, one must conceive of "innovation" in a new way. When viewed from the perspective of cultural innovation theory, markets, competition, opportunities, and innovation itself get turned upside down. Now that we have analyzed a number of key cases, let us take a step back and build the general model.

A cultural innovation is a brand that delivers an innovative cultural expression. As we have demonstrated, some of the most powerful and valued brands in the world have become so by offering an innovative cultural expression. So, to understand cultural innovation, one needs first to understand the central role of cultural expressions in creating customer value. And then one needs to understand how particular cultural expressions target a new kind of blue ocean—what we call ideological opportunities—to leapfrog competitors pursuing more conventional product-innovation and marketing strategies.

Cultural Expressions Are Key

Throughout history, people have valued the "right" cultural expressions because they play such an important role in organizing their lives within societies. Cultural expressions serve as compass points, organizing how we understand the world and our place in it, what is meaningful, what is moral, what is human, what is inhuman, what we should strive for, and what we should despise. And cultural expressions serve as linchpins of identity: they are the foundational materials for belonging, recognition, and status. Cultural expressions permeate society, providing us with the building blocks with which we construct

CULTURAL INNOVATION THEORY

meaningful lives. They give guidance on all the key social, political, and existential constructs: from the nation, social class, gender, race, sexuality, and ethnicity, to constructs like beauty, health, religion, nature, compassion, generosity, ethics, the body, work, competition, the market, and success.[1]

In modern society, traditional sources of cultural expression—religion, the state, the arts, education, and other social institutions—have been superseded in large measure by the mass media and commerce. Since the beginning of the twentieth century, companies in the West have competed to monetize this rich source of economic value. And brands have become the prime commercial vehicles for marketing cultural expression.

Cultural Expressions Consist of Ideology, Myth, and Cultural Codes

Cultural expressions are composed of ideology, myth, and cultural codes. Consider Jack Daniel's and Marlboro as examples. Whiskeys and cigarettes have both long competed to champion the best cultural expression of one particularly important construct—masculinity. Both brands offered innovative cultural expressions of masculinity, by which we mean that both brands surpassed their competitors in ideology, myth, and cultural codes.

An ideology is a point of view on one of these important cultural constructs that has become widely shared and taken for granted, naturalized by a segment of society as a "truth." Ideologies profoundly shape our everyday evaluations and actions. We all hold dear many ideologies, which allow us to function consistently, coherently, and effectively in our social lives. Ideologies also serve as the foundation of consumer markets. Strong brands sustain ideologies—a particular point of view on a cultural construct that is central to the product. Jack Daniel's and Marlboro both advocated reactionary working-class frontier masculinity, a particular point of view on masculinity that incited American men to embrace the historic self-reliant, vigorous type of masculinity that existed before the country became overrun with soft, sedentary organization men. Yet, ideologies are concepts, not expressions; and an ideology can be expressed in any number of ways. Consumers experience ideology through layers of cultural expression, not as a declarative intellectual proposition.

So ideologies enter culture when they are conveyed via myth and cultural codes.

Myths are instructive stories that impart ideology. In American commerce during the 1950s and 1960s, the revitalization of the country's historic frontier masculinity was dramatized using two different myths, each of which spun off major cultural innovations. Jack Daniel's proffered a myth, which was drawn from America's hillbilly subculture, romanticizing a small distillery in the Tennessee backwoods that had survived untouched by industrialization and the post-war ideology of the organization man. Jack Daniel's men proudly and stubbornly continued to uphold time-honored, frontier ideals of masculinity with their whiskey making. Marlboro finally struck gold when it hit upon the ranch subculture of the America West to convey a myth about hardworking cowboys herding their cattle with determination and skill on the desolate, weather-threatening range. In each case, the ideology became comprehensible, viscerally felt, and resonant only because it was embedded in myth; it would have made little sense as a conceptual statement.

For a myth to resonate with consumers, it must be composed using the most appropriate and compelling cultural content—cultural codes, to borrow an academic term. All mass-cultural expressions—whether a film or a retail store design or packaging graphics—rely on elements for which the meaning has been well established historically in the culture. It would be impossible to compose an expression from scratch, because, with no historic conventions to fall back upon, each and every element in the composition would have to be defined for the audience in a way that would allow for the proper interpretation. Cultural codes provide a shorthand for consumers, allowing them easily to understand and experience the intended meanings. (What usually differentiates more "artistic" and avant-garde expressions is that they ignore, challenge, play with, or purposely mangle cultural codes.)

The most apt ideology embedded in a potentially powerful myth will backfire if it is composed with culturally illiterate, clunky, off-strategy codes. An adroit and precise use of codes is essential. To signify a preference for old-world craft over modern machines, Jack Daniel's advertising romanticized the process of assembling the staves of the oak barrels and charcoaling their insides. To signify the old-time frontiersman, the antithesis of the organization man, the advertising showcased hefty, rural, Southern men in old-fashioned denim overalls. To signify the celebration of active outdoor labor over sedentary office work, the advertising showed men burning huge ricks of maple for the charcoal filtering. To celebrate the "tell-it-like-it-is" plain speaker over the glib city slicker, the advertising used folksy, parochial, phrases like "welcome to the holler." All of these codes worked together in a redundant manner to create the intended meaning.

The adept use of cultural codes was also crucial to the success of Marlboro. In Marlboro's case, it took Leo Burnett a decade to get the cowboy codes right—the portrait of cowboys on the range without any bosses or machines, happy to rely on their own know-how and industry to complete their grueling, often dangerous, work—for the myth finally to take off. Jack Daniel's and Marlboro both needed to settle upon the correct cultural codes before their myths were able to convey the ideology that target consumers so yearned for.

Cultural competition spans across all three elements of cultural expression. Cultural innovations break through when they bear the right ideology, which is dramatized through the right myth, expressed with the right cultural codes.

How Cultural Expressions Create "Emotional Benefits"

Consider Starbucks. Starbucks succeeded because it provided a particularly resonant cultural expression of a very important construct— social class. Starbucks competed to deliver a type of status that academics call cultural capital, more commonly termed sophistication. To understand the powerful resonance of Starbucks' cultural expression of "sophistication," we need to break it down into its three constitutive elements: ideology, myth, and cultural codes.

Ideology: Artisanal–Cosmopolitanism

Starbucks adapted an artisanal–cosmopolitan ideology advanced first by Peet's and then copied by the original Starbucks and Il Giornale. The artisanal–cosmopolitan movement took on anonymous industrial foods to champion their antithesis: culinary pleasure, terroir beans, skilled hand-crafted coffee, small lots, idiosyncratic and exotic sourcing,

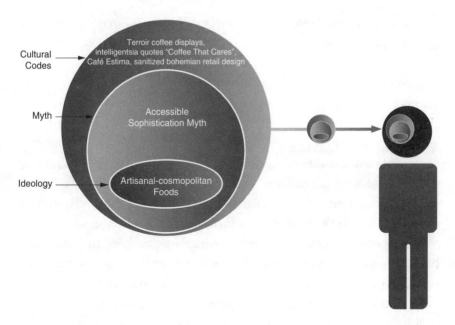

Figure 7. Starbucks' Cultural Innovation

and pre-modern agricultural traditions. Artisanal–cosmopolitanism was one of the most compelling and important ideologies for expressing sophistication (cultural capital) in 1990s America. Starbucks did not just express "sophistication"; it conveyed a very specific ideology of sophistication. Any other ideology would not have worked.

Myth: Accessible Sophistication
At the ideological level, Starbucks was hardly original. The same ideology had been pioneered two decades earlier by Peet's and had become the bedrock of the elite artisanal–cosmopolitan subculture. Starbucks broke with its predecessors in the way it embedded the ideology in the coffee experience: specifically, in the myth and cultural codes it used to stage the ideology. Instead of the rarified and difficult coffee experience on offer by subcultural brands, Starbucks promised its customers that they too could have a sophisticated coffee experience, but one that was accessible to them, that was not alien at all. "I can imbibe in artisanal–cosmopolitan coffee sophistication without risk, without awkwardness, while enjoying the kinds of drinks I have always liked." This myth is an influential example of what we call the *cultural capital trickle-down* tactic, because it packages the sophistication found in elite subcultures

and acts as a fast follower, trickling it down in a way that the non-elite can easily enjoy.

Cultural Codes

To make this myth work required nuanced deployment of the right cultural codes across the marketing mix. This is where Starbucks excelled. Its success was in large part due to the coherent and compelling "accessible sophistication" codes used for every consumer touchpoint: the use of whole-bean coffee as a visual retail prop, the Italianized barista language, the sanitized Bohemian-café design codes, the appropriation of sustainable production politics for in-store signage, and so on.

A mindshare perspective would reduce our analysis to "Starbucks branded sophistication"—end of story. But, from a cultural perspective, this is no explanation at all. Yes, Starbucks became *the* sophisticated coffee brand in the USA, but not because it associated the concept of sophistication with the brand. In fact, other brands—beginning with International Coffees, then Peet's and the original Starbucks, and then Shultz's Il Giornale—built themselves around "sophistication" and yet failed to dominate the mass market. They failed because their particular cultural expressions of "sophistication" did not resonate with the target.

Starbucks worked because it got the cultural expression right—sophistication conveyed by the right ideology, myth, and cultural codes to resonate with the new cultural-capital cohort in 1990s America. When a prospect walked in the door and placed an order, she was engulfed in a very accessible artisanal–cosmopolitan experience that made her feel more sophisticated than if she had bought a coffee from a competitor. The expression was right because Starbucks nailed the ideology, myth, and cultural codes. If it had failed to execute on any of these three components, the entire expression would have been sabotaged.

Because Starbucks delivered the right cultural expression, cultural-cohort consumers responded predictably. They came to depend on Starbucks, developing strong emotional attachments to the brand. Starbucks became highly relevant and desirable to them. They identified themselves with the brand and so attributed desirable qualities to it: Starbucks was "hip," "cool," "fun," "adventurous," and so on. In other words, cultural expressions drive all of the key brand metrics that businesses strive for. So-called emotional benefits are a consequence of effective cultural expression.

How Cultural Expressions Create "Functional Benefits"

Consider Nike. Nike had a minor success selling shoes via a better-mousetrap strategy when selling to the subculture of professional runners. Knight and Bowerman conveyed the shoe's superior performance by emphasizing their improvements in design and materials. However, when they applied this strategy to the expansive mass market, it did not work. They tried to market Nike shoes based upon performance, but customers outside the technocratic domain of the runners' subculture were not interested in "performance." This claim was an engineer's abstraction.

Nike's first breakthrough came when the company celebrated the combative solo willpower psyche of its competitive runners, which resonated with mass-market customers who were anxiously searching for a new motivational tool to pursue the American Dream. Many consumers found value in this cultural expression and, as a result, readily came to believe that Nikes would help them perform better. In the late 1980s, Wieden + Kennedy revised how Nike expressed this ideology in a highly provocative and compelling manner. The branding showcased the combative solo willpower of determined athletes who, with their Nikes, were able to overcome seemingly insurmountable societal discrimination, such as racism and poverty.

More formally, Nike's cultural expressions were composed of:

- *Ideology.* Combative solo willpower.
- *Myth.* "Just Do It." Athletes facing the most severe forms of social discrimination rely on Nike's combative solo willpower to overcome these barriers and win. So Nikes will allow you (the consumer) to overcome the adversities you face, especially the dog-eat-dog labor market, to achieve your American dream.
- *Cultural codes.* Wieden constructed the ads with cultural codes that nailed the vernacular of each discriminated sports subculture. For instance, spots set in the American ghetto appropriated the bleak public housing high-rises, the beat-up basketball courts with chainlink

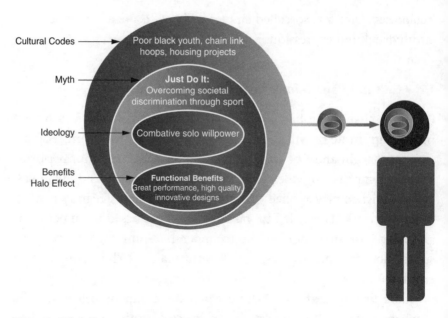

Cultural Codes — Poor black youth, chain link hoops, housing projects

Myth — **Just Do It:** Overcoming societal discrimination through sport

Ideology — Combative solo willpower

Benefits Halo Effect — **Functional Benefits** Great performance, high quality, innovative designs

Figure 8. Nike's Cultural Innovation

nets, even the garbage drifting on the street, all of which combined to convey the harsh reality of ghetto life, and the huge barriers that one would have to overcome to break out of this environment.

Advocates of the better-mousetraps model claim that Nike effectively marketed "performance" through excellent shoe designs. But very few consumers—only professional runners and other competitive athletes—actually evaluated the technical performance of Nike shoes as a shoe engineer would do. Rather, Nike won over mass-market consumers with cultural expressions that they identified with because these expressions served a functional role in their identity projects. And, once they had identified with Nike's expressions, consumers readily made strong inferences about how Nike shoes would improve their performance.

We find this same phenomenon across our research cases. For example, when Anheuser-Busch launched the "This Bud's for You" campaign, Budweiser's functional brand-equity scores leaped: taste and quality perceptions went way up. Similarly, when Ford Explorer was launched with new product design codes and new advertising, the autos were perceived as safer than the Ford Bronco II, the functional equivalent that had preceded it. This is a complex idea, directly at odds with orthodox economic and psychological models of markets, but it is central to understanding how cultural expressions create value.

Why Mindshare and Mousetraps Ignore Cultural Expression

The central role of cultural expression in consumer markets is poorly understood because of the dominance of the mindshare and better-mousetraps models. Most companies, under the spell of mindshare marketing, fill their strategies with abstract mindshare concepts— "fun" or "sophisticated" or "youthful" or "high quality" or "respon-sive" or "built-to-last." This approach implicitly asserts that consumers value abstract concepts such as these, and, so, when a brand conveys such concepts effectively, consumers will value the brand.

Companies like to focus their marketing strategies on mindshare concepts because they are easy to understand, measure, and manage (as we demonstrate in Part Three). But the idea that consumers find value in such abstractions, as abstractions, is a figment of the marketing

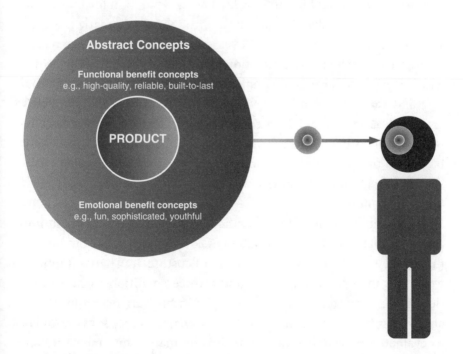

Figure 9. Mindshare Marketing

technocrat's imagination. One can force consumers to think in these terms by requiring them to do so with highly structured market-research instruments. But, from the consumer's perspective, the concepts do not exist as independent entities. Rather, what consumers buy, experience, and value in a brand is a particular version of the abstract concept—its cultural expression. Rather than "fun," consumers experience a particular expression of fun—for example, dancing around the house in joyful abandonment to a favorite tune on one's iPod. iPod's version of fun is different from Audi's version of fun, which is different from Club Med's version of fun. Each brand's "fun" comes to life as a full-blown cultural expression. While they are considerably harder to understand, measure, and manage, cultural expressions, not mindshare concepts, are where the action is in the marketplace. So we need to build theory accordingly.

Better-mousetraps models conceive of brand value in terms of functional benefits—how well the product or service works (often termed *rational benefits* in marketing). As long as functionality is properly built into the product, then its value will be directly and readily perceived by consumers. The brand becomes valued as its reputation for impressive functionality and reliability advances throughout the market. Mindshare marketing problematizes the ease with which consumers recognize and experience these functional benefits—it takes some work, which is why we have marketing, and perceptions can be twisted this way and that with framing devices. But mindshare marketing holds exactly the same view as better-mousetraps theories with respect to what is valued by consumers. Both assume that what consumers are buying is the perceived technical functionality of the offering: consumers buy a Honda because they believe that it will break down less often than another car.

This is another kind of technocratic view of markets. In this case, it is an appropriate lens for a small subset of consumer markets, but not for most, and even then only for a segment of customers. The assumptions work well in consumer markets under three conditions: where functionality is important, where there is significant variance in functionality across brands, and where that functionality is easy for consumers to evaluate (or technocratic evaluations by market intermediaries are very credible and widely disseminated). In such categories—say kitchen knives or carpeting or bicycles—we usually find a segment of consumers who respond to better mousetraps in the direct technocratic manner that engineers and economists assume. But, even in such categories, many consumers tend not to be technically engaged in the category. And, more importantly, only a small minority of consumer markets can be characterized by the three conditions that allow for technocratic consumption. Most consumer markets are characterized by functionality that is less important to consumers, or by small incremental differences in functionality across brands, or by functionality that is difficult for consumers to evaluate. In such cases, culture takes over in guiding consumers' perceptions of functionality. As we argue above, cultural expressions strongly influence how consumers understand and value the functional aspects of the offering.

Avoiding Red Oceans: Breaking out of the Cultural Orthodoxy

Since cultural expression is such a potent driver of customer value, it should be no surprise that innovating in cultural expression—what we call cultural innovation—is a powerful tool for building new businesses and reviving failing ones.

Competitive red oceans are today understood as spaces where there is a great deal of overlapping functionality across current offerings and, therefore, little opportunity to innovate. Innovators need to look for blue oceans (or white spaces) that provide significantly improved value propositions for a brand, whether they are created by new technology or by mixing-and-matching value propositions across categories.

Few businesses—whatever the physical product or service they sell—understand that their offering is understood, experienced, and valued by consumers as a cultural expression. Few businesses, therefore, are managing their cultural expressions. As a result, incumbents in a category tend to arrive at a conventional idea of what is good cultural expression and then copy one another. This is a common phenomenon in business and other types of institutions, well documented by academics who call it mimesis. While businesses compete to outdo each other in providing different benefits, at the cultural level they imitate each other, developing their marketing initiatives as minor variations of the same ideology, myth, and cultural codes. As certain cultural expressions become dominant, businesses come to treat these conventions as durable taken-for-granted "facts" of the marketplace.[2]

This is exactly what happened in the 1950s' whiskey market. The major whiskey-makers all assumed that middle-class American men wanted their whiskeys to express the "classy" modern lifestyle of the well-to-do organization man. Competition between whiskey brands was based largely upon which brand could represent the organization man's lifestyle in a more interesting and credible way. Likewise, in post-war America, it went without saying that coffee should be marketed as a middle-class staple. In the health-drinks market, the big beverage companies all assumed that the way to innovate on health was to devise drinks with the newest most popular "secret-bullet" ingredient. We call these taken-for-granted cultural expressions that are widely imitated the category's *cultural orthodoxy*.

The fact that incumbents tend to market their wares using the same well-worn cultural expressions creates a great opportunity for agile cultural entrepreneurs. Categories that are red oceans from a better-mousetraps perspective are often blue oceans from a cultural perspective precisely because the most powerful competitors are focused on fierce product-level competition, ignoring the cultural aspects of their businesses.

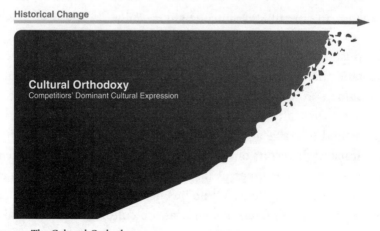

Figure 10. The Cultural Orthodoxy

Social Disruptions Produce Ideological Opportunities

The engine of cultural innovation is historical change in society that is significant enough to destabilize the category's cultural orthodoxy, creating latent demand for new cultural expressions. Markets often sustain these orthodoxies for years at a time, occasionally a decade or longer. But at some point, as history unfolds and social structures shift, one or more of these shifts will be disruptive, challenging the taken-for-granted cultural expressions offered by category incumbents, and creating emergent demand for new cultural expressions. This is what we call a *social disruption*. These are moments when once-dominant brands lose their resonance and when innovative brands take off because they deliver the right expression.

Social disruptions create *ideological opportunities*. The category's cultural orthodoxy no longer adequately delivers the cultural expressions that consumers demand. Consumers yearn for brands that champion new ideology, brought to life by new myth and cultural codes. For Jack Daniel's, the organization-man myth propagated by the mass media and political elites rubbed against the country's historically dominant myth of the gunfighter on the frontier. The

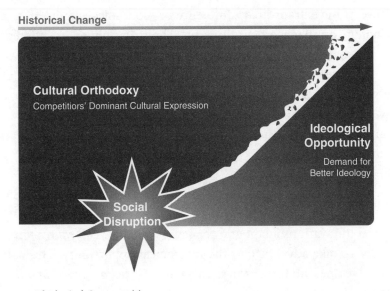

Figure 11. Ideological Opportunities

success of the organization man created a backlash: a widely shared belief that the organization man was too wimpy and effeminate to serve as a model for American men, especially in the midst of the cold war, and a yearning to resuscitate what the gunfighter stood for. In our terms, a massive ideological opportunity was created. Yet, because the major whiskey brands were locked into the category's cultural orthodoxy, they could not imagine giving up their "modern" "aspirational" positioning to return to whiskey's rough-and-tumble rural heritage.

This way of thinking about blue oceans is radically different from the better-mousetrap models. According to technological and mix-and-match models, opportunities are always out there in the world, lying dormant, until the right new technology or creative mix-and-match offering comes along. People always want better functionality. Ideological opportunities, in contrast, are produced by major historical changes that shake up cultural conventions of the category. These shifts unmoor consumers from the goods that they have relied on to produce the symbolism they demand and drive them to seek out new alternatives. It is an emergent kind of opportunity that is specific to a historical moment and a particular group of people.

Ideological opportunities provide one of the most fertile grounds for market innovation. Yet, these opportunities have gone unrecognized because of the extraordinary influence of economics, engineering, and psychology on management thinking. These disciplines, as different as they are, share a common assumption—in order to simplify the world, they purposely ignore cultural context and historical change. They remove all the messy bits of human life in order to present a tidy view of consumption that allows for corporations to function in a streamlined fashion. But it is in these untidy parts that innovation opportunities lurk.

Cultural Innovations Repurpose Source Material

Cultural innovations adapt and repurpose what we call *source material* in order to take advantage of the ideological opportunity. This source material comes in three types: *subcultures*, *media myths*, and *brand assets*.

Subcultures

Innovations adapt alternative ideologies, myths, and cultural codes that are lurking in subcultures and social movements (which we shall refer to jointly as subcultures to simplify).[3] For our purposes, subcultures are groups or places that cohere around an ideology that is antithetic to the category's cultural orthodoxy. Social movements are the same, except that they have an explicit agenda to change society, and so often seek to challenge dominant ideologies directly. The organic-foods, slow-food, and fair-trade movements are all good examples. Subcultures provide great credibility as foundations for brand expressions because they "prove" that the ideology actually exists in the world as a viable world view that has value for its participants.[4]

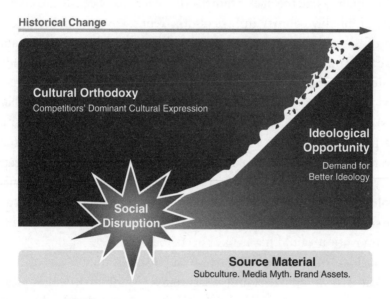

Historical Change

Cultural Orthodoxy
Competitiors' Dominant Cultural Expression

Ideological
Opportunity

Demand for
Better Ideology

Social
Disruption

Source Material
Subculture. Media Myth. Brand Assets.

Figure 12. Repurposing Source Material

Media Myths

Often, the mass media are quicker than other forms of commerce to borrow from subcultures in order to promulgate new cultural expressions. Media myths come packaged in all types of popular culture products: in films, television programs, music, books, magazines, newspapers, sports, politics, even in the news. In addition to the direct appropriation of subcultures, cultural innovations often draw inspiration from the media's mythic treatments of these subcultures.

Brand Assets

Businesses usually have cultural assets that can be leveraged as well. These assets include both the company's business practices that have significant cultural potential, as well as the brand's historic cultural expressions that people still remember. One of the central objectives of *How Brands Become Icons* was to document these equities and to show how they are reworked as the brand evolves historically.

The Jack Daniel's innovation was sourced from the rural hillbilly subculture—denigrated in American culture at the time as backwards, parochial, unmannered, and lower class, the antithesis of the organization man. That the Jack Daniel's distillery had been located in the heart of hillbilly country in Lynchburg, Tennessee since the region was part of the country's frontier, and that distilling whiskey had remained since the frontier days a backwoods hobby in this subculture, made Jack Daniel's a particularly credible brand to champion this ideology. The mass media performed the inversion of the myth of the hillbilly whiskey-maker—from backwoods bumpkin to recalcitrant frontiersman. The fact that the brand had a storied existence amongst insiders as a tiny regional distillery cranking out the same quality whiskey year in and year out gave tremendous credibility to the brand's anachronistic ideology. The subculture, media myth, and brand assets were all crucial sources for the Jack Daniel's innovation. Without these components, the innovation would never have occurred.

Consider other extraordinary cultural innovations, all of which advocated frontier masculinity: cigarettes (Marlboro), whiskey (Jack Daniel's), motorcycles (Harley-Davidson), jeans (Levi's, Lee), and SUVs (Jeep). The historic uses of these products within a particular subculture—frontiersmen drank whiskey, wore denim, and liked to smoke; soldiers, the modern frontiersmen, drove Harleys and Jeeps in the Second World War, and liked to smoke and drink whiskey as well—gave these brands their credibility. And then the mass media turned these subcultural ideologies into myth—the rebel films with Marlon Brando and James Dean, and the Western films and television programs—providing valuable fodder for brands to repurpose.

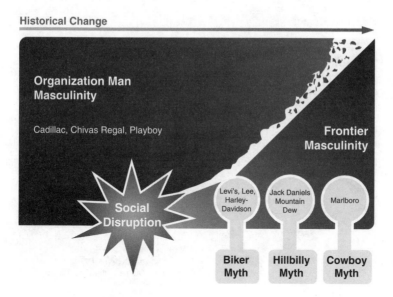

Figure 13. Postwar Media Myths

Cultural Design

The final stage of cultural innovation involves designing a concept that responds to the ideological opportunity in a compelling and original manner, drawing upon appropriate source materials. Executing the design requires that each important consumer-facing element of the brand conveys the cultural expression in an original and artful manner. This transformation of source material into design is the "creative" aspect of cultural innovation, but—as we shall see in Part 2—it is a creative act that is far more directed and constrained than typical "out-of–the-box" tabula-rasa creative projects in the industry today. Once the prospective innovator has understood the right ideology, myth, and cultural codes, instilling these elements into the offering across the marketing mix is usually a straightforward task that is much more susceptible to constructive management than typical creative assignments.

Brands that deliver innovative cultural expressions become powerful cultural symbols—what we call iconic brands. What makes these brands so powerful is that they become collectively valued in society as a widely shared symbol of a particular ideology for a segment of the population. People use the brand in their everyday lives to experience

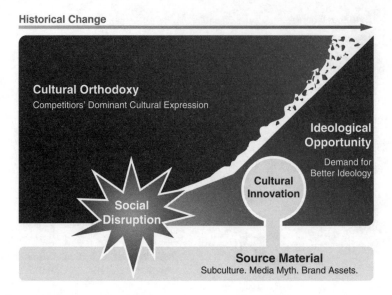

Figure 14. Cultural Innovation Theory

and express this ideology. The brand's cultural role in social life becomes conventional, and so is continually reinforced.[5] Cultural innovations generate three kinds of value, all interrelated:

- *Symbolic value.* Cultural expressions sort out the most important aspects of human life and provide concrete direction and motivation, acting as symbolic anchors for questions of identity, purpose, aspiration, and value. Consumers of branded cultural expressions viscerally experience these desirable ideas and values in everyday life (what anthropologists call *ritual action*).
- *Social value.* Cultural expressions stake out social identities, often based upon key social categories such as social class, gender, race, and ethnicity. They can buttress important political identities as well—for instance, ideals concerning environmentalism, nationalism, and social justice. These social and political identities are used to convey status—demonstrating one's superiority to others, and building solidarity and community with others.
- *Functional value.* When people find symbolic and social value in a brand's cultural expression, they tend to perceive that the brand provides better functionality, is higher quality, and is more trustworthy. Foods and drinks taste better. Companies are trusted. Services

are performed with more consistency. Durable goods are more reliable. When consumers resonate with a brand's cultural expression, they want to believe the branded products and services are excellent, and so the expression strongly influences their perceptions of seemingly functional qualities. Functional benefits are social constructs, not objective facts as assumed by economists and engineers.

Doing Cultural Innovation

In the past, cultural innovation has been a random event. The goal of this book is to turn it into a systematic discipline. We have outlined the theoretical underpinnings of this discipline in Part 1. But more work is required to transform a historically focused academic model into a forward-looking strategy framework. In Part 2, we describe the discipline we have created—what we call *cultural strategy*—which is informed by a distinctive set of cultural research techniques. Cultural strategy is, necessarily, a different animal from the conventional strategy used in most companies. Today, strategy is a language of abstraction. To effect cultural innovation, strategy must specify highly contextual opportunities and direct traffic on specific cultural content. It is this task to which we now turn.

Notes

1. Markets for cultural expression are, by definition, much broader than typical product markets. So, rather than view brands as located within market "spaces," instead we need to understand that all brands are embedded in these broader cultural marketplaces. Fortunately, though, only a small subset of these constructs will be "in play" for any given brand. Brands can engage only in topics that are credible from the consumers' viewpoint, which usually depends on how the product, benefits, uses, and its consumers are represented in the mass media. A careful analyst can easily ascertain the cultural constructs that are relevant for a given category.
2. Here we are referring to what Berger and Luckman call "sedimentation," Pierre Bourdieu calls "doxa," and other social theorists call "reification."
3. In Douglas B. Holt, *How Brands Become Icons: The Principles of Cultural Branding* (Boston: Harvard Business School Press, 2004), we used the term "populist worlds"

to reference these pockets of alternative culture that brands use as source material. We found that this term was difficult for many managers and students to understand, so we have shifted to more conventional terms.

4. We develop this point in detail in Holt, *How Brands Become Icons*.

5. Of course, individuals' experiences with brands are more complicated. People routinely overlay brand ideologies with their own personalized stories, images, and associations. And, of course, non-customers can directly challenge the brand ideology. As companies, entrepreneurs, and movement organizers are usually interested in aggregations of customers, these idiosyncratic meanings have little managerial relevance unless they aggregate to transform conventions. The same holds true with challenges, which become important when they become a communal activity, used to advance a counter-ideology. See, e.g., Craig J. Thompson, Aric Rindfleisch, and Zeynep Arsel, "Emotional Branding and the Strategic Value of Doppelganger Brand Image," *Journal of Marketing*, 70/1 (2006), 50–64.

Part 2

Applying the Cultural
Strategy Model

Introduction

In this part we explain how to adapt cultural innovation theory for use as a strategic tool—what we call *cultural strategy*. We have spent the last eight years working to transform what began as an academic theory into a strategic discipline that guides the development of cultural innovations. We have pursued what we like to think of as an "ideas laboratory" approach. Over this time we have tacked back and forth between academic research cases, applications of the theory to strategy projects, and turnkey branding applications of the theory, with each iteration seeking to improve the model.

We began to apply the model in 2003—the Fat Tire project we discuss in Chapter 11 was our first significant application. Along the way, we have been fortunate to have the opportunity to take on cultural strategy projects across a wide range of brands, categories, and countries. Space constraints limit us to the four cases that follow to illustrate these applications: Clearblue pregnancy tests, Fat Tire beer, Fuse music television, and Freelancers Union. But our work for a variety of other brands has been equally helpful in allowing us to develop cultural strategy as a new innovation discipline. Our work for several entrepreneurial companies was particularly useful for helping us to advance applications of the model to grow start-up businesses in cut-throat red-ocean environments. For Spirits Marque One, we developed a cultural strategy that built its challenger vodka brand, Svedka, into the sixth largest imported vodka in the USA. In 2007, Svedka sold for $384 million to Constellation Brands. For Mark Antony Brands, we developed a cultural strategy to restage Mike's Hard Lemonade. The brand had been declining for five years previously, but with the restaging Mike's gained ten share points in two years, leaping from number three in its category to the top-selling brand.

Our work for multinational corporations such as BMW, The Coca-Cola Company, Brown-Forman, PepsiCo, and MasterCard Worldwide has been extremely useful for advancing our understanding of applications for which the charge is to revitalize an incumbent brand, often marketed globally. For instance, we developed a cultural strategy that revitalized Coca-Cola's historic ideology of healing social fractures, which supported the company's successful efforts to re-establish the brand as a global icon. Several assignments for Microsoft allowed us to apply the model in technology-driven categories very different from the typical lifestyle categories where we had previously done much of our work. Regional assignments in Asian, European, and Latin American markets have been similarly instructive in working out how to apply the model in countries outside the USA. International applications have included developing strategy for Georgia Coffee in Japan (The Coca-Cola Company's most profitable brand), Sprite and Aquarius in Europe, and Cazadores tequila in Mexico. Finally, our ongoing work for the social enterprise Ben & Jerry's has been extremely helpful in allowing us an opportunity to adapt the model to social innovation.

The Six-Stage Model

We build cultural strategies by assembling six complementary types of cultural analysis. We assemble these components like pieces of a puzzle. In the cases to follow, we present these analyses as linear stages for ease of exposition. But, in reality, the development of cultural strategy proceeds by moving back and forth between these six analyses and making ongoing comparisons. These real-time juxtapositions across tentative analyses continually sharpen the interpretation. In each of these iterations the strategist rules out alternatives, further refines the preferred strategy, and builds confidence in this direction through triangulation.

Map the Category's Cultural Orthodoxy

We begin by mapping the cultural red ocean that our strategy must circumnavigate—what we call the cultural orthodoxy. The cultural orthodoxy is the conventional cultural expression (consisting of ideology,

Historical Change

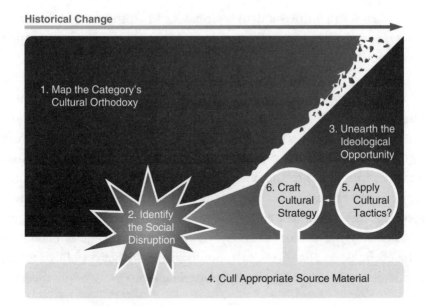

Figure 15. Applying the Cultural Strategy Model

myth, and cultural codes) used by most incumbents as they compete to create customer value. Cultural codes are to be found in every marketing activity, from product design, retail, communications, packaging, and service scripts, to CEOs' speeches that get picked up in the media. In the cases that we profile in this part, we identify the cultural orthodoxies that were producing red oceans in the four respective categories: the patriarchal medicine ideology in pregnancy tests (Clearblue), the artisanal–cosmopolitan ideology in craft beer (Fat Tire), the teeny-bopper dream of the rich, famous and beautiful life promoted by MTV in music television (Fuse), and the corporate professionalism ideology in the health insurance industry (Freelancers Union).

Identify the Social Disruption that can Dislodge the Orthodoxy
Social shifts eventually disrupt consumers' identification with conventional category expressions. At any historic moment in any locale, there are a myriad societal changes taking place. We focus on those changes that unsettle the category's ideology, that lead consumers to desire a new ideology or to feel uncomfortable with the existing ideology. These disruptive social shifts can be led by technology, the economy, social structure, demography, social movements, or the mass media. In the

four cases we identified a demographics-led disruption (Fat Tire), an economy-led disruption (Freelancers Union), a social-movement-led disruption (Clearblue), and a mass-media-led disruption (Fuse).

Unearth the Ideological Opportunity

Once we have specified the social disruption, we then detail precisely how this disruption is impacting on category customers. In this phase, we dig into customers' identity projects to ascertain their collective desires and anxieties in relation to the disruption. What is the emerging desire for new cultural expressions caused by the disruption? What is the emergent ideology that customers are gravitating toward? In the four cases, we describe how we unearthed: body positive feminism (Clear blue), the ache of the Bobo (Fat Tire), the populist backlash against MTV (Fuse), and leftie workplace solidarity (Freelancers Union).

Cull Appropriate Source Material

Cultural innovations are never created from scratch. Rather they repurpose cultural expressions lurking in subcultures, social movements, media myths, and the brand's own assets. This is what we call source material. Cultural innovation is not about "futuring" or brainstorming pie-in-the-sky visions of what may come to be in ten years. Rather, successful innovations repurpose existing ideologies, myths, and cultural codes—which have already been embraced by some people, however dated or marginal—to address the ideological opportunity. The ideological opportunity usually provides strong clues as to what is the most appropriate source material. And sometimes the business is embedded in a movement or subculture, and so the right source material is obvious.

Apply Cultural Tactics?

In our research and consulting we have developed a number of specific techniques that work as tactical embellishments of cultural strategy. These tactics can be particularly powerful in certain applications. So we review the laundry list of tactics to see if there is a good fit, and import into the strategy iterations any tactic that seems promising. The six tactics we review in this book include:

- provoking ideological flashpoints (Ben & Jerry's, Fuse)
- mythologizing the company (Jack Daniel's, ESPN)
- resuscitating reactionary ideology (Jack Daniel's, Marlboro)
- cultural capital trickle-down (Starbucks, Vitaminwater, Fat Tire)
- crossing the cultural chasm (Nike, Starbucks, Fat Tire)
- cultural jujitsu (Ben & Jerry's, Fuse)

Craft the Cultural Strategy

As we emphasize throughout the book, cultural strategy demands a different approach from the conventional strategies found in both the better-mousetraps and mindshare-marketing models. This is so because cultural strategy requires identifying a specific opportunity that opens up at a particular historical moment, within a particular societal context; and then responding to this opportunity with a particular cultural expression, made up of ideology, myth, and cultural codes. Not only are the components of cultural strategy necessarily different. Crucially, cultural strategy must be far more specific and directive as well. While conventional strategies work with generic benefits and emotion words, cultural strategy directs everyone involved in the innovation to craft a particular cultural expression into every component of the offering. The acid test is whether or not the strategy document directs those involved in the design of the innovation toward a promising cultural expression and warns them away from cultural dead-ends. Typical strategy documents are a page or two with a summary architectonic figure (box, house, onion, key, and so on). Such strategies are far too vague for this purpose. Cultural strategies are detailed documents that specify nuanced direction in terms of ideology, myth, and cultural codes. In cultural innovation, details matter.

Triangulating across Seven Cultural Research Methods

One of the most important aspects of our "idea laboratory" approach has been to devise a set of systematic cultural research methods that inform the strategy development process in an effective and efficient manner. We have devised the appropriate cultural research methods to inform each component of the model. These methods are straightforward applications of academic research techniques. We have helped to pioneer some of these academic methods, in fact.[1] We also make

Historical Change

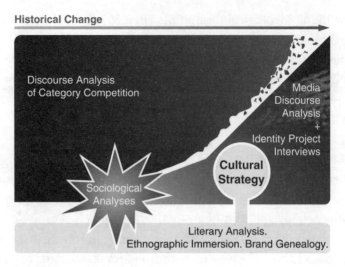

Figure 16. Cultural Research

extensive use of academic and learned journalistic literatures as secondary data. These literatures can be used either as a substitute for some of the primary research, or as initial leads upon which the primary research builds.

As with the strategy itself, doing cultural research to inform cultural strategy is not a plug-and-play method but, rather, must be customized for each project. The research follows the iterative path of the strategy: digging into one facet of the model using one research technique provides strong direction to other facets, and vice versa. The most challenging aspect of doing this research is to determine which methods to emphasize and downplay for any given project, and to determine the most effective iterative pathway through the methods. We begin with the pieces of the strategic puzzle that are the most important, the most self-evident, and the ones that will provide the tightest initial parameters to focus the remaining components of the analysis. If a reader would like to learn more about these techniques, they are widely discussed in the academic literature.

Applications

In addition to demonstrating how the cultural strategy model works in practice, the cases we have selected give us a chance to develop additional threads of our argument. The Clearblue pregnancy test case provides an excellent proving ground for our claims regarding the power of cultural innovation to complement technological innovation. Pregnancy tests are, ostensibly, a technology-driven category. Yet we show that cultural innovation was key to attaining category leadership on a new technology. Fat Tire provides a grounded example of a common innovation problem—what we term *crossing the cultural chasm*—for which cultural strategy is a very effective antidote. Fuse allows us to demonstrate a powerful yet counter-intuitive cultural tactic: taking on the dominant incumbent directly, using what we call *cultural jujitsu.* Freelancers Union demonstrates how our model can drive social innovation. And, as well, the case allows us to challenge Clayton Christensen's adaptation of his economic approach to social innovation.

Notes

1. For instance, the identity project interview is an adaptation of a technique that Craig Thompson, Holt, and others developed in the consumer culture theory literature. And the brand genealogy is a technique Holt developed in *How Brands Become Icons: The Principles of Cultural Branding* (Boston: Harvard Business School Press, 2004).

10

Clearblue Pregnancy Tests: Branding a New Technology

Cultural strategy can unearth significant opportunities in categories that have been dominated by technological innovation. Companies doing business in such categories tend to act just as the better-mousetraps model recommends: they constantly push for the next big technological breakthrough that will create novel functionality in order to provide their brand with a substantial advantage over competitors. The problem is that breakthrough technologies are hard to come by, and, when a technology is introduced that really improves performance on an important category benefit, it is quickly copied by competitors. So, while incumbents imagine themselves to be innovation focused, in reality brand competition in these categories is dominated by benefits slugfests. Competing brands duel it out in red oceans using mindshare branding, often commodifying the category in the process. Many packaged goods categories unfold in this fashion. These categories are dominated by big marketing companies (what we will come to term brand bureaucracies in Part 3)—such as Procter & Gamble, Pfizer, L'Oréal, and Henkel—that are dedicated to technological innovation and swear by the mindshare marketing model.

Technology-driven categories offer excellent opportunities for cultural strategy, for two reasons. Because incumbents are so focused on developing new product technologies, they are usually blind to the social and cultural value that the brand is capable of delivering. That blindness creates opportunities for a brand to outflank the benefits battle with an innovative cultural expression. In addition, developing a cultural innovation is an effective tool to forge a durable claim to an innovative technology. When companies compete using the same bland mindshare approach to make technological claims, consumers rarely pay attention. Despite huge marketing expenditures, none of the brands owns the innovation from the consumer's perspective. Cultural innovation makes technological claims much more sticky and persuasive, as we demonstrate in this case.

Pregnancy tests provide a constructive example. Since its inception, category competition has been structured around four technological innovations: a new immunoassay isolated the presence of the pregnancy hormone (hCG) in urine, without cross-reaction from other hormones, and allowed for accurate home testing; a new paper strip coated with monoclonal antibodies led to simplified, one-step testing, and spared women from the messy chore of trying to pee into a cup and then mix her urine into a test tube; more sensitive hCG detectors enabled testing earlier after a missed period; and, most recently, digital readouts made test results much easier for women to interpret. Each time, the innovator brand enjoyed a short period during which it led the market with a demonstrably better value proposition. But competitors, including store brands, quickly mimicked the innovation, and the category soon returned to conventional mindshare competition, in which brands competed by exaggerating slight differences in product benefits.

For decades, the major pregnancy test brands tried to convince consumers that their product was superior in delivering one or more of three benefits: "accurate," "early," "easy." In the summer of 2003, Clearblue launched the first digital readout for its test—a major technological innovation that made the test much easier to use than the prior analog versions. The breakthrough lasted four months. Then e.p.t., Clearblue's top competitor, launched its own digital test, and within a year the private labels followed suit. So the category quickly returned to benefits-as-usual mindshare warfare: accurate, early, easy.

Given the dominance of mindshare marketing, we were not surprised when our research told us that women treated pregnancy tests as a low-involvement purchase. From a cultural perspective, however, pregnancy tests are anything but boring. They are intimately related to woman's efforts to reproduce, or to keep from reproducing. One would be hard pressed to find a more culturally charged topic. We soon discovered a major ideological opportunity that incumbents had missed because they were so focused on technological advances. We restaged Clearblue as champion of body-positive feminist ideology, and the immediate result was huge sales gains, gains of the sort that are rarely seen in packaged goods.

Benefits Slugfest Creates Red Ocean

In the early 1970s, research sponsored by the National Institutes of Health led to the development of the home pregnancy test—a paper strip coated with anteserum that identified the presence of the "pregnancy hormone" human chorionic gonadotropin (hCG) in urine. In 1978, four home pregnancy test brands were launched in the American market, allowing women to test before or instead of visiting a doctor. The tests were virtually identical: they used the same technology and performed to the same 99 percent level of accuracy. Despite the product parity, these brands tried to convince consumers that they were different, each making benefit claims in an attempt to outmaneuver the other brands.[1]

- Warner-Chilcott's *e.p.t.* (a.k.a. Early Pregnancy Test) claimed in its brand name the benefit of early knowledge, while its advertising touted the product's accuracy ("its high accuracy rate has been verified here in America by doctors") and ease of use ("that means you can confidently do this easy pregnancy test yourself"). An end line summarized things by cramming in all three benefits together: "At last early knowledge of pregnancy belongs easily and accurately to us all."

- A second brand, *ACU-TEST,* claimed accuracy in its brand name, while its advertising claimed early knowledge of result ("the sooner you know you're pregnant, the sooner you can take proper care of yourself"), and its ease of use ("simple urine test that requires no internal examination"). To personalize the message, ACU-TEST added an image of a woman biting her fingernail and looking pensively off-camera, playing up the drama of the wait for results.

- Ads for the *ANSWER* claimed earliness and accuracy, but focused on the "confidence" that comes from its results.

• *Predictor*, the fourth brand, pursued a "best of all benefits" strategy, proclaiming to be the most proven ("the only test used in 3000 hospitals and nine million laboratory tests"), the most accurate ("tests confirmed a 98.9% accuracy"), easy ("as easy as A.B.C."), safe ("only a urine specimen is required"), and early ("early detection is important").

When one brand introduced a technological advance, competitors quickly copied it, and used the new technology as additional ammunition in the ongoing benefits war. With the new digital technology, all the brands promoted that their digital product delivered some combination of accurate, early, easy, and (now) clear. Some branding also sought to add "emotional benefits" by dramatizing the wait in a vein similar to ACU-TEST's nail-biting ad. Companies wanted to convey "confidence" as well, and all did so using the same cultural codes in their branding: alluding to doctors' expertise, clinical testing, or a technological advance.

When the management of Clearblue came to us in 2006, sales were a distant third place in the USA. While Clearblue was the number-one brand in most European markets, it was rapidly losing share to private labels. Recent brand communications had focused on the benefit of "clarity." Clearblue's ads sought to elicit emotion through the conventional nail-biting imagery. It used the director David Lynch to ratchet up suspense, and it claimed that "When you're waiting to find out if you're pregnant or not, nothing else matters in the world... only Clearblue gives you a clear yes or no in one minute." Other ads relied on metaphors to dramatize clarity. For instance, Clearblue's unambiguous results were compared to clear car directions and unambiguous furniture building directions. In another spot, a man gives increasingly confusing directions to a woman traveler, until the ad helpfully explains how clarity is a good thing, especially when it comes to pregnancy tests.

Fortunately for us, Clearblue was at the time owned by Inverness Medical Innovations, a small, entrepreneurial, healthcare-products company that had purchased the business from Unilever in 2001. As a result, Clearblue's management team was much leaner and more independent in its thinking than the typical brand bureaucracy. The global marketing and innovation team consisted of three women, all of whom had little patience or temperament for brand bureaucratic logic. In their first meeting with us, they projected the word vagina on a PowerPoint screen, explaining that they were a women's health company, and if we were to work with them, then we would have to get used to using the word in business meetings. In their brief to us, they stressed that the most important part of the assignment would be to move beyond the benefits game. They knew that the slugfest had commoditized the category, leading consumers to believe that all the tests were pretty much the same. Private labels had replicated category benefit claims on their lower-priced packages and, as a result, reaped a 33 percent share of the market.

By 2006, they had become utterly frustrated by the branding process that they had inherited from Unilever. It had been lengthy and expensive: first a segmentation study, followed by idea-generation sessions let by management consultants, then months of concept testing and concept optimization, and, finally, the reduction of all key findings into the eight text boxes of a brand strategy diagram, in a shape they called the "brand key." The process was similar to the standard brand strategy process used by all the blue-chip consumer marketing companies, as we describe in our analysis of the brand bureaucracy in Chapter 14. With headings such as "benefits," "reasons to believe," and "consumer discriminator," the brand key's text boxes ensured that managers built the strategy around category benefits. Like the brand houses, brand pyramids, and brand onions used by other elite brand bureaucracies, the brand key forced managers to distill all component benefits and insights into an abstract "essence" located in a privileged text box—in this case, the keyhole at the center of the diagram.

After conducting an elaborate survey, listening to numerous focus groups, testing a variety of concepts, optimizing a final concept, and diligently filling in the brand key, the Clearblue team had ended up with a brief singling out *early knowledge of result* ("test 5 days sooner"), *accuracy* ("over 99% digital accuracy"), *ease of use* ("one step," "easy to grip"), and *clarity* ("easy to read the results"). The elaborate process had led them to replicate the laundry list of category benefits used by all competitors for the previous twenty-five years! This was precisely the type of strategy they had hoped to avoid: "the best of all benefits." The consumer insight was said to be, "I feel nervous and I need to know right now if I am pregnant or not"—the old nail-biting story. The brand essence distilled all this into the emotional benefit of "confidence," just what other pregnancy tests had been championing for decades. Rather than uncovering an opportunity to innovate, the process had led Clearblue back into the red ocean of the benefits slugfest.

Clearblue's managers were intrigued by the possibility that our cultural strategy model could uncover opportunities for innovative branding, and sidestep the processes that continually forced them toward category clichés. They challenged us to use our framework to develop an innovative concept for Clearblue. So we started by conducting cultural research that would reveal the best ideological opportunity for the brand to leapfrog the category's cultural orthodoxy.

Cultural Orthodoxy: Patriarchal Medicine

We first mapped the category's cultural orthodoxy, which had served as the tacit foundation for twenty-five years of benefits wars. We discovered that the two leading pregnancy test brands, e.p.t. and First Response, consistently relied upon the rhetoric of what we termed *patriarchal medicine.*

Their branding addressed women in a superior and condescending voice, leaning on pseudo-scientific language. The ads portrayed the idealized customers of pregnancy tests as prim-and-proper mothers who seemed as thought they had been transported from a 1950s television show. The branding implied that these women were embarrassed by talking about their bodies and bodily functions in public. Reproductive health is an indelicate subject that should remain private, and so public forums like an ad must revert to polite 'ladylike' euphemisms.

One e.p.t. ad featured a woman waiting nervously to check the results of her pregnancy test. Her husband sits next to her and comments in a somewhat patronizing tone. In one version, he says, "Better luck next time." In another, he simply shrugs when the test proves negative. The men and women all look as though they came straight out of *Family Circle* or *Good Housekeeping.* The ads seem purposefully to avoid any hint that the need for the product is a direct consequence of having sex. Rather, the ads present the "good" woman's desire to get pregnant and realize her dreams of family with her husband, projecting 1950s-era ideals of stable motherhood and nuclear family. e.p.t. women typically tear up with happiness when they discover they are pregnant, or stiffen with anxiety when they discover they are not. The idea that the tests would be used to avoid pregnancy, their predominant use, is studiously ignored.

Similarly, the First Response advertising relied upon narrators speaking in the voice of "doctor knows best." Announcers, often wearing lab coats, speak with medical authority: "Imagine! Knowing you're pregnant the moment it happens. Science is getting close!" The message is driven home with graphics that evoke a similar pseudo-scientific aura, albeit pinked-up. In one, a dot labeled with the word pregnant appears on a Cartesian plane. A line then travels to a second dot that is labeled "pregnancy hormone variant." We then see the profile of a woman silhouetted against a rising line graph; this time the line connects from the woman's vagina to a bar that reads "Missed Period." The movement of the line on the graph is punctuated by vibraphonic chimes and other sound effects that would not be out of place in a documentary about the wonders of science.

Both brands unknowingly championed the ideology of *patriarchal medicine*: women are passive and married. Their primary role is procreation. Only male professionals ordained by the medical profession have the proper expertise to make health decisions about women's bodies. So women are expected to defer control of their bodies and responsibility for their health to the mostly male medical establishment. These bodily issues are to be kept private and treated in a clinical manner, free of any taint of sexuality.

Source Material: Body-Positive Feminism

Next in our research we looked for a subculture that has effectively challenged the patriarchal medicine ideology. We were particularly interested in identifying a subculture that had been picked up by the media and turned into a media myth. We found that a powerful movement that had long challenged patriarchal medicine and its alternative gender ideology had recently bled into popular culture and become very influential amongst our target of 16–40-year-old women. The research involved the examination of academic research on feminist social movements that have challenged patriarchal medicine, a discourse analysis of the third-wave feminist subculture, and a discourse analysis of mass media that have drawn upon this movement.

Second-Wave Feminism's Alternative Health Movement

Patriarchal medicine was first challenged in the United States by a book published in 1971 by the Boston Women's Collective called *Our Bodies Ourselves*. The book urged women to take control of their bodies and their health, and advocated complete openness and honesty when it came to talking about women's sexual health and reproductive issues. The book was hugely influential in the feminist movement of the era, often referred to as the second wave.

This health movement was part of a broader "personal is political" call to reclaim women's bodies from the dominant misogynist patriarchal ideology found throughout society. Catharine MacKinnon and Andrea Dworkin's crusade against pornography is indicative of how second-wave feminists often dealt with issues of sexuality. Wherever patriarchal relations were promulgated, such as in the objectification of women in pornography, second-wavers made stark criticisms and sought out institutional change. They raised these issues in the court-rooms and in the universities, launching a new women's studies curriculum.

The Third Wave's Body-Positive Feminism

Beginning in the early 1990s, a "third-wave" feminist ideology began to emerge in younger women's subcultures, distinguished from the second wave primarily around issues of sexuality. Rather than taking women's bodies out of the bedroom and making them political objects in the classroom and courts, third-wavers found it much more empowering to reclaim sexuality. Third-wave feminism directly challenged the second wave's approach to heterosexuality. Instead of seeking to isolate women from men's imposition of sexual relationships, the third wave celebrated sexuality as a means of female empowerment. For women to overcome patriarchal oppression, then they must be able to enjoy their sexuality freely rather than build a wall around it.

Third-wave feminists called out the label "slut" as a double standard: why should women be disparaged for being promiscuous if men were applauded for it? Behaviors and speech that were traditionally thought unladylike or unfeminine were suddenly embraced as empowering—from sexual aggressiveness to locker-room-style lewdness. Women began to take pride in using the same openness in discussing their bodily functions, genitalia, sexual desires, and sexual conquests as had been accorded to men.

Further, the third wave rejected as dictatorial their predecessors' orthodox ideas of what it meant to be a feminist. Instead, they encouraged women to make use of whatever identities empowered their own sexuality and confidence in rebutting patriarchal incursions—whether girly girl or bitch or sex symbol or tomboy or stripper or sweetheart or lipstick lesbian. Many of these identities were taboo to the women's lib generation, but third-wave feminism was all about shattering taboos.

The emergence of this ideology was driven by a generational shift. The women who identified with third-wave feminism tended to be the children of baby boomers. Unlike their baby-boom parents, whose generation fought tough political battles for basic rights, many third-wavers grew up believing that institutional equality had been for the most part achieved. Third-wavers were part of a generation in which women were better represented in elite schools of medicine and law than were men. This younger generation waited longer and longer before getting married and increasingly chose to pursue competitive careers. Being more media savvy than their parents, they enjoyed a playful relationship with popular culture, often taking ironic pleasure in female stereotypes in the media, ranging from Paris Hilton to *America's Next Top Model.* They preferred to approach gender issues with a sense of humor, eschewing what they saw as the humorless feminism of their parents' generation.

This body-positive feminism was promoted by several influential subcultural magazines and websites. *Bust,* the "magazine for women with something to get off their chests," advertised itself as "the Voice of the New Girl Order," and, with its sections on careers, pop culture, and sex files—including sex toys and porn guides—offered an edgy alternative to the likes of *Cosmopolitan* and *Vogue.* The magazine spoke with extreme openness about sexuality and reproductive issues and took on an emphatically anti-prudish tone. The magazine ran an online shop called the Boobtique. *Bitch*, published out of Portland, Oregon (the home of the third wave's riot girrrl subculture), described itself as "a feminist response to pop culture," and provided a third-wave commentary on everything from fashion to music to sex to the color pink. The magazine celebrated the likes of burlesque and lesbian sex scenes in films. It offered the view that pornography could be empowering to female actors. Some of the magazine's more popular articles included Jennifer Maher's "Hot for Teacher" on the "erotics of pedagogy," Julia Scheeres's "Vulva Goldmine" on the new culture of vaginal reconstruction, and Lee Shoemaker's "Standing Up to Pee" on gender "urinalysis." The website Nerve.com attracted hundreds of thousands of young professional women through its mixture of erotica, graphically sexual photos, daring Internet dating, and notable literary contributors such as Naomi Wolf, Joyce Carol Oates, and Norman Mailer. The site described itself as "a smart, honest magazine on sex, with cuntsure (and cocksure) prose and fiction" and encouraged its members to go out and have sexual encounters.

Ideological Opportunity

Finally, we conducted identity interviews with a group of women who were representative of the most opportune target for Clearblue: 16–40-year-olds in professional and managerial jobs. We learned that, while few of them were activists in the feminist movement, many had come to embrace the third-wave ideology when it came to being open about their own bodies, celebrating sexuality, and pursuing femininity in whatever identity fit best. They very much embraced the body empowerment message of *Our Bodies, Ourselves*, but were much less comfortable with second-wave feminism's take on sexuality. Growing up in an age of sexual frankness and promiscuity, second-wave views came across to many women as strident and even prudish.

We found triangulating evidence that the third-wave ideology had permeated some segments of the mass media. A small off-Broadway play called *The Vagina Monologues* opened in 1996. The play comprises a series of monologues, each of which relates somehow to the vagina, whether through sex, menstruation, masturbation, pregnancy, or tools used by OB/GYNs. The play sought provocatively to dramatize that the female body and women's reproductive health are nothing to be ashamed of and should be talked about freely and forthrightly without stigma. It trod exactly upon the second-wave versus third-wave fault line, championing the latter. As a result, it quickly garnered a cult following and in the early 2000s grew to become a national and then international cultural phenomenon. The play was performed by Whoopi Goldberg at Madison Square Garden and televised on HBO. Numerous touring companies performed the play worldwide in more than 120 countries. We learned that the play continued to be extremely popular in our key markets, especially the United Kingdom, where it was in constant rotation across more than fifty cities.[2]

The most powerful popular expression of body-positive feminism was the television show *Sex and the City*. The show put forth a pro-vocative model of womanhood that women in Europe and the USA had never before experienced on the television screen. Arguably, it was the single most influential work of mass culture that shaped feminine ideals for the post-baby-boomer generation of women. The show dramatized the everyday lives of four women in their mid-thirties living profes-sional lives in New York City. These women openly pursued and took pride in their sexual adventures, and frankly discussed such issues as sexually transmitted diseases, birth control, promiscuity, "fuck bud-dies," erectile dysfunction, and gynecological disorders. The show was venerated for its candid discussions about sex and womanhood. Young professional women emulated the four friends on the show in the way they dressed, spoke, and socialized with one another, while members of the religious right skewered the show for its lewdness and impropriety.

Launched in 1998, the show evolved from an HBO hit in the USA to become an international phenomenon. Channel 4 in the UK picked it up in 1999, and soon the show was syndicated around the world, from Germany to South Korea to Brazil. The DVD box set became a best-seller, and *Sex and the City: The Movie* was an international hit, the top-grossing romantic comedy of all time.

We also found a number of innovative commercial endeavors that were responding to the growing demand for body-positive feminism. For instance, national gym franchises in the USA such as Crunch began to offer striptease classes, where women could trade in their workplace identities as lawyers or public-relations executives for the sexually empowering identity of a stripper.

Our interviews and discourse analysis revealed that, by 2006, when we took over Clearblue branding, body-positive feminism had diffused from the third-wave feminist subcultures to become the dominant gender ideology of our target. The women we studied treated sexuality in a very frank and often sassy and ironic manner that was completely alien to most older women. And body-positive feminism had a direct impact on how these women pursued motherhood, and how they avoided it, and what they expected for reproductive health. Like the feminists of the era of *Our Bodies, Ourselves*, they insisted upon having complete charge over their bodies; but they had their own expectations about how their bodies were to be talked about in public discourse. Bodily pleasures and problems were now part of everyday life, something to talk about, laugh about, deal with, never to hide.

We viewed this generational embrace of body-positive feminism as a substantial ideological opportunity for Clearblue. For simple biological reasons, women from this younger generation were the most frequent buyers of pregnancy tests. So the two leading brands in the category, First Response and e.p.t., were upholding an ideology that had become anachronistic, appealing only to older women, who each year were becoming less important consumers in the category. Through our analysis, the ideological opportunity became obvious—Clearblue should champion body-positive feminism in women's reproductive health.

Designing the Cultural Innovation

Clearblue's managers were excited about this opportunity, even though their initial briefing document had prohibited any cultural expressions that might be understood as feminist. Clearblue's managers shrugged off the breach. They recognized that the issue was semantic. As one of them put it, "That brief was talking about angry, hairy armpit feminism." They urged us to write up the strategy in a way that the rest of their organization would understand. So we created a manifesto that included:

Clearblue champions a body-positive feminist view of reproduction and women's health. Clearblue celebrates women's bodies. We are not embarrassed by them. We see reproductive health as playful and fun, not "sinful" or "unladylike." We talk about reproductive issues directly; we have no secrets and we do not hide behind euphemistic language. We view gender issues with humor, not with earnestness. We see women who are dealing with reproduction issues as strong and empowered, not deferential to men or nervously awaiting test results. We celebrate what's natural, we don't hide it. We will have fun pointing out patriarchal medicine's double standards in its treatment of women's sexuality and sexual health. We will be reflexive and ironic about the taboos around women's bodies.

After writing this manifesto, we began work on how to bring this ideology to life in as provocative a way as possible. What myth should we dramatize? What cultural codes should we repurpose? The challenge was that we were branding a category few women paid attention to. We also had a very small media budget. So we had little margin for error in designing cultural expressions that would resonate with our target. We had to incorporate just the right body-positive feminist codes in just the right way to provide our target with the knowing wink that told them that we shared their views. All in 30 seconds, or on an 8½ x 11 piece of paper.

This situation was a natural for applying our "provoking an ideological flashpoint" tactic, which we had developed through our analysis of Ben & Jerry's (see Chapter 4). The body-positive feminist ideology was still highly contested in both European and American society. Flashpoints abounded. And, if we hit the right flashpoint with a provocative creative idea, we could get our target enthused even with a minimal media spend. We researched what was the most contentious issue championed by body-positive feminism? We first identified the overt blunt talk of sexuality, but sexualized chatter had become widespread in the social media age and so was quickly losing its edge and feminist meaning.

We moved on to consider celebrating frank public conversation about women's bodily functions. Because other women's health companies were so prudish when it came to portraying bodily functions, often using abstract blue fluids to represent urine, or pouring beakers to represent urination, we recognized that puncturing this taboo would be particularly provocative. And this flashpoint was equally contentious in both the USA and Europe, our two key markets. Also, this cultural strategy fit organically with how Clearblue products were actually used. As Clearblue's managers were fond of pointing out, we were in the business of marketing "pee-sticks." For a pregnancy test to indicate if you are pregnant, you have to pee on it.

Pregnancy Test: Pee Ship

Our first assignment was to brand the digital technology on the Clearblue pregnancy test. While all competitors including the store brands offered digital technology, their mindshare branding had been so perfunctory that many women had not paid attention. So, even though this innovation had been on the market for several years, we felt there was an opportunity to establish Clearblue as the leader in digital pregnancy testing by using cultural strategy. To mock our competitors' patriarchal medicine ideology, we made a film that bluntly and dramatically visualized what women do when they check to see if they are pregnant. Because we wanted to announce in as loudly and proudly a way as possible that women's bodily functions are nothing to be ashamed of, we decided to give our lead television spot an anthemic quality. We set the spot in outer space, with a dramatic build-up using a soundtrack and visual of an enormous approaching "spaceship" that paid homage to *2001: A Space Odyssey*.

A baritone-voiced narrator speaks with more than a little hyperbole to heighten the satire of the category's scientific ads: "It has arrived...the next generation of pregnancy test. Its design...breathtakingly simple. Its circuitry...incredibly accurate." The soundtrack hisses theatrically as the pregnancy test's cap begins to float away, as though disengaging from a docking station.

The narrator continues, speaking slowly, loudly, and emphatically: "It is without a doubt the most sophisticated piece of technology...". And now, just as the ad is about to climax, a clear fluid pours down from the top of the frame, descending toward the tip of the pregnancy test. The narrator finishes: "...that you will ever pee on. Introducing the Clearblue digital pregnancy test. It's so advanced, it's easy."

The unexpected stream of pee splashing all over the digital pregnancy test powerfully expressed, as words could never do, that Clearblue championed body-positive feminism over the antiquated patriarchal medical view of women's reproduction. In thirty seconds, we made the category leaders e.p.t. and First Response seem antiquated, because they treated women's bodies with embarrassment and modesty, hiding them behind euphemisms.

Ovulation Test: Innuendo

We also applied the body-positive feminist cultural strategy to restage Clearblue's secondary product line of ovulation tests. While the pregnancy tests were by far the company's best-selling product line, the ovulation test represented a major growth opportunity, since Clearblue was the category leader. Clearblue's managers focused on the US market, because Americans, compared to their counterparts in other countries, were not very knowledgeable about reproduction issues. The majority of American women were unaware that they have only a few days every month in which they can conceive. Their odds of getting pregnant are very low during most days of their menstrual cycle, but then go up dramatically during the two days when they ovulate most heavily. Many fertility problems in the USA stemmed from lack of knowledge about the ovulation cycle.

Not only was knowledge limited; testing for ovulation was highly stigmatized. The dominant discourse in the USA painted ovulation tests as a procreative crutch for women who had physical fertility problems. Women in our research reported being extremely embarrassed about either inquiring into ovulation testing or making purchases in the store. They did not want to talk publicly about ovulation testing, since they felt that it was associated with women who were desperate to get pregnant. The sense of taboo surrounding ovulation testing made it a perfect fit for our "provoking ideological flashpoints" tactic. We decided Clearblue should work to shatter this taboo, and open up the conversation about ovulation in American culture.

Furthermore, we discovered that there was an interesting sexual angle that allowed us to use the third wave's take on sexuality in a manner that was fresh and provocative. Because the best way to get pregnant was to have sex as many times as possible during the two high-ovulation days, the product offered an organic opportunity to champion women's sexual dominance.

For the ovulation tests, we had an even smaller budget than we had had with the pregnancy test. So we chose to work with radio and print. The radio spot set an aggressively sexual woman protagonist in direct conflict with an absurdist male voice of prudishness. The radio spot, titled "Sexual Innuendo," begins with a woman educating the listener on the Clearblue Digital Ovulation Test: "You see, every woman has just a few days each month for conceiving and Clearblue can help you figure out exactly when it's baby-making time." Suddenly, her voice shifts into a sexy tone as she repeats "Sweet, sweet, baby-making time." A soundtrack of slow funk suggestively starts up, referencing the codes of 1970s pornography.

No sooner has the music started, than it comes to a grinding halt when the prudish male intrudes: "Ahem. I'm worried this is going somewhere dirty." The woman responds: "What?! I can't say baby-making in an ovulation ad?! Oh, I'm sorry. Clearblue's Digital Ovulation Test will tell you when it's time to..." We then hear a loud, sexy, exhaling sound. The prudish male voice interrupts again, "Come on...stop that." The woman responds, "Stop what? That was just a woman lifting a piano." She continues mischievously, "She's getting in shape, because she knows in advance her best days for...". We now hear the sound of bedsprings squeaking suggestively. The prudish male voice interrupts, exasperatedly, "Hey! Quit it! That's offensive." The woman responds, "What's so offensive about a border collie prancing on a rusty trampoline?" The man responds, "That doesn't even make sense for an ovulation ad." The woman explains, "Of course it does. It makes you smile. Like the smiley face that appears on the Clearblue Digital Ovulation Test to let you know your most fertile days."

Unconvinced, the prudish male mutters, "I don't know. Something's up here." The woman responds suggestively, "Something is up. And just in time, too!" The prudish male voice protests, "Hey, that's sexual innuendo!" The woman retorts in conclusion, "I didn't say it, you did."

Results

Our restaging of Clearblue's pregnancy test provided a near perfect field experiment to evaluate the effectiveness of our cultural strategy. The digital pregnancy test had been launched in 2003 with considerable promotion spending to support the rollout. Product sales had quickly leveled out and no additional promotion spending had been planned. So the only change in Clearblue marketing was the broadcast of our television advertisement. We were able to measure the weekly sales impact at the chain-store level in each market. In the first weeks after the spot had been aired in the United Kingdom, sales shot up 74 percent, reversing nine months of decline. Weekly sales in Germany shot up 364 percent in the month that our campaign ran, reversing nearly a year of decline. In the United States, in the month following the ad's launch, sales of Clearblue's digital pregnancy test increased 80 percent. Clearblue achieved record sales at Wal-Mart—with sales up 53 percent versus the same period in the previous year—despite taking a 9 percent price increase, and following a year and a half of declining sales. Needless to say, it is exceedingly rare for a stand-alone ad campaign to achieve this level of incremental sales in a mature category.

Conclusion

We applied our cultural strategy model to make a provocative ideological statement in what had been a technology-driven category. Competitors had long relied upon mindshare branding to promote product benefits, and so had advanced an increasingly dated ideology without knowing it. We crafted the body-positive feminist strategy using cultural research that cost much less than the traditional research that Clearblue managers had been using and that took only a month to execute. We had only a small budget for research, strategy, and creative development and we had to get it right the first time.

The key in applying cultural strategy to a technology-driven category is to understand that benefits and symbolism are deeply intertwined. One of the most dysfunctional aspects of the mindshare branding model is that it treats the product's functional aspects and the product's image and emotional qualities as separate and independent components of the brand's value. This faulty logic leads to the conclusion that, if the product incorporates a new technology that really enhances functionality, then, to capture the value of this enhancement, the branding should make a direct rational claim to consumers, embedded in a creative idea that provides a nice emotional feel. In the pregnancy test category, this is what the incumbents had done for twenty-five years, and the result had been to hand the category over to private labels.

Our research has revealed over and over again that this assumption is dead wrong. Innovative cultural expressions work as a prism to reshape consumer perceptions of the product's features and benefits. This prismatic effect is particularly powerful in establishing the brand's dominion over a new technology. This is precisely what we were able to accomplish with Clearblue. Because Clearblue persuasively drama-tized body-positive feminism, consumers perceived that Clearblue was the digital technology leader, that it was the most reliable pregnancy test available, that it provided earlier results than the others, and that it was easier to use.

Notes

1. The Office of NIH History, *A Thin Blue Line: The History of the Pregnancy Test Kit* (National Institutes of Health, http://history.nih.gov/exhibits/thinblueline).
2. See www.vaginamonologues.co.uk/default.asp?contentID=576

11

Fat Tire Beer: Crossing the Cultural Chasm

Kim Jordan, the CEO of the New Belgium Brewing Company, had taken an educated gamble. The brewery's flagship Fat Tire Amber Ale was a favorite in the Rocky Mountain states. The brewery's sales topped a 3 percent share in Colorado, impressive numbers for a microbrewery, with total sales approaching $50 million. The beer had become wildly popular amongst Colorado's outdoor enthusiasts, who flocked to the mountains to mountain bike, hike, Nordic-, downhill-, and backcountry-ski, road bike, mountain climb, kayak, and fly fish. However, Jordan and her husband, Jeff Lebesch, owners of the privately held company, had much more expansive ambitions—to win over mass-market beer drinkers, to roll out distribution throughout the country, and eventually to trump Sam Adams as the nation's number one craft beer. So first the brewery expanded distribution into Texas; and then, in 2002, New Belgium entered Washington state and Oregon, with its sights set on the massive Californian market to the south. To support this expansion, the company invested in a risky and expensive expansion of the company's bottling lines that doubled the brewery's capacity.

But the expansion soon hit a snag. While Fat Tire sold well at first in Washington and Oregon, as drinkers were excited to try a new style of beer from an out-of-state brewery, sales soon began to sink. Local micro-breweries, which were much loved by beer drinkers, introduced copycat Belgian brown ales, and Fat Tire's share immediately went into a tailspin. Jordan worried that, unless Fat Tire sales picked up, she would not be able to pay out her capital costs, and, even worse, the brand would begin to lose the new distribution that her sales team had worked so hard to achieve. The company was struggling to figure out a strategy to translate its success in the mountain states to the larger market. In 2003, she hired us to develop a brand strategy that would allow the company to compete effectively in these major metropolitan markets.

Crossing the Cultural Chasm

New Belgium faced a problem that is common amongst entrepreneurial companies with successful niche businesses—what we call the *cultural chasm*. We review how social enterprises can hit cultural chasms in our analysis of Patagonia (see Chapter 6). We find that small niche companies and start-ups often run into the same problem. New Belgium had done very well in cultivating outdoors enthusiasts in the mountain states, the drinkers who had embraced Fat Tire from the beginning. But the company was struggling to extend this niche popularity to the mass market. In this sense, New Belgium's problem was no different from Jack Daniels in the early 1950s and Nike in the 1970s. Nike stalled because the company knew how to sell running shoes only to runners. But, when it culled from the runners' subculture one particular ideological facet that had tremendous appeal to the mass market—the runners' stubborn competitive tenacity to push themselves even though they were training alone—and presented it in a simple, inviting manner, Nike took off amongst mainstream consumers. The principle is a kind of cultural alchemy: the company converts an ideologically charged element of subcultural experience into a broader marketplace myth, to be enjoyed ritually by less-engaged mass-market consumers.

Cultural strategy offers a powerful tool for entrepreneurs looking to break into the mass market. By crossing the cultural chasm, young companies and niche businesses can transform their offerings into mainstream successes. We put this strategy to work for Fat Tire, a former niche offering, and it became the third largest craft beer in the USA, gaining rapidly on the two top brands, Sam Adams and Sierra Nevada. With minimal resources, we developed a cultural strategy, implemented it, and turned New Belgium's troubled markets around, putting the company on course to surpass its ambitious sales goals.

Background

Jeff Lebesch fell in love with Belgian beers on a bike tour of the famous monastic breweries of Belgium and became a dedicated home brewer, trying to emulate classic Belgian styles. He proved to be a talented brewmaster, impressing friends. So he and his wife, Kim, founded the New Belgium Brewing Company in 1991. Jeff, an engineer, constructed a brewery in their basement from old dairy equipment. Kim, a former social worker, sold beer to local merchants from the back of the family station wagon. She sold the beer as anyone in small business would do, by knocking on doors at bars and restaurants and building relationships. She spread the word at beer festivals and got as many drinkers as possible to try their beer. A decade later, the company still relied on this grass-roots approach for its marketing. As the brewery grew, Kim hired a sales team of "Beer Rangers"—gregarious young beer enthusiasts who wore ranger hats bearing the New Belgium trademark—to arrange events in local bars and hand out free beers to the prospects they encountered on the road. The company mounted a touring bike-centric festival, the Tour de Fat, which included a bicycle parade, indie music, vaudeville acts, and the usual beer tasting. Kim hired a marketing director, Greg Owsley, who had previously worked in sales for a Colorado organic produce company. We were intrigued to learn that New Belgium had only two senior managers who had professional training and experience for their current jobs: the brewmaster, whom they had hired from one of Belgium's famous breweries, and the national sales director, hired to coordinate the rollout, who had previously worked for the Boston Beer Company (brewer of Sam Adams).

For the West Coast expansion, Jordan and her team tried to execute the same sort of grass-roots relationship marketing approach that had worked so well in their mountain-state markets. But the problem with this approach was twofold. First, it was logistically impossible and far too expensive to reach a critical mass of prospects with these small, labor-intensive efforts. Second, whatever the scale of the approach, New Belgium was just hawking another craft beer in markets where there were already many dozens of excellent, well-established, local beers made by equally dedicated craft brewers. Fat Tire was just another great beer, and a non-local one at that. Without effective branding,

Fat Tire was doomed to fail. As the Washington and Oregon markets began to slip, Jordan assigned Owsley to find a consultant to help crack this problem.

Before he found us, Owsley had tried out two conventional marketing consultancies. The first of these specialized in unearthing "higher-order" "unconscious" feelings and metaphors—the approach that we critiqued in Chapter 1 as leading to the *commodity emotions trap*. Like many other qualitative market research firms, this firm relied upon "laddering," projective techniques, and visual imagery to push informants to elicit the most abstract concepts that they associate with the brand under study. This technique, called ZMET©, produced results that were similar to other mindshare market research techniques we have encountered: it led to concepts that were so abstract that they could have been applied to almost any brand. Because these laddering techniques force participants to rationalize their preferences in more and more abstract terms (by continually asking "why" to any response), they inevitably lead to very generic strategy advice.[1] In this instance, ZMET© churned out the following deep, tacit, consumer meanings that New Belgium should emphasize in Fat Tire branding:

BALANCE

CONNECTION

NATURE

JOURNEY

TRANSFORMATION

While such "feeling words" might have been embraced by a more typical MBA brand manager, Owsley immediately spotted the problem. The terms had no specific relation to beer, much less Fat Tire. They would have fit equally as well with a brand of yoga mats, a granola bar, a sports bra, or the state of Hawaii's tourism efforts. Rather than stake the brewery's financial health on this list of abstract adjectives, Owsley and Jordan felt it best to see what a second brand consultancy had to say.

Owsley hired another consulting firm, which conducted extensive market research in order to develop a different emotional branding strategy. The diagnostic work centered on a large quantitative branding study in the new Western markets. The research mostly focused on psychological concerns such as the awareness of New Belgium and its

Fat Tire brand, and the recall of the benefits that these brands "owned" in consumers' minds. The consultants discovered that West Coast beer-drinkers had some modest associations with Fat Tire, but no idea about the company brand, New Belgium Brewing. This was hardly surprising, since the name Fat Tire was present in big letters on the six-packs, but the New Belgium name could hardly be found, and the same was true of the tap handles in bars, which used the single-speed bike used to reinforce the Fat Tire name visually. The consulting firm's first recommendation, then, was to rename the brewery the Fat Tire Brewery to take advantage of this awareness.

They also discovered that Fat Tire was associated with the Rocky Mountains and so recommended that the branding should make effective use of that linkage. By owning this emotional territory, the consulting firm suggested, Fat Tire could significantly enhance its branding in the West Coast markets. Owsley had even less trouble spotting a fundamental problem the second time around. It would be at least as difficult for Fat Tire to "own" the emotional territory of the Rocky Mountains as it would be for the brand to own generic metaphors such as "balance," "connection," and "transformation." Coors had spent the previous thirty years developing its own association with the Rocky Mountains through mind-numbing repetition. By now, such branding would strike even a neophyte customer as an obvious cliché.

Out of frustration, Owsley and Jordan reverted back to their old ways, but gave it their own emotional branding spin—they wrote a manifesto for New Belgium stating that the company branding would be built around "relationships." When we signed up, New Belgium was focusing its entire marketing effort on building relationships with consumers. While certainly an improvement over "balance" or "Rocky Mountains," "relationships" was just as generic and just as unlikely to distinguish New Belgium from a crowd of craft brews whose owners were also very customer-relationship oriented.

Owsley found us through a *Harvard Business Review* article one of us had written. He thought that a cultural approach made a lot more sense than the conventional marketing ideas offered by the other two consultants. As on-again-off-again home brewers, we were excited to sign on. We set up the focal strategic problem in terms of the cultural chasm: how do we selectively leverage Fat Tire's considerable credibility in the mountain states to craft a cultural expression that would resonate powerfully with the mass-market target in the major metropolitan areas on the West Coast?

Cultural Orthodoxy: Artisanal Connoisseurship

In 2003, the American craft beer segment consisted of nearly 1,500 breweries that together produced about 3 percent of the beer consumed in the United States. This incredibly diverse group of small breweries represented a remarkable turn of events. Previously, the market had been dominated by mass-market industrial beer produced by a handful of conglomerates, such as Anheuser-Busch, Miller, and Coors, which marketed extremely "light lagers" that were cheap to produce and offensive to no one. These virtually indistinguishable beers were the result of long-term efforts to eke out higher margins in a price-sensitive category, which forced the big breweries to shift to cheap fillers such as rice and corn. Beer was an industrial commodity, just as was coffee in the post-war era, as we report in our analysis of Starbucks in Chapter 5.

We detail in the Starbucks analysis the social disruption that drove Starbucks' success: the demographic shift beginning in the late 1980s in which a large *cultural capital cohort* entered the adult marketplace demanding more sophisticated cultural expressions in their lifestyle goods. Craft beers catered to this same cohort, but skewed toward males, because men drank a lot more beer than women. The revolution in craft beer followed precisely the same path as coffee, diffusing out of the artisanal–cosmopolitan subculture whose epicenter formed in the Bay Area in the late 1960s. In 1965, Fritz Maytag, a Stanford University graduate and heir to the Maytag white goods fortune, rescued San Francisco's tiny Anchor Steam Brewery from imminent bankruptcy and brewed beers using a frontier-era "steam" recipe that resulted in a more flavorful beer than the typical light lagers. The artisanal–cosmopolitan crowd loved this odd beer. A decade later, in 1976, Jack McAuliffe launched the New Albion Brewery in Sonoma County north of San Francisco. McAuliffe was the Alfred Peet of craft beers, launching the brewery that would inspire hundreds of beer aficionados to start their own micro-breweries and brewpubs.[2] He produced beers that were more distinctive and esoteric than Maytag's brews.

New Albion Porter became known for its extremely complex layers of flavor. New Albion Stout was the only domestically brewed stout for sale in the country at that time, and its taste was challenging even to beer connoisseurs.

Inspired by these pioneers, beer-crazed entrepreneurs started up dozens of new craft breweries, each one small, independent, and offering its own twists on old-world brewing recipes. The craft-brewing renaissance took off in California, spreading northward up the coast, then in the mid-1980s eastward to Colorado, Vermont, and beyond. By the time New Belgium was considering its regional rollout, craft beer was an established segment in every state in the country, with most liquor stores and bars offering a good selection. And these beers did particularly well in the pioneering markets of northern California, western Oregon, and Washington state.

From the beginning, this segment organized around the same ideology as Peet's coffee and the original Starbucks: what we term *artisanal–cosmopolitan connoisseurship.* It is no coincidence that the Bay Area was the initial epicenter. Beer and coffee were two of the early and most important food and drink categories to be aestheticized as the tastes of cultural elites trickled down to an increasingly educated middle class looking to express a new kind of cultural sophistication.

Craft brewers and their insider customers were motivated by the same ideology that Alfred Peet was advancing in coffee. Their goal was to make the most flavorful and interesting beers, not lowest-common-denominator swill. They gave their attention to ingredient provenance, not bland, anonymous filler. They made use of pre-modern styles and brewing techniques, not mass industrial technology. Scale was much less important to them than making a delicious and intriguing beer of the highest quality. They rejected the processed, the artificial, and the preserved, while celebrating the perishable, the fresh, and the natural. They scorned corporate notions of consistency and standardization and championed the idiosyncratic and the "flawed," often adding personal touches to each beer. One eccentric Bay Area brewer, for instance, became celebrated for his fall Pumpkin Ale. Craft brewers celebrated the handmade over the factory produced, the small batch over the mass scaled, and patience over speed. They defended brewing as a craft skill, learned over years by apprenticeship, and rejected the notion that it could be reduced to an assembly-line process.

All the major craft beer brands became proficient at communicating this ideology, using very similar cultural codes. The Boston Beer Company—an aggressive marketer—soon dominated the category with its flagship Sam Adams brand. While selling nearly ten million cases of Sam Adams Lager a year, the company still conveyed the artisanal–cosmopolitan connoisseurship ideology across all its marketing. James Koch, the company founder, narrated low-fidelity ads in which he recounted how the recipe for Sam Adams was handed down by his great-great-grandfather, a St Louis brewer. He explained that his beer adhered to rigorous German purity laws that limited the beer's ingredients to hops, malt, yeast, and water, and boasted about the prizes that Sam Adams had won in various beer festivals. The brewery engaged in an aggressive insider strategy, creating a range of increasingly esoteric "competition beers"—such as beers laced with Belgian chocolate—aimed at sustaining the brand's credibility in artisanal–cosmopolitan insider circles. In media coverage, Koch knocked the industrial brewers for using inferior ingredients and lowest-common-denominator recipes and for being motivated more by money than by any real interest in brewing.

Sierra Nevada, the number two craft beer in 2003, advanced the cultural orthodoxy without resorting to mass media. The brewery conveyed its artisanal–cosmopolitan connoisseurship through their choice of old-world brewing styles and recipes, their product names, their label design, their brewery location and design, their brewery tours, and their entry into competitions at craft-beer festivals. The folksy, hand-painted watercolor labels communicated connoisseur details such as the use of generous quantities of Cascade hops that give the ale its fragrant bouquet and spicy flavor. To further communicate artisanal connoisseurship, the brewery launched a variety of specialty brews, such as a hoppy and potent Celebration Ale, a porter, a wheat beer, a stout, a barley wine, a blonde ale, and a pale bock.

Most craft breweries emphasized the craft skills of their brewers and their preference for fresh, natural, fussed-over ingredients. They attributed their creative experimentation and personalized idiosyncratic signatures to their pre-industrial, old-world brewing traditions.

As once-esoteric beers such as Pale Ale became standard craft fare, brewers pushed toward ever-more obscure recipes, such as German Kosch and Marzen styles, Belgian "white" beer, French "farmhouse" ales, and Belgian abbey ales. As well, a hop arms race broke out, as breweries raced to make the most bitter ale possible. The brand leading the hophead revolution, Dogfish Head, relied upon exactly the same cultural codes as the first wave of craft breweries.

When we signed onto the strategy project, New Belgium was playing the same game, mimicking the cultural orthodoxy of the craft beer category. The brewery did its best to invest its beers with the aura of artisanal–cosmopolitan connoisseurship. It glorified old-world beer recipes, created defiantly challenging beers, experimented with esoteric ingredients not usually found in beer such as lemon verbena and Thai kaffir leaf, and aged beer in barrels, just as wineries do. Its 1554 "black ale" came from a centuries-old recipe that New Belgium brewers had discovered in an old Belgian brewer's manual. New Belgium's labels were produced in the same folksy handmade style as many of its competitors, with the same range of cute homespun names. They produced comedic, amateurish posters and coasters typical of a craft brewery. New Belgium did make great beer. But, then, so did dozens of other top-notch craft breweries. Their Belgian recipes, once distinctive, were no longer so, as dozens of breweries were even more experimental and esoteric, outplaying New Belgium on these key dimensions of cultural capital.

Fat Tire was different though. It did not play the cultural capital game. Rather it happened to be a very palatable slightly sweet beer that many drinkers who were not connoisseurs liked to drink. So it had the potential to break out of the craft category and become a mass-market beer. But, as Fat Tire won some initial accolades, local craft breweries were quick to offer their own take on the Belgian brown style, with knock-offs that drinkers often liked just as much as Fat Tire. Many craft beer drinkers favor local breweries, and these breweries also had powerful distribution clout, controlling a high percentage of the bar and restaurant taps. So Fat Tire was handicapped. If New Belgium was to compete outside Colorado on the quality of its beer alone, it would probably lose. Instead of trying to convince drinkers that New Belgium had better beer, our approach was to build an innovative cultural expression that outmaneuvered a marketplace saturated with artisanal–cosmopolitan beer branding.

Ideological Opportunity: The Ache of the BoBo

Our aim was to develop a new ideology for craft beer, one that would powerfully resonate with our target drinkers if we expressed it through the right myth and cultural codes. Demographically, our target drinkers were highly educated male professionals and managers, mostly between 25 and 45 years old, who made a good income and so could afford craft beer priced 50 percent higher than domestic brands. The import demographic was important to us as well, as there was considerable switching between craft and import beers; import drinkers were similar to our target drinkers, but not quite as wealthy or as well educated. The bullseye customer in our major metro areas would be the Microsoft designer in Seattle, the Silicon Valley IT engineer, the Dallas lawyer, or a Los Angeles creative director—a successful career-oriented male urban professional who drinks beer after work and on weekends when socializing. By 2003, craft beers had become widely diffused, expressing cultural capital through their artisanal-cosmopolitan ideology. So our specific goal was to devise an innovative new expression of cultural capital. To do so, we needed to pay close attention to emerging desires for ideology amongst this group.

The Dot-Com Era's Creative Rebel Discourse

The dot-com boom of the late 1990s fundamentally changed how the cultural capital cohort envisioned their careers, setting afire the "bohemian" aspects of their identity project with respect to their occupations. Previously, the upper-middle-class occupational goal had been to snag a prestigious and well-paying job: a great investment banking house, a powerful law firm, a reputable research hospital, an industry-leading engineering firm. All that changed when the business press began to fill with stories of super-smart young entrepreneurs who were rejecting the rigid bureaucracies of big companies and their incrementalist approach to business in favor of entrepreneurial start-ups pursuing wildly imaginative ideas with reckless energy and creative willpower. Their "offices" reflected their imaginative mindset:

replacing rows of glass-walled offices and cubicles, they favored bare spaces equipped with foosball tables, bean-bag chairs, chill-out spaces, whiteboards, and other brainstorming supplies.

The godfather of this bohemian takeover of management was Steve Jobs. The 1998 launch spot of Apple's "Think Different" campaign captured Jobs's "creative rebel" ideology perfectly:

Here's to the crazy ones, the misfits, the rebels, the troublemakers, the round pegs in the square holes...the ones who see things differently—they're not fond of rules...You can quote them, disagree with them, glorify or vilify them, but the only thing you can't do is ignore them because they change things... they push the human race forward, and while some may see them as the crazy ones, we see genius, because the ones who are crazy enough to think that they can change the world, are the ones who do.

Prestige and a good salary were no longer sufficient. The cultural capital cohort were inspired to find fulfillment by expressing their passionate creativity, unorthodox sensibilities, and intellectual fire-power in their work and avocations. In other words, in the late 1990s, the social class game for those who aspired to cultural capital hit an inflationary inflection point. Whereas the 1990s had been dominated by the cultural capital cohort's quest for culturally sophisticated goods to sprinkle across their lifestyle, now that was no longer good enough. With the consecration of Silicon Valley upstarts as the new ideal, this cohort were given a strong cultural push to "live" their ideology in their work life, rather than simply to buy goods that expressed it. They felt it necessary to do something—in the words of Jobs—"insanely great" with their lives.

Trapped by Technopoly

This new identity project ran head-on into a basic structural problem, however. The dot-coms went bust, and, once the foosball tables, pinball machines, and espresso bars had been cleared out, few jobs remained that allowed for this kind of work, much less demanded it. The careers that offered good salaries and prestige were the same as before: these were jobs that required the rote application of professional skills, which needed to be done well, but were seldom particularly creative or likely to change the world. Even more problematic, many of these occupations were now subject to the same rationalizing forces of process engineering that had made blue-collar and service work so stressful and unsatisfying in the previous two decades.[3] The rationalizing calculi used by private equity investors and M&A bankers as they sought to "extract value" from assets in the market were industriously applied to all professions, instilling a new form of competition to push the efficiency of middle-class labor as far as it could go. Rationalizing management technologies had taken over with no countervailing forces in sight—what critics called *technopoly*.[4] Even doctors, once the most protected of professionals, were now squeezed by HMOs, insurance companies, and hospital management. They were booking patients in fifteen-minute increments, 8 a.m. to 6 p.m., and watching the clock to keep them moving through. No more Wednesday golf outings. The life of lawyers, engineers, and middle managers was no different.

On the job, technopoly created extraordinary competitive pressures. If you did not work harder than others and constantly keep up with the new knowledge and techniques required to do your job most effectively, your position was at risk. Americans now worked the longest hours in post-war history, and professionals and managers worked the longest of any class of American workers. Mobile information technology meant that professional jobs were increasingly a 24-hours-a-day, 7-days-a-week proposition: at first laptops and affordable home Internet, then Blackberries, then WiFi (and now iPhones). Work became virtually inescapable, regardless of how far one traveled away from it.

Despite these pressures, escape was never a legitimate possibility for most of the cultural capital cohort, for the pay was often excellent and golden handcuffs tied them to their jobs: the luxury dining and exotic vacations, the mortgages on townhouses and urban lofts. Not to mention that they relied heavily on their friends in the same predicament, for it was these rat-race-infested social networks that provided them with respect and secured their place in the status hierarchy.

The Ache of the BoBo

How was one to be a creative rebel, pursuing the insanely great, in a world of work dominated by technopoly? The cultural capital cohort had no time or mental capacity to devote themselves to what they most yearned to do: the construction of self through creative acts. They suffered from a kind of attention-deficit disorder, the cultural economy of distraction. Carving out time from technopoly jobs to dedicate oneself passionately to creative acts seemed to be a pipedream. Many had become cultural dilettantes, heavily dependent on the various cultural intermediaries who act as specialists directing their tastes and activities. To characterize this widespread anxiety for our clients, we borrowed David Brooks's felicitous phrase for the cultural capital cohort—the Bourgeois-Bohemian, or BoBo for short. Hence we termed this profound contradiction *the ache of the BoBo.*

Media Myth: "I Downshifted to Pursue my Passionate Avocation"

We were convinced that we had discovered a great ideological opportunity, but how to respond to it? We next looked for clues in our target's mass culture preferences to see if we could find the salves they were relying upon to mend their BoBo ache. We did not find the usual books and films and television programs (though, soon after, many avocation-focused cable channels and websites would jump into this space). Instead, we found that our BoBos were very inspired by a particular kind of story that they enjoyed reading in their newspapers, magazines, and favorite websites. The stories fitted a consistent formula: they featured BoBos who had ditched their successful big city careers finally to pursue their creative passions by committing themselves full-time to avocations that promised little in the way of economic rewards. For instance, an investment banker who had thrown in the towel, was apprenticed with a famed cheesemaker in Normandy, purchased 50 acres in rural Maine, and located a heritage breed of goats to populate the pastures, with the goal of making the most interesting chèvre ever to grace American tables. Such stories usually took place somewhere in beautiful pastoral places such as mountain towns, the quaint New England countryside, coastal beach towns, or the desert.

We noted that this genre was taking off amongst BoBos in the United Kingdom as well. Hugh Fearnley-Whittingstall launched his River Cottage television series in 1998. Hugh was a well-pedigreed upper-middle-class citydweller (Eton College, then Oxford) who abandoned the conventional Oxbridge lifestyle to buy an old farm in the West Country and pursue a downshifted lifestyle. However, ever the BoBo, he applied his passionate interest in food to become an extremely energetic and knowledgeable advocate for the return of preindustrial agricultural practices, cooking techniques, and tastes. An early advocate of eating every part of the slaughtered animal, Hugh made it his goal to sensualize and aestheticize this kind of cooking. BoBos in London were enthralled, and soon enough Hugh was imported into the USA, taking off just as our project began. This genre provided us with a very helpful clue as to how to compose a cultural strategy for Fat Tire that would respond to the ache of the BoBo.

What to Do with the Mountain Outdoor Adventure Subculture?

Beginning in the 1980s, American mountain states were increasingly overrun with outdoor enthusiasts, sporting the latest hiking gear, riding handmade mountain bikes, carrying fly-fishing rods, driving with skis and kayaks mounted to their car tops. Mountain towns such as Crested Butte, Telluride, Durango, Jackson, Moab, Truckee, and Flag staff became conspicuously transformed by kayak festivals, white-water rafting operations, mountain-biking stores, and snowboard rental shops. Nearby college towns such as Boulder, Fort Collins, Missoula, and Bozeman experienced the same transformation.

For Coloradans, what was most important about Fat Tire was that it served as a fits-like-a-glove prop for these adventures. You had your Yeti mountain bike and Black Diamond back country skis, and a duffel full of REI gear, all of which you stuffed into and onto your Subaru wagon. When the CFS on the Upper Ark hit 4000, when fresh powder dumped in the backcountry, or when the bike trails were tacky and snow free, off you went. Thanks to the beer's name, its watercolor of a single-speed bicycle on its label, its Colorado mountains provenance, and its artisanal production, Fat Tire perfectly evoked this mountain outdoor adventure subculture. As a result, subculturalists had adopted Fat Tire throughout Colorado and the surrounding states as a stalwart prop for their adventures. You took along a six-pack of Fat Tire, or ended a great outing with the draft that was waiting for you at the local mountain-town bar.

We knew that Fat Tire was a flag for the mountain outdoor adventure subculture, and that Bobos felt ideological yearnings for beautiful pastoral places such as mountain towns. Our cultural strategy model encouraged us to mythologize the elements of the subculture that were most ideologically resonant with our BoBo target, just as Nike had done with the running subculture in the late 1970s. This was the consumer "truth" within the subculture. And, if we had followed this path, we would have hit a dead end.

The problem was that the world of outdoor mountain sports was already extremely commercialized, having become one of the most pilfered subcultures throughout the 1990s. It was the natural ideological terrain for outdoor-adventure sports brands; Patagonia, North Face, Oakley, Nike, Reebok, Adidas, and Burton had been mining these cultural materials long before we started our project. And so were brands like Mountain Dew, Heineken, Shell Oil, Gatorade, and a whole range of automobiles, none of which had much relation to mountain sports.

Instead of building the brand from the "subculture outwards," we returned to the opposite question: what is it about the ideological stew that was so distinctive in these mountain-town subcultures, woven into the activities of the locals, that our BoBo target finds so appealing? Our study of BoBos and their fascination with "downshift to pursue my passionate avocation" stories revealed the best linkage. Our last analysis examined the brewery itself to see how the company should figure in the concept.

New Belgium's Cultural Assets

We spent a great deal of time at the brewery interacting with the staff and watching the company operate, and our experience reinforced and embellished the strategic direction in which we were moving. Few of the brewery employees were active participants in the mountain outdoor adventure subculture—the senior managers seemed to have little time ever to escape the Front Range. However, the company was an exemplar of the media myth that BoBos so loved.

The brewery's founders were both professionals who had given up their careers to pursue the avocation that they were passionate about, regardless of where it took them. They viewed brewing as an eclectic pursuit, where the fun came from experimenting with beer styles and improvising brewing equipment. Very few of the staff were trained professionally for their jobs, and Kim and Jeff liked it that way. For instance, the COO (promoted from CFO) joined the company as a graduate student in philosophy.

A Company of Amateurs

The company widely adopted Jeff's DIY all-consuming passion to become an excellent brewer. It was assumed that people could become superb at whatever was their company assignment through DIY learning and trial and error, if only they were given the free rein to do so. One of the company's key employees told us a story about how Jeff had pushed him to disassemble and rebuild a piece of complex German brewing equipment with no instructions or direction from Jeff (though Jeff kept a diagram in his desk just in case he messed up). He was eventually able to do so, inspiring his passion to become expert in the seemingly most trivial details of the brewing process.

Pastoral Organization as Antidote to Technopoly

New Belgium was organized as an extended family of people drawn together to work in a much more communal and humane way than the dominant technopoly model. Drawing on her social-work background, Jordan opened the brewery to families and advocated humane work hours. The company provided employees with stock and encouraged nonstop participation in its local community and the markets it serves. The brewery looks more like a modern ski lodge than a corporate facility, sitting near the banks of the Poudre la Cache River with dozens of single-speed bikes parked out front (employees receive a free bike on their first anniversary). Prospective employees were required to perform a creative act of some sort to get hired. They painted, they played music, they wrote essays.

The Single-Speed Cruiser

This idea of the pastoral antidote came to life in New Belgium's design icon—the single-speed fat-tire bike. The bike was a powerful symbol of human-scaled technology: simply designed, easy to work on, the antithesis of high-end bikes decked out with gizmos the riders do not need. The cruiser was a mythic time machine, harkening back to an era when technology was far less invasive in human life.[5]

Cultural Strategy: Community of Pastoral Amateurs

We synthesized the insights from all these analyses to develop a novel ideology for Fat Tire to champion that would respond directly to the Ache of the BoBo—what we called the *community of pastoral amateurs*. To focus our efforts, we wrote a twenty-page manifesto that we summarize here.

The Amateur

An amateur pursues an art, science, craft, study, or athletic activity for the joy of doing it, because it is intrinsically interesting. Amateurism is the opposite of professionalism. Amateurs are not interested in formal institutions and status therein. Rather they are organized informally. They approach the activity with a particular attitude: playful, whimsical, zealous, even obsessive. Amateurs are willing to take risks and plow down blind allies because theirs is not a careerist profession. They are not trying to climb to the top of the hill the fastest. The fun is in the creative pursuit. Because they do not identify themselves with a formal profession or set of institutional guidelines, they can be stubbornly iconoclastic. Our ideal type is the iconoclastic British amateur often portrayed on BBC documentaries: a bureaucrat by day, he fills all other available hours of the day with the pursuit of a singular lifelong eclectic passion. Say, early Mesopotamian oil jugs. The interest is entirely intrinsic and leads to wild opinions and sometimes strange diversions. However, because his passion fires such industrious and sustained efforts, our hero becomes one of the world's leading experts on the topic, all without a degree.

Pastoral

Pastoral is, in the first instance, a place of natural beauty where man exists in perfect harmony with nature. In the United States, the mountain towns of the West are quintessential pastoral places. Even more important is the idea that our avocations should free us from the constraints of technopoly, allowing us to pursue our passions free of the iron cage of rationalizing technologies. Pastoral pursuits are those that express a utopian resolution of man's interactions with technology. Pastoral activities are activities that demonstrate that technologies can be harnessed and humanized to improve the quality of human life in harmony with nature.

New Belgium is a community of pastoral amateurs who brew beer amongst other avocations. We approach pastoral amateurism as a life philosophy, an approach to living that can be applied to any craft or activity.
We celebrate quixotic playful exploration. Pastoral amateurs investigate their chosen domain with intensity. But this is not a masculine conquest. This is a playground, not a frontier.
We champion wildly non-instrumental investments of time. Pastoral amateurs' inquisitive ethos means that they will take whatever time it takes to learn what needs learning, pursue the paths of inquiry that are open, experimenting to get things right, attending to the details.
We believe in humanizing technology. Pastoral amateurs assert human control over technology.
We embrace brash iconoclasm. Pastoral amateurs are not afraid to do something for the first time. "An enamored amateur need not be a genius to stay out of the ruts he has never been trained in." (D. Boorstin)
Our approach is communal, not competitive. Pastoral amateurs live their passion amongst fellow travelers, excited and supportive of the accomplishments of fellow traveler amateurs.
We prefer childlike innocence to jaded professionalism. Untainted by professionalism, pastoral amateurs have a naive innocence about them.

We built a comprehensive brand platform, which directed everything from the names of new beers, to communications, sales protocols, and the design of tourists' experience when they visited the brewery. The ethos of amateurism extended to everything from website design to coasters to events such as a "ride-in" film festival that featured amateur film-makers, an array of new products such as highly idiosyncratic seasonal beers, and the presentation of online videos celebrating local amateurs as friends of New Belgium. But, to turn around the West Coast markets, we needed to create some sort of mass cultural expression of the pastoral amateur ethos. Our creative challenge was to devise a pastoral amateur call to arms, calling out to BoBos in Seattle, Silicon Valley, Santa Monica, San Diego, and points beyond, allowing them to dream a bit that they too might some day have a chance to give it all for their avocation rather than their 8-to-8 job. Given the vast target we needed to talk to, and the kind of story we needed to tell, we knew that we needed to be working with film, still by far the most compelling storytelling medium. So we convinced New Belgium to invest in its first (and probably only) ad campaign.

Selecting Cultural Codes: The Tinkerer

The Tinkerer Character
We wanted to tell a story of quixotic exploration, the humanizing of technology, and the kind of freedom with time that only a child now has. We thought that the best way to tell it was through a simple character study. It would feature a man engaged in his avocation, working at a leisurely pace with no time pressures, no intrusions from the outside world. He would be driven by his love for the hobby as opposed to status. The study would show him existing in harmony with nature, in a rural setting, and living in a slow-paced locale—the antithesis to fast-paced city life. The study would romanticize manual, get-your-hands-dirty, tinkering activity—the antithesis of abstract, cerebral, professional work. To cast this character, whom we came to call "the tinkerer," we wanted to avoid a stereotypical mountain out-doors character, or any other stereotype for that matter. To heighten the mythical nature of the spot, that it could be about anyone, we found a young Czech man who happened to be traveling through Boulder, Colorado, and used him in all the spots as our lead character, never speaking a word.

Single-Speed Bikes
We decided upon old single-speed bicycles as the object of his obsession—he is a man who strips down old multi-gear bicycles and converts them into single-speed cruisers (an esoteric hobby at the time, which has since become much more popular—building what is now known amongst bike enthusiasts as a "fixie" for fixed speed). The single-speed bicycle was a powerful pastoral amateur

symbol, and Fat Tire owned it, so it was an obvious choice. Around this time, people who imbibed in the pastoral amateur ethos around the country had begun to embrace single-speed bicycles as a symbol of human-scaled technology, a statement against the encroachment of technology on their cultural traditions and on nature.

Mountain-Town Setting

We wanted to romanticize the pastoral aspects of mountain towns in an utterly authentic but also very romantic way that would pull at the heartstrings of our BoBo beer-quaffing prospects. We worked with New Belgium to assemble a short list of quintessential Colorado mountain towns. The director for the ads, Jake Scott, spent several weeks driving around the state scouting the locations. Most of these were old mining towns in the middle of the mountains, now settled by anyone who could scratch out a living to stay in such beautiful places: Creede, Silverton, Salida, Crestone, and Paonia. We vetoed the most popular destination cities such as Aspen, Vail, Steamboat Springs, and Telluride, because these places had been so heavily commercialized and overtaken by the rich. We settled upon Paonia, Colorado, a town of 1,497 on the Gunnison River, at the foot of the Grand Mesa. The highlight of the Paonia calendar was a three-day Mountain Harvest Festival with music, poetry, an art show, and classes on canning and raising livestock. The town's combination of beautiful natural scenery, rusty old farm equipment, and dilapidated miners' homes evoked a period in American history when life was much simpler and less rationalized, when technology was held at bay. The setting evoked an era that seemed artfully imprecise in time: it brought to mind the early twentieth century as much as it did the current day.

Psych-Folk Soundtrack

To enhance the mythic nature of the campaign, we decided against dialogue. Instead we would run a soundtrack from beginning to end, which would need to work as hard as the visuals to conjure up the ideology. In recent years, a new genre of lo-fi folk-influenced rock had emerged, reinvigorating the original 1960s genre of Graham Parsons, The Byrds, The Grateful Dead, and others. These musicians often celebrated the pastoral in their lyrics and sometimes directly critiqued the encroachment of technology. They also celebrated the ideal of amateurism through their production values and instrumentation. Artists would employ conspicuously DIY production techniques—for instance, recording with a handheld cassette machine and leaving in the tape's hissing sounds, or trying out new instruments with which they had little familiarity. One of the new indie folk musicians who particularly evoked the pastoral amateur ethos was Devendra Banhardt, then a Colorado-based artist. Devendra's combination of steadily thrumming, finger-style guitar, lo-fi production techniques, and naive musings about the likes of crows, cows, pigs, and flies embodied precisely the pastoral amateur ideology that we wanted to convey, so we made arrangements with him to use his music for all our spots.

Tagline: Follow Your Folly, Ours is Beer

Because our creative idea would focus on pastoral amateur avocations other than beer, we felt that we needed a tagline that would make the linkage back to the brewery and the beer very explicit. We wanted to say "here's the kind of ideology we aspire to, we celebrate all who pursue the same kind of thing, and this is exactly the ideology that is at the heart of our brewery and the beer that you're drinking." Through lots of creative brainstorming, we came up with a call-to-arms declaration— "Follow Your Folly"—that was our part-serious part-tongue-in-cheek response to Nike's "Just Do It" and other hypercompetitive taglines so common at the time. To this we added a hook to say that we were part of this movement as well, not the leaders but fellow travelers who shared the same ideology: "Ours is Beer." So each spot would end with a very simple low fidelity shot of a Fat Tire poured into a glass with the tagline.

The Tinkerer Anthem

We made four ads, but our efforts were focused particularly on one anthemic launch spot, since we had such a small media budget. The Tinkerer relied upon a whimsical, childlike song performed by Devendra called "At the Hop." The spot begins with our protagonist—the bicycle tinkerer—arriving at a yard sale in front of a rural Colorado home. He waves a neighborly hello to the house's owner, a 70-year-old man who is relaxing on his porch with his wife. He wanders through the yard looking at discarded picture frames, distressed cabinets, and vintage soda-pop cases until he spots a rusted old bicycle. The bicycle clearly requires a lot of work, but he sees potential in it, gets a gleam in his eye, and motions to buy it. The owner waves him off, refusing payment for the bike. He returns the wave and leaves.

We next see the Tinkerer at home in his workshop in a converted barn. It appears to be well used—this is clearly a place where he spends a lot of time. He looks at the bicycle studiously and then begins methodically to take it apart. We cut between long ponderous shots that show him captivated by his hobby and short, quirky shots that show him following his whims. In one shot, he tries on a hat that he has made from handlebars. In another, he looks out from atop his barn.

The Tinkerer removes the old racing handlebars and inspects a new crankshaft. We see parts drop to the floor as he works. He lovingly polishes the old frame and installs an old leather saddle. A series of cuts demonstrate that many hours have passed. We see through the window that night has fallen. We see the warm light of the barn under a dark midnight sky.

Finally, the next day, we see the Tinkerer, his toils finished, heading out to try his restored mid-century red cruiser. We see him push down on the pedal, then ride the bike out into the road. His dog follows for a few steps, but soon the Tinkerer is on his own. He picks up speed and feels the wind in his hair. As we see the Colorado countryside rise up around him, the spot cuts to a Fat Tire poured into a glass with the end line "Follow Your Folly, Ours Is Beer."

A second spot in the series called "Night Ride" carried the mysterious Tinkerer's story forward. It is shot at night, under a starry Colorado sky, and through the entire spot we hear a quiet, lyrical, song by Devendra. The spot opens with the Tinkerer toiling away in his workshop. He is working on his bicycle again, this time tinkering with another symbol of human-scaled technology—the old-fashioned headlamp connected to a dynamo power generator, the kind that generates electricity as it rolls against a spinning tire. We then see him heading out into the night on his bicycle to try out the headlamp. He peddles down a dark mountain road, lit only by his bike light. We see that he is approaching a steep climb. Because the headlamp is powered by the bicycle's speed, it becomes faint as the tinkerer slowly pedals his way up the hill. As he struggles in his climb, the light flickers on and off. We see the strain in his face as he approaches the top, but, as he crests the hill, he is overcome by a sense of satisfaction. He coasts down the other side of the hill into the darkness. As he picks up speed, the whole road begins to light up. Then, just as he reaches the bottom, he leans back in his seat and swings his legs out, experiencing again a moment of pure bliss. "Follow Your Folly, Ours Is Beer" the title reads, as we cut to the tinkerer smiling in the light of the bicycle headlamp. The spot ends with a Fat Tire poured into a glass.

Film and Editing

In both spots, we infused a sense of amateur experimentation through the editing, camera work, and visual stylings. Handheld camera techniques and the montage editing gave the stories a spontaneous, idiosyncratic feel: the cutting between images followed the flow of the music and explored artistic visual juxtapositions rather than adhering to a scripted structure. The camera lenses, the film stock, and the color-correcting gave the films a grainy, timeless feel, romanticizing the golden pastoral daytime scenery and the expansive Colorado nighttime skies.

Results

Our clients at New Belgium were brave to take on the great expense of this effort and, even more important, to embrace a marketing technique—mass advertising—that they initially disliked and dreaded, no different from Phil Knight back in the day. We needed to demonstrate that we had accomplished what we had claimed we could do from the beginning: crossing the cultural chasm to bring Fat Tire's ideology to a mass market of beer drinkers far removed from the mountain towns of the Rockies. So we set up a field experiment, dividing ten media markets into two sets of five that were equivalent in terms of both demographics and Fat Tire sales. We ran the campaign in five markets and ran no advertising in the other five. Sales in test markets increased 37 percent in the first six months versus a modest 2 percent increase in control markets, even though the campaign ran for only fourteen weeks. We calculated that the campaign would pay for itself with an 11 percent increase and so the campaign was making money for the brewery from the start. And there were other benefits as well. Part of the initial lift-off in the first month was that the grocery trade was so impressed by the effort that the New Belgium's sales force was able to drive many more feature ads and displays for Fat Tire along with the brewery's secondary beers such as Sunshine Wheat beer and 1554 black ale. In addition, the momentum of the ad campaign allowed it to convince grocers to cut in new distribution points for these secondary beers. Sales of New Belgium's top secondary beers increased by over 50 percent as a result.

Conclusion

New Belgium is a great example of an entrepreneurial venture trapped in a niche market because the company had hit a cultural chasm. New Belgium had become so adept at relationship marketing that it had trouble seeing that another approach was needed to build the Fat Tire brand on the West Coast. In this respect, New Belgium's position in the early 2000s was no different from Starbucks in the 1980s, Nike in the 1970s, or Jack Daniel's in the early 1950s. All four companies delivered a high-quality product that sold predominantly to a niche subcultural market. Because these companies understood their appeal as offering a better mousetrap—connoisseur coffee, the smoothest whiskey, the most technologically advanced shoe, the most interesting and finely crafted Belgian beers—they could not envision that the mass-market prospects were much more interested in an innovative cultural expression than in fine-grained product differences. This is what we term the cultural chasm. As a result, all four companies struggled to compete in the mass market with competitors that had superior resources.

Crossing the cultural chasm requires moving from a marketplace dominated by *insider* customers, who often hold considerable expertise in the category, to what we call *follower* customers, who simply want an accessible way to tap into a valued cultural expression that the product can credibly represent.[6] For New Belgium, this shift required stepping away from the hardcore beer aficionados, who were the opinion leaders in the craft brew market, and their artisanal–cosmopolitan ideology, to consider what value the brand could offer to the cultural capital cohort in order to satiate their particular ideological thirst.

Notes

1. For an academic critique of this sort of market research technique, see Douglas B. Holt, "Post-Structuralist Lifestyle Analysis: Conceptualizing the Social Patterning of Consumption in Postmodernity," *Journal of Consumer Research*, 23 (Mar. 1997), 326–49.

2. Maureen Ogle, *Ambitious Brew: The Story of American Beer* (Orlando, FL: Harvest Books, 2007), 297.

3. Jill Andresky Fraser, The *White-Collar Sweatshop: The Deterioration of Work and its Reward in Corporate America* (New York: Norton, 2002).

4. This idea was most effectively formulated by social theorist Jaques Ellul in his *The Technological Society* (New York: Vintage, 1967), which in turn harks back to seminal ideas offered by Lewis Mumford decades before, as well as by Max Weber. Cultural critic Neil Postman's excellent *Technopoly: The Surrender of Culture to Technology* (New York: Vintage 1993) covers similar ground in a more updated and reader-friendly manner. We use his better-coined term to represent the ideas in both books.

5. These exciting discoveries nearly led us down another cultural dead-end. Our immediate conclusion was that, because New Belgium "walked the walk" so convincingly and in ways that were distinctive enough to work with creatively, this was a perfect assignment to apply the tactic that we call mythologizing the company (see our analyses of Jack Daniel's, Chapter 3, and ESPN, Chapter 16). We have argued that, since consumers are increasingly cynical about corporate myth-making (rightly so, as there are many abuses), if the company actually delivers on the brand ideology in its everyday business practices, then one should use the company's actions as the source material to brand. However, as we started to explore what the branding might look like using New Belgium's renegade brewers and non-professional employees and pastoral complex, our creative development circled back to the category's cultural orthodoxy: expressions that conveyed artisanal–cosmopolitan connoisseurship. Instead of leapfrogging the category, we were in danger of entering a cultural red ocean. We recognized that, to speak to the ache of the BoBo, we had to open up the branding to something beyond beermaking. New Belgium was but one example of many avocations one might pursue.

6. These customer constructs are developed in the ESPN analysis in Douglas B. Holt, *How Brands Become Icons: The Principles of Cultural Branding* (Boston: Harvard Business School Press, 2004).

12

Fuse Music Television: Challenging Incumbents with Cultural Jujitsu

Entrepreneurs must often compete against a powerful incumbent that dominates the market and commands far superior resources. Better-mousetraps models urge entrepreneurs to avoid direct challenges to incumbents. Such turf wars are supposedly red oceans, where start-ups are destined to be eviscerated by the big fish. Cultural strategy reveals that in many cases just the opposite is true. Sometimes, categories are rife with entrepreneurial opportunity precisely because a powerful incumbent dominates and at the same time has a cultural weakness to exploit. In such categories, taking on the incumbent directly is often the best approach. The challenger uses the popularity of the incumbent against itself, what we call *cultural jujitsu*. The more hefty the incumbent, the greater the leverage. For instance, Ben & Jerry's took off as a successful business only when it mounted a direct challenge to the Pillsbury Company's Haagen-Dazs, and leveraged the heft of the super-premium ice cream giant to astounding effect.

MTV is the goliath of music television. The network launched in 1981 and quickly established itself as the dominant arbiter of taste in American youth culture, promoting new musical acts, showcasing provocative music videos, mining new youth subcultures, and presenting youth-related news. It offered the hottest new youth cultural programming offerings, from animated slacker cartoons such as *Beavis and Butthead* to prankster comedies such as *Jackass* and *The Tom Green Show*. To corner the music television market, MTV Networks bought up competitors such as Country Music Television and the Black Entertainment Network, and it spun off niche networks such as VH2 and MTV2. By 2003, MTV Networks owned thirteen domestic cable

245

networks, including MTV Hits, MTV Jams, MTV Tr3s, a Latin-oriented network, and mtvU, a college-oriented network. The unit's $27 billion global business was the single largest asset in the media conglomerate Viacom's portfolio of companies.

Rainbow Media launched MuchMusic in the USA in 1994 as a simulcast of a Canadian music television network with the same name. The tiny network soon began to offer its own music video programming. Management conscientiously followed the principles of better-mousetraps innovation: it sought to carve out a blue ocean niche by championing "alternative" musical genres, such as indie, heavy metal, punk, and emo that MTV had largely abandoned because they were too small. Yet the concept never took off. Nine years later, in 2003, the network still had minuscule awareness amongst its youth target and virtually no important national advertisers. Nielson ratings remained low, hovering around a 0.3 percent share. Cable operators saw little reason to give the network prominent billing in their channel line-ups and typically tucked it away in their systems' triple digits.

In 2003, Rainbow Media hired us to help restage the network, which it had renamed Fuse, to compete more successfully against MTV.[1] We were given the assignment with a tiny marketing budget that limited us to on-channel advertising and a small amount of guerrilla marketing. Nonetheless, using the cultural strategy model, we were able to turn around the network. We identified an ideological opportunity that took advantage of MTV's Achilles heel. We developed a cultural strategy that led to numerous provocative challenges to MTV, setting up Fuse as the behemoth's ideological counterpoint. In the first year of its relaunch, the network attracted unprecedented media attention, doubled its ratings, significantly grew its subscription base, and attracted dozens of new national advertisers.

Cultural Research

Rather than focus on identifying the category's cultural orthodoxy and leapfrogging it, instead we focused exclusively on MTV's cultural expressions with the goal of pinpointing an ideological Achilles heel that we could exploit. Because of MTV's dominance, we knew that our best chance was to use cultural jujitsu tactics. So, we began our research with a brand genealogy of MTV.

Most youth music is, from an ideological viewpoint, an expression of youth rebellion, flaunting adult bourgeois norms. MTV originally operated as an adept clearing house for this kind of ideology, aggregating a diverse range of rebellious expressions. In the early 1980s, the network celebrated underground New Wave acts that had largely been ignored by the radio industry, introducing audiences to their provocative dayglo fashions, androgynous make-up, and audaciously sculpted haircuts. In the mid-1980s, the network presented Americans with Boy George's provocative mix of camp and drag and Madonna's then-shocking combination of sexuality and religious iconography. In the early 1990s, MTV recognized the potential of gangsta rap as a rebel myth for mainstream white youth, introducing them to the likes of Ice-T, Ice Cube, Dr Dre, and Snoop Dogg. The network titillated teenagers and shocked parents with these artists' unprecedented celebration of gang violence, illicit drug use, police resistance, misogyny, and verbal profanity. Around this time, MTV also helped to popularize the defiant slacker subculture, through Beck's lo-fi "Loser" video and Mike Judge's hyper-cynical *Beavis and Butthead* cartoon. The network had become expert in programming ever more provocative expressions of youth rebellion, serving up massive ratings while maintaining credibility as an authentic youth cultural player. In this way, MTV became the single most powerful youth brand in America.

MTV's Ideological Achilles Heel

In 1997, MTV President Judy McGrath launched an ambitious new strategy, shifting the network's emphasis from music videos to longer-format programming. MTV executives had always known that music videos were poor vehicles to generate ratings because they encouraged channel surfing after each four-minute video ended, compared to longer-format programs that could lock in the viewer for thirty minutes or an hour. Yet, since music videos were the founding *raison d'être* of the network, no one had questioned their continued presence.

McGrath changed all that. Enter the era of teen soap operas, with their schlocky yet sticky content. The most successful of these, *Undressed*, followed the romantic relationships of young, good-looking, and often well-to-do Los Angeles teenagers. The network began to run and rerun episodes of *Undressed* with stunning frequency. Enter the era of reality programming. Whereas MTV once used reality shows such as *The Real World* as a novelty to round out the music video programming, McGrath's strategy had reality programming dominating the network's programming line-up. To replicate the ratings success of *The Real World*, MTV launched a slew of vapid reality shows such as *Sorority Life* and *Room Raiders* and celebrity gossip programs such as *The Mandy Moore Show*. Enter the era of pop princesses such as Britney Spears, Jessica Simpson, and Paris Hilton, who now began to make appearances on MTV with greater and greater frequency and were trotted out with much fanfare at key network events such as the *MTV Video Music Awards*. Eventually, the network gave Simpson her own show, *The Newlyweds*, which showcased her life with Nick Lachey, chauffeured cars, starter mansions, and vacation villas. The show delighted in details that revealed the couple's privilege, such as Simpson's unfamiliarity with canned tuna and her inability to do laundry on her own.

Enter the era of celebrity glamour and fame worship. In 1998, *Total Request Live* was MTV's prime outlet for airing music videos, but the network compromised its integrity by having celebrities show up as hosts. Instead of focusing on the musical or artistic details of the videos, *TRL* became a vehicle for promoting the upcoming movies of the celebrity co-hosts, pandering to the hundreds of screaming teenagers who showed up outside the studio to catch a glimpse of the rich and famous. Other shows were even more explicit about their celebrity glamour and fame worship. *MTV Cribs* gave viewers glimpses into celebrity mansions, and *Punk'd* featured model-turned-actor Ashton Kutcher playing pranks on other celebrities, intruding on them in their expensive homes or mock-arresting them in their luxury cars.

All this added up to a radical remaking of MTV's ideology, from an advocate of youth rebellion to a promoter of a teenybopper dream of the rich, famous, and beautiful lifestyle. MTV no longer idealized youth as rebels and provocateurs, but instead celebrated them as beautiful, rich, polished mini-adults. Romanticizing life on the margins was replaced by worshipping jet-setter celebrities doing glamorous things. MTV no longer gloried in oddball and often lo-fidelity production values, but instead presented itself as the polished, slick, orthodoxy of upscale fashion.

This radical shift made economic sense for MTV, the category's dominant brand. The United States had entered a period of turbo-charged expansion of the upper class, spurring a society-wide infatu-ation with "making it," becoming rich, and then "living large" on the proceeds.[2] And the wealthy were becoming younger and younger if you believed news reports. The media had shifted from celebrating long-haired slackers who were pissed off at the world and formed under-ground bands to help vent their anger (Nirvana, for instance, in the early 1990s), to heroizing teenage tech entrepreneurs who made tens of millions before they were of legal drinking age.

By 2003, the bloom of the wealth-frenzied dot-com-driven late 1990s had shriveled up. In that go-go era of teenage millionaires, the lifestyle of rich, famous, and beautiful had seemed attainable for anyone. But, with jobs disappearing and incomes stagnating, a class divide was setting in. The United States had produced a huge upper class with over seven million millionaires. So, if you were a teen growing up in a well-to-do household with parents who could afford to send you to a good college—perhaps 15 percent of households—this dream remained very attractive. MTV's ideology remained extremely popular with some American youths, especially appealing to younger middle-class teenage girls. But, for teenagers who were growing up at a distance from these monied circles, the rich, famous, and beautiful lifestyle now seemed light years away, a dream that had lost all credibility. These teens' parents were working harder than ever, and yet their combined real incomes were no different from thirty years earlier. Most American teenagers were now forced to take on part-time menial jobs with low pay and no benefits, just to keep up with the fashions, video games, mp3 players, and social lives of their peers. They could not afford a four-year college and suspected that at best they could expect a very routinized and poorly paying job in a few years. These non-elite teens were caught in a bind: they were bombarded with MTV shows that attempted to entice them with the elite lifestyle, yet they had become increasingly aware that they were heading down a decidedly less glamorous path. With this research in hand, we concluded that MTV's abandonment of the foundational rebel ideals of youth culture to embrace its bourgeois antithesis was its Achilles heel, the point of vulnerability for a cultural jujitsu maneuver.

We discovered in our research that MTV was increasingly rubbing non-elite teens, especially males, the wrong way. A backlash against MTV was surfacing on the Internet. One Internet forum titled *MTV Sucks* elicited plenty of comments declaring that MTV had lost its rebel edge and was instead relying upon celebrity idols to shore up ratings.[3] As one forum participant explained:

Don't expect MTV to do anything controversial. Complaining that MTV won't show a politically charged video makes about as much sense as complaining that "Everybody Loves Raymond" hasn't done a show on bondage. MTV is the safe haven for Britney and N'Sync fans—it's not where you are going to find cutting-edge stuff. Go to your local independent record store.

As another participant put it:

Now it seems as though MTV (and all the countless channels initially inspired by MTV) is bashing individuality and replacing it with a message of conformity and trend dictation. "Cribs" tells us to get a big pimped-out house.... What happened to the initial message of individuality and music. Does the money now lie in endorsing conformity and material gain? Of course it does, and MTV sold out to that idea years ago.

Or, as a participant on www.jumptheshark.com put it: "In conclusion, I think somebody murdered the original idea of MTV, and it [sic] MTV is now headed by money hungry idiots and their teeny-bopping daughters."

Seeking better to understand the ideological underpinnings of this backlash, we interviewed teens and young adults who agreed with, amongst other things, the statement "MTV sucks." When we asked our interviewees what they hated most about MTV, they complained about "expensive parties for spoiled brats," "whiny rich kids," "millionaire teenage pop idols," and, more generally, "shiny, happy, people all dressing and acting the same." One interviewee, when asked to describe the typical MTV viewer, posited, "dumb, rich, frat guys and shallow girls who drive their daddy's Saab." The backlash, we determined, was an angry expression of the growing class divide. Our research allowed us to make a straightforward inference: the best ideological opportunity for Fuse was to challenge MTV with an ideology that channeled this deep disgruntlement with the lifestyle of rich, famous, and beautiful by mounting a populist counterpoint. Nailing down the specifics of this counterpoint was the goal of our next phase of research.

Source Materials: Culture Jammers as Populist Pranksters

With a significant ideological opportunity in hand and a brand entirely lacking in any kind of equity, we went in search of the most compelling subculture, social movement, or media myth to mine for cultural content. We concluded immediately that we would need to look beyond the network's loose confederation of subcultural programming efforts. We needed a broader and more rebellious platform. Youth music subcultures were not only fragmented, but had by this time become far too predictable and overused as expressions of youth rebellion. By 2003, corporations had become adept at paying off once-rebellious musicians in order to trade on their subcultural credibility. As a result, the rebel value of youth music subcultures had plummeted. We needed a more compelling platform, and one that specifically informed the teen class divide we had discovered. We asked: what subcultures or movements have the most resonance and credibility at this moment in history to mount a populist challenge against the world of the rich, famous, and beautiful?

We hypothesized that the anti-globalization movement would be a good place to dig. Not only did the movement offer a potent critique of the corporatization of youth subcultures, but its angry populism was a better fit with our target than, for instance, the constructive optimism of the green movement, which resonated primarily with elite youth. At the time, the anti-globalization movement was rapidly gaining influence amongst our target. Naomi Klein's book *No Logo*, a controversial anti-multinational screed, had shot to the number one position on best-seller lists in 2001, and sold more than one million copies by 2002. The book's primary angle—a populist attack on big business—was helpful. It allowed us to think about how we could position MTV as part of the greedy global oligopolists that Klein dissed so aggressively. Even more useful, though, was the particular movement that she lauded, illuminating a contingent that had existed on the margins for decades—the culture jammers.

Culture jamming is a cultural form of resistance. Activists attack powerful institutions by sabotaging their public image. They added their own ironic additions and playful satires to the advertising of multinationals, and G8 meetings, and corporate headquarters buildings.

The history of such subversive cultural pranks goes way back, as Greil Marcus recounts in his seminal book *Lipstick Traces: A Secret History of the Twentieth Century.* These techniques were largely "hidden"—existing in the margins with little publicity—for decades until the idea caught fire amongst youth resistance efforts across Europe and North America in the social movements of the 1960s and 1970s. These activists were inspired by the Situationists, a group of political and artistic pranksters that had formed in Europe in the late 1950s. The Situationists enacted a series of absurdist media stunts designed to subvert social institutions and create unrest. For instance, in one of their early pranks, a member dressed up like a priest and denounced God from the pulpit of Notre Dame cathedral in Paris.

The Situationists invented a strategy that they called *detournement*— the do-it-yourself repurposing of a well-known image or message to create a new work with a new meaning—what would come to be known as culture jamming two decades later in North America. They claimed that detournement turned the expressions of the capitalist system against itself, reclaiming individual autonomy and creativity from the passive "spectacle" that the system produces.[4] The most important theorist of Situationists, Guy Debord, wrote a book *The Society of Spectacle*, which became one of the bibles of 1960s activists. At the same time, in the United States, labor activist Saul Alinsky was working with similar ideas, advocating "mass political jujitsu," which involved "utilizing the power of one part of the power structure against another part...".[5] Perhaps the most influential application of Situationist principles came at the end of this era, as music and fashion impressario Malcolm McLaren molded The Sex Pistols straight out of the Situationist textbook. Launching the band's breakthrough single, *God Save the Queen,* he introduced it to the public on the day of Queen Elizabeth II's Silver Jubilee by promoting it in a press conference in front of Buckingham Palace, having the band perform the tune on a boat outside the British Parliament, waiting for the police to arrive, inviting the press to watch as he and others were arrested, and then explaining to the press that the arrest was an example of the country's blind deference to the dominant royal social order.

Around the same time, the Media Foundation in Vancouver launched a culture-jamming venture based around the magazine *Adbusters*, which had built up a small but highly influential base of activists. Adbusters—"the journal of the mental environment"—published anti-corporate salvos and "subvertisements," parodies of corporate advertisements. The magazine's founder, Kalle Lasn, later published a book, *Culture Jamming*, in 2000, as part of the group's continuing efforts to push culture jamming into the mainstream. But it was Klein's book that actually accomplished this goal, putting cultural jamming on the map as one of the most compelling and credible ways to "fight the system."

Klein showcased the work of the Media Billboard Liberation Front, who defaced a massive Levi's billboard, the largest in San Francisco, by pasting the image of Charles Manson over the denim model's face. She applauded the activists who painted "Shit Happens" onto an Exxon billboard after the Valdez oil spill and the artists who turned Joe Camel into Joe Chemo, hooking the character up to an IV machine. She lauded the online "hacktivists" who broke into corporate websites and left their own anti-corporate messages behind, and the creators of *Uncool*, a photocopied zine that included a full-page mock ad for Philosophy Barbie, who wondered: "What came first? The beauty or the myth? If I break a nail, but I'm asleep, is it still a crisis?"[6] Circulation of the magazine *Adbusters* soared as Klein's promotion of culture jamming caught on, becoming an influential read amongst youth seeking out alternative means of rebellion.

Klein's book also set the stage for the rise to prominence of the most impressive and famous culture jammers of the era, the audacious Yes Men, heroes of several of the youth we interviewed. The Yes Men impersonated high-level executives from multinational companies. They dressed in business suits and snuck into top-level meetings of economic elites to sabotage them in classic Situationist style. They proposed the most preposterous schemes imaginable to subvert what they viewed as the predatory behind-the-scenes machinations of multinational corporations. What made their pranks particularly funny and powerful was that most of the time their corporate audiences totally bought into the wacko ideas they presented. For instance, the activists posed as positive-spirited McDonald's executives at a major conference and proposed a plan to recycle first-world waste into hamburgers for Third World consumption. The corporate audience nodded appreciatively as the speakers explained that hamburgers made of waste would be both environmentally responsible and very profitable.

Culture jamming offered a very contemporary and resonant movement that we could repurpose to craft a populist rebuttal to MTV. We just needed to reframe the target a bit, and extend the mockery so that it took aim, not at the business practices of elites, but at their lifestyles as well.

Cultural Strategy: Populist Prankster

We sketched out a memo that posited a new ideology for Fuse, in which the music network would take on MTV's celebration of elite lifestyle, using culture-jamming as the primary weapon.

Fuse stands by teens who think that MTV is only for elite snobs and celebrity sycophants and has abandoned everyone else. Fuse is about music, plain and simple, stripped bare of all the fake lifestyle glitter. Whereas MTV idealizes youth who live the rich, famous and beautiful lifestyle, we at Fuse think this is a bad joke. Who gets to live this life after all? Fuse tears down this ridiculous façade to reveal life as it really is: not always beautiful, rarely rich, and often raunchy and seedy rather than glamorous. Hip is NOT a bunch of shiny happy people who all dress and act the same. We respect people who don't give in to elite norms, even if they end up being distasteful or lewd according to some. We think *anyone* could be a better celebrity than the overpaid fakes that MTV throws at us. Even MTV's production values drip money: super slick with a well-oiled style that spreads from graphics to set design to sonic signatures. We at Fuse don't have much money, just like you. But we can have a lot of fun making do with what we've got.

With only a couple months to go before the restaging, our Fuse team met in Rainbow Media's Manhattan offices. We recognized that we needed to bring the new concept to life in as noisy a way as possible.

We had only $1 million to launch the new network into a highly saturated media environment, cluttered with youth culture, youth marketing, and youth products. By using culture jamming to communicate provocatively our populist anti-MTV ideology, we believed that, even with a minimal budget, we could get the attention of music journalists, ad trade journalists, youth cultural bloggers, television news producers, and music fan communities. We figured that we could multiply the efficiency and effectiveness of our media buys on a vast scale by applying the principles we had discovered in the guerrilla branding efforts that launched Ben & Jerry's—the tactic we call provoking ideological flashpoints.

Culture Jam No. 1: Save the Music Video
One issue particularly annoyed our target teens, surfacing again and again in our interviews. Jaded interviewees loved to accuse MTV of abandoning its roots by drifting away from playing music videos. We knew from our discourse analysis that it would be easy to frame MTV's abandonment of music videos in order to embrace rich, famous, and beautiful lifestyle programming as a large corporation's "selling out" youth culture for the sake of corporate profits. By designing an ideologically charged prank to assert our counterpoint, we could strike MTV in its cultural Achilles heel.

We came up with an integrated cultural idea that we called "Help Save The Music Video".[7] The first component was a week-long on-air telethon in the style of a charity fundraiser. But, instead of asking our viewers to pledge their financial support, we asked them to pledge hours of slacking in front of their television, watching music videos. We invited as co-hosts various musicians whose videos MTV judged too offensive or distasteful to air. Marilyn Manson, for example, explained to the camera that "Music videos are really important because young children can be exposed to themes of violence and devil worship." We constructed a large digital board to keep viewers apprised of the number of music videos saved.

To turn this idea into a media event, we decided to hire Sally Struthers as spokesperson for our cause. Sally originally starred as a plump hippie in *All in the Family* and had more recently become known for her public advocacy of Save the Children, the African poverty charity. As a has-been celebrity, Sally was the perfect antithesis of MTV-style glamour and

APPLYING THE CULTURAL STRATEGY MODEL

fame worship. And "save the children" provided distasteful wordplay for our tagline. In billboards, we juxtaposed Sally's image against the headline "Please Help Save Music Videos. Watch Fuse." For youth magazines, we created the headline "By Watching 3 Minutes a Day, You Can Show a Music Video that You Care." For youth cultural websites, we created the headline "Right Now a Music Video is Being Neglected." For trade magazines, we tweaked the message with the headline "The Children Are Hungry. For Music Videos."

We bought a billboard in Times Square, directly across from MTV's headquarters. MTV's show *TRL* was shot live from MTV's headquarters in a studio that looked out upon several billboards in Times Square. *TRL* had become one of the prime symbols of MTV's reorientation toward celebrity bubblegum glamour, with this show overtly catering to screaming teenyboppers hoping to catch a glimpse of star guests. What better way to draw attention to our new network's populist prankster ideology than to place a billboard mocking MTV's abandonment of music videos so that it would show up as a backdrop to one its most popular shows?

When we discovered that MTV's parent company, Viacom, owned one of these billboards directly across from *TRL*, we saw the potential to up the ante on this prank. We thought it was very likely that Viacom's managers would try to block our use of this billboard, once they had figured out that we were using it to deride the crown jewel of their media empire. Framed in the right way, Viacom's attempt to suppress our "Saving the Music Video" campaign could be exposed to the public as a monopolistic effort by a large, cynical corporation to subdue a cheeky, populist upstart—along the same lines as Ben & Jerry's "What's the Doughboy Afraid Of?" campaign. To make sure that Viacom would take the bait, we also placed ads on every available Viacom-owned phone booth in Times Square, and commissioned street teams to parade outside Viacom and MTV's headquarters with sandwich boards, urging as many pedestrians as possible to help save the music video. We also supplied local coffee vendors with thousands of Fuse coffee cups to hand out in place of their regular coffee cups. Each Fuse coffee cup prominently featured a culture jam of MTV's logo. One of these extended the logo's prominent M into the word Monopoly. Another used the M to ask, "Where's the M in emptee-vee?"

The day before the billboard was slated to go up, we sent its content to Viacom media executives for approval. Our team simultaneously leaked the content to MTV executives, hoping that this would increase the chance that somebody at MTV or Viacom would try to do something to stop it. By mid-day, Viacom and MTV had taken the bait. First, MTV's COO telephoned the CEO of Fuse's parent company, to complain about the anti-MTV cups that had begun to appear in Times Square earlier in the day. He described the message on the cups as a "personal affront." Then, a top Viacom media executive telephoned Fuse president Marc Juris to say that they would not run the billboard, given its content and its location as a backdrop for *TRL* studios. The prank was underway.

Throughout the afternoon, the Fuse PR team leaked the 'breaking news' to the press, painting Viacom as a corporate goliath out to crush a little start-up that had the gall to challenge MTV. To escalate the prank, we then called Viacom ad sales executives to explain that we had leaked the story to the press and that they would get some very negative coverage unless they allowed the billboard to go up. Viacom then had little choice but to reverse its decision.

We invited the press to show up in Times Square the next morning to watch as the billboard went up. This became the second part of the story. The sight of workmen putting the billboard up piece by piece made for a compelling visual for helicopter television news cameras as well as for ground photographers.

With the most influential newspapers, music journals, youth culture magazines, and television news networks all rushing in to break the story in real time, it became clear that the prank had struck a nerve. Our extremely frugal campaign to restore music video to its rightful place in youth culture generated phenomenal national coverage via editorial and PR pick-up of our efforts. Rolling Stone wrote about Fuse as a "small but flourishing" channel taking aim at MTV, applauding Fuse for the idea that "Music television should play music videos." National news sources such as *TV Guide, Entertainment Weekly,* and the *New York Times* amplified Fuse's cause with such headlines as "Fuse under MTV," "The Music Channel that's Giving MTV Competition," and "Brash Music Network Rocks the Establishment." In a matter of days, we had seduced a wide range of media to give powerful expression to Fuse's populist prankster ideology, free of charge. The stunt was beginning to paint MTV into a corner as the slick, cynical, corporate behemoth.

Culture Jam No. 2: Tacky Poverty-Stricken Beach House Mocks MTV's Spoiled Rich Kids
To follow up, we considered what other content would allow us to dramatize our populist social class critique of MTV. Summer was approaching, and MTV's airwaves would soon be filled with those "expensive parties for spoiled brats" that stuck in the craw of our target. We knew from our research that the MTV Beach House was one of the most salient examples of all that was wrong with the network.

Every summer, MTV threw parties that the network broadcast from a multi-million dollar mansion on the beach in a famous upper-class vacation spot. In 2002 and 2003, the MTV Beach House was located in East Quogue, one of the most wealthy and glamorous sections of the Hamptons. The MTV Beach House broadcasts featured expensive parties, screaming teenyboppers, and celebrity appearances. The 2003 MTV website described the beach house as "buff boys, bodacious babes and the swimsuits that make them sizzling." This spectacle was centered on the rich, famous, and beautiful people showing off.

From a cultural strategy standpoint, this was low-hanging fruit. We designed a communications idea that would mock MTV's annual beauty culture overdose in as provocative a way as possible. We decided to create our very own beach house: *the Fuse Beach House.*

We located the Fuse Beach House in a run-down motel in an anonymous suburb off the New Jersey turnpike, surrounded by concrete, and miles from the beach. We then chose to populate the house with a motley assortment of people, clearly without much money: some had serious guts, several were senior citizens, and all were shabbily dressed. Most appeared to be socially marginal in some way or another: one was a geeky fantasy video gamer with a ponytail; another was a nerdy amateur karate expert; another sported uneven tan lines that suggested a leather S&M corset.

Instead of VIP events and celebrity visits, we had our vacationers engage in the most mundane activities that we could conjure up. The launch spot featured the Fuse Beach House revelers lining up to use a single porta-potty, set up in a parking lot, next to the beat-up swimming pool where they hung out. They wait impatiently, grimacing on account of their urinary discomfort. When someone opens the door to hassle the dawdler, and discovers that the porta-potty is empty, everybody in line gets ticked off. An end line declares, "Tons of music videos, but only one bathroom. The Fuse Beach House." A second spot showcased several of the beach-house members playing the kiddie pool game Marco Polo, in the motel's fetid, nearly empty, pool. "Watch music videos and take a dip in our Olympic-sized fun puddle," the end line urges. A third spot featured a Fuse Beach House music performance: a mild-mannered 60-year-old man tries and fails to find a guitar chord for the better part of a minute. Behind him, an octogenarian woman scrubs one of the motel room's mildewed walls.

We then erected a billboard opposite the TRL studios to see if MTV executives would once again take the bait. The billboard featured the Fuse Beach House marquee in front of a dark, dirty, hotel room with our diverse cast of characters sitting around and looking bored. The ad's headline, "It's not the Hamptons. It's not near the beach. It's not even a house." Reportedly, executives at MTV had been so rattled by the "Help Save the Music Video" billboard that they had set up an internal task force whose sole function was to monitor Fuse advertising. In this instance, they apparently had the billboard owner—the multinational music company Bertlesmann—reject the placement on the grounds that it was too "tacky." We could not resist telling the press about this, and once again the press delighted in covering the story.

We continued to extend the idea across a variety of non-traditional media. We erected a pop-up version of the Fuse Beach House in Times Square and had Fuse VJs broadcast from inside. The Beach House then traveled along with the WARPED tour, an underground music and extreme sports festival that featured alternative, punk, and hardcore bands. Fuse Beach House toiletry kits were handed out, which were of actual use to festival goers, and Fuse Beach House postcards were passed around, for people to send to family and friends. As part of this mobile Beach House, we set up a giant, Music Video Make-Out Couch. To draw further traffic to this interactive space, we erected *The Fuse Music Video Slut,* a large inflatable slide shaped like a giant blow-up doll. By the end of the Fuse Beach House campaign, Fuse audience ratings had increased 450 percent with no significant change to the network's programming.

Culture Jam No. 3: F-List Celebrities Mock MTV's Fame Worship
We continued to look for the most opportune MTV content to mock as we moved into the fall of our first season. Using our cultural strategy lens we identified the MTV Video Music Awards as another obvious target. A much-hyped annual event for MTV, the VMAs had become a "wannabe" version of the Oscars and the Grammies: its pre-show provided glimpses of the rich and the famous arriving and walking up the red carpet; its main event featured celebrities introducing acts and handing out awards; its after-parties supplied fodder to the celebrity gossip sections of newspapers, magazines, blogs, and websites. In the early 2000s, the spectacle focused on boy bands such as N Sync and the Back Street Boys, pop princesses such as Britney Spears, Christina Aguillera, Beyonce Knowles, and Jennifer Lopez, and celebrities who had little to do with music, such as Lindsay Lohann, Drew Barrymore, Gwyneth Paltrow, and Selma Hayek. By 2003, the VMAs had become a major celebrity gossip event, attracting significant coverage from the likes of Access Hollywood, E!, and Teen People.

To mock MTV's snobby celebration of A-List celebrities, we set up a series of endorsements by people that celebrity culture had cast out as uncool, unglamorous, and crass. We signed up Sy Sperling, president of the Hair Club for Men. Sy's hair club was one of the largest companies in the hair-replacement industry, and his infomercials had become a staple of late-night cable television. He was widely known for his obnoxious trademark sign-off, "I'm not just the president, I'm also a client." In our communications, we had him declare, "The only thing better than a club about hair is watching music videos on Fuse."

We signed up Tammy Faye Bakker, an evangelist, Christian singer, author, and television personality. Her fame peaked in the late 1980s and early 1990s when her televangelist husband Jim Bakker became one of the most influential fundamentalist celebrities, opening the Heritage Village USA amusement park and heading up the widely syndicated Praise the Lord (PTL) Club television show. He was indicted for defrauding this evangelical organization, and directing millions of dollars of funds for his personal use and sexual escapades. Perhaps because of her tendency to wear heavy make-up, Tammy Faye enjoyed a lingering presence in popular culture, albeit as the butt of jokes of late-night talk-show hosts, and of youth cultural cartoons such as *South Park*. We had Tammy endorse our new network by saying, "I saw the light. It was a TV and it had music videos on it."

We then brought Miss Cleo on board. Miss Cleo was a self-proclaimed psychic and shaman who rose to fame in the early 2000s through her numerous ads for her psychic hotline. She was particularly appealing to us because she had recently made headlines when she had been accused of deceptive advertising, billing, and collection practices. We talked Miss Cleo into endorsing Fuse with the statement, "Will you find love?...No. Will you be rich?...No. At least you have music videos on Fuse."

Finally, we recruited Robin Byrd to our cause. Robin was a former porn star, most notably featuring in the porn classic *Debbie Does Dallas*. She was also a staple of late-night television through her public-access cable television show *The Robin Byrd Show*. By 2003, the show had run for nearly thirty years and had become known for its less-than-glamorous stripper guests, its cheesy graphics, and its lo-fi production values. For Robin, we created the headline, "When I'm not making porn, watching porn, downloading porn, or hanging out with porn stars, I like to watch Fuse." This culture jam also generated phenomenal national media coverage, announcing to non-elite youth that Fuse offered a populist sanctuary from MTV's bombardment of aspirational wealth and glamour.

Extending the Populist Challenge beyond MTV

By the end of the first year, our MTV culture jam had gained enormous traction. However, we were worried that, if we continually pranked MTV, our efforts would become predictable and stale, just the opposite of what a talented populist prankster should do. We needed to keep surprising the teens who were now paying attention to Fuse. So we made a decision to extend our populist culture jamming to other sacred icons of the rich, famous, and beautiful lifestyle. The first choice was easy—the Apple iPod.

Culture Jam No. 4: The Populist Prankster Takes on Apple
In the spring of 2004, iPods became the must-have fashion statement for upper-middle-class youth and young adults. (Of course, the iPod would eventually diffuse much more widely, but, at its high initial price point, it first gained traction amongst the upper middle class.) The media buzz was deafening: iPod was the single most fawned-over, talked-about, and written-about phenomenon in the music industry. From our cultural lens, the iPod was perfect fodder for a populist culture jam. Apple was an elite, expensive brand that was conspicuously consumed by the most educated segment of society. Apple was a "sacred cow" in America, a company that was so good at what it did and so cool that no one would dare critique it—a perfect example of the kind of lemming-like attraction to fame that Fuse should challenge.

The iPod "Silhouettes" advertising was one of the most famous campaigns of this era. But, to us, it seemed to celebrate a world view of clean-cut, bourgeois, pseudo-individuality. The silhouetted images featured iPod listeners either dancing by themselves or playing air guitar. Each character sported a clichéd hipster haircut. The ads seemed to imply that air guitaring or dancing while wearing headphones was somehow a cool, rebellious gesture.

These immediately recognizable graphics provided the point of leverage for our culture jam. We hijacked the design code to invert Apple's stylish upper-middle-class ways. Ours would be an affront to polite middle-class society—as dumb-ass and vulgar as we could get past the media censors. In one ad, we featured the silhouette of a young man watching television with a match, lighting his fart on fire. In another ad, a silhouette of another young man watches television with his pants around his ankles and a jar of hand cream by his side. In another, a woman watches television naked while hanging upside from a stripper pole. In a two-page spread, a man performs fellatio on a woman on one side, and then the woman reciprocates on the other side.

Once again, we decided to orchestrate a real-time news media stunt. We leaked our ads to Steve Jobs, CEO and founder of Apple Computer, just as they were going up on billboards and showing up in magazines. Almost immediately, we received a 'cease and desist' letter, in which Apple threatened a lawsuit. We then circulated Apple's letter to the media, giving it our populist spin. The press bit on the story, turning an extremely frugal media buy of less than $500,000 into a national media phenomenon. One newspaper headline read "Apple Blows Fuse over Ads." Another read "Apple Fussy; Accuses Fuse over Parody Ads."

Conclusion

Using culture jams to provoke ideological flashpoints, our frugal guerrilla branding efforts consistently generated phenomenal national coverage. With a budget that could only be a rounding error for MTV, Fuse became the cultural leader of music television, along the way repositioning MTV as a slick, cynical corporate behemoth out of touch with today's youth.

The impact on advertisers was stunning: Fuse won more than sixty new advertisers in the first year of the campaign, while ratings quadrupled in the months following the network relaunch and doubled overall year on year. Fuse sustained these gains until our clients Marc Juris and Mary Corigliano left to run Court TV, and we moved with them to help revitalize that network.

Our success in launching Fuse demonstrates that blue oceans can exist at the very heart of mature categories, if you view such opportunities in terms of ideology instead of better mousetraps. Innovation opportunities do not necessarily require searching for unorthodox value combinations outside existing categories, or waiting for a new-to-the-earth technology to drop out of the sky. One particularly efficient way to break through in mature categories is to play off the well-known cultural expressions of a powerful incumbent. We take advantage of the market power of the incumbent to provide a platform for the challenger, what we call cultural jujitsu. In this case, the jujitsu relied on culture jamming, a technique borrowed from activists' challenges to society's power structures. But there are many other ways to apply the same jujitsu technique. In the 1970s and early 1980s, Stolichnaya rapidly grew to the No. 2 position in the vodka category by challenging the cosmopolitan authenticity of Smirnoff, and pointing out that the category incumbent hailed from the distinctively uncosmopolitan town of Hartford, Connecticut. Apple's breakthrough cultural innovation came with its "1984," an anthemic TV spot that provocatively painted IBM as a stifling bureaucracy. Leveraging the cultural heft of the dominant incumbent by attacking its ideological Achilles heel, Apple became one of the most valuable brands in the world.

Notes

1. The team consisted of Marc Juris, the young president of MuchMusic USA, who organized a small unorthodox team including Dave Carson, from Heavy, who acted as a creative director, Mary Corigliano, a former MTV marketing executive, and Kim Jacobs, a former advertising copywriter who was eager to establish her career as an on-air promotions director. We at Amalgamated were hired to do the relaunch communications. It was a motley crew, but it immediately gelled into what we describe later in this book as a *cultural studio*.
2. See Juliet B. Schor, *The Overspent American* (New York: Harper, 1999); Robert H. Frank, *Luxury Fever* (Princeton: Princeton University Press, 2000).
3. www.winamp.com
4. Guy Debord and Gil Wolman, *A User's Guide to Detournment* (1956), www.bopsecrets. org/SI/detourn.htm
5. Naomi Klein, *No Logo* (New York: Picador, 2000), 282.
6. Ibid. 287.
7. As with all the cultural studios we have studied and participated in, rolls blurred and thinking evolved iteratively and collectively. Dave Carson spearheaded the naming and logo design for the network, and developed a logo concept that was novel at that time: for every on-air network identification, the logo design would be entirely different. Each logo presented the Fuse name as a visual detournement of a familiar design, illustration, or animation style, ranging from video-game graphics to Japanimation to Soviet propaganda posters. Carson proposed various culture jams of the MTV logo, and this led to discussions about various culture jamming that we could carry out in Times Square. Mary Corigliano, the Marketing Director, came up with the idea to put a billboard on a building opposite MTV. When we presented the idea about "Saving the Music Video," President Marc Juris—himself a former creative—blurted out, "you mean like Sally Struthers?" After a good laugh, we decided in the affirmative, and began to riff on ideas that used Sally as a spokesperson.

13

Freelancers Union: Branding a Social Innovation

The cultural strategy model also offers a powerful tool to launch *social innovations*—ideas that aim to solve social and environmental problems. Social innovation, also known by synonyms such as social entrepreneurship and social enterprise, has taken off around the world. Efforts to harness the enterprise and resources of the marketplace to solve the challenging problems of the world have exploded—from spurring development in the global south, to halting the spread of infectious diseases, to motivating commitment to a low-carbon society. When the global elite of business and political leaders meet in Davos, they routinely look to social entrepreneurs to play a key role in tackling systemic global problems. Many foundations and universities are rushing to fold social enterprise into their missions, and most of the leading business schools now fund research centers and offer courses in this area.

But, as many a social entrepreneur has discovered, mobilizing people to solve social problems is even harder than motivating new consumers to buy a commercial product. While social enterprises have proliferated widely, few have scaled to the size needed to make an appreciable social impact. Social innovation concepts are a great fit for the cultural strategy model because they are devised explicitly to address a social disruption. In one of our first opportunities to apply our cultural strategy model to social innovation, we rebranded Working Today, a very promising but as yet unsuccessful social-enterprise concept. This is a particularly interesting case to consider, since leading better-mousetraps theorist Clayton Christensen has used Working Today as evidence to argue that his disruptive innovation model is a powerful tool for doing social innovation.

Working Today

In 1996, Sarah Horowitz, a third-generation labor activist, was troubled by the health-care dilemma facing the outsourced workers that the American economy was then producing at an historic rate. So she founded Working Today, an Internet-driven not-for-profit organization that offered independent workers better health-insurance rates than they could secure elsewhere. Most insurance in the United States was delivered through big corporations that negotiated group rates for their employees. People who did not work for a company that carried health insurance had to finance their own health care. Horowitz recognized that the new "knowledge economy" relied on a rapidly expanding workforce of outsourced part-timers, freelancers, and contractors. These workers had no corporate health benefits because they were not full-time employees. Facing huge premiums in the market for individual policies, many of them rolled the dice and lived without any medical insurance at all. The idea behind Working Today was to aggregate these independent workers and use their collective bargaining power to negotiate much lower group health-insurance rates. The concept was truly innovative, a clever solution to a major social problem that had recently emerged. Horowitz received a MacArthur genius award in 1999 in recognition of her creative activism.

However, the award was more an act of wishful thinking than recognition for a successful social innovation. During its first six years of operation, Working Today was a modest niche organization. When Horowitz sought out our help in 2002, Working Today had pulled in less than 2,000 independent workers to buy into its health-insurance plan. The organization purchased a meager $1.2 million worth of health-care insurance policies each year. In 2003, we applied the cultural strategy model to reconfigure Working Today as the Freelancers Union. And the business took off. Five years later, the social enterprise was buying $70 million in group insurance for 93,000 active members, becoming the fastest-growing individual health-insurance provider in the USA. Sarah Horowitz now presides over one of the most famous

American social innovations of the past decade and has become an icon of the social entrepreneurship movement.

Category Orthodoxy: Corporate Professionalism

The US health-care market was dominated by a small group of enormous insurance and health-management companies that offered policies ranging from traditional health insurance to vertically integrated health maintenance organizations (HMOs) with services delivered by their own doctors. They competed to get their products on the list of plans that major corporations offered their employees. So these companies were focused on their business-to-business markets, selling group policies to a wide variety of big organizations, public and private. These organizations made their health insurance selection using conventional economic criteria: what are the cheapest plans that offer the greatest range of choice and the best quality of care.

Since corporations typically offered their employees a variety of plans, often from several carriers, the health-insurance providers engaged in some consumer branding, but of the most pedestrian variety. They used standard mindshare logic, communicating their offerings by focusing on particular benefits that they deemed to be important to consumers—breadth of coverage, affordability, access to physicians, user-friendly service, efficient processing of claims, or some combination thereof.

Oxford HealthCare, for instance, differentiated its offering by focusing on superior coverage and affordability. "I deserve prescription drug coverage," says an indignant customer in one of its television ads; "I refuse to pay a monthly plan premium," says another; "I demand 100 percent hospitalization," says another. HIP focused on its superior access to physicians. It ran a $10 million print campaign featuring customer close-ups under headlines like "No referrals to see specialists? Niiiice!" and "Now more doctors. Now more choices. Now that's for me." Humana featured its user-friendliness, asking consumers in a print ad to "Imagine health insurance less complicated than, well, health insurance" and "Forget the common cold. We've cured persistent on-hold music." United offered live online chats with medical experts, dental coverage, and faster customer service.

The big providers reinforced their benefits claims with constant invocations of what we call the ideology of corporate professionalism. They projected their customers as rational buyers who believed that the most dependable and highest-quality medical care was provided by large, substantial, well-resourced, and well-managed insurance providers. Their ads made their benefits claim in glossy, impersonal imagery and clichéd big business logo designs like Empire's blue butterfly and Oxford's vector art. To portray their employees and network physicians, these companies used generic stock photos of middle-class parents and workers, along with darkly handsome physicians armed with stethoscopes, assurance, and concern. The providers' very names—HIP, CIGNA, Empire, Blue Cross Blue Shield—projected the aura of a huge conglomerate entity, spliced together through mergers and consolidated into acronyms.

Struggling in a Red Ocean

When Horowitz came to us in 2002, we soon identified why her Working Today concept was not working. She had mimicked all the cultural codes of the category's cultural orthodoxy—corporate professionalism—in an effort to brand her innovative service. The organization's name, Working Today, expressed a sense of mundane professionalism. Its tagline, "Benefiting the Way that you Work," echoed the cloying attempts of larger insurers to present their benefits claims from their consumers' perspective. Working Today's logo, with its unobtrusive abstract vector art, invited prospects to imagine that they were dealing with an anonymous, risk-averse, conglomerate. Its website used the conventional corporate stock imagery that other health-insurance providers featured on their sites: workers dressed in professional attire, the image intentionally blurred, as if to maintain a sense of anonymity.

We viewed Horowitz's revolutionary business model as an ideal foundation for a cultural innovation. Yet Working Today failed to deliver on the ideological transformation that this health innovation made possible. By following conventional mindshare branding dictums to portray Working Today as a professional, dependable corporate provider of affordable insurance, Horowitz had actually stripped her offering of its enormous cultural potential. Given the vastly superior financial resources of its competitors, Working Today was fighting a losing battle. Whereas health-insurance conglomerates typically spent tens of millions each year on advertising and employed large sales forces to respond to inquiries, Working Today had an annual communications budget of less than $100,000 and no sales force to speak of.

This competitive imbalance posed a serious dilemma for Horowitz. On the one hand, she recognized that she could not win the uphill battle against her huge competitors. On the other hand, she was worried about abandoning the category's orthodox codes. If Working Today gave up on trying to convey its corporate professionalism, would the start-up risk being seen as a small fly-by-night organization—not professional, not corporate, not dependable enough to be trusted?

Frustrated by her lack of success following the conventional mindshare approach to developing her business, Horowitz was particularly receptive to working with us to restage Working Today as a cultural innovation, even if that meant abandoning the ideology and attendant cultural codes of the health-insurance category.

Ideological Opportunity: Leftie Solidarity for Freelancers

Good social enterprise concepts are distinct from commercial branding in that the offering explicitly addresses a social disruption, usually in the form of a serious social or environmental issue. For commercial brands, we have to unearth the social disruption through research. Horowitz had already designed Working Today to attack a major economic dislocation in the labor market. By the late 1980s, as Wall Street finished dismantling the country's postwar conglomerates, a new organization form—the networked firm—took shape. These agile new companies outsourced production around the globe, constantly moving to the lowest-cost suppliers. They also aggressively outsourced all functions that were not core to the firm's business. To manage salary and health-insurance costs, companies pushed whatever labor they could to contingent workforces: freelancers, independent contractors, temporary workers, or consultants. Through the 1990s and early 2000s, this outsourcing gravitated from blue-collar to middle-class jobs.

We refined Horowitz's sociological insight to sharpen her target. Horowitz had been targeting all outsourced workers. By the early 2000s, outsourcing was hitting commercial arts workers with particular force. Companies were cutting costs by outsourcing disciplines such as graphic design, web design, interior design, journalism, architecture, advertising, web programming, technical writing, illustration, and 3D animation. These actions produced a large workforce of commercial arts contractors who made a living by combining piecemeal freelance jobs.

We conducted identity interviews with commercial arts workers in New York City to understand how these prospects coped with outsourcing. Many of our informants had attended art schools and, before the economic realities of making a living set in, had dreamed of becoming artists. So they readily identified with the bohemian ideology of the art world. Many resided in neighborhoods known for their bohemian artist communities, such as Manhattan's East Village and Lower East Side, and Brooklyn's Williamsburg, Fort Greene, Greenpoint, and Boerum Hill. Even those who lived elsewhere idealized the bohemian lifestyle that these neighborhoods offered.

They not only embraced the cultural side of bohemia, but also favored bohemia's leftist politics, in which social activism has replaced the revolutionary fervor of old. In the early 2000s, the center of bohemian activism was the "anti-globalization movement"—a diverse range of groups opposed to the way in which giant global corporations exerted tremendous power to dominate industries such as food, water, weapons, health care, even education, prisons, and the military, to the detriment of basic social welfare. The anti-globalization movement frequently called out the hypocrisy of large corporations for putting on a friendly, trustworthy face in their branding efforts while exploiting workers and degrading labor standards behind the scenes. Our informants abhorred George W. Bush, in part because of his support for the unregulated political power of corporations at the expense of worker welfare and rights.

Given their anti-corporate sentiment and poor experience with health care, it came as little surprise to learn that these commercial arts workers were extremely cynical about the incumbent health-insurance companies. They mocked health-care marketing that portrayed such companies as trustworthy and dependable. And they accused these health providers of taking advantage of independent workers, charging them exorbitant prices because they had nowhere else to get insurance.

When it came to their freelance labor arrangements, the commercial arts freelancers had deeply conflicting experiences. They welcomed the autonomy that freelance work offered, and valued their independence from big corporations. Because commercial arts freelancers operated outside the constraints of mainstream institutions, they were able to paint themselves as free-spirited mavericks, modern bohemians who worked in the margins. Maybe they did not make much money, but they could work when they wanted and where they wanted. If the muse struck them, they could hop in the car for a middle-of-the-week road trip.

However, the freelance labor arrangements left a material and social void. Freelancing denied them the security of corporate health-care and unemployment benefits. And freelancers yearned for the group solidarity found in more stable organizational configurations. Because they worked on short-term projects, moving from workplace to workplace, freelancers rarely experienced the organizational camaraderie that other workers enjoyed. At the same time, because their work required long hours working alone at home or in a coffee shop, freelancers missed out on the joie de vivre of the bohemian arts community in their everyday work life. Our discovery of this collective yearning for group solidarity built around a bohemian-leftist ideology offered a powerful ideological opportunity for Working Today.

Source Material

To generate source materials for how a revamped Working Today could harness this opportunity, we researched the history of worker solidarity and labor struggles against the unregulated power of large corporations, beginning with the anti-globalization movement and then eventually digging into the halcyon days of the labor movement in the USA in the early twentieth century.

The Anti-Globalization Movement
We began our investigation with the anti-globalization movement, since many of our informants identified with its ideology, and Horowitz's concept fitted so perfectly with its critique of the global

economy and big business. We sifted through the most influential personalities, films, books, radio shows, and media stunts. Michael Moore mocked the greed and inhuman labor practices of large corporations such as General Motors and Nike in his documentary films *Roger and Me* and *The Big One*. MIT linguist Noam Chomsky was a tremendously influential public intellectual amongst this group, formulating ongoing Marxist critiques of world events that he felt embodied the inhumane nature of neo-liberal capitalism. Naomi Klein's book *No Logo* became hugely influential for calling out new economy companies that relied on cheery brand imagery to gloss over their behind-the-scenes exploitation of workers. The World Social Forum organized the splintered anti-globalist groups around the world into a rhetorical counter to the global elites gathered at the neo-liberalist Davos World Economic Forum. In 2003, a group of anti-globalist pranksters called The Yes Men released a DVD documenting their rise to notoriety as they falsely impersonated officials from the WTO and various large multinational corporations on news shows and at business conferences. The Yes Men were particularly renowned for satirizing how modern-day global corporations exploited workers. This same year, the provocative film *The Corporation* became a hit within anti-globalization circles for arguing that modern corporations exhibited the traits of a psychopath.

This dig into the anti-globalization movement provided us with important clues. But for two reasons it was not a bull's eye. First, by the time we began our work, the movement was losing the credibility it had earned in the wake of extensive media coverage of the protests at the WTO meeting in Seattle in 1999 and subsequent meetings in Europe. By 2003 the anti-globalist sympathizers were beginning to realize that what the media had presented as a seamless and coherent movement was actually a heterogeneous assemblage of groups rife with internal conflict. Second, the movement's cultural expressions were focused more on global media spectacle than on local worker solidarity. The Yes Men, Michael Moore, and Chomsky engaged our target more as onlookers than as participants. So we determined that the movement was not a good fit with our commercial arts contractors' intense yearning for bohemian-leftist workplace community. Perhaps inspired by Horowitz's family history, we began to think that the only way to crack this cultural puzzle was to start a union.

Early Twentieth-Century Labor Movement

Unions had been the most influential form of worker solidarity in the USA, until they were decimated by the same economic forces that had produced the networked firm so reliant on outsourced labor. So seeking out source materials from a time when unions were powerful seemed to us an excellent alternative. In the period from about 1900 through the Great Depression, labor activism hit a peak in the USA. It was a time when union activities were the site of political radicalism, with anarchists and socialists in the mix. It was a time when labor leaders strove to form an international labor movement, working with their counterparts in the Soviet Union and Europe. In 2003, the union movement of the early twentieth century remained etched in America's collective memory as one of the most powerful expressions of worker solidarity, celebrated in films by left-leaning producers and directors. This was the only time in American history that a labor movement was truly influential, so it is not surprising that this era received such mythic treatment.

We saw the potential to restage Working Today as the organizing nucleus to rally freelancers in support of a non-corporate form of collective health insurance. Unions of the day, such as the AFL, the CIO, and the Wobblies, used a wide variety of evocative cultural expressions to advance their ideology. We were particularly interested in the movement's songs and slogans, which called for collectivism and emphasized communal bonds. The Wobblies chanted "An Injury to One in an Injury to All," while other organizers used "Solidarity Forever!" and "The Union Makes us Strong!"

The directness and combativeness of some of the movement's slogans had a special appeal. In 1931, the challenge "Which Side are you on?" rallied striking coal miners in Harlan County, Kentucky. In 1937, organizers challenged General Motors laborers to "Sit Down and Watch your Pay Go up" to sit at their work stations and refuse to work. Because this language was so different from the safe, kowtowing, marketing gestures of the health-insurance category in 2003, we believed that it offered great potential for helping us to express the alternative ideology desired by our target.

Our target held considerable nostalgic affection for the old protest songs of the era, such as in the very popular recordings of Woodie Guthrie's lost songs by Billy Bragg and Wilco. They also loved to mine the design codes of the art associated with the early twentieth-century labor-union movement. Perhaps the most iconic expressions of worker solidarity came from the constructivist art movement of the Soviet Union in the period following the Russian Revolution, and continuing through the 1930s. Constructivist artists made visually striking posters using abstract and angular geometric design to communicate messages about worker solidarity. The designs remained incredibly popular seventy years later, influencing major designers, and artists.

The union logos of this era also provided promising material for us to work with. Their slogans evoked the bonds of community using words like "united" and "brotherhood." Their design often featured the union's core craft skills or its collectivist bonds. Images of craft tools such as wrenches, saws, and framing squares evoked a pride in the sort of highly skilled craftsmanship that companies in the New Economy were outsourcing. Other logos used images of handshakes or clenched fists to express the collective strength that results from organizing. As we researched these cultural codes, we realized that we could repurpose them in a way that would engender pride amongst commercial arts freelancers. Appropriating the codes of the old American union movement to suggest that it was time to start another could inspire our target to come together around the bohemian-leftist ideology they identified with.

This idea of drawing from the union movement to reinvent Working Today leveraged one of the social enterprise's prime brand assets: Horowitz herself and her family story. Virtually every major press article about her organization mentioned her family's tradition of labor organizing. Sara's grandfather had been the Vice President of the International Ladies' Garment Workers' Union. Her father was a labor lawyer. Her mother, a schoolteacher, was a union activist in the American Federation of Teachers. Sara had graduated from Cornell University's School of Industrial and Labor Relations and then created Working Today with the goal of advocating on behalf of new economy independent workers. Since Sara had received considerable press, in our cultural innovation model we considered her cultural equities as source material for the innovation. The union revival ideology was an authentic and credible extension of her personal mission.

Designing the Cultural Innovation

To respond to the identity desires of independent commercial arts workers, we proposed that Horowitz's organization should champion an ideology of *independent worker solidarity*. We wanted to create a rallying call to commercial arts freelancers to come together as a defiant new community that would push to revamp how the United States treated outsourced labor in the New Economy. Championing afford-able health care as a right for all workers would become our core issue to organize the union.

Our first decision was to change the name Working Today to Freelancers Union. The name change proved to be a controversial recommendation. Our cultural research had revealed that, because the name Working Today imitated the bland corporatist ideology of the incumbent health-care pro-viders, the organization had not even registered with our target, despite seven years of marketing efforts. Nonetheless, Horowitz considered the term "freelancer" to be problematic. She had been using "independent worker" to reference her target, because her conventional marketing research had indicated that this term was more aspirational because it expressed its "professionalism." But our cultural research revealed that commercial arts workers wanted to distinguish themselves from corporate types. So using the cultural code "freelancers" as a tongue-in-cheek reference would work much better at engendering group solidarity and cultural value.

The term "union" was even more controversial. Horowitz had purposely avoided talking about her organization's offering in terms of unionism. To do so would not only violate the marketing conventions of the health-insurance category, but would also flout the juridical rules of the AFL-CIO. To call Horowitz's organization a union would challenge labor laws dating back to the 1930s that barred contingent workers from joining unions. We viewed this challenge as a great strength of the idea: pushing to extend unions to outsourced workers in the New Economy hit an ideological flashpoint. It was a truly innovative and timely position to take, one that fitted the organization's mission and would also provoke great interest. After much discussion and some hesitation, Horowitz decided to defy the labor establishment and restage her organization as a union.

To develop a visual identity for the Freelancers Union, we conceived of a new logo that playfully riffed on the well-known design codes of early twentieth-century union logos. We designed a badge-like logo with the union name inscribed between the outer two circles, the date of the union's founding inside near the bottom of the inner circle, and, at the center, iconographic etchings that symbolize craft labor practices and worker solidarity. We considered featuring commercial artist tools in the iconography, such as a pen, a ruler, and a computer keyboard. But in the end we settled on the image of three bees, to represent the independent workers, and a beehive, to represent the greater community that free-lancers could now belong to, despite operating as free agents.

To launch the new Freelancers Union brand, we created an advertising campaign on the cheap. Outdoor and print ads featured a new design template that evoked the abstract geometry and the stark fonts of early twentieth-century constructivist poster design. We wrote short, pro-vocative headlines that framed the push to expand collective health insurance to freelancers as a mobilization for a new social movement. The copy angrily winked at the health-care problems that freelancers faced. One headline read "Health Insurance vs. Paying Rent." Another headline alluded to the fact that many freelancers were forgoing health insurance entirely: "Echinacea is not an acceptable form of health insurance." Yet another alluded to the widespread use of WebMd to self-diagnose because doctors were unaffordable: "Your primary care physician should not be a website."

We wrote the ads so that they would feel as though they came from a knowing peer who shared the same frustrations and fears about health care. This persona was the antithesis of the category's predominant cultural codes, which spoke to customers from on high as the authori-tative big company. We ended all the ads with the tagline "Welcome to Middle-Class Poverty," which served as humorous political satire, put-ting a name to the problem that freelancers had to date experienced anonymously and autonomously. We knew that talking about college-educated white-collar workers as suffering from "middle-class poverty" would get lots of local media attention and resonate with our target, because it deviated so radically from existing stereotypes of poverty. The ads urged freelancers to join the union now to get access to "health insurance and other benefits for today's mobile workforce."

The print and out-of-home advertising efforts were rounded out by a sponsorship campaign on National Public Radio and a guerrilla stickering campaign. The guerrilla stickering campaign was inspired by the Wobblies. They had printed up hundreds of thousands of stickers with labor slogans, and urged members to stick them wherever they went, from workplace equipment to streetcars (a technique that was later appropriated by many an unsigned rock band). For Freelancers Union, we recruited both union members and guerrilla street teams to place stickers with our satirical headlines in commercial arts workplaces, on subways, in taxi cabs, and on lamp-posts around the city. Our media budget for these combined branding efforts was $85,000.

We also leveraged the Freelancers Union strategy to make recommendations for the redesign of the organization's website. We suggested shifting the emphasis from touting health-insurance benefits to recruiting visitors as union members. Horowitz redesigned her homepage with a front-and-center call to "join the movement." Now visitors were urged to become a member, even if they were not currently in the market for health insurance.

Horowitz then drew upon the strategy to add new "bells and whistles" on the website that were designed to forge prospects' identification with Freelancer's Union: website freelancer job postings, freelancer-to-freelancer discussion groups, a calendar of union events at which freelancers could network, sales of union T-shirts, and an offer for a "union card" that triggered freelancer discounts with participating retailers. These offerings transformed the relatively static website into a prototypical Web 2.0 social media community, visited regularly by large numbers of engaged participants.

This website redesign supported our broader goal—to transform Working Today's business model. Before the relaunch, Working Today had had no systematic means for acquiring leads and then converting these leads into paying health-insurance customers. The Freelancers Union relaunch, with the focus on joining a union to support a very relevant cause, allowed us to attract a much larger number of prospects than would normally be interested in a health-insurance website. We were able to sign up large numbers of recruits before they were actively shopping for health insurance. The union membership system allowed us to remain engaged with this list through customer relationship marketing until their health-insurance needs arose (for example, when rates from existing insurers went up or benefits from previous employers ran out).

As these health-insurance needs arose, we could then convert the prospects into customers. The union membership model proved to be a highly effective sales funnel for Horowitz's organization. As union membership swelled, so did the number of extremely well-qualified leads in the Freelancers Union database. As the number of well-qualified leads exploded, so did sales of Freelancers Union health-insurance packages.

Results

Our restaging of Working Today as Freelancers Union was particularly comprehensive. We used our cultural strategy to transform virtually every aspect of the offering: from the organization's name, to its logo, to its design template, to its advertising, to its social media offering, to its system of managing its relationships with online customers. The response was overwhelming. In its first six years in business as Working Today, the organization had attracted 2,000 members and billed $1.2 million in health-insurance policies. In the five months following the 2003 relaunch, 4,000 new members signed up. For the year, revenues from writing health insurance policies shot up 619 percent to $7.6 million. By 2008, six years into the restaging, Freelancers Union had attracted 93,000 members and was generating $66 million in annual revenue.

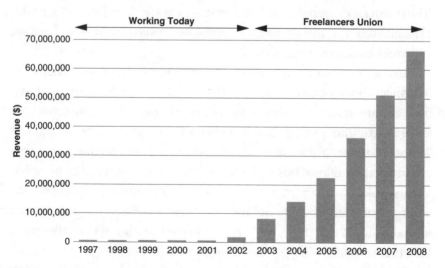

Figure 17. Revenues, 1997–2008

Source: Working Today, IRS Form 990, 1997–2008.

Conclusion

Our transformation of Working Today into Freelancers Union demonstrates how the cultural strategy model can be applied to scale social innovations. And, since Clay Christensen and his colleagues use Freelancers Union as a key example to support their better-mousetraps approach to social innovation (summarized in Chapter 6), the case provides a useful acid test. Do social innovations scale simply by providing a cheaper, more effective, or more convenient solution to a social problem, as Christensen and his colleagues argue? Or does cultural innovation play an important role?

A superficial examination might corroborate Christensen's argument for the centrality of better mousetraps. After all, Horowitz's business model delivered much cheaper health insurance to a niche population that was too small to interest the big insurance companies. So Horowitz's success would seem to support Christensen et al.'s idea that cheaper "good-enough" solutions are the path to address social problems. This interpretation falls apart, however, when one looks more carefully at the evidence. To arrive at this interpretation, Christensen and his colleagues had to ignore the historical trajectory of Horowitz's organization. Horowitz's social innovation failed for six years when it was branded using her original Working Today strategy, which emphasized professionally delivered health insurance at a better price. The social innovation took off only when we rebranded it as Freelancers Union, tapping into prospects' yearning for lefty-bohemian solidarity by starting a union that advanced affordable health care for freelancers. During its six years of sputtering, the organization provided the "cheap but good-enough" solution that Christensen and his colleagues laud. The organization took off only when we rebuilt this "better mousetrap" into an ideologically innovative organization with cultural expressions that resonated strongly with the target.

Christensen's model applies an economic calculus to social innovations: innovations succeed when they provide better economic value to underserved markets. Our work on Freelancers Union demonstrates that this economic approach is insufficient. Promoting social change inevitably involves an ideological contest—a newer ideology challenging an older one. For the new ideology to catch on, it must provide significant cultural and social value to participants and supporters, not just economic value. In the variety of social innovation cases that we have researched and worked on, this social and cultural value counts for at least as much as brute calculations of rational interest. Further, as we argue throughout this book, people's perceptions of functional benefits are strongly influenced by the social and cultural value of the offering. Because Freelancers Union offered up cultural expressions that freelancers yearned for, the group insurance product was judged to be of a higher quality and a better value. To be successful, efforts at social change require cultural strategy to give meaning and value to the innovative concept. Strategies that treat social issues as only pragmatic problems of functionality and cost are bound to fail.

Part 3

Organizing for Cultural Innovation

14

The Brand Bureaucracy and the Rise of Sciency Marketing

The holy grail for managers is to create the next Nike. Or Ben & Jerry's. Or Jack Daniel's. Or Vitaminwater. But, somehow, despite ritual genuflection to the most successful cultural innovations, the world's best consumer marketing companies rarely come close. These companies are under intense pressure from stockholders to improve their performance, and senior managers press hard to institute systems that will improve the ROI of marketing investments. So why do they have such a uniformly mediocre track record in cultural innovation? Firms run by founding entrepreneurs do much better, and so do medium-size enterprises that are not dominated by professional marketing organizations, even though both of these types of companies typically devote far fewer resources to marketing. We have discovered that large professional consumer marketing companies are trapped in a management model that systematically derails cultural innovation—what we call the *brand bureaucracy.*

While innovation has flourished in most every other area of these firms—from supply chains to service delivery to IT—when it comes to developing new brands, the modus operandi has not budged for some thirty years. Take, for example, the two leading soft-drinks marketers in the world, PepsiCo and The Coca-Cola Company. Both companies excel at day-to-day marketing, but they are equally mediocre at cultural innovation. They have devoted hundreds of millions of dollars to introduce an army of clunkers to the world: Tava, Pepsi Blue, Surge, Vault, Enviga, OK Cola, Coke Blak. Meanwhile, entrepreneurs with little financing and no distribution power but with far more sensitivity to ideological opportunities have built huge franchises out of Snapple,

Gatorade, Arizona, Red Bull, Vitaminwater, Innocent, and Odwalla. Coke's senior management has all but given up on the organization's innovation capabilities and acquired an innovation pipeline instead, paying premium prices for Odwalla, Fuze, Vitaminwater, Honest Tea, and Innocent, all developed by entrepreneurs.

We find that this innovation sluggishness—a general inability to respond to major shifts in consumer preferences—becomes endemic once companies reach a certain size and level of professionalization. We have also discovered the antidote to this impoverished innovation capability—what we call the *cultural studio*. We have found cultural studios in all the cultural innovation successes we have studied. They flourish in the cracks and crevices of the marketplace where the brand bureaucracy has less influence. Many of the cultural innovations we have studied come from entrepreneurial start-ups (Vitaminwater, Patagonia, ESPN, Snapple) and from firms that rejected professional marketing management at the time of their successes (Nike, Puma). Cultural studios can exist at big marketing companies (Levi's, Volkswagen, Tango, MINI, Lee), but they are orchestrated as skunkworks projects by renegade managers who are able to deflect the influence of the brand bureaucracy.

Method

In this chapter, we explain why the brand bureaucracy so regularly fails at innovation, and why, despite this failure, it remains deeply entrenched in all the big consumer products and services companies. We conducted detailed organizational research on eleven cultural innovation cases to uncover the organizational barriers that keep companies from innovating culturally, and the organizational passkey that allowed cultural innovations to flourish:

Snapple	ESPN	Tango (UK)
Lee Jeans	Levi's (EU)	PUMA (EU)
Budweiser	Mountain Dew	MINI
Volkswagen	Got Milk	

In an age that heroizes entrepreneurship, bureaucracy is often a damning term. However, the successful application of bureaucratic principles is crucial to the success of every major company. Bureaucracies, as Max Weber wrote, have "technical superiority" because they function like a machine—optimizing precision and speed while minimizing ambiguity. Many aspects of the marketing function—rolling out products, fine-tuning the product offering, managing channels, orchestrating service delivery—benefit greatly from bureaucratic norms. For a number of companies—consider FedEx, Toyota, GE, Southwest Airlines, and Wal-Mart—their competitive advantage comes from particular excellence in well-honed bureaucratic structures. But, while bureaucracy can generate enormous benefits for businesses, when it comes to cultural innovation, it can be profoundly dysfunctional.

What is a Brand Bureaucracy?

Max Weber's analysis of the characteristics of bureaucracy proved invaluable to us as we sought to understand why professional marketing companies hang on so tenaciously to an approach to brand innovation that rarely works. His analysis also reveals how bureaucracies lead to dysfunctional results when commerce meets up with culture. We have adapted six key criteria Weber used to define bureaucracy in order to conceptualize the institutional logic of what we term the brand bureaucracy.[1]

Calculable Rules

For Weber, "calculable rules" are the primary feature of bureaucracies. Managing large and complicated projects—fighting wars, building technically complex products, serving geographically dispersed populations— requires a simplified standardized set of management tools. Three aspects of "calculable rules" are central to modern marketing:

Abstraction and Reduction

Bureaucracies require simple heuristic descriptions of their brands and customers so that managers can quickly understand the management issues at stake, share information, and make efficient judgments. Brands and customers are expressed in a concise and generic language that any manager can quickly understand, regardless of their specific experience with the brand. Brand strategies are reduced to a short set of adjectives and phrases, usually fitting on a single page, and often further reduced to a single sentence.

Standardized Procedures for Consistency and Control

In bureaucracies, consistency is insured by the application of objective rules and standardized procedures. Brand bureaucracy pushes toward a single mechanical logic—for research, strategy, and creative development—that is applied uniformly to every brand in every situation.

Scientific Management and Quantification

Scientific management is a core feature of bureaucracies, since science provides legitimatized tools to standardize problems, to monitor them, and ultimately to control them. Bureaucracies push for efficiency by applying scientific logic to make continual improvements in procedures. Since the rise of Taylorist management principles in the 1920s, the application of scientific principles to management problems has caught on as the means for improving bureaucratic efficiency. Its impact can be seen in the quality-control revolution in production of the 1980s, the process engineering frenzy of the 1990s, and the decision science-driven behavioral incentive models in the 2000s. Scientific management has also been crucial in the development of the brand bureaucracy, and so we examine its influence below.

Rationalized Management

Bureaucracies work through intensive rationalization, carried out by managers who are well versed in the objective application of rule-like procedures. Large companies have devised management systems to deliver this sort of consistent decision-making process to marketing. Ideally, marketing managers should be interchangeable. Managers in brand bureaucracies are selected and socialized so that they will consistently deliver the same decisions using the same process across the bureaucracy. For the brand bureaucracy, three qualities of rationalized management are particularly important:

Specialized Expertise

Bureaucracies are, first and foremost, a way of organizing complex projects. Bureaucracies break down the complex market offerings of the company into specialized tasks. Managers are pushed to excel at completing their tasks efficiently. Bureaucracies do this through specialization—dividing the project into discrete tasks and creating roles and departments to manage each task, and allocating these roles "to functionaries who have specialized training and who by constant practice increase their expertise."[2]

Hierarchical Chain of Command

Brand bureaucracies favor tightly orchestrated procedures, hierarchical systems of supervision and subordination, organized around a unity of command. Weber states: "The bureaucratic structure goes hand-in-hand with the concentration of the material means of management in the hands of the master."[3] Professional marketing organizations rely upon a hierarchical chain of command in which the widely distributed tasks of the organization are integrated under singular and consistent management direction. In marketing companies, brand managers ostensibly have profit-and-loss responsibility. In reality, they sit at the bottom of a pyramid. Senior management controls all major decisions to ensure that the organization's goals are consistently pursued.

Dehumanized Application of Rules

Bureaucracies are staffed by professionals who are committed to the orderly functioning of the organization's rationalized processes. In order for bureaucracies to run smoothly, this administration must be impersonal: "interference" of human emotion and individual idiosyncrasy is minimized. Weber notes that "Bureaucracy develops the more perfectly, the more it is 'dehumanized,' the more completely it succeeds in eliminating from official business love, hatred, and all purely personal, irrational and emotional elements which escape calculation."[4] This dehumanizing characteristic of brand bureaucracies is at odds with cultural innovation, which requires a nuanced understanding of collective "irrational" desires that pulse through society, and the ability to respond to these desires with cultural expressions that are profoundly "human." Brand bureaucracies must deal with this basic problem in their quest to innovate: once you have stripped out the humanity, how do you put it back in?

The Rise of Sciency Marketing

The comedian Stephen Colbert caused a little media sensation in 2005 when he used the word *truthy* on his television show *The Colbert Report*. By *truthy* he meant "something that seems like truth—the truth we want to exist."[5] Mocking George H. W. Bush's decision to send troops to Iraq as a prime example of truthiness, Colbert satirized the "feeling of truth" that Bush sought to convey when he asked Americans to trust his gut. Doffing our caps to Colbert, we coin a word of our own, *sciency*, by which we mean "something like science—the science we want to exist." Professional marketing companies dream of converting inherently humanistic aspects of marketing into a predictable mechanistic science, leading to the creation of what we term *sciency marketing*.

Sciency marketing's fixation on imposing scientific terms and methods to all marketing problems is the foundation of the brand bureaucracy. Sciency marketing arose gradually, beginning in the 1920s and finally achieving hegemony in the 1980s. Marketing was once viewed as an art and craft, dominated by entrepreneurs with an empathetic "feel" for the market and a knack for seducing prospects with their communications.[6] Beginning in the 1920s, leading consumer marketing companies such as Procter & Gamble, Colgate-Palmolive, and Lever Brothers began to apply to marketing the same bureaucratic procedures and scientific methods that had taken root in the Taylorist management of mass production. Later, scientific methods of market research spread from social scientists working to shape public opinion during the Second World War into commercial marketing. After the war, scholars such as Paul Lazerfeld, Robert Merton, and Elihu Katz began formalizing both quantitative and qualitative market-research techniques that marketers could use to study their consumers. In the 1950s, Rosser Reeves at Young & Rubicam and David Ogilvy became influential advocates for applying marketing science to creative expressions.

At this time, advocates of a more humanistic perspective still had great influence. Adman Leo Burnett effectively resisted the encroachment of science, often relying upon so-called motivation research that drew upon humanistic academic traditions. In the 1960s, the humanistic approach to branding temporarily won out. On the heels of DDB's renowned work for the Volkswagen Beetle, charismatic admen such as Howard Gossage and George Lois led advertising's "creative revolution," which was propelled by the anti-authoritarian zeitgeist of the 1960s.[7] But, as the counter-culture burned out, and as it became clear that the creative "artists" of Madison Avenue had overstepped their reach, the pendulum hurled back toward science and has been stuck there ever since.

Since the 1970s, marketers have sought to apply to the management of brands the same meticulous precision that scientists apply to the natural world. This effort was spurred by marketing's "information revolution." Until then, marketers had waited patiently for their monthly "Nielsen audits," in which the A. C. Nielsen Company sent an army of auditors into a random sample of stores across the country to hand-count inventories on the shelf. For a marketing scientist, the audits produced terrible data: the data were thin and fraught with significant human and statistical errors. So the introduction of UPC codes and retail scanning at checkout was scientific nirvana. Marketers could now get extremely detailed and accurate information on purchase behavior within days of the transaction. These huge datasets were mined like gold by a booming cohort of academic marketing scientists, and the market research and consulting firms they spun off, who imported methods from operations research to develop algorithms to make sense of these data.

In the 1980s and 1990s, marketing science greatly increased the profitability of pricing, sales, and promotion policies. With these clear results in hand, consumer marketing companies became devoted to expanding the scientific approach to rationalize the entire marketing mix. Companies sought to optimize marketing expenditures just as they had done with the rationalization of production and supply chains.

Marketing science has yielded brilliant results in a few sectors. Grocery retailers and "club"-oriented service providers like hotels and casinos are now using complex field experiments to do what is being called "behavioral marketing." They test various promotional schemes, which allow them to tailor the most profitable offering for each of their customers. When the consumer context fits—in situations where consumer decisions can be approximated by brute economic calculus, where highly detailed data are available, and where marketers can run low-cost experiments on alternative marketing schemes—scientific marketing works wonderfully. But in contexts where these conditions do not hold, all bets are off. Many of the most important marketing strategy decisions do not allow for a scientific approach. In particular, market innovation is an exceptionally poor fit. But that has not stopped the brand bureaucracy.

Sciency Marketing

The scientific approach now dominates marketing, not only in those areas where it works well, but also in areas where it clearly does not. Scientific marketing is very useful for tasks such as pricing, promotions, and sales-force allocation. This functional application of science to marketing deserves the moniker *scientific marketing*. However, the tenacious application of marketing science in domains where it clearly does not work is the product of ideology, not effective management. We use the term *sciency marketing* to reference the misuse of science in the quest for legitimacy and certainty.

The brand bureaucracy thrives on the veneer of science, regardless of the results. Without the requisite data and orthodox analytic techniques in your holster, you are not prepared to hold a "serious" meeting at any of the big marketing companies. Managers assume that, even if the scientific approach does not seem to work at present, at least flawed science is better than no science at all. And, regardless, sooner or later the right technology will come along, which will generate the right data, which will be analyzed with appropriate scientific rigor, so that in the end all marketing decisions—even market innovation—will succumb to marketing science.

The MBA and the Construction of the Credentialed Marketing Professional

The MBA confers professional legitimacy. Like other professionals such as lawyers and doctors, managers earn the MBA to gain access to a body of consecrated knowledge that one must master to be properly credentialed, and mastery of which allows one to claim expertise over laymen. It was not always so. Until the 1960s the MBA was explicitly a trade degree, with education focused on learning real-world applications through case studies. In the early 1960s, a review of the MBA by major foundations delivered a scolding blow, declaring the MBA to lack academic integrity, implying that it was an illegitimate credential.

The report recommended that the MBA deliver scientific theories of business, thus launching a half-century march to scientize the MBA.

The reconstituted MBA required that each functional discipline define a coherent scientific body of knowledge and techniques that defines professional competence. The business disciplines borrowed liberally from the natural sciences and the closest imitators in the social sciences, especially economics, since these fields were the most academically prestigious sources of such credentialed knowledge. As a result, MBA education has shifted over time to deliver this sort of "rigorous" education, rich in formal mathematical skills and scientific frameworks. In a mathematized area like finance, professionalization is straightforward, as there is an accepted body of economic concepts and mathematical techniques that one needs to know in order to be a competent hedge-fund manager or investment banker.

For marketing, establishing this scientific pedigree required more creativity. In the 1970s, as the ideology of marketing as science took hold, a large cohort of experimental psychologists migrated into marketing departments at business schools to colonize the elite tier of the discipline, determined to create this missing scientific foundation. The first wave of research, intent upon producing a "general theory of consumer behavior," was a flop. But the psychological wing of the field eventually won out by importing the subdisciplines of "decision science" and "behavioral economics" in the 1990s. They were joined by an influential influx of engineers and statisticians with operations-research training. Beginning in the 1980s, this second cohort began intensely to mathematize any and all marketing phenomena.

So for three decades these experimental psychologists and operations research "modelers" have dominated the marketing faculty at all the elite business schools. All the other disciplines in the academy, many of which are central to marketing—including sociology, anthropology, history, political science, geography, media studies, and the humanities— have been systematically excluded from these schools. These psychologists and engineers retain a vice grip on what is defined as knowledge in marketing, not only in the elite MBA curriculum but also in all the top academic journals.

In such an academic environment, it should not be surprising that market innovation is studied and taught using sciency assumptions that align perfectly with the axioms of the brand bureaucracy. The academy provides a continual supply of the ideological glue that holds together the brand bureaucracy.

Co-Dependents: Market Research Firms, Consultants, and Ad Agencies

The brand bureaucracy has spawned an enormous supporting infrastructure of market-research companies, ad agencies, design firms, and consultancies that make their money by playing to its institutional biases. There is a global oligopoly of firms that control the delivery of sciency market-research techniques such as "concept testing," "volumetric" forecasting, conjoint analysis, simulated test markets, and the like. Brand bureaucracies have aligned with these firms because they provide the "objective" metrics they demand for evaluating and controlling their brand innovation efforts.

Never mind that such tests actually work against the development of successful innovations. In our research, we have yet to come across an innovation that this kind of research has identified and advanced. Rather, sciency innovation research inevitably favors generic and superficial cultural codes that evoke a quick and predictable response from respondents. These methods are easily manipulated by savvy creative industry firms. Yet brand bureaucracies remain addicted to them because they fit so well with the bureaucratic logic. Wayward brand bureaucrats who harbor devious thoughts that perhaps these methods are not all that helpful are scolded and warned that any deviation from the sciency approach is risky, not just to their brands but to their careers.

MBAs are groomed to become sciency marketers and, upon landing coveted brand management jobs, face untold pressure to cleave to their expertise. Yet they find that, in the pursuit of innovative new businesses, their scientific aspirations never come true. So they are susceptible to "the next big thing"—the breakthrough that will finally allow them to routinize innovation. Consultants are some of the most agile marketers around. They are highly adept at developing consulting "products" that hit brand bureaucracy sweet spots. In the 1980s, consultants sold brand bureaucracies on the idea that research could predict people's response to creative brand expressions by measuring changes in the body's electrical impulses. Marketers spent a fortune to have their prospective customers hooked up to what looked like an electric chair to see if their communiqués inspired blips on the impulse monitors. In recent years, consultants are shopping MRI scans to tap into the brand bureaucracy's utopian impulses to control its customers. Marketers have spent millions with these consultants, who promise that the splashes of color on their scans that illuminate different sectors of the brain will allow the company—at last!—to align brand innovations perfectly with customers' hard-wired desires.

As for the ad agencies that work for the big consumer goods companies, they have responded defensively, as they must, given their subordinate position, to the dominance of the brand bureaucracy. All the big agencies are set up to mirror their clients' prerogatives, so clients' brand bureaucracy principles are replicated throughout the agency. Agencies are more than happy to express publicly the profound wisdom of their client's branding initiatives, but behind the scenes they subject these efforts to constant ridicule. Agencies obligingly structure their entire work product to the beat of the client's innovation assembly line, which we describe below, despite private acknowledgment that this structure is self-defeating.

How the Brand Bureaucracy Stifles Innovation

The brand bureaucracy dominates the innovation process at all professional consumer marketing companies. We have demonstrated in Parts 1 and 2 that succeeding at cultural innovation requires nuanced and detailed engagement with cultural changes in society throughout the innovation process. Cultural innovation requires five key steps:

- analyzing the category's tacit cultural orthodoxy;
- uncovering ideological opportunities by analyzing the social disruptions that create demand for new cultural expressions;
- locating and understanding the appropriate source materials for the innovation to leverage, which are to be found in subcultures, social movements, and media myths;

- formulating a cultural strategy for the innovation, specifying its ideology, myth, and cultural codes;
- designing the innovation: creating a coherent cultural expression across the marketing mix that brings the cultural strategy to life.

The brand bureaucracy organizes innovation to guarantee failure in each of these stages. The priorities of sciency marketing and command-and-control management lead to the systematic stripping-out of culture in the research and conceptual stages. And in the design phase, where cultural content is unavoidable and crucial, the brand bureaucracy engages in strategically bereft "cultural-injection" processes.

Stripping out Culture: Reducing the Market to Generic Abstractions

Reductionist Research: Keeping Culture out of Marketing
Cultural innovation demands nuanced understanding of society and culture. Brand bureaucracies strive for just the opposite. They are organized to avoid context and historical detail in favor of simple highly distilled portraits of the marketplace. Opportunities are described in a few pithy diagrams or a few bulleted lists of a Powerpoint presentation. The brand bureaucracy rationalizes the marketplace into simplistic "insights" that management across the company can digest with little effort.

Brand bureaucracies demand present-tense research. They act as if their customers live in the "infinite present." Customers and markets are presented in snapshot form, offering a simple steady state world in which to sell one's wares. To understand the future, they demand "trend reports" that present generic ideas (often sold by research firms to many clients across many industries) and treat societal change in the most superficial manner. Trend reports focus on the surface-level changes in the market—surf gear is hot, millennial youth rely on cell phones for dating, upper-middle-class women are increasingly concerned that their purchases are "green." This is the fads-and-fashions level of change. Trends reports ignore the structural shifts in society, their impact on culture, and their potential to transform the benefit structure of a given category.

Brand bureaucrats are sequestered in corporate offices, from which they outsource all market intelligence work. Direct engagement with the marketplace is usually limited to the ritual of attending the occasional focus group, sitting behind the mirror and grabbing a few random phrases that prove handy for "I was there" storytelling back at headquarters. Brand bureaucracies have customer insights departments filled with specialists who manage the effort to identify brand opportunities. But the actual work is almost always outsourced to market-research firms. The primary job of customer insights staffers is to ensure that all reports circulated to management are standardized according to the highly distilled and simplified format that management demands for all data. The research firms gather and analyze the data, and then condense and standardize "findings" into Powerpoint slides. The raw data—interviews, observations, focus groups, photos, and so on—as well as more detailed analyses, are seldom included. Any raw data that do show up are summarily moved straight from the mailroom into the archive, gathering dust until they are routinely scrapped. For the brand bureaucracy, the only relevant data are contained in the highly distilled presentation, which, in turn, is distilled further into a summary chart or two. Once this distillation of a distillation is consecrated by senior management, it becomes the company's *lingua franca* for marketplace knowledge.

The most successful market-research firms have shaped their capabilities and deliverables to respond to this logic and so are particularly good, as a result, at delivering slick summary charts, puffing them up ceremoniously, and selling them as profound market insights. Firms favored by brand bureaucracies offer methodologies that bypass the complex socio-cultural details required to succeed at innovation. The contextual detail required for cultural innovation is systematically expunged before it has a chance to enter the front door of the brand bureaucracy.

Mindshare Marketing: Debating Abstract Adjectives
The reductionist words and phrases concocted in the brand bureaucracy's "insights" process travel straight into the innovation strategy. Brand bureaucracies love strategy, because it provides them with a tool to perform bureaucratic alchemy: magically turning a messy

complicated marketplace into a simple standardized management template. Developing innovation concepts takes the same form as strategy for ongoing businesses: a simple diagram or statement consisting largely of abstract adjectives. Different companies use different geometrical shapes—diamonds, onions, houses—but the logic is always the same.

In *How Brands Become Icons*, we called this form of strategy-making "mindshare marketing" to reflect the idea—dominant since Trout and Ries made it famous in their book *Positioning: The Battle for your Mind*—that branding success requires colonizing cognitive real estate in the mind of the consumer. You reach branding nirvana when you link your brand to a preferred category adjective in lots of consumer synapses. In this way of thinking, innovations stake out a gap in the category's cognitive associations and fill it with a new combination of adjectives.

The production of a brand strategy can take six months to a year. It is informed by reams of expensive research and proceeds across dozens of meetings. Brand bureaucrats spend months dueling over synonyms: should the new product be *quirky* or *fun-loving*? Should we instill *fun* into it? Or should it be *rebellion*? How about *playful*? Or *energetic*? Or *individualistic*? Or *optimistic*? The debate is essential, since brand bureaucrats believe that the success or failure of an innovation rests on choosing the right handful of abstract terms.

Because brand bureaucracies rely on hierarchical decision-making, to get a new concept signed off—to commit R&D or production moneys, especially prior to launching a test market—requires many repeat performances as the idea creeps up the organization chart. Junior managers develop the provisional concept in the form of a written document or Powerpoint presentation, usually with the help of creative suppliers. They make a presentation to their immediate superiors, the strategy is tweaked, and then they present it upward again. Recommendations by junior managers are always provisional and subject to change, often radically so, as the recommendation moves up the chain of command. The process continues until the strategy reaches senior management, usually the CMO, the President, or even the CEO, who has the final say and, as often as not, puts his or her mark on the recommendations.

Once approved, the concept is usually converted into some sort of blueprint or rule book—sometimes called a "brand bible"—that provides explicit formal direction on the crafting of the innovation. These strategy documents, once they are blessed by senior management, take on a life of their own. They anchor all subsequent decisions: they are used to brief creative partners and to judge all aspects of the design. The process is linear: research bequeaths strategy, and strategy bequeaths design.

DEBATING ABSTRACT ADJECTIVES AT A BLUE-CHIP MARKETING COMPANY

This example draws from one of our experiences consulting for some of the world's most respected consumer marketing companies. We have fictionalized the corporate branding objective, and we have disguised all the specific terminology debated by managers, in order to maintain confidentiality. However, the adjective-debating process we describe actually happened. This case is not an outlier. In our experience this process is standard operating procedure in many brand bureaucracies.

The company was eager to launch a new fruit-flavored tea brand across Latin America, and perhaps then globally. To do so required nailing the "concept," which required lots of adjective debates, sandwiched with sciency research to test each iteration of adjectives. Dozens of the company's managers worked with a small army of consultants and market-research firms for a year and a half, spending millions of dollars, to debate the "brand vision," the "core proposition," and the "brand personality."

They started out with the brand vision: this drink was to "Enable a life lived absolutely, completely, and totally fulfilled." The core proposition was "A new thirst-quencher that empowers you to achieve far more than you ever thought." But some managers disagreed; they did not think this was quite right. So more research was commissioned and the brand vision changed. Now the brand would champion "Up for Adventure." And, in the next iteration, they moved on to "Energy to Enjoy Life Everyday." And then on to "Refresh your Day." Then to "Refreshing Vitality," "Refreshment for an Active Lifestyle," and "Fuel for Life." The company's managers eventually settled upon "Refresh for Life."

They had similar debates over the "brand personality." What began as "mature, approachable, surprising, understated, current, and vibrant" soon changed to "mature, surprising, vibrant, light, and uplifting." Numerous discussions, multiple rounds of research, and two management consulting firms later, the brand team settled upon "adult and balanced, 'a breath of fresh air,' inner strength, approachable, zest for life, passionate, upbeat, spontaneous, fun loving and playful, vibrant yet natural."

Participants spent the most effort debating what the company terms the "core proposition." This effort was informed by several rounds of concept testing, both qualitative and quantitative, that used sophisticated concept-optimization methods designed to identify the most advantageous combination of words. The lengthy debate was also informed by a massive research project, again qualitative and quantitative, that focused on identifying psychological "need-states" that were underserved in the category, with input from three market-research firms and two management consultancies.

First, the core proposition changed from "A new thirst-quencher that empowers you to achieve far more than you ever imagined" to "A new kind of tea that unlocks your rhythms, fueling you every day so that you can be up for all of life's challenges." After several further

(cont.)

iterations and much research, it became "A unique tasting, better for you drink that helps recharge you to bring out your natural best." After more research, "unique tasting" was changed to "great tasting." After yet more research, the proposition was changed to "A line of great tasting, healthy beverages that replenish your body and refresh your thirst, providing hydration and keeping you charged for your active lifestyle" and then "A new line of delicious, invigorating beverages that help you be your natural, energetic best, both physically and mentally." The team then settled upon "A new line of deliciously refreshing good-for-you beverages that help you be your natural, energetic best, both physically and mentally, every day!" With the help of the management consultants and further concept testing, the proposition became "A delicious new fruit tea that refreshes the body and mind to help you see things with fresh eyes and stay positive during the day." On and on it went, until a consensus gelled around the final core proposition—"an invigorating replenishing drink that helps you feel *refreshed for life.*"

All these variations were intended to inject emotion into the brand, but they did so by reshuffling a laundry list of generic adjectives. These adjective lists could reasonably depict virtually any existing drink brand, leaving enormous degrees of freedom for creative partners to make up almost anything they wanted and claim that it was on strategy. The company's senior managers inadvertently encouraged this extremely shallow debate by insisting that middle managers focus their efforts on filling in the various boxes of the company's "brand pyramid" schematic. Like the onions, houses, trees, and keys of other brand bureaucracies, the brand pyramid enabled senior managers to manage brands at a glance. As a result, middle managers spent month after month obsessing over minute differences in the words that fit into the pyramid, which could not possibly have had any impact on the result.

Concept Testing

Brand bureaucracies often devote more time to "concept testing" than to any other part of the innovation process. It is not unusual for a brand bureaucracy to spend only a day or two generating innovation ideas, often in "brainstorming sessions," and then spend the better part of a year trying to measure consumers' reactions to these concepts. Through qualitative and quantitative research tests, these concepts are ranked, screened, optimized, and then fed into sophisticated statistical models that are supposed to predict sales and market share.

Each concept is represented as a "concept formulation." Old-fashioned brand bureaucracies still use "stripped" concept statements that are similar to the positioning statements one reads about in marketing textbooks: factual, non-emotive, written descriptions of rational benefits, physical performance, and reasons to believe. For instance, "A new suntan lotion that blocks out the sun's damaging rays while keeping your skin healthy with protective anti-oxidants such as Vitamin E and Zinc." Modern brand bureaucrats have come to terms with the fact that such rational concept statements are too far removed from the offering's eventual presentation in the marketplace, through the likes of product design, advertising, packaging, and in-store display, to predict how consumers will respond. These more sophisticated brand bureaucrats seek to inject emotional content into the concept, what we will term *emotioneering* below. The process for developing these more "emotive" concept statements has become an art unto itself at many large companies—the brand bureaucrat's version of the creative act. Here, otherwise scientifically oriented marketers flex their artistic muscles to imbue their offering with emotionally persuasive claims. For instance, "A new energy drink boosted with even more anti-oxidants, to help you get more out of life. Whether at work or at play, with a crowd or going solo, it refreshes in a way that will help you see more, do more, and experience more." Some brand bureaucrats prefer to try their hand at making mock advertisements, while others prefer to construct "mood boards"—collages constructed from stock photos or clippings from other companies' print advertisements. Despite these dedicated efforts, the concepts fail to escape the weaknesses of mindshare marketing—they are full of vague generic phrases that could mean just about anything, and certainly do not point the way to an innovation.

The lack of innovative content is not a problem, though, for in the brand bureaucracy the quality of the concept is far less important than the rigor of the process used to test it. Concept testing has become a goldmine for research firms, which have created ever more sciency systems of measurement, metering, and statistical mapping. For example, Kelton Research has developed what it calls "dial testing": a technique that

validates the effectiveness of your communications with our Instant-Response dial technology... These handheld dials enable participants to provide instantaneous and constant feedback on the information presented to them, providing us with an exact gauge of each respondent's reaction, in real time, to the words and phrases they see and hear.[8]

Other brand bureaucracies are turning to "biometric feedback research," which involves hooking consumers up to biometric sensors in what one firm describes as a comfortable, unobtrusive garment that detects and integrates key biomeasures that form the basis of human emotions: respiration, motion, heart rate and skin conductance. In conjunction, state-of-the-art eye-tracking technology precisely identifies where a person is looking during any time/response period. These biomeasures are time-locked to the media stimulus and analyzed using [our] proprietary analysis and report generating software that aggregates the biometric data into easy to interpret reports of emotional engagement.[9]

As of 2009, at least ninety market-research firms in the USA offered biometric response services.

These measurement systems yield graphs and statistical maps that encourage brand bureaucrats to remove lower-scoring benefit phrases from one concept statement, and replace them with higher-scoring phrases from other concept statements. This process is called *concept optimization*. One large market research firm describes concept optimization in sciency terms as "the opportunity to remove a part of the stimulus that is undesirable and replace it with something more advantageous. The client then has a chance to maximize market share, response rate, and or attention span, which ultimately turn into profit."[10] Following this logic, a brand bureaucrat might observe that the words "confidence to be your shiny best" scored well in one concept test, and the words "deep cleansing" scored well in another, and so create a new, optimized, concept that reads, "deep cleansing that gives you confidence to be your shiny best." Of course, by this same logic, one might extract *Mona Lisa*'s smile and place it in Munch's *The Scream*. Still, few brand bureaucracies would approve an innovation concept that has not been optimized.

For the next stage of concept testing, the brand bureaucracy has come up with an equally sciency term: "volumetric" testing. In this stage, brand bureaucrats use concept formulations, now optimized, to forecast the sales and profitability of their innovations with complex statistical methods. Although some brand bureaucrats create their own forecasting systems, most outsource these expensive services from research firms such as Nielsen's BASES. The number crunchers at these firms input concept scores into sophisticated algorithms, which are intended to estimate trial and repeat purchase. But these highly sophisticated statistical techniques cannot possibly yield useful results because they rely on flawed inputs: abstract adjectives and clichéd stock images that have often been mechanically mixed through optimization. But such is the allure of these ultra-sciency procedures that brand bureaucracies often launch new brands entirely based upon volumetric test results.

Command-and-Control Management

The operational imperatives of bureaucracy reinforce this highly reductionist approach to innovation strategy. Managers value concepts that are easy to understand, apply, and measure. For the revolving door of managers who oversee the development of a new concept, a good concept is one that is easy to grasp and plays well to top management, which has no time to explore more complicated concepts. Hence, the contextual nuance and details required for cultural innovation must be expunged from strategy documents. The bureaucratic demand for simplicity and control seals the innovation's fate.

A brand bureaucracy is a demanding corporate environment: reports are constantly due, meetings and presentations fill the calendar. Managers are required constantly to implement: to meet retailers and suppliers, to perk up the sales force at a regional meeting, to submit the promotion analysis to senior management, to make sure labels get printed. Brand bureaucrats have expansive responsibilities and they switch assignments regularly. They are encouraged to build generalist management competencies to manage large businesses within complex organizations, and with myriad partners throughout the value chain. Getting the major marketing tasks done on time and on budget leads to promotions. They have no time and no incentive to get their hands dirty in the contextual complexities of their marketplaces. While these generalist decision-making skills can be very useful for other kinds of marketing decisions, when it comes to managing cultural innovations, just the opposite is true.

Until we developed this analysis, we were routinely frustrated by the superficial stereotypes that count as state-of-the-art consumer insights and brand strategies in many blue-chip consumer marketing companies. But, within the logic of the brand bureaucracy, viewing the market in highly reductionist generalizations is entirely sensible. In fact, given work constraints, there is no other option. It is no wonder that brand bureaucracies are thrilled by "neural marketing"—plugging consumers into MRIs to see what sort of branding lights up the right corridors of their cerebral cortex. Such standardized technology neatly avoids all the messy cultural detail to provide easy-to-grasp blueprints for managers.

Unfortunately, squeezing out culture in order to produce digestible presentation bites cannot possibly produce a cultural innovation. These distilled abstractions are far too vague, blunt, and abstract. Instead, the command-and-control process tends to produce me-too trend-chasing ideas, even clichés.

Trying to Inject Culture back into the Innovation

Brands are inherently cultural expressions. In the end, even if the concept consists entirely of abstract phrases, the actual market offering must make use of concrete cultural content in the formulation of the marketing-mix details: the product design, service encounter, packaging, retail environment, and communications. So, when it comes to the actual design of the new or restaged brand, cultural content must be "injected" back in. However, because such messy content has been systematically excluded from the insights and strategy stages, when cultural content is finally added back in, it happens without any sort of strategic guidance, governed instead by an odd combination of sciency procedures and reliance on stereotypes.

The Innovation Assembly Line

Brand bureaucracies organize innovation as an *assembly line*. In pursuit of efficiency, the brand bureaucracy compartmentalizes research, concept, and design. Once the concept is fixed in a brand bible of some sort, the brand bureaucracy uses it as a blueprint to control the design phase. The concept is treated as a fixed set of rules that must be followed strictly in order to achieve success. The assumption is that creative outputs should flow out of a production line: a systematic linear process that begins with structured inputs—customer insights—that beget a blueprint for the innovation, which is then used to vet design ideas. The brand bureaucracy views design ideas as an abundant, unpredictable, even random input. So it is the power of the vetting process—using the concept blueprint to cull "on-strategy" ideas and toss out "off-strategy" ones—that in their view leads to a successful innovation.

One problem with this linear innovation assembly-line process is that it creates barriers to the iterative learning that is essential for cultural innovation. Brand bureaucracies routinely make big bets on a single direction, leaving no opportunity for feedback loops to improve the design, and no provision to shift gears when a dead end is hit.

But the biggest problem is that it privileges a culture-bereft abstraction as the definitive guide for designing the brand. Such blueprints require creative partners to produce bland expressions of generic abstractions. Any truly innovative cultural expression developed by creative partners is systematically eliminated by the innovation assembly line.

Paint-by-Numbers Literalism

Brand bureaucracies use the brand blueprint to micromanage the design of all marketing elements, usually in a very literal paint-by-numbers fashion. Their sciency understanding of these concepts leads them to demand that each brand expression reveal the concept in the most unambiguous manner. Brand expressions are always to be "aspirational" in the most stereotypic manner—younger, more beautiful, wealthier, and with plenty of charisma. Desired emotions should be on display in a way that even an inattentive child would comprehend. Managing cultural expression as if it were subject to the scientific method, brand bureaucracies break the execution into minute discrete parts and apply literalist criteria to each. The necessary result is that the humanistic aspects of the design—those aspects that forge resonance through artistry, metaphor, ambiguity, and storytelling—are discarded. The basic toolkit of figurative techniques—metaphor, trope, fantasy, imagination, tone, sensibility, satire—without which it is impossible to generate a meaningful cultural expression, is absent from the brand bureaucratic mindset. It is not surprising, then, that brand bureaucracies tend to launch brands with marketing that comes across as a didactic lecture rather than expressive culture.

HOW PAINT-BY-NUMBERS LITERALISM KILLED THE SNAPPLE CULTURAL INNOVATION

Snapple became an iconic brand in the USA in the early 1990s as the result of a brilliant cultural innovation.[11] Many non-elite Americans had become cynical about Reagan's promises of trickle-down prosperity because they observed the huge gulf between the good life enjoyed by the country's elites and their own economic struggles. Snapple had a cheap label, funny flavors, some of which tasted bad, bizarre ads that seemed to have been made for under $1,000, and promotional support from Rush Limbaugh and Howard Stern. These expressions together advanced a kitschy populist ideology that mocked the slick ways of big corporations and celebrated everyday people instead. At a time when Americans had had more than enough of powerful companies making big profits, they loved Snapple as the underdog counterpunch.

Rolling out Snapple as a national grocery brand while keeping its kitschy populist ideology intact was a huge challenge. It was done artfully by the ad agency Kirshenbaum & Bond, led by Snapple's non-traditional marketing manager Jude Hammerle. The team developed advertising featuring a large and brash woman from Long Island named Wendy, who was actually a Snapple employee charged with answering fan mail. They made Wendy "the Snapple Lady" the brand's spokesperson. The Wendy ads were cheaply produced silly documentaries featuring the stories that real customers had written in to the company. Snapple visited their homes to check out their stories or to follow up on new oddball Snapple flavors that fans had suggested. Snapple sales tripled in two years, from $232 million in 1992 to $674 million in 1994. The Quaker Oats Company acquired Snapple for $1.7 billion, intent upon doing even better.

In devising the Wendy campaign, Hammerle, an advertising creative with no formal brand management training, and the Kirshenaum & Bond team had violated every rule of the brand bureaucracy: no brand onions, no focus groups, no concept testing, no positioning statements, no linear assembly-line process. Rather, they worked together experimenting with ideas, and learning from their mistakes, until they had developed a sophisticated tacit knowledge on how to express Snapple's kitschy populism in advertisements, grassroots events, PR stunts, talk radio sponsorships, and new products. Thirty spots were filmed for every eight that aired. Ads were selected for their perceived cultural resonance rather than their expression of what Jude derisively referred to as "objective product benefits." In other words, they were a consummate example of the organizational structure we term *the cultural studio*, which we develop in the next two chapters.

Then the Quaker Oats brand bureaucracy took over. Before the acquisition, Quaker management had researched key executives at Snapple. They had decided early on that Hammerle did not have the proper marketing credentials. So they replaced him with a team well schooled in brand bureaucracy. Thereafter, Kirshenbaum & Bond was forced to create work that aligned with mindshare briefs and that was developed, approved, and tested according to brand bureaucratic procedures.

First, the brand bureaucracy conducted extensive consumer research. "They were very big on doing research," says one of Snapple's original marketing team who stayed on long enough to see how Quaker worked:

> I mean qualitative, quantitative, again and again. They would put the existing campaign into research, and of course pick apart the results. I mean, they did so many research studies, tracking studies, the first year I must have traveled the whole focus-group-city route nearly every week for months on end. I think they just felt they had to have research to back up every decision they made.

The research frenzy was intended to inform Quaker's primary fixation: developing a positioning statement. Quaker management found it unbelievable that Jude and his team could possibly develop effective branding without one. Quaker executives visited the agency to lecture them about what a positioning statement was, and how to write one. The agency pushed hard for the shorthand phrase they used for the Wendy's concept—"you love us, we love you back." In addition they proposed the campaign's tagline "Made from the best stuff on Earth." Quaker management agreed to test Kirshenbaum's two positioning concepts along with a variety of others generated by Quaker's brand bureaucrats.

> You can just imagine trying to test the concept, 'You love us, we love you back,' and then really trying to break it down. I remember having endless debates about this, because you can interpret the research in hundreds of different ways. I often felt like we were just like rats in a cage, spinning our wheels, because people were interpreting the research really literally. I can just remember having endless meetings and feeling as though I had been in this meeting fifty times before. The positioning statements were debated for months; we were spinning our wheels for about a year.

While spinning its wheels doing the positioning research, the brand bureaucracy worked concurrently to rationalize creative development on the existing Wendy campaign. So it devised a strategy checklist for Kirshenbaum to use to evaluate whether ideas were on strategy. These directives pushed for ads on particular features (the wide-mouth bottle) and flavors, and regional variation of letter writers. No mention was made of the brand's ideology, or the particular cultural expression of that ideology that the "100% Natural" campaign had nailed so effectively. Kirshenbaum's scripts now not only had to meet the dreaded checklist but also had to be approved all the way up a hierarchy: from the Snapple National Marketing Manager, to the Snapple Director of Marketing, to the Vice-President of Advertising for the combined Snapple and Gatorade unit, to the Vice-President of Marketing for Snapple, to the CMO for the combined Snapple and Gatorade unit, to Don Uzzi, the President of Quaker Oats Beverages, to Phil Marineau, President and Chief Operating Officer of Quaker Oats. Since these executives had no understanding of Snapple's cultural resonance, and no time to catch up, they naturally relied on the handy checklist that their junior managers had prepared for them. The result was a series of clunky Wendy spots that tried to wedge the mindshare directives into the creative work.

Quaker's extremely literal understanding of how branding works meant that it could never comprehend the success of Wendy. Management was embarrassed by the campaign, seeing only poor-quality film and a lead character who was the antithesis of an aspirational figure like Quaker's "I Like Mike (Jordan)" campaign for Gatorade. Likewise, it found many of the Snapple fans cast in the ads, as well as their homes, to be unappealing. "They didn't like a lot of the people in the ads," explains Risa Mikenberg, Kirshenbaum's key creative working on the Snapple business, "especially if they looked weird. Like, Ralph, from one of the most popular ads, had a lazy eye and a pompadour. They didn't like the houses that our people live in. The drapes. We always called them Drapes People. But the main thing was Wendy. They were, like, 'Couldn't you find somebody more attractive?' "

In one of their first meetings with Kirshenbaum, Quaker management expressed concern that the advertising was amateurish and asked the agency to produce fewer spots and spend more on them. The creative team had in fact used considerable professional expertise to give the TV spots their kitschy feel, using super16 film so that it looked grainier than standard 35mm, creating an oddly tall reception desk to dwarf Wendy, framing shots from humorously clumsy angles, using color correction techniques to make the film look substandard. Hammerle and Kirshenbaum had become masters at expressing kitschy populism with Wendy and the pseudo-documentary films of Snapple drinkers. They went to great lengths to imbue the TV spots with the verité indirection, and lo-fi charm of a cable access show. Wendy, pudgy and loud, delivered wonderfully on this ideology when viewed

(cont.)

next to an onslaught of ads with the beautiful people that brand bureaucracies worldwide deem crucial to sell product.

Quaker managers were also very concerned that the campaign was "too New York" for a drink that was sold nationally. They thought Wendy's loud Long Island accent and Borscht Belt style of humor would backfire on a nationwide basis, despite the fact that the ultimate portrayal of New York life from a Jewish point of view, Seinfeld, was the number one show on the air, appealing to Americans coast to coast. The brand bureaucrats became convinced that Snapple's communications did not reflect the brand's "average consumer."

Kirshenbaum's arguments that the oddball casting was crucial to convey the brand's ideology fell on deaf ears. Quaker wanted beautiful people in the ads. The agency finessed the issue by appointing a second more attractive character as Wendy's "assistant." But this was not enough. Quaker fired Wendy and launched an entirely new campaign based upon its new strategy. It adopted a new positioning statement, one that tested the best in the focus-group research.

Kirshenbaum resigned the Snapple account because Quaker's brand bureaucracy was so adversely affecting agency morale. So Quaker produced a series of poorly received campaigns with its roster agency, Foot Cone Belding. Snapple's sales, which had been climbing at an obscene rate, quickly turned around and tanked just as fast. After several desperate moves to salvage the business, replacing existing brand bureaucrats with new ones, Quaker was forced to unload the business for $300 million dollars—destroying $1.4 billion in brand value in three years.

Emotioneering: Reducing Cultural Expression to Feeling-Words
Cultural innovations in commerce work just like other creative products—books, films, music, and art—that break through culturally. Cultural innovations advance ideology through myth; and myth in turn is conveyed via cultural codes that stir emotions along the way. Yet, bureaucratic principles necessarily strip away all the cultural aspects of the innovation concept—the myth and the cultural codes used to bring the concept to life, the very qualities required to generate emotion—in favor of mechanized "feeling-words" that have all the evocative power of children's flash cards.

Brand bureaucracies are able to operate efficiently by treating customers as simply as possible, stripping out their history, social life, and culture. Yet marketers know that emotional connection with their consumers is critical, and they discovered long ago that most attempts at innovation fail to spark much of an emotional connection. So the brand bureaucracy has been on a decades-long vision quest to shovel emotion into the process. Terms such as "emotional branding" and "emotional benefits" have littered the branding landscape for over a decade, as brand bureaucracies have sought to "engineer" emotion into their creative work. The misbegotten solution uses sciency research to identify the emotions that need to be embedded in the product. Strategies today are incomplete without "emotional benefits"—words such as *irreverent, funny, playful, warm, spirited, sincere*—which we critique in Chapter 1. Managers demand that their partners bolt these emotions into the offering through their creative work.

HOW EMOTIONEERING GUTTED THE LEE JEANS BRAND

In the 1980s, Ronald Reagan seeded a revitalized version of the frontier myth, which would continue to flourish and grow over the next two decades to dominate the American mass media. This new mythology created a huge opportunity for brands that could credibly play off this myth. This frontier revival provided the ideological opportunity that allowed for a wide variety of successful innovations: from the Ford Explorer, Harley-Davidson, and Levi's to Budweiser, Patagonia, and Mountain Dew.[12]

Lee Jeans faced an equally promising opportunity. Since the jeans had actually been worn on the frontier (along with Levi's and Wrangler), and, so, were appropriated as a frontier symbol in the last revitalization of the frontier in the 1950s and 1960s, the brand could easily play on this cultural asset to exploit this emerging demand.

The spectacularly popular album *Born in the USA* featured a close-up of Bruce Springsteen's backside encased in a pair of beat-up Levi's, and *Rolling Stone* pictured Springsteen on its cover wearing a Lee denim vest. The images announced that the frontier myth was back and that you could sign on to it if you wore the right jeans. No longer were Lee and Levi's nostalgic brands. Lee sales soared to record levels.

But Lee's management had no interest in deciphering why Lee jeans suddenly had such cultural resonance, and so it failed to restage Lee to take advantage of this opportunity. Lee faced one of the most attractive business opportunities of the decade. Why did the company miss it? Management's faith in sciency research is to blame.

Lee conducted research that "proved" that its mindshare strategy—which positioned Lee as "the jeans brand that was comfortable because they really fit"—was exactly right. Its quantitative study ranked "comfortable" as the single most important benefit that consumers sought in an ideal brand of jeans. Of the twenty-eight benefits listed, "comfortable" scored highest, with 94 percent of respondents claiming that it was either "essential" or "important but not essential." Focus groups backed up these findings. Respondents consistently agreed that comfort was one of the most important benefits that they were looking for in jeans. Lee managers reasoned that their brand could "own" this benefit. After all, did not Lee jeans fit well when compared with the fashion brands? And had not Lee advertising built equity in this benefit after years of hammering it home?

Next, management commissioned a segmentation study, which revealed that middle-aged women were the best statistical fit with Lee's "comfort and fit" positioning. So management decided to ditch the youth target altogether in favor of older women. As a result, the company and its agency, Fallon McElligott, spent the next decade championing Lee as sensible, wholesome pants for middle-aged women.

The Fallon ads of this period were not only "on strategy," communicating over and over again the benefits of comfort and fit. They were also creative and entertaining enough to win major ad industry awards. A typical ad from the late 1980s, "Silhouette," opens with a red convertible sports car squealing round a corner. The ad cuts to a woman in undershirt, alarmed that she is not dressed yet for her date. As she tries to squeeze into her jeans, she is unsuccessful, and begins to dance around trying to pull them over her hips. When the man

(cont.)

in the sports car sees the woman's silhouette in the window, he smiles, and then raises his eyebrows to the camera. We then see the woman dancing around increasingly frantically in the room, until she finally trips, and then falls into a coat and hat stand. From the outside silhouette, the coat and hat stand looks like a man bending down to kiss her. The man from the sports car now looks disappointed, shrugs to the camera, and the flowers he is holding all instantly droop. "Trouble fitting into your jeans?" asks the voiceover, "Try Lee, the brand that fits." The ad ends with a close-up "bum shot" of the Lee logo patch, and a super that reads "The brand that fits."

But, despite the awards, Lee's market share plummeted from 20 percent to 8 percent. Lee managers had relied on mindshare marketing to reduce their brand to a set of generic cognitive associations: *attractive, comfortable, confident.* Such reduction was unavoidable; the "rigorous" quantitative testing they valued demanded simple concepts to work with. Then they used these associations as the foundation for all the research they conducted for over a decade. This sciency research blinded management to the fact that Lee's equity was based upon the perception that the brand was an authentic expression of the ideology of American frontier. Likewise, this research blinded management to the fact that Reagan's revitalization of this ideology presented Lee with an extraordinary opportunity.

By 1995, Lee managers had grown desperate for an innovation to resuscitate the brand. At the urging of a Fallon account planner, they decided to try their hand at what we term *emotioneering*. They changed the communications strategy to what they called "a more *emotional,* value-oriented positioning." The strategy shifted from "heavy on rational/light on emotional" to "heavy on emotional/light on rational." Because they viewed the old benefits as too functional, the task now was to find benefits that would be more emotional.

Lee went through an elaborate process with Fallon to identify these emotional benefits. They discovered through a series of focus groups that "looking attractive" was one of the key emotional benefits that customers wanted from their jeans. While it is hard to believe that extensive research could produce such a generic and uninspiring result, such is the nature of emotioneering. The brand bureaucracy decided to probe for "higher-order emotions," asking the focus groups *why* they wanted to look attractive, in a typical laddering exercise. The groups told them that looking attractive would help them "feel confident." So an even more abstract emotional benefit emerged:

Makes me Feel Confident
Makes me Look Attractive
Good fit

Following months of research and strategy meetings, Lee management distilled the new strategy into a one-page brief, which was further distilled into what they termed the "creative key idea":

Lee Jeans make you feel confident and look attractive.

Management also wanted to articulate Lee's "brand personality." This was necessary because "looking attractive" and "feeling confident" could more or less be claimed by any brand. The team articulated a brand personality that was supposed to be distinctive to Lee: "real," "down-to-earth," "natural, yet sensual," "sexy," "romantic," "vital," "hip," and "fun." Management then distilled this list of adjectives into a phrase that articulated the Lee brand essence:

Wholesome Sexuality

As requested, Fallon's creatives delivered on the strategy, creating beautifully executed black-and-white ads that told sexy but homespun romantic stories with Lee jeans center stage. One television ad, "Ferry Boat," opens on a sleepy mid-western ferry terminal, at the edge of a beautiful lake. The spot cuts close to a rusty Ohio license plate, and then cuts back to show a beautiful and wholesome-looking woman stepping out of an old pick-up truck. As the woman stretches suggestively, we see a close-up of her Lee jeans. We then cut to a second pick-up screeching to a stop. This time, a ruggedly handsome man jumps out of it and begins to run toward the ferry launch. The music builds as he races to make the departure. The man then leaps onto the ferry just as it is pulling away, and walks toward the woman. "Excuse me," he says shyly, "You dropped this back there." The woman is surprised to see that the man is holding out a necklace. "Where?" the woman asks. "Nebraska," the man sheepishly responds. As the boat speeds out over the lake, the film cuts artistically to the view of the black water from the back of the ferry. A super appears: "Lee. The Brand that Fits." Audiences found Fallon's campaign to be entertaining, but this cultural expression was totally at odds with the ideological opportunity to revitalize the brand's frontier ideology. As a result, Lee sales continued to stall.

This case provides a representative example of how brand bureaucracies miss even the most obvious ideological opportunities because they reduce the brand and the marketplace into psychological constructs that erase from view all historical change and cultural context. In its focus first on functional and then on emotional benefits, the brand bureaucracy's mindshare push to focus on abstract "high level insights" and "emotional truths" necessarily led to generic words and phrases that had no chance of inspiring consumers, much less directing an innovative restaging of the brand. Lee management followed brand bureaucracy directives to ignore the brand's place in history and society. So they could not possibly see the opportunity to leverage the brand's frontier heritage to offer a revised version of this myth, even though evidence was everywhere that Americans yearned for this sort of cultural expression.

Encouraging Random Creativity through Cultural Outsourcing

Because the brand bureaucracy systematically strips away culture in the early stages of the innovation process, managers are forced to allow culture to sneak back in at the end. Managers experience the design phase of innovation as particularly challenging and often frustrating because their brand bibles are inadequate filters, and so they struggle to make good decisions. They realize that, despite their attempts to micromanage all aspects of the branding, using sciency techniques wherever possible, in the end there are key aspects of the design that are out of their control.

The brand bureaucracy tells itself that all the arduous and expensive work prior to the design phase provides a crucial, if mundane, foundation for the innovation. The final step, then, requires outsourcing the addition of cultural content to virtuoso creative talent to add the final spark. This is an idea that ad agencies and design firms like to perpetuate, because it is their one source of power in what is otherwise a very unequal relationship. However, the results are perpetually mediocre. The problem is that, because the brand bureaucracy's direction is so vacuous, the outsourced creative partners routinely deliver what we call *random creativity*: design elements that are often artful and stylish and clever, but fail to deliver any sort of cultural innovation.

Brand bureaucrats insist upon micromanaging all brand expressions using the vacuous abstractions of the brief. Creative partners know well that the generic terms in the brief are useless at best, and so following the brief in literal fashion would negate any possibility of developing innovative cultural expressions. So, backstage they do their best to work around the brief—building cultural expressions based upon impromptu "strategies" that creatives are forced to concoct on the fly to give their work product some direction. The resulting ideas are necessarily a crapshoot. Lacking credible strategic direction, creatives often work to finesse their work product so that it meets the parameters of the brief while also impressing peers who will evaluate the work as artistic. This is a game that the most successful communications and design firms have mastered, one that greatly pleases brand bureaucracies. But composing random cultural material to suit a generic brief seldom delivers an innovative cultural expression.

The design elements of the brand, regardless of how seemingly "creative" (that is, impressive to other commercial artists and award shows judges), can be successful culturally only if they deliver an innovative ideology, dramatized with accurate and compelling myth and cultural codes. Because the brand bureaucracy does not understand that cultural expression should be strategic, it treats these design elements as pure creative inspiration. The result is "creativity" run amok—random creativity. Without a cultural innovation process that effectively manages cultural expression, creatives pursue expressions that they like, that they think are cool, that they hope will wow their peers. Brand bureaucracies try to rein in random creativity by instituting market-research tests. But testing random creative work is a very poor substitute for nurturing the right cultural expressions in the first place.

The Brand Bureaucracy's Iron Cage

Max Weber famously described the institutional inertia of bureaucracies as an "iron cage." Once the rationalizing force of the bureaucracy has been installed into organizational ideology and routines, it becomes highly constraining and very hard to change course. Since the 1980s, the brand bureaucracy has become an iron cage. The scientific approach to marketing is very effective for some aspects of marketing, and massively dysfunctional for others. Beyond its effectiveness as a management tool, the most prized function of the brand bureaucracy is that it allows big companies to be big and to continue to grow. Over time, as the brand bureaucracy has been enthusiastically embraced as an organizational solution for big companies, it has become an end in itself.

The brand bureaucracy has become a powerful institutional logic that permeates all aspects of the marketing enterprise. It provides the taken-for-granted assumptions that undergird everyday discussions, plans, and the arguments that win the day in big meetings. It is central to the education, hiring, training, and promotion policies of all large consumer marketing companies. Managers working in brand bureaucracies have no choice but to embrace it if they are to succeed. Like all strong institutions, the brand bureaucracy is deeply conservative, easily repelling threats. Direct challenges to the brand bureaucracy are dismissed as naive, incoherent, lacking proper rigor.

The brand bureaucracy is the "common sense" of the industry: it dominates nearly all the major consumer marketing companies, ad agencies, and research firms, along with all the top MBA programs. Decades ago, a handful of blue-chip marketers, research firms, and ad agencies created a sciency folklore: myths that "demonstrate" that the brand bureaucracy is the way to go. Once a generation of scientific marketers had been installed in the senior ranks of consumer marketing companies—who have the power to institute the procedures and structures and training that pertain to branding—the ideology of the brand bureaucracy became self-perpetuating. The brand bureaucracy has seeped into their organizational cultures: its assumptions pervade the company's planning process, on-the-job training programs, promotion requirements, and recruiting strategy.

Once the brand bureaucracy had been established as the taken-for-granted "truth," managers found it much easier to follow the social norms of the most respected marketing companies than to act as a heretic and challenge these norms. In other words, branding operates according to what organizational sociologists call *mimetic isomorphism*. Once everyone is imitating everyone else (mimesis), it is nearly impossible to break out of these shared assumptions (isomorphism).

Brand bureaucracies have been able to normalize consistently medi-ocre results because it is difficult to establish direct causal links between marketplace results and the way in which companies organize their innovation efforts. So brand bureaucracies routinely pass the blame to their creative partners. For example, in an article on Chief Marketing Officers in the trade magazine *Adweek*, Laura Klauberg, Vice-President of Marketing at Unilever, is quoted on what the article terms "the innovation gap": "She says the problem is that agencies and media partners have yet to be a consistent source of innovation. While she sees this slowly changing—'We are getting more [breakthrough ideas] than we had in the past,' she says—the company was far from satisfied."[13] Brand bureaucrats assume that they have the right innovation process. So if only their creative partners would respond to their directives, voila!

In our research, we discovered that an informal organization struc-ture that is antithetic to the brand bureaucracy—what we term *the cultural studio*—was responsible for every cultural innovation that we studied. Small companies and entrepreneurs have a natural advantage at cultural innovation because they are not embedded in the brand bureaucracy. For large companies that aspire to breakthrough market innovations, it is necessary to set the brand bureaucracy aside and organize in a very different way. In the last two chapters of Part Three, we develop how cultural studios operate.

Notes

1. Max Weber, *Economy and Society* (Berkeley, CA: University of California Press, 1978).
2. Ibid. 975.
3. Ibid. 980.
4. Ibid. 975.
5. www.newsweek.com/id/56881
6. See Nancy Koehn, *Brand New* (Boston: Harvard Business School Press, 2001).
7. This transformation is nicely chronicled in Thomas Frank, *The Conquest of Cool: Business Culture, Counterculture and the Rise of Hip Consumerism* (Chicago: University of Chicago Press, 1998). Frank is much less convincing in arguing that the creative takeover was an "end of history" done deal that has not changed since. Rather, it was a brief experimental moment that was quickly squashed by the soon-to-be hegemonic brand bureaucracy, driven by sciency marketing.

8. Kelton Reasearch Research Tools, "Communication and Advertising: Language Dial Testing," www.keltonresearch.com/research-methods/capabilities/advertising-market-research (Jan. 11, 2010).

9. Innerscope Research Website, "Our Approach: Innerscope's Biometric Monitoring System2," www.innerscoperesearch.com (Jan. 11, 2010).

10. Zogby International, "Market Research: Dial Testing / Perception Analyzing," www.zogby.com/Products/ReadProduct.cfm?ID=96 (Jan. 11, 2010), her-reports/e3ifc7db5bf2ea46d9541582b0844cddaa3

11. We analyzed Snapple's cultural innovation in more detail in Douglas B. Holt, *How Brands Become Icons: The Principles of Cultural Branding* (Boston: Harvard Business School Press, 2004).

12. We analyzed this transformation in the Mountain Dew, Budweiser, and Harley-Davidson analyses in *How Brand Become Icons.*

13. Janet Stillson, "CMOs Demand Command Performance," *Adweek.com*, Mar. 2, 2009, www.adweek.com/aw/content_display/special-reports/ot

15

The Cultural Studio Forms Underground: Levi's 501s in Europe

Levi's—the iconic jeans brand of the post-war youth counter-culture—was collapsing in Europe. By the early 1980s, the brand had lost all its cache amongst the youth. The jeans had become a commodity: they were sold at cut-rate prices at bargain-basement stores, and even so the brand was losing share each year. In the United Kingdom, Levi's had hired an ad agency that had just been launched, Bartle Bogle Hegarty (BBH). But the Levi's brand bureaucracy remained in place, and BBH readily succumbed to its structure and process. As a direct result, its first effort for Levi's consisted of a set of beautiful ads that had zero impact on the brand, failing to budge sales. At corporate headquarters in San Francisco, top management was giving serious consideration to pulling out of the European market. Instead, it decided to have one last go at radically renovating the brand.

Management sent over a troubleshooter, Bob Rockey, from the USA to take over management of the European market. Rockey was impressed by BBH and gave the agency the entire European account while instituting a radically different branding process. Gone was the brand bureaucracy. Instead, Rockey granted BBH total control over the restaging of the Levi's brand. He also decided to focus the turnaround effort on an almost-forgotten model—the 501s.

With Rockey's protection, a cultural studio emerged organically, consisting of BBH creative head John Hegarty, designer Ray Petri, director Roger Lyons, copywriter Barbara Nokes, account director Nigel Bogle, and later on director Tarsem. The cultural studio artfully appropriated some of the most provocative gender-bending ideas circulating at the time in the British art world to create a subversive and very European interpretation of Levi's American myth of youth rebellion. European youth flocked to the restaged Levi's—one of the most exciting and unique expressions of rebellion of the era.

Levi's Brand Bureaucracy Enforces a Mindshare Campaign

Levi's was one of the first new business pitches for BBH, a London agency founded in 1982 by John Bartle, an Account Planner, Nigel Bogle, an Account Director, and John Hegarty, a Creative Director. They had split off from TBWA after transforming it into one of the top British agencies. From the beginning, the team recognized that it needed to engage with Levi's heritage as an iconic brand symbolizing post-war youth rebellion. Hegarty and Bogle recalled their experiences with the brand in the 1960s when both had been obsessed with their 501s. Hegarty summoned the imagery that defined Levi's to him back then:

Jeans here arrived as Americana. The icons were James Dean and Marlon Brando. At the time, all things great and young came from America—great movies, great music, great clothes. That's where we went for our youth culture. The 501 had this moment when it was at a changing point in youth culture— when it was sort of part of the rallying cry of this enormous seismic change that was going on—with music, fashion and film.

Bogle had similar memories. He recalled ritually drying his Levi's on the rocks of a beach in southern France while he was on vacation in the 1960s. Together, he and Hegarty set about articulating what the brand had expressed as an iconic brand of the rebellious American masculinity that so appealed to British youth back in their day.

Bogle had been pouring over various mindshare research documents on the Levi's brand since the beginning of the pitch. Study after study reported that Levi's was associated with "America," "Quality," and "Original." But such studies not only missed the brand's most critical meanings— the particular characteristics of masculine rebellion and personal freedom that Levi's had embodied. They also missed the historical dynamics of Levi's symbolism. What had once been a culture-leading icon was now a nostalgic cultural has-been. So the only way to revive Levi's was somehow to revitalize its faded assets.

While Hegarty and Bogle intuitively understood that the restaging idea needed to build from the cultural space that Levi's once owned, they were less clear about how actually to do this. After all, British youth had by now rejected American culture in favor of a myriad home-grown forms of rebellion. Alone, Hegarty and Bogle did not have the cultural insights to crack this tricky problem. And, predictably, Levi's brand bureaucracy, redefining the brand's problem in a much more pedestrian and inaccurate manner, would insist that they not even try.

Trends Advice

BBH first hired a famous trends expert, who would give them misleading advice, twice over. Peter Wallis, working under the name of Peter York, was the style editor of the leading fashion magazine *Harpers and Queen*, co-author of the immensely popular *Sloan Rangers Handbook* and owner-manager of a consultancy, who billed himself as an expert on cultural trends. Wallis's opinions challenged Hegarty and Bogle's initial vision. He described how, in post-punk Britain, mass fashion trends were dead. Hegarty summarized Wallis's overview of youth culture:

Fashion was all about underground movements, was all about little brands coming along. You dressed the way you listened to music, so if you were into Dexy's Midnight Runners, you dressed in overalls, if you were a Culture Club fan, you literally might wear a dress. You had the Goths. You had the New Romantics, represented by Adam Ant. Kids were fracturing all over the place. Where before you might have had three subcultures, you now had around 55.

The idea, soon to become a cliché, that mass culture was fragmenting into such things as brand tribes, brand communities, and brand subcultures was just becoming popular marketing advice in 1982. Wallis argued that, as these diverse subcultures emerged, big brands like Levi's were paying the price for having become universally acceptable—they were now seen as "conformist." The profusion of new brands not only made Levi's seem "dated" and "unfashionable," but also made the Levi's fit seem wrong. Everybody wanted tight jeans. So, in order to be relevant at all, Wallis argued that Levi's needed to embrace one of these subcultures, even though Levi's had no credibility in any of them.

As BBH began work on the initial campaign, the Levi's brand bureaucracy kicked into gear, rejecting both Peter Wallis's subcultural recommendation and Hegarty's and Bogle's intuitions about engaging the brand's historical symbolism. Instead, in assembly-line fashion, Levi's brand managers conducted research to input into a conventional marketing brief that would drive the brand communications. Levi's management insisted on a series of strategy meetings with BBH— extending over five months—in order to hash out, in conventional marketing phrasing, the "key consumer benefit."

With brief in hand, BBH once again turned to Peter Wallis, this time to conduct focus groups to help evaluate a number of brand concepts with 16–24-year-old males, who were the brand's target. Most of the concepts directly played off the brief: they were framed in conventional marketing terms as positioning statements, emphasizing product quality, durability, and various emotional benefits. But, in addition, BBH sneaked in some of its original ideas as well. One of the test concepts, a montage of "legendary American heroes from Brando to Eastwood," nodded to Hegarty and Bogle's vision. According to Wallis's analysis, the research results confirmed his initial view that tapping into Levi's heritage would falter. His debrief stated:

- capitalizing on "the past" is problematic because the respondents' interest in different periods of youth culture was largely segmented along subcultural lines;
- capitalizing on "Americana" is problematic for a generation that grew up with punk, Nixon, and generally anti-American sentiments;
- capitalizing on "heroic icons" is problematic for a generation with no role models. ("Now, the conventional wisdom among kids is that major trends are made by their own groups and tribes, and not by rock stars.)

All Wallis's conclusions—which derived from the responses that British youth gave to conventional positioning statements—would later prove to have been exactly wrong. This kind of analysis typifies the literalism that continues to dominate conventional marketing. Yet, Levi's used Wallis's research to devise a concept based upon durability, firmly rejecting any sort of cultural approach.

For the next five months, BBH engaged in mindshare debates with Levi's management to work out the right abstract phrase to guide the creative idea. BBH continually revised the benefits terminology used to describe Levi's, in presentation after presentation, debating minor variations in these abstract adjectives and for pushing subtle shifts in emphasis between functional benefits and emotional benefits.

BBH creatives worked from the final brief, which emphasized the jeans' durability, to create visually stunning and funny ads. "Rivets" was a humorous visual documentary about the source of Levi's rivets, depicting, with fantastic visual treatments, the mining and smelting of the rivets. This spot was followed by "Stitching," which playfully suggested that one could go deep-sea fishing with the Levi's thread.

Despite its visual appeal, the campaign failed to have any impact on how youth valued Levi's; sales fell 11 percent in 1982, 2 percent in 1983, and 13 percent in 1984. Levi's Europe was hemorrhaging, yielding its share of a shrinking market to a variety of smaller, trendier brands of jeans. The Levi's team at BBH became extremely concerned. With the division losing close to $80 million per year, Levi's management was openly discussing whether it should "pull the plug."

Enter Bob Rockey

Instead, Levi's top management in San Francisco inserted Bob Rockey to see if he could rescue the company's troubled European operations. Rockey was a retail clothing veteran who since college had learned the business working his way up the ladder at Federated Department Stores. He had established a reputation at Levi's as the turn-around expert, having revived faltering youth and women's apparel lines in the USA. He was not a professional marketer and did not have an MBA, and so had learned branding in the trenches.

Following an extensive review, Rockey gave the entire EU branding assignment to the start-up agency BBH, replacing McCann-Erickson in continental Europe, because he was impressed by BBH's strategic thinking. From that date forward, Rockey made it clear to BBH that he was empowering the agency to create the strategy for Levi's that it believed had the best chance of reviving the brand. As a result, Rockey quickly established an enormous amount of trust with BBH. He did this through his actions, if not through his personality. As BBH Account Director Tim Lindsay put it: "Bob was a nice guy, but perhaps as a result of his military background, not the most warm and effusive guy. You just felt that he thought what you were doing would be great and therefore it was your responsibility to make it great."

He quickly made a number of important strategic decisions, in part based upon BBH's assertive recommendations. He moved the brand upscale, raising prices where Levi's jeans were sold on the cheap, he limited distribution to higher-quality retail accounts, and he began the rollout of Levi's retail stores. These were necessary but hardly sufficient moves to get the brand out of its commoditization spiral; youth needed once again to perceive Levi's as rebellious enough for them to seek out the brand and pay premium prices.

To lead this restaging effort, Rockey chose to focus on Levi's classic 501 jeans, which had just been restaged very successfully in America. When he asked Levi's EU managers for their thoughts on this idea, none of them gave him a convincing answer. Rockey estimated that eight out of ten managers had predicted that the restaging would not work, but without offering a rationale other than that the 501 design was very different from current fashion. The conventional market research conducted by Levi's was not going to help Rockey either:

Each country had a market research budget with which they were funding annual research. Trouble was that they were primarily trying to defend why they weren't doing as well as they should. The thing we *didn't* have was research that could help us gauge whether it was possible to make a success out of something as crazy as 501. And quite frankly, we couldn't find a way to develop compelling research that could give us an answer to that. It was such a crazy product. We asked the McCann research group and two or three other market research companies. We asked our US agency, Foote Cone Belding, to come up with a proposal. Quite frankly, nobody had a very good idea.

501s certainly must have looked rather odd in the early 1980s with their straight outseams, baggy rear, and distinctive "bunching" around the crotch. This design contrasted with the prevailing "tight" look of the day. But, BBH recognized that—if they were able to develop the right brand concept—the 501s' oddball design would be a big help. Not unlike the VW Beetle in the 1960s, the 501s' conventional "ugliness" was potentially a better product from a cultural perspective: it provided a unique design that BBH could use to push provocative new ideology into the jeans category.

Rockey also wondered if he should insist that BBH adapt the successful approach used in the USA, which played off contemporary American culture. But BBH was adamant that the Levi's brand was very different in Europe. The agency told Rockey that Levi's should try to disassociate itself from contemporary American culture, which Europeans disliked. As BBH's Tim Lindsay put it: "We found that modern America, the America of Reagan and Tom Cruise, of the middle-of-the-road music and pappy TV, had many negative aspects. The US 501 commercials expressed this modernity, and showed the product worn in a way that young European consumers poured scorn on." It was clear that the US commercials were not the way for Levi's Europe to go, but finding the right cultural idea to market the 501s proved more difficult.

Rockey's insistence that BBH should be allowed to work autonomously effectively dismantled Levi's brand bureaucracy. Levi's managers did not want Rockey to blame them for interfering if BBH failed. The organizational void created by Rockey's strong-arm tactics allowed a cultural studio to emerge organically, as BBH focused its efforts on Rockey's challenge.

First Source Material: Revamping the Myth of Post-War Youth Rebellion

In Europe, Levi's was a quintessentially American brand, representing youth counter-culture in the halcyon days of the 1950s and 1960s. So Hegarty and Bogle were correct from the start with their intuition that the restaging would need to engage these powerful historical assets.

But from the literalist perspective of Levi's brand bureaucracy (not to mention their trends researcher), this direction made no sense. After all, BBH executives had noted that British youth particularly despised American culture in the 1980s. Not only was Ronald Reagan's chest-thumping hawkishness—forcing nuclear missiles into Europe, threatening

Russia, funding "freedom fighters" in Central America—the object of many a European youth protest. Perhaps even more offputting was Reagan's return to "morals" and "decency," built around the nuclear family, which reinforced European youths' perceptions that America was a land of moralistic (and often hypocritical) prudes. So how should the branding deal with Levi's Americanness? BBH creatives quickly homed in on what seemed obvious given Hegarty's and Bogle's nostalgic memories: instead of thinking of the United States in such literal terms, they should latch onto the potent myth of post-war youth culture. Flashing back to post-war America, when the country was widely admired in Europe and when the role models for youth rebellion were at their most influential, made sense. This interest in 1950s America provided a natural point of cultural contact for Levi's, given its long-standing cultural assets.

Europeans still found much to admire in these historic figures, from James Dean and Marlon Brando to Gene Vincent, Elvis Presley, and Buddy Holly. A rockabilly renaissance was afoot, led by the Stray Cats, while George Michael of Wham! effected a clean-cut James Dean look with white t-shirt, jeans, and leather jacket. Likewise the music of the era never seemed to lose its appeal, and remakes were continually near the top of the charts in these years. So John Hegarty and his crew set about constructing scripts that relied on authentic reconstructions of youth culture in post-war America, even including original soundtracks from the day, an unusual move in 1985 but a perfect bridge to transport European youth back to the days of Dean and Brando.

Mining post-war rebel youth mythology was an obvious choice, but what to do with it? If the new Levi's 501 advertising was simply to ride the coat-tails of this nostalgic interest, the brand would be charting a conservative, even reactionary, course. Levi's would never win back the allegiance of teens as the ultimate symbol of youth rebellion.

Superficial First Iteration: Fetishizing Dressing Rituals

The initial ad concepts were straight applications of Hegarty's and Bogle's nostalgia. Hegarty noted: "People went through a tremendous amount of effort to get their jeans just right. One way to do that was to wash them with stones. I thought: I must turn that idea into an event. Hence the launderette."

Hegarty made a typical advertising move. He built the 501 creative idea as an entertaining dramatization of what marketing people like to call a "product truth." Such ideas can lead to pleasant and entertaining ads, but, lacking any sort of ideology, they cannot possibly create significant cultural value. Playing with the ritualized care with which people looked after their Levi's jeans would provide useful content for two ads in the campaign. But the breakthrough cultural idea was yet to come.

This initial concept—ritualizing the jeans in period setting with period music—offered a nostalgic throwback to the 1950s that probably would have appealed only to the baby-boomers who grew up in that era (no different from the Volkswagen Beetle relaunch of the late 1990s). The research conducted at the time revealed as much. Several creative routes were tested qualitatively, including the early incarnation of "Launderette." Hegarty recalls that none of the ideas tested particularly well. Lindsay notes: "The research had been 'ok'—it wasn't like 'wow'... people didn't get excited."

The cultural studio's breakthrough would come later, once BBH had moved forward with some of the rituals scripts and begun to work on production. The new members who then joined the cultural studio nudged the work in an entirely different direction. Instead of treating Levi's heritage in a nostalgic manner, they subjected the heritage to artistic subversion, upending the seemingly documentary reconstructions of 1950s America by injecting a provocative new gender ideology then bubbling up in London's artworld.

More Source Material: Buffalo Gang and Gender-Bending Avant-Garde Art

To produce the scripts, Hegarty collaborated with one of his acquaintances, Ray Petri, who worked from a neighboring office in Soho. Petri was a renegade stylist who had become the impresario of an underground avant-garde fashion movement in London and eventually one of the most influential designers of the 1980s. He found high fashion to be a bore. Inspired by some of the more provocative ideas churning in the avant-garde art world at the time—this was the era when photographer

Robert Mapplethorpe and others created a major stir with graphic homoerotic shots—Petri and his "gang" of collaborators developed a rogue male style drawn from the street, a direct challenge to the fashion show runways filled with haute couture. He found further inspiration in the cultural melting pot of Portobello Road in Notting Hill, then Britain's center of Caribbean culture, with dreadlocks and reggae the order of the day. Petri pioneered an aesthetic that borrowed the sensuality and street-savvy toughness of this milieu and melded it into an androgynous look. The term "Buffalo" was a Caribbean expression to describe people who are rude boys or rebels with the hard edge and tough attitude that Petri's style invoked. Buffalo's provocative stance came not only from its cele-bration of racially charged Caribbean styles, but especially from in its transgression of conventional gender codes. Petri dressed men in skirts and women in bomber jackets. One of Petri's key collaborators Judy Blame (a man) went on to become a stylist for Boy George.

BBH and Buffalo were inextricably linked through the networks of designers, photographers, directors, and such who worked both for the fashion industry and for advertising. Petri brought Buffalo's ideas of a new gender-bending rebel masculinity into the cultural studio, as he collaborated with Hegarty and his team. But it was Hegarty's choice of director, the next new member of the studio, who had the most influence on injecting Buffalo's gender radicalism into Levi's nostalgia.

Cultural Strategy: Provoking Gender Codes by Objectifying the Male Body

Hegarty and Nokes brought in Roger Lyons to direct three of the launch ads when the spots were still germinal, in rough sketch form. Lyons quickly became a key innovator in the cultural studio. In their initial meetings, BBH gave Lyons an unusual amount of time to think through his treatment. He went to the meetings with BBH armed with old movies, reference books, and research. Much of their work involved a straightfor-ward search for the most authentic cultural codes to convey the European mythology of 1950s American youth culture: casting, hairstyles, wardrobe (down to the use of boxers in "Launderette"), and the set.

But the key innovation evolved from Lyons's discussions with Hegarty on how to portray the male lead who would be stripping off his clothes in the "Launderette" spot. They came to envision the ad as a kind of male striptease. The model and singer Nick Kamen was to be filmed as a male sex symbol. His body would be displayed in a voyeuristic fashion, provocatively undressing for an unflinching camera, in a way that had previously been reserved for women. Under Hegarty's and Lyons's direction, the camera would linger sensuously on close-ups of Kamen's belt unbuckling, his boxer shorts, his rippled stomach. The direction incorporated cuts to admiring glances of female onlookers, which would make the voyeuristic nature of the story impossible to ignore. The complete lack of dialogue would force the audience to focus exclusively on Kamen's body.

By the 1980s, the conventional rebel posturing of the 1950s—the macho dangerous bad boy who could get any girl he wanted— had long become a mass-marketed cliché. Young men who had grown up with these icons were now sedate family men, so the rebellious connotations of the Deans and Brandos had long since evaporated. The only way to reclaim them would be to subvert the 1950s ideal. With Lyons's prodding, the BBH cultural studio created a radical inversion of the 1950s male rebel. While all the cues were period authentic—from the dress and hairstyle to the music and props—our rebel hero's presentation of the self was anything but. James Dean surveyed women from a distance; he did not strip for them.[1]

Kamen's striptease was a disturbing provocation that challenged adult middle-class European gender mores. Messing with age-old gender norms by inverting a cultural code previously reserved for women was startlingly risqué. Such a heated and seemingly heterosexual interlude, with Kamen performing a striptease for his female voyeurs, would have been interpreted as gay, until this ad was broadcast. It was not until the early 1990s that Calvin Klein ads would mainstream this sort of display of the male body. So this "objectification" of Kamen's body offered up an innovative ideology of youth rebellion.

The spots were all the more provocative—and very funny besides— because they were set in 1950s America, where prudery was thought to run rampant. That the ads obliquely made fun of American culture while at the same time acknowledging its cultural power made the campaign particularly intriguing for European youth.

Initial Results

The 501s campaign rolled out on Boxing Day 1985. The impact of the cultural innovation was so rapid and powerful that the commercials had to be taken off the air because Levi's garment manufacturing plants were unable to keep pace with the unprecedented demand. Levi's 501 sales in 1986 grew 600 percent, and in 1987 rose another 1,000 percent. The campaign had single-handedly catapulted the jeans brand back to its former leadership position as a potent symbol of youth rebellion, becoming the decade's must-have jean.

Rockey aggressively raised prices, delisted the non-core lines, and cut distribution points in 1986, causing total volume to fall by 11 percent while profits soared. By 1987, on the back of the 501 restaging, sales had also recovered, increasing by 13 percent versus 1985 at the much higher price point. So profits—the team's primary goal—skyrocketed. As late as 1984 the head buyer for one of Levi's major retail customers insisted that no one would ever willingly pay £20 for a pair of jeans in the UK. Levi's 501s were relaunched at a target retail price between £27 and £30. So Levi's average price for the entire line increased 18 percent in 1986 and another 13 percent in 1987, increases that dropped directly to the bottom line. Bob Rockey recounted proudly the striking economic impact of the innovation:

We got direct and immediate results. By the end of the first year, the European Levi's business was profitable again. We turned the corner at the end of our fiscal year in 1985 and made a million dollars. By 1986 we made 85 million dollars. By 1987, we made 200 million dollars. 501 went from being almost the smallest product in terms of volume in Europe to being the largest in the second year. By the end of the second year of the campaign, we were either the number one or number two brand in every European country. International went from being a profit drain to being the largest profit contributor to the entire company.

Sustaining the Cultural Innovation

From the mid-1980s through the mid-1990s, BBH's cultural studio evolved this cultural strategy through iterative experimentation into one of the most effective rebranding efforts in European business history. But through this entire period, the cultural foundation of the innovation remained unarticulated, and resided primarily in the tacit, situated learning of the cultural studio.

BBH planners and Levi's management formally interpreted the campaign in conventional marketing terms—"brand truths" such as "authenticity" and "American heritage." So, when Levi's conventional marketers jumped in after the launch in an attempt to control the campaign's evolution, they forced it toward literal expressions of these generic concepts. Not surprisingly, these initial extensions misfired.

"Eddie Cochrane"
In 1988, BBH produced the spot "Eddie Cochrane." Like "Launderette," "Eddie Cochrane" is set in 1950s America, features a classic American music soundtrack, and is filmed in beautiful color that suggests period authenticity. Unlike "Launderette," the spot features a conventional marketing narrative that centers on the benefit of appearing attractive to members of the opposite sex. "Eddie Cochrane, how to get Eddie Cochrane," the female narrator of the ad begins, as we see a beautiful woman deciding what clothes in her wardrobe to wear. "I just put on my Levi's and sweatshirt and went down to that party," she explains, as we cut to a wild-looking 1950s New Year's party filled with handsome American rockers styled similarly to Nick Kamen in "Launderette." "I can remember how embarrassed I was," the narrator explains as we see her walking sheepishly around the party, turning heads. "But," she continues, as the spot cuts to Eddie Cochrane smiling at her, "Eddie asked me to stay!" The spot closes with a product shot and an end line that reveals that the narrator is Sharon Steeley, who went on to become Eddie Cochrane's girlfriend.

Feedback from the marketplace was poor, and the spot failed to achieve anything near the influence of BBH's first 501 ads. "Eddie Cochrane" went down in BBH lore as an extraordinary failure. So the cultural studio was allowed to regain control of the creative idea. With freedom to collaborate and make their own decisions once again, Hegarty and his cultural studio evolved the strategy in highly original directions, making provocative cultural expressions that kept the ideology vital for a full decade.

"Refrigerator Man" and "Pick-Up"
The 1988's "Refrigerator Man," set in a family-run 1950s-era roadhouse, features dropping jaws, turning heads, and raunchy music, referencing the usual stereotypes. Then the camera cuts to a close-up crotch and stomach shot of a man walking down the stairs, toward the camera, wearing only a pair of tight white underpants. He struts across the room, playing to the gaze of the proprietor's daughter, and retrieves his jeans from the refrigerator. In 1989's "Pick-up," the denim-clad hero stops for a couple whose car has broken down. He determines that they need a lift and so proceeds slowly to strip out of his jeans to the gawk of the stranded wife, and to the gaze of the camera. The hero then ties his jeans to the bumpers of the two cars and proceeds to tow the couple's car with his improvised rig. These straightforward extensions of the original cultural strategy were warmly received by Levi's new teen and young adult fans in Europe. However, the creative work was becoming formulaic, which would surely discredit the ideology of a brand that relied so heavily on avant-garde art to cultivate a new form of rebellion. So the cultural studio pushed the strategy in a new creative direction.

"The Swimmer"
In 1992, Hegarty and his creatives created a script based on the 1960s American cult film *The Swimmer*. The script was innocent enough: a man clad in jeans runs from suburban backyard to suburban backyard, swims through each pool that he finds, and then arrives at a backyard wedding, where he steals the bride-to-be away from her older fiancé. An end line reads: "The more you wash them, the better they get."

The creative team then collaborated intensively with Tarsem Singh (known professionally simply as "Tarsem"), a music video director known for his flamboyantly baroque visual style. Tarsem saw the potential for homo-eroticizing the "Swimmer" spot. Tarsem's treatment begins with an innocent scene of kids playing with a hose in a suburban backyard in a period that appears to be the early 1960s. Then the kids' jaws drop and the camera cuts to a close-up shot of the denim-clad crotch of a man walking toward the camera in slow motion, as the water sprays him suggestively. The camera follows the man's torso into the neighboring yard, where a conservatively dressed family is having a barbeque behind their suburban home. Again, all jaws drop, and this time we see a plump sausage from the barbeque placed suggestively in the foreground as the hero's denim-clad crotch again heads toward the camera. The man then slowly peels off his undershirt to reveal a perfectly sculpted torso. To the gaze of onlookers, he performs a lavish slow-motion dive into the pool, and then emerges, eyes closed, on the other side, with water dripping off his body. In the background, the neighbor wife grabs his discarded undershirt and draws it toward her chest. The spot cuts to scene after lavish scene of the man diving into backyard pools. With each dive, we see the swimmer's body from a different angle. Each time he emerges, we see water cascading off his body. When the swimmer finally seduces a woman following one of these invasive pool borrowings, he does not so much as look at her—rather he walks past her in slow motion and she mechanically follows him as the camera focuses on his muscular back.

The soundtrack choice for "Swimmer" was equally provocative. The cultural studio decided to use Dinah Washington's 1953 performance of the show tune "Mad about the Boy." The song's passionate lyrics about unrequited love for a man on the silver screen further objectifies the protagonist's body. Dinah Washington's dramatic and seductive voice repaints the entire spot with the campy sheen of a drag show. Indeed, for those in the know, Noel Coward originally wrote "Mad about the Boy" in 1932 for a Broadway revue in which a businessman confesses his unre-quited homosexual love for a male film idol. By the early 1990s, the song had become a staple of London's burgeoning drag-queen cabaret scene. "Swimmer" had such an effect on audiences in Britain that Mercury Records rereleased Washington's performance of "Mad about the Boy." The 1930s show tune became so popular that it shot to the top of the singles charts in the UK.

"Creek"

Hegarty's cultural studio kept pushing the gender code provocations further and further, which was crucial to sustain leadership as an avant-garde rebel brand. As the team came to understand that it was the gender-bending cultural codes that were driving Levi's provocative new ideology, it gained the confidence to move away entirely from post-war America, which opened the door to some of its most creative and provocative work. The 1994 "Creek" was the most homoerotic spot to date, this time setting the extreme objectification of the male body in an overtly puritanical American setting. For this spot, the cultural studio added Vaughan and Anthea, a music video director duo known for their gorgeous use of black-and-white film as well as their mastery of camp in videos. The spot is filmed in black and white and set in the 1870s. Two bonnet-clad daughters sneak away from a picnic with a stern Mennonite father and a bible-reading mother to find a seemingly naked man bathing in a creek, splashing water on himself, rubbing water over his chest, splashing it over his shoulder. The anticipation builds to the moment when the man comes out of the water. The camera zooms in twice on the man's lower abdomen. The cultural studio brought in a music composer, Peter Lawlor, to write an original soundtrack. In the editing suite, he provided a musical overlay to the lower abdomen close-ups, composing music that builds to a sonic explosion as the man finally bursts out of the water and the water cascades off his jeans. The campy soft-porn effect is as startling as it is funny. When Levi's audiences demanded to know the track, Lawlor formed a band named Stiltskin, turned the soundtrack into a single, and the single shot to number one in the UK charts.

"Taxi"

The 1995 "Taxi" spot was the first mainstream television ad to treat a transvestite as an object of desire. For "Taxi," Hegarty and his team brought into the cultural studio Baillie Walsh, a director who was adept at capturing gritty street settings in his music videos, and was at the time filming a documentary about Consuella, a transvestite prostitute with AIDS. "Taxi" features a checker cab zipping around a seedy 1970s-era New York of street prostitutes and hustlers. We first see our heroine from the rear, trying to hail the cab, wearing high heels, tight jeans, and a short silk halter-top that leaves most of her mid-section exposed. The camera cuts close to her rear end as she gets into the cab. As she sits down, she bats her eyelashes at the driver, and the driver leers back at her, smacking his lips. As the driver watches in the mirror, she puts on a show, slowly caressing her breast, licking her lips as she removes her make-up, and provocatively puckering for the driver. The driver thinks that all is going swimmingly until our heroine pulls out an electric razor to shave the stubble on her chin. The driver realizes what is going on at the same time as the viewer: he has been erotically enticed by a cross-dressing man. The spot ends with a beauty shot of our heroine's sexy behind as she gets out of the taxi and walks through the steam of the New York City sewers. Again, the spot's soundtrack, in this case Freakpower's "Turn on, Tune in, Cop out," immediately shot to the top of the UK charts.

For as long as the cultural studio continued provocatively to reinvent the cultural codes that conveyed Levi's ideology of messing with society's gender norms, sales continued their annual double-digit climb.

What is a Cultural Studio?

The restaging of Levi's in Europe is a great example of how cultural studios form as a kind of corporate underground—a skunkworks operating in the midst of a company dominated by the brand bureaucracy. While underground cultural studios tend to last only a few years, because they are dismantled by the brand bureaucracy when a crisis passes or when a renegade manager moves on, they can have a very powerful impact on innovation during their life span. The Levi's cultural studio is by far the longest-lasting underground we studied. Three key organizational features distinguish cultural studios from brand bureaucracies.

Brand Community of Practice Accelerates Cultural Learning

BBH's great success was due to a unique organizational configuration that unleashed the cultural skills of the assembled team. The same BBH team had worked on the Levi's account for several years before and had failed to make any progress. With Bob Rockey's support, the participants were able to work in a very different mode. John Hegarty brought in the right collaborators to iterate quickly through a wide range of ideas. He assembled participants with a range of expertise in the cultural space of interest and organized them so that they could quickly and efficiently discover the most provocative new ideology and bring it to life with the right myth and cultural codes.

The cultural studio is a cultural variant of a distinctive organizational form—a *community of practice*—widely recognized by management experts as central for other kinds of innovation. This concept originated in cognitive anthropological studies of apprenticeship,[2] which pointed to a particular kind of learning (situated) and knowledge (tacit) that emerges in groups of practitioners who are focused intensively on applying particular skills to a problem at hand. In organizations, communities of practice can emerge in situations where participants are able to work collaboratively over time on a particular issue. Communities of practice emphasize the open-ended sharing of expertise, participation that is constant and not role-bound, and an emphasis on evolving an ever-improving collective body of knowledge as the team iterates toward solutions. The community of practice concept has been applied previously to characterize effective organizational structures for producing better mousetraps. Like technological innovation, cultural innovation is also a complex, nuanced, and dynamic task, creating a very challenging knowledge and learning problem. What we call a *brand community of practice* is the optimal organizational configuration to meet this challenge. Cultural studios rely on flat collaborative teams, purposely blurring assignments based upon formal expertise and title, which naturally leads to a mode of investigation in which the members of the group push each other to advance the collective project.

The Brand Bureaucracy's Siloed Assembly Line

The *siloed assembly line* favored by brand bureaucracies, in contrast, effectively erases any chance of the rapid collaborative learning required. In brand bureaucracies, innovation efforts are organized to follow three discrete and linear stages: first research insights, then strategy formulation, and finally creative development. A specialized group with the right credentials is formally assigned "ownership" of each stage. There are market researchers who derive the insights, brand managers and planners who concoct and enforce strategies, and creatives who craft the actual design of the innovation effort. While, in theory, they make up a team, in practice, their roles are quite specialized. Each task is completed one at a time and presented as a finished product (a sub-assembly) to the next group to pick up and carry forward: research begets strategy begets design.

The siloed-assembly-line model counts on a fixed timeline: contributions to the innovation must arrive fully formed and on a schedule, easy to explicate for the remaining team members further on down the assembly line. Because the participants "downstream" have not been part of the previous process and because the insights and ideas must be represented formally, usually in the form of a Powerpoint presentation, what is passed along at each stage is necessarily a stripped-down version of the large body of tacit insights and ideas that exist within each silo. As a result, the only recommendations that travel easily between the silos are the simplest and most superficial results.

The nuanced insights and unorthodox conclusions that result from the concerted efforts of a community of practice could never survive the assembly line, because they would create bottlenecks and confusion. Assembly-line participants quickly learn that catering to stereotypes and conventional opinions is a much better career strategy than gumming up the works. The siloed assembly line simply does not allow for the speedy accumulation of tacit knowledge that is critical for cultural innovation.

Emergent Strategy through Iterative Experimentation
The work process in the Levi's cultural studio centered on iterative experimentation, trialing half-baked ideas based upon muddy and often off-track ideas, which allowed for great learning, so that over time the group zeroed in on a powerful cultural strategy. There was no formal strategy blueprint that it was required to implement. Rather, participants treated the assignment as a cultural puzzle that intensive collaboration would eventually crack.

The first idea, reconstructing American youth culture of the 1950s, would have been a bomb as a stand-alone concept. But, as an initial palette from which to reinvent youth rebellion, it proved essential. Similarly, the idea of focusing on dressing rituals was formulaic advertising that would not have kick-started the brand. However, because this creative path focused the cultural studio's efforts on the male bodies that performed these rituals, it provided the essential lead that allowed the studio to conjure up the far more powerful idea—using the sexually conservative world that Levi's inhabited in 1950s America as an ironic setting for turning contemporary gender norms upside down.

Cultural studios rely on the iterative improvements that result from collaborative improvization. The work of the studio consists in large part in playing off each other's ideas, building on them, pushing against them, refining them with new reference material. The more iterations, the better the idea.

The Brand Bureaucracy's Literal Enforcement of Static Blueprints

This meandering semi-structured process would never fly in a brand bureaucracy because it violates the axioms of sciency marketing. Brand bureaucracies devote enormous resources up front to market research that is supposed to provide rigorous scientific specification of the market opportunity and the requisite design of the innovation. Brand bureaucracies treat their innovation concept—usually a list of abstract phrases that comes out of the research process—as a static blueprint. Strategies always precede creative development and, once they have been approved by senior management, they become the crown jewels of the innovation effort, to be sustained at all costs.

Brand bureaucrats are assigned to orchestrate the innovation process, to ensure that all decisions made by otherwise unpredictable creative talent directly convey the concept. These managers regularly intervene in the design process to enforce their abstract phrases upon the many dozens of decisions that must come together to make the innovation effort successful. So, rather than nurturing a better strategy through creative exploration, brand bureaucrats see it as their mission to ensure that their first and only strategy remains immovable.

In cultural studios, strategy forms as the emergent result of a long run of design explorations. Even when the Levi's strategy seemed to be finished—as the breakthrough success of "Launderette" seemed to suggest—there were more nuances to discover. It would take the cultural studio a few more years to discover that provocative gender-bending that mocked Levi's American heritage was the strategic key to Levi's claim to a new kind of rebellion, leading to a decade-long breakthrough. In cultural studios, strategy is treated as a provisional summary of the studio's thinking, which participants assume will become obsolete and require revision as the studio develops a more sophisticated understanding through its ongoing collaboration.

Decision-Making Authority Rests with the Studio
Until 1984, Levi's European management had organized its efforts according to the logic of the brand bureaucracy. Decisions in strategy, design, creative idea, and production were all subject to command-and-control principles. Decisions flowed from practitioners to provisional approval by middle managers in different disciplines, regions, and product categories, and on to final approval from several layers of senior management. As sales and prices fell, year after year, and losses built, nobody deviated from what supervisors and senior managers expected. Researchers recommended harnessing the key benefit deemed by focus groups and quantitative tests to be the most relevant to consumers: the jeans' durability. Strategists laddered this functional benefit into various generic emotional territories. Agency creatives and directors expressed this benefit in highly artistic and emotive ways. Following the conventional marketing rule book, Levi's elaborate command-and-control organization churned out branding effort after branding effort that met the hurdles of various sciency research metrics, but failed to have any positive impact on Levi's perceived value.

Troubleshooter Bob Rockey took a different approach. He was obsessed with putting the best team in place. He spent far more time than is the norm, before assigning an ad agency to revive the brand, interacting with the team and holding conversation after conversation during which he drilled team members for their views and rationales on all sorts of challenging strategic issues. Once he had decided upon BBH, he placed his bet on the agency. He gave Hegarty and his team full responsibility to make the best work, and demanded full accountability. He asked plenty of probing questions, but he never second-guessed the team's judgment, much less micromanaged their work product to fit a mindshare blueprint.

Rocky made his decisions publicly and took full responsibility for them. Similarly he made clear to everyone at Levi's that BBH had full control over the restaging and that it would be accountable. In brand bureaucracies, roles, responsibilities, and "ownership" of a particular project are fragmented and ephemeral. So often, enough "ownership" is credited post hoc to the brand bureaucrat with the most clout; everyone working on the project realizes this and so develops a risk-averse approach.

Brand bureaucracies enforce a command-and-control process that is dominated by the "final word" of senior management, despite formal assignment of these projects to mid-level managers and their creative counterparts. As a result, the brand bureaucracy tends to produce innovation opportunities, concepts, and executions that align with the prejudices of senior managers. Since senior managers have no time to delve into the contextual details of the innovation work, this means in practice that the work is edited to favor stereotypes, conventional opinions, and platitudes, hardly the stuff of innovation.

Brand bureaucracies believe that, the more control they exert over the innovation process, the better the chance that the results will be positive. Rockey's organizational model demonstrated that just the opposite is true. By keeping the brand bureaucracy's command-and-control decision-making at bay, Rockey allowed BBH to form a cultural studio. By putting trust in the cultural studio to make all the important calls, he enabled it to flourish. And Rockey's empowering management style created a virtuous circle of effort: it engendered the trust, devotion, and hard labor of all the studio members. Once Roger Lyons and Ray Petri understood that they had unusually broad decision-making power, they put unusual amounts of effort into innovating on behalf of the Levi's brand. Rockey set the bar we find throughout our cases: senior managers who wish to join the cultural studio as practitioners need to decide if they can commit enough of their own time to immerse themselves in the team's day-to-day learning. If they cannot participate fully, then they should function, after the team has been assembled, primarily as facilitators of process or as the team's liaison with external stakeholders.

This case illustrates just how crucial organizational models are to cultural innovation. Before its reorganization, Levi's in Europe had had at its disposal all the key talent that would eventually go on to produce the cultural innovation—Hegarty, Nokes, Petri, and Lyons had all been involved in earlier Levi's efforts. Organized into a command-and-control decision-making structure, these individuals were able to contribute only to the brand's stagnation and demise. Given the power to make their own decisions as a team, they were able to develop a cultural innovation worth billions in brand value. We found these same organizational qualities across all the cases we studied. While cultural studios emerged for reasons that are often idiosyncratic, the properties of the studio itself were consistent in all of our cases.

At the big professionalized marketing companies dominated by the brand bureaucracy, cultural studios occasionally form "underground" when a well-placed manager is able to create enough autonomy within the organization for a project team to gel into a cultural studio, often taking advantage of a crisis situation within the firm that allows for unorthodox moves. These cultural studios are typically short lived, since eventually the brand bureaucracy overruns the autonomous space that has been created. In addition to Levi's, we found underground cultural studios at Britvic UK (Tango), Anhauser-Busch (Budweiser), Lee Jeans, and Volkswagen.

For smaller companies and start-ups that lack a formal MBA-driven marketing function, cultural studios can form organically "above ground," as participants iterate to the best organizational structure to pursue their innovation goals. Companies such as ESPN, Nike, Ben & Jerry's, Puma, and Snapple—all of which avoided domination by professional MBA marketing—allowed for the above-ground version of the cultural studio to form. It is to this above-ground version of the cultural studio that we now turn.

Notes

1. On the provocative new gender codes emerging in the 1980s and 1990s, see Mark Simpson, *Male Impersonators: Men Performing Masculinity* (New York: Routledge, 1994), Frank Mort, *Cultures of Consumption: Masculinities and Social Space in Late Twentieth-Century Britain* (London: Routledge, 1996); Kenneth MacKinnon, *Uneasy Pleasures: The Male as Erotic Object* (London: Cygnus Arts, 1997); and Sean Nixon, *Hard Looks: Masculinities, Spectatorship & Contemporary Consumption* (New York: St Martin's Press).

2. Jean Lave and Etienne Wenger, *Situated Learning: Legitimate Peripheral Participation* (Cambridge: Cambridge University Press, 1991). Etienne Wenger, *Communities of Practice: Learning, Meaning, and Identity* (Cambridge: Cambridge University Press, 1998).

16

The Cultural Studio Forms
above Ground: ESPN

ESPN went on air as a 24–7 sports cable channel in 1979, the first of its kind. A poorly financed seat-of-the-pants start-up, the network had to fill airtime with whatever cheap programming it could acquire, which led to hour after hour of Australian Rules football amongst other sports previously obscure to the American sports spectator. By the early 1990s, the channel had built a loyal niche audience of hardcore sports fans, but faced what we called a *cultural chasm* in earlier chapters (see, in particular, the analysis of Patagonia in Chapter 6). Casual sports fans— the fans that made up the vast majority of sports television viewership—did not care about the network's esoteric sports expertise and were not tuning in.

The channel's breakthrough began in 1992 when Keith Olbermann teamed up with Dan Patrick to take over ESPN's hour-long sports news report, *SportsCenter*. They nicknamed the program *The Big Show*. Between highlights, the two offered commentary on the world of sports that was at the same time very smart, very critical, and very funny. Often they would intertwine references to a wide range of popular culture to keep the audience on its toes. Amongst hardcore sports fans, Olbermann and Patrick became heroes, the high priests of the tribe. But beyond the coterie of enthusiasts, few sports fans knew much about ESPN. With *SportsCenter*, ESPN had an ace in the hole, but did not know how to play it to win a larger audience. The sports-spectating mass market was still habitually watching sports reporting on the big three networks (ABC, NBC, CBS) and their local station's nightly news, as they had done for several decades.

In 1995, ESPN launched a major branding effort created by Wieden + Kennedy—"This Is SportsCenter" (hereafter TISC)—which leveraged *SportsCenter* with the intent of winning over the mass-market sports audience. The campaign had an immediate and profound impact. ESPN became much more than an entertaining and informative conduit for sports. The network became the center of sport for many American men, not only the nexus of information but, even more important, the moral authority for sport. ESPN emerged in the 1990s as the epicenter of one of the biggest and most potent brand communities in the USA. (When we interviewed ESPN fans—all men—a number of them greeted us at the door proudly wearing ESPN paraphernalia, as if they were announcing to us that they were fellow members of some secret society.) ESPN became the most dominant and profitable cable channel in the country, the crown jewel of the Disney media empire, estimated to deliver 40 percent of the Disney Company's gross profit.

This cultural innovation was not the result of the collective brilliance of Wieden + Kennedy, despite the fact that Wieden was and remains one of the most able agencies in the world. Nor was it produced by a lone act of creative genius. Nor can we attribute the success to great strategic insights produced by ESPN management. Rather, as we discovered in our research, TISC was created by the collaborative work of a relatively autonomous *cultural studio* that combined a junior copywriter, an ESPN brand manager, a director, and a film editor. It was the particular structure of the cultural studio that allowed TISC to flourish. ESPN demonstrates how cultural studios can come into being "above ground" in young organizations that have not yet succumbed to the brand bureaucracy.

Initial Learning in the Embryonic Cultural Studio

ESPN's management awarded its branding assignment to Wieden + Kennedy in 1993. The move came as no surprise. Wieden's spectacularly successful "Just Do It" campaign for Nike made the agency irresistible for another sports brand. Wieden gave three of its experienced creatives—Larry Frey, Jerry Cronin, and Stacy Wahl—tactical assignments in order to explore a new voice for ESPN. For instance, Cronin created small-print ads for newspapers that connected the brand with pronouncements such as "The food at Hooters is actually pretty good," or "We will, we will rock you—Enough Already." Through these early efforts, the trio developed the idea that ESPN should speak as if it was itself a sports fan, showcasing the humor and sensibilities of its own most ardent viewers. When ESPN management requested a brand strategy from the agency, Frey and Cronin, in a couple of pages, summed up what they had learned. "It came down to two lines," says Cronin:

> ESPN isn't a large network.
> It's a huge sports fan.

Rather than treat sports as the American TV networks typically did, with reporters acting as dispassionate journalists just reporting the facts, Frey and Cronin suggested that ESPN communicate the passionate knowledge and stubborn opinions of the sports fan. ESPN management loved this idea and ran with it. Frey's and Cronin's positioning statement remained at the heart of ESPN's brand strategy a decade later. However, this supposed strategic breakthrough had little to do with the cultural innovation that propelled ESPN *SportsCenter* into an American institution. Rather, the strategic breakthroughs came later, as a cultural studio formed and pushed in a different direction through its creative explorations.

The National Hockey League Campaign

Hank Perlman joined Wieden + Kennedy as a junior copywriter in 1993, just as Wieden was taking over the ESPN account. Perlman's first task was to write spots promoting the National Hockey League (NHL) games televised on ESPN. While most Wieden creatives would have been disappointed to be assigned to a backwater project, hockey, on a backwater account, ESPN, Perlman was elated. He loved sports. The work consisted mostly of producing 15-second "tune-in" spots, teasers that ran on ESPN, which were supposed to entice viewers to tune into a particular NHL game.

Conventionally, tune-in spots would use highlights from each of the two teams' recent games, or perhaps from the last head-to-head game they had played. If the teams enjoyed a rivalry, the ad emphasized that fact. The male announcer typically shouted at the audience, hyperactively informing them that the upcoming match would be "a war," "an epic battle," "a grudge match," history-in-the-making. None of this made sense to Perlman. The bombastic promotional style was shopworn, and the truth at the heart of the cliché—that the players would battle each other—was a given and therefore unworthy of mention. Few games equaled their advance billing, he thought, and most fans knew it.

As he became involved in hockey, Perlman came to think that the players, many down-home characters from rural parts of Canada, could be an intriguing and funny point of departure for better advertising. Perlman assembled a like-minded production crew—Bryan Buckley and Frank Todaro as directors and Paul Norling as editor. Bryan and Frank were sports nuts. Norling was not, and so he brought an outsider's perspective to the group, spotting the characters and lines that worked outside the fan idiom. Producing dozens of NHL spots together, the four soon gelled into a cultural studio. With the addition of one more key partner and several important collaborators, they would go on to invent TISC.

Experimenting with Cultural Codes: Saturday Night Live in the Locker Room

Perlman's NHL idea relied on an improvised documentary style rather than scripted fictions. Perlman was a long-time fan of *Saturday Night Live*, and the *SNL* mode of improvisational comedy had a deep influence on the campaign. He particularly liked the late-night comedy show's fake documentary skits. So he chose a low-tech documentary approach, shooting on black-and-white film. He set up silly skits and convinced the hockey players to improvise around his basic concepts. He filmed the skits in the teams' training facilities, catching them during free time and coaxing from them improvisational banter to flesh out his comedic treatments. Perlman also captured the unexpected oddballs who worked at the arena: the equipment manager, the driver of the Zamboni (the machine that smooths the ice between periods), the old guy whose job it is to flash the buzzer when a goal is scored. In one of the funniest spots of the campaign, Perlman gets the

Zamboni driver to catalogue the unusual items that people throw onto the ice, showing off the Tupperware collection he had recently acquired.

The scripts were developed collaboratively. Perlman and his three comrades would get together and improvise ideas, each trying to outdo the other in telling an *SNL*-styled treatment that would be hysterical for a hockey fan. Drawing on their sensibilities as fellow sports fans, the members of the cultural studio evolved a distinctive comedic sensibility that fit the NHL perfectly. "Why don't we get Ranger player Alexi Kovalov," Perlman thought, for a New York Ranger–New York Islander game. The reason? Kovalov had just started to speak English, and Perlman had heard him on an interview and his thick accent sounded funny. So he set him up with the appropriate line dissing the rival team and filmed him as he walked out onto the ice. Kovalov looks into the camera and says with his almost impenetrable Russian accent "If there's one thing I really can't stand, it's a Long Island accent." The players quickly grew to admire Perlman's spots, because the humor captured their kind of masculinity so well: hypercompetitive, even violent, more than happy to do some damage, but caught behind the scenes they were everyday guys with cute smiles, adolescent senses of humor, and working-class values.

Perlman's concept invited fans to take a backstage look at the players and their world, to see that, behind the uniforms and media glare, hockey players were just ordinary guys. Whereas Nike played up athletic intensity and competitive tenaciousness, ESPN now took the athletes off the pedestal and offered them up as populist figures, normal guys with a playful, self-deprecating side.

Cracking the "Backstage-Pass" Myth
While ESPN management continued to believe that their sports-fan strategy was guiding the brand, the creative work of Perlman's embryonic cultural studio was taking the brand in a new direction. The NHL ads no longer configured ESPN as a sports fan, but instead turned the viewpoint inside out. No longer speaking *as* a fan, ESPN spoke *to* fans as the ultimate insider, opening the door to them, inviting them to come in. ESPN was now the trusted confidant and fellow traveler of the world's most admired athletes, completely at home in the world behind the games, the world inaccessible to sports fans. In the ads, ESPN gave fans a backstage pass

to the real world of professional athletes, providing them with a portal, up-close-and-personal, to the athletes' idiosyncrasies. The cultural studio imagined athletic life as a "working guy's world," where playful, adolescent humor is the obverse side of physical domination. This myth would prove critical in the development of TISC.

To make "This is SportsCenter," Perlman's cultural studio made full use of the cultural expression insights gleaned from the NHL campaign—the backstage-pass glimpse of athletes as everyday people and the improvisational *SNL* documentary-styled satires. Nonetheless, TISC still required several additional innovations. After all, the NHL campaign, while a very effective vehicle for promoting the NHL, did little branding work for ESPN. The ads heroized the athletes while relegating ESPN to the role of a conduit through which fans could access sport. The athletes were still the stars.

Alan Broce Cements the Cultural Studio
ESPN hired a new Advertising Manager, Alan Broce, to oversee Wieden's work. Broce joined from PepsiCo, where he had been a brand manager for four years. Before that, he had been an ad agency account executive. Despite his pedigree, Broce was the antithesis of a brand bureaucrat, which is one reason why he left PepsiCo for a start-up. A Duke alumnus, Broce was a hardcore sports fan and ESPN was his favorite sports channel. Thanks perhaps to his dissatisfaction with PepsiCo and his earlier agency experience, Broce did not set up a conventional client–agency relationship. He immediately took to forging direct relationships with Wieden creatives rather than working through the usual brand bureaucracy channels. Noting that his favorite ESPN advertising was the NHL work produced by Perlman, he quickly sought him out and began to work directly with him. In the brand bureaucracy, this is not only a breach of the delicate rules of etiquette that delineate roles and responsibilities—since it bypasses the account director and planner—but it also sets off political alarms at agencies because, without careful handholding and management, a client, when faced with the informal random comments that creatives routinely let fly, is likely to behave unpredictably. But, because Wieden + Kennedy was a much looser agency than the full-service shops that typically served brand bureaucracies, no alarms sounded.

The incipient cultural studio quickly embraced Broce. He demonstrated that he shared their understanding of ESPN and its role in sport and American culture, and happily jumped into their improvisational mode for developing ideas. With additional help from a few other collaborators, especially Rick McQuisten, Perlman's partner and art director in the first year, the team was responsible for the astounding success of TISC.

Making "This Is SportsCenter"

By 1995, ESPN's success had spawned fierce competitors: FOX Sports (FOX Sports Net) and CNN (CNN-SI) were launching ambitious efforts that mimicked ESPN's all-sports formula. While ESPN had developed a strong franchise amongst hardcore sports fans, the channel was still little known in the mass market for sports. So Bornstein and his senior staffers decided it was time to launch the network's first "off-channel" brand campaign.

ESPN had a lot to brag about. Had it decided to build the business using conventional marketing, it could easily have communicated what ESPN did best: the wide range of sports it covered, the excellent live reporting, the expertise to be found on its various highlights and talk shows. Instead, Broce argued that the campaign had to be rooted exclusively in what he considered the soul of the network—*SportsCenter*. Keith Olberman and Dan Patrick's *Big Show* had jelled into ESPN's signature program and was attracting a cult following amongst a contingent of hardcore sports nuts. Bornstein supported him, as he understood well *SportsCenter*'s connection with hardcore fans. And Broce insisted that Perlman and his cultural studio take on the branding campaign. Since Perlman's hockey ads had won him credibility at ESPN, especially with Bornstein, there was no argument. The rest of the studio—including Broce's own contributions—lurked under the radar, mostly hidden from the client's view. Hank served as the creative "author" in the minds of ESPN management.

Broce never proposed a conventional strategic brief. He did not gather a laundry list of ESPN's key benefits and associations, he did not map out ESPN's "personality," nor did he spend much time thinking about the emotions that viewers ascribed to ESPN. Instead, he empowered the cultural studio to experiment toward a creative solution that would supercharge fans' identification with *SportsCenter*. The studio's strategy process was simply an ongoing conversation, primarily between Alan and Hank, in which they refined their understanding of *SportsCenter*'s peculiar sensibilities and its seriousness of purpose toward sport.

While Wieden planners working on the account sought to direct the creative process by writing up standard marketing briefs, their documents had no influence on the process. "We never sat down with a planner," said Perlman. "We never sat down in strategy sessions. We never asked them to tell us 'what's ESPN, the brand?' " Perlman and Broce well understood the connection between ESPN and the subculture of hardcore sports nuts because they were fellow travelers who inhabited the fantastic world created by ESPN's announcers, a world in which sport was the moral center of the universe. As Broce joked, when all other channels were covering major news-making events like the invasion of Iraq, ESPN would quickly mention it and then move back to sports programming. Perlman and Broce understood *SportsCenter* as a special place where American men gathered together to commune. *SportsCenter* provided viewers with a lingua franca, a sensibility, and a world view. This general observation came easily to them as long-time fans. Because *SportsCenter* was so deeply embedded in the world of sport, the cultural studio intuitively latched on to the cultural tactic that we call *mythologizing the company*. Rather than borrow from sports subcultures as source material, as did Nike, *SportsCenter* itself would serve as the locus of the concept.

Discovering the Bristol Studio as Cultural Source Material
For the first round of ads, Perlman joined up with art director Rick McQuisten and headed out with Broce to ESPN's headquarters in Bristol, Connecticut. For four days the two hung out with Broce and watched how *SportsCenter* was made. From this immersion, Perlman knew that there was something odd but very special about the fact that ESPN was broadcast from a low-budget studio in Bristol, Connecticut:

One thing that was great is that it was kind of geeky: shot in Bristol, the announcers don't dress that well. Cool was the one thing ESPN never was. There was no cache, no coolness. We thought that was funny. Bristol is this horrible part of the earth, an industrial park of a town. These guys were good looking young guys who were willing to live in Bristol just because they wanted to work at ESPN. Part of what's cool about ESPN is how uncool it really is. How geeky it is, how nerdy it is. So we thought we should celebrate that.

Perlman also could not believe the old-school style of journalism he witnessed. "We were blown away when we went there," Perlman says. "Blown away by the way the show was produced." He had no idea how much of what he loved was the result of the ESPN staff's skills and dedication. The anchors wrote their own copy and then ad-libbed around it on air to suit the quickly changing, real-time sports world. Perlman loved this working man's approach to sportcasting. The cultural studio also discussed the production values, which it considered to be extremely low budget and cheesy. It made fun of the sets, the sportscasters' wardrobes, their make-up, and the way none of the amateurish surroundings seemed to affect the way the on-air personalities presented sports. "I loved that they pick out their own ties and shirts and weren't very good at it. It comes from Bristol. Its not hip, unless you were a hardcore sports fan."

Perlman started sketching spots around the elements that he found fascinating and revelatory: ads about anchors writing, about anchors doing their own make-up or selecting their own wardrobes, about overworked Production Assistants, about the chaos around selecting highlights each day on deadline. The cultural studio was looking not for "benefits" that must be sold, but for cultural source material within this subculture of hardcore sports nuts. And they found a goldmine.

Saturday Night Live *Skits Evolve into Mockumentary*
As Perlman and McQuisten brainstormed on the *SportsCenter* campaign, they pushed Perlman's original *SNL*-inspired cultural codes a step further. Considering other mass-culture references, the two soon latched onto the new "mockumentary" genre as the most viable creative platform for unfolding *SportsCenter* stories. Perlman devised a format inspired by the seminal mockumentary *Spinal Tap*, where the spot started with an ESPN announcer speaking to camera in a serious, straight voice, framing the story as "real" documentary. Then the stories would unfold into ridiculous scenarios, all performed straight, as if real. This mock documentary humor was the only creative platform

that the cultural studio ever seriously considered, and the only idea that it ever pitched to ESPN.

The first round of ads brought the audience backstage into the drab Bristol facility—fluorescent lighting, cubicle cities, dropped ceilings, monotonous office carpet—to experience everyday life at ESPN. The spots developed two themes, which we call "athletes in the house" and "sportscasters at work." The sportcasters-at-work spots played on the idiosyncratic behind-the-scenes observations that had so fascinated Perlman and McQuisten on their visit. We find Keith Olberman and Dan Patrick applying make-up in the men's bathroom, debating whether they have got the mascara right. In the athletes-in-the-house spots, the camera follows the *SportsCenter* personalities doing their jobs, wandering down the halls, in and out of their colleagues' offices, and along the way they happen to run into star athletes, who seem to be just hanging out. In one spot, Roger Clemens is in the house, helping out on the copying machine. In another, Mary Lou Retton happens by, doing backflips down the hallway. George Mikan and Gordie Howe, the ancient basketball and hockey greats, seem to be taking retirement in Bristol. Jason Kidd delivers the day's highlights via helicopter. Most absurdly, the Syracuse University "Noodge" mascot—a large orange with legs—is presented as a Bristol fixture. (In later rounds, the Florida Marlin appears, another notoriously odd mascot with its stiff body and ominous beak.)

The first spots, such as the Clemens and Kidd ads, showed athletes contributing to the work done at ESPN. But the cultural studio soon discovered that it was a much more powerful idea—because it was even more absurd—to suggest that athletes simply hung out at the trashy Bristol digs because *SportsCenter* was so thoroughly knitted into their lives. In the most popular of these ads, Dan Patrick wanders into the office lobby speaking to the camera about how ESPN works, when he happens to run into Pistons superstar Grant Hill. Hill is sitting behind a grand piano, tinkling the ivories in lounge-lizard fashion. Patrick stuffs a dollar into the tip jar as he passes by.

The ads did not shine the spotlight on famous athletes and try to ride the coat-tails of their popularity, as most sports brands did. Just the reverse. They featured athletes who hung around *SportsCenter* in their free time simply because it is the epicenter of sport. Cultural innovation works through various tropes. This is a classic example of hyperbole: by wildly exaggerating the importance of *SportsCenter* in a humorous way, the campaign leaves the audience to ponder that a somewhat less exaggerated version—that *SportsCenter* really does occupy a special, even sacred, place at the center of sport—is quite plausible.

Selling in the Campaign

The cultural studio's innovative concept would have been for naught without senior management's willingness to grant the studio the freedom to take the work to market with little interference. In most cases, even when cultural studios form effectively on the ground, they are quickly squashed by the brand bureaucracy, or even by the agency's senior management, who act pre-emptively as surrogate voices for the client's prerogatives. Selling cultural innovation to senior management requires a delicate dance: they necessarily lack the nuanced tacit knowledge that has evolved within the cultural studio, but, yet, they are ultimately accountable for its performance. As well, senior managers often want to put their mark on the work. So the norm is for senior management to meddle in, and even reject, the output of the cultural studio. In the case of ESPN, serendipitous circumstances allowed Perlman's studio to secure a safe passage for its work.

When the spots were finally finished, Perlman, McQuiston, and Broce showed the entire reel of twenty-seven spots to the senior creatives at Wieden. The reception was not unkind. People in the room laughed, but did not seem to love the spots nearly as much as their creators did. Only the creatives who were hardcore sports fans and ESPN aficionados thought the spots really funny. Perlman recalls that Jim Riswold, the brilliant creative and sports nut who had led development of the Nike "Just Do It" campaign, laughed the loudest. Perlman's creative director Larry Frey liked the ads but was concerned that only a minority dealt effectively with what he considered to be *SportsCenter*'s most important benefits. Dan Wieden echoed Frey's concern. But, since Perlman's studio already had the clients' blessing, and since Broce was deeply involved, Frey and Wieden were fine with allowing the reel to be presented to ESPN's senior management. Broce recounted the reception at ESPN: "We showed them to Bornstein and other assembled brass. The response in the room was significantly worse than at Wieden. After they talked politely about the ads for awhile, Bornstein said he thought the spots were funny and edgy but then asked 'Are you sure you want to replace the *SportsCenter Fantasy* campaign with this?' My heart sank." "There was a lot of nervousness," recalled Broce. Not only were they apprehensive about the creative idea. Management was also concerned that the campaign would make stars out of the announcers and put them in an unfavorable negotiating position on salaries. In the end, Bornstein green-flagged the campaign purely as a matter of trust in Broce and Perlman. After a few months on air, of course, everybody loved them and always had.

While TISC was influential out of the blocks, this cultural innovation did not reach its apex until more than a year later, after the cultural studio had learned from the launch ads and pushed the idea further. The first round of ads conveyed the cultural strategy—that *Sports-Center*'s beat-up Bristol studio, filled with geeky sports aficionados, is the spiritual center of American sport—in hysterical scripts. The ads relied mostly on the gag humor of Perlman's earlier NHL spots, but now with *SportsCenter* as the center of attention. As the campaign matured, the cultural studio discovered a crucial additional cultural code that cemented *SportsCenter* as an irresistible ideological force amongst American men.

Asserting "Pure Sport" Ideology
The cultural studio's most important advance was the discovery that TISC resonated best when the satire was directed at the moral order of sport—when *SportsCenter* used biting humor to advocate for the integrity of competitive sport, untainted by business interests, overpaid athletes, Hollywood celebrity, sports bureaucracies, or performance-enhancing drugs. In "Shoe Contracts," the cultural studio wanted to scold the exploding market for pro athletes' contracts for shoe endorsements. At the time, even relatively minor stars were earning millions of dollars per contract for agreeing to wear a company's shoes and appear in their ads. A number of these endorsers managed very brief or uneventful careers in pro leagues, shorter in some cases than the duration of their endorsement contracts. For hardcore sports fans, these marketing efforts insulted the purity of the game. So in "Shoe Contracts," Dan Patrick is courted by a shoe executive whose company makes wingtips, traditionally part of conservative business attire, to wear their shoes on air for a

handsome fee. This spoof generated a big laugh and, at the same time, established ESPN as the guardian of "pure sport."

ESPN's judgments sometimes flipped the other way, as when the league bureaucrats tried to enforce rules that were tangential to how the game was played. Perlman recalled: "Allen Iverson was getting shit from the NBA for wearing his shorts too long. We thought 'that's stupid.' So we asked: what's the equivalent at *SportsCenter*? So we made "Suit Policy," in which we had a guy going around *SportsCenter* measuring lapels and cuffs to ensure that the talent went on air with league-approved wardrobe.

One of the campaign's most successful spots was "The Kid." At the time, professional sports teams were competing in a race to the bottom, drafting high-school kids far too young to handle the rigors and competition of pro sports. Kevin Garnett had just signed a massive NBA contract before he went to college, the traditional pool from which professional players were selected. More often, the brilliant youngsters failed, and the team would announce it was cutting its losses and ending its relationship with the player, saying that, regrettably, the kid was good, but too immature to navigate the difficult world of pro sports.

This degrading of the purity of sport was perfect fodder for TISC's moral satires. So the cultural studio wrote a spot about a kid "drafted" by ESPN to be a sports anchor immediately after he has completed high school. The draftee character was selected from an unusual casting call: Buckley and Perlman showed up at Bristol High School and announced over the intercom that they were casting for an ESPN ad. They picked a youngster who displayed an astonishing knowledge of the Boston Red Sox. The cultural studio structured a skit where the youngster improvises as an over-the-top smart ass. In the spot, a regular *SportsCenter* co-anchor sits beside the adolescent on the *SportsCenter* stage. The co-anchor barely begins his commentary on Yankee pitcher Jimmie Key, when the kid blurts out, "Jimmie Key?! I could hit Jimmie Key. What is he, a hundred? Jimmie Key sucks." The anchor, who had no idea what was coming, looks stunned. The improvised spot, about a young hothead with great game knowledge but no edit function, was a hit with fans.

Another spot picked on baseball star Albert Belle, who was always getting into fights. Papers reported that he was even threatening sports reporters. His unruly behavior was another no-brainer issue for the cultural studio to riff on. The idea unfolded like the others, according to Perlman: "So Albert Belle is beating up reporters, what would *Sports-Center*'s response be? Okay, they would take self-defense classes. And, in the *SportsCenter* world, what would their self-defense classes be? Of course, they'd get the guy from Kung Fu. That's literally the way the logic would work. So let's see if we can get David Carradine." And they did, producing another hysterical ad that pulled no punches in its send-up of violent players who could not control their tempers off the field.

Perlman describes how studio members began to think about *Sports-Center*'s role in the world of sport: "When the Marlins won the World Series and then dismantled the team piece by piece, *SportsCenter* needed to comment. We made a spot. What we're really saying is that we love sports. We care about sports to the point where bullshit like that pisses us off. But we did it in a way where we made fun of it."

From a mindshare branding perspective, these communications were incomprehensible. What possible benefit could they be promoting? How could they possibly be advancing an aspirational status? What sort of brand personality was this? But, in cultural terms, they were perfect. At a time when sports fans were becoming more and more upset by the commercial takeover of sport, ESPN stood up to champion the integrity of athletics in its purest form.

The cultural studio, which had now worked together for several years, had become a well-oiled cultural innovation machine, able to craft poignant spots at will from within *SportsCenter*. Members never reflexively examined the basis of their satire, which we have analyzed in a formal manner in this chapter. Rather, they had so internalized ESPN's ideology and had become so in synch with the *SportsCenter* sensibility, that creating with these materials came naturally. Concept and execution unfolded together, in the act of collectively hammering out the ads. What the cultural studio had discovered was that *Sports-Center* was the prophetic voice of "pure sport," giving sermons on the world of sport with tongue firmly in cheek. TISC brought fans "inside" the world of sport and gave them a language and moral ammunition to feel as though they played an important role in sustaining the sports community. The ESPN cultural studio's structure and processes were diametrically opposed to the structure and processes demanded by the brand bureaucracy.

The ESPN Cultural Studio

The ESPN cultural studio violated virtually every "best practice" followed by brand bureaucracies. The distinctive aspects of the ESPN cultural studio, as an organizational form that is particularly suited for cultural innovation, are identical to the cultural studio that we discovered in researching the restaging of Levi's in Europe in the previous chapter, as well as the rest of the organizational cases that we studied.

Collaboration in a Brand Community of Practice

In the ESPN cultural studio, research, strategy, and creative ideas were purposely jumbled together to inform what the members saw, holistically, as their task: to express the brand in such a way that it would become the acknowledged leader of American sports culture. Members added value to this project however they could, which almost always involved contributing across the board to insights, strategy, and creative work in no particular order and regardless that everyone but Alan was supposed to be focused solely on creative tasks. As Perlman recounted: "It was a total collaboration. There were no boundaries. We all helped each other out. Bryan and Frank wrote a lot of the spots. I was the writer but I was involved in directing. The lines were very blurred. Alan Broce would write some of the spots; he would even direct some of them. We were all producers, writers, directors. An ideal set of circumstances; really a great way to work."

This seeming disorganization dissolved the territorial dysfunctions that stems from the formal roles and responsibilities of the brand bureaucracy. In brand bureaucracies, strategists defend their abstract phrases, insisting that creatives deliver precisely on their briefs. Researchers defend their insights as the only legitimate empirical basis from which to make inferences about consumers. And creatives insist that everyone else defers to their creative genius, disallowing ideas that come from others.

The ESPN cultural studio placed great value on the collective learnings of the group, many of them quite subtle and tacit, which cumulated as they worked together making many ads. Over the course of less than two years of intensive collaboration, the ESPN cultural studio developed a highly nuanced understanding of ESPN's ideology of pure sport, and how to create hilarious cultural expressions of this ideology in a way that captured ESPN's hammy sensibility. While participants we interviewed were able to offer partial slivers of this collective wisdom, they struggled to make explicit their tacit knowledge. Said Perlman: "It's intuitive. I never said to Allan Broce: this is the voice of ESPN. A wide variety of work got produced and some of the stuff starts to feel like ESPN and some of it doesn't. What happens over time is you begin to discriminate: 'That ad feels like us.' " As the members of the cultural studio worked together, they developed their own language for talking about *SportsCenter* and its audience, full of nuanced observations about what was distinctively "great" about the program and the best cultural codes that would allow them to dramatize this "greatness."

ESPN and Wieden managers who did not participate in the collaboration had trouble understanding what the creatives were up to, and struggled to converse with them about the ongoing creative development. The same thing happened when it came to evaluating finished work. Lacking access to the cultural studio's nuanced conversations about *SportsCenter* and its central place in the moral order of sport, others did not have the wisdom to grasp the humor's ideological sweet spot. So they had to guess from afar and hedge their bets. In so doing, Weiden creative directors lapsed into mindshare thinking, attempting to anticipate the criticisms they expected the work to receive from the client. When Perlman showed the launch ads to Larry Frey and Jerry Cronin, he recalled that they were nonplussed: "It doesn't say enough about the show. They're funny, but it doesn't tell you what the show's about. Dan Wieden said more or less the same thing." Similarly, Judy Fearing and other senior ESPN executives struggled to judge the potential effectiveness of the campaign.

Emergent Strategy through Iterative Experimentation
The studio did not derive an a priori brand strategy and then consider how to execute the strategy creatively. Instead members continually changed course because of cultural leads, crucial insights that were inferred from empathetic immersion into ESPN and its hardcore fans rather than through distilled Powerpoint presentations. The ESPN cultural studio was noteworthy for its collaborative

improvisation, in which each iteration pushed the idea forward, adding insight and nuance, and the participants became more adept as a result. All the elements of the campaign came together as a product of this iterative mode of work. The studio continually refined the cultural strategy by using the ads it was making as benchmarks to interpret weaknesses and then make real-time adjustments. Likewise, studio members immediately spotted the Bristol studio and the sportscasters' work routines as valuable cultural assets precisely because the research was conducted in the midst of strategic and creative discussions, which allowed them to "see" much better than would have been possible for researchers working independently to discover "brand truths."

This improvisational mode was applied from soup to nuts: from exploring research and cultural reference material to changing lines on the set. In the brand bureaucracy, improvisation is supposed to happen in creative development. But the iron hand applied by brand managers as they use the strategy to micromanage the creative process usually means that such exploration is a feeble and half-hearted effort. In contrast, in the ESPN cultural studio, improvisation pervaded the entire process.

Strategy was built into the iterative process rather than treated as a stand-alone static document. Perlman's studio began with provisional ideas, executed content around the ideas to experiment with cultural codes to bring the strategy to life, reflected on the work and the target's reaction to it, and then revised the strategy based upon this learning. For ESPN's cultural studio, strategic thinking was always provisional, and could always be improved upon based upon the iterative work of the group.

Decision-Making Authority Rests with the Studio

TISC succeeded because ESPN senior management never pulled rank and asserted command-and-control authority over the brand communications. Perlman acknowledges:

There weren't too many people involved. On the ESPN side, there was only one client: Alan Broce. He had Judy Fearing above him, the head of marketing. We had to take Judy through it and then hear a few comments through Alan. But ultimately she trusted Alan, and Alan trusted us. The other thing is, if we ever heard advice that we didn't believe, we ignored it. If we'd taken all of the direction we received, we would have ruined the campaign.

ESPN CEO Steve Bornstein never meddled; he never micromanaged. He made suggestions but never insisted that the cultural studio follow them. In the end, it was Bornstein's trust in the cultural studio's capabilities—both in Broce's stubbornly confident enthusiasm for the work and in Perlman's proven abilities to do great work that his on-air talent loved—that allowed TISC to thrive. This is a consistent attribute of the role of senior managers in our cases: once they have empowered a cultural studio and are convinced that the group is collaborating productively to develop interesting work, they clear out and facilitate the process rather than force the studio to work through the typical bureaucratic hurdles.

While Hank Perlman was clearly the cultural studio's leader, Allen Broce's role was crucial. Broce was unique in that, as a brand manager, he became a key member of the cultural studio, a real creative collaborator. This is rare and certainly not necessary for a cultural studio to succeed. In our other cases, brand managers rarely play such a role. What is of critical importance is the role Broce played in encouraging the cultural studio to work according to its own methods, to defend the autonomy of the cultural studio, and to assert ultimate authority to decide on the right brand content. From the beginning, he encouraged the studio to produce the content that would have the greatest cultural impact—the funniest material for which the laugh would "prove" the strategic point that *Sports-Center* was sitting at the epicenter of sport culture. Rather than serve as the enforcer micromanaging content to deliver on strategy bullet points, he joined in the collaboration to figure out more intriguing and provocative ways to deliver on the studio's overall objective.

The antithesis of the extreme fragmentation of responsibility in the brand bureaucracy, Bornstein's approach placed full responsibility for the success of the campaign on the cultural studio and then gave it lots of leeway to get the job done. Perlman paraphrases Bornstein as saying "you're on your own, you believe in this idea, make it work. You are either going to succeed or fail. We hired them to do this work, so good luck." This quotation is nearly identical to Bob Rockey's declarations to BBH in the Levi's case.

THE CULTURAL STUDIO FORMS ABOVE GROUND

Other Cultural Studio Cases

The unsung heroes uncovered by our research were the managers who kept the brand bureaucracy at bay to pursue collaborative work in a brand community of practice, and the organizers of the cultural studios who facilitated its iterative experimentation to develop a breakthrough cultural strategy. Here are some additional examples in short form.

Snapple
The Quaker Oats Company would never have paid $2.3 billion for Snapple without the brilliant work of Jude Hammerle, the former ad agency executive who was assigned by Thomas H. Lee Partners (the private equity company that had bought Snapple in 1992) to manage the brand. Hammerle worked from a cultural perspective inspiring his cultural studio collaborators at the ad agency Kirshenbaum and Bond to uncover what it was about Snapple—its ideology—that had created such unyielding affection amongst a group of core loyalists. Then he demanded intensive iterations over many months to discover the best cultural expression to convey this ideology when the brand went national. The focus was never on devising a simplistic strategy document. Rather he was interested in more subtle learning that would come only from intensive collaborative iterations that he allowed to drag on for months beyond deadline until a real cultural solution was derived.

Yet, when Quaker acquired Snapple two years later, instead of ensuring that the organizational glue that made Snapple branding work so well was sustained, Quaker's managers fired Hammerle and undid the brilliant cultural strategy that he had engineered in his cultural studio with Kirshenbaum. Quaker's brand bureaucrats went on to destroy $1.8 billion in brand value in three years, which must be some sort of record.[1]

Volkswagen
Volkswagen AG would have pulled the plug on the entire North American market, as sales plummeted below 70,000 autos in the early 1990s, had it not been for the rebellious gumption of the US Vice-President of Sales. Steve Wilhite pleaded for one last chance to revive the cultural value of

Volkswagen in the United States. He fired the agency that had created Volkswagen's breakthrough cultural innovation in the 1960s, Doyle Dane Bernbach, and at the same time he dumped the brand bureaucratic practices that had ensured for many years that DDB could never regain its edge. Wilhite created the organizational space for Lance Jensen, a junior copywriter who won the subsequent pitch for dark-horse Arnold Communications and would go on to become a very effective cultural-studio organizer. Jensen and his studio, with Wilhite as their guardian member, crafted advertising in 1994 and 1995 that was good enough to pull Volkswagen out of its death spiral. But it would take another two years of intensive collaboration and iterative experimentation to discover the breakthrough ideology, myth, and cultural codes that made "Drivers Wanted" one of the most impactful cultural innovations of the 1990s in the USA.[2]

Puma
Puma's extraordinary comeback (in the 1990s in Europe and then in the 2000s in the USA) would never have happened had it not been for the startling organizational insight of Jochen Zeitz, installed at the age of 30 as CEO of the struggling company following eight straight years of losses. Zeitz had spent a decade at Colgate-Palmolive, a quintessential brand bureaucracy, and so knew from experience that the conventional marketing model would never salvage this once great brand. So he made a radical decision. He blew up Puma's brand bureaucracy in Herzogenaurach (the town where Puma and Adidas had been formed by feuding brothers who split up the family business) and built from scratch a very different kind of organization—modeled more like a design and fashion company than an athletics-wear marketer. He moved all the key design and communication work from corporate headquarters in Germany to a new design center in an urban loft space in Boston. And he hired Antonio Bertone, a young skateboarder who had been retailing alternative music and cartoons in Boston, to seed Puma with opinion-leading urban youth. Bertone was so successful, and so impressed Zeitz, that Zeitz soon appointed him Director of Global Brand Management (and then later promoted him to Chief Marketing Officer), despite his total lack of any of the seemingly requisite MBA skills to succeed in such a position. Bertone had no

interest in command-and-control decision-making or sciency marketing. Instead he hired the most culturally savvy people he could find and
organized them into cultural studios around the sports/lifestyle spaces
in which Puma wanted to compete. Zeitz is the only professional
marketer we have encountered who had the foresight to recognize the
weaknesses of the brand bureaucracy and, so, purposely created the
organization antithesis—reinventing the entire Puma marketing organization as a cultural studio. This seemingly odd structure was the central
reason that Puma's stock price increased 8,000 percent in the fifteen
years following Zeitz's appointment.

Budweiser

Budweiser's "Whassup!" was a crucial cultural innovation that helped
to pull the brand out of an eight-year slump in the USA. The concept
started as a short film created by Charles Stone III, which his rep had
sent around to a bunch of ad agencies. Bud's ad agency, DDB in
Chicago, thought the film could be turned into a great Bud ad and
pitched the idea to Anheuser-Busch. The idea was approved, but the
brand bureaucrats at Anheuser-Busch immediately gummed up
the works. They micromanaged the cultural expression. Following the
literalist world view of mindshare marketing, they insisted that the all-
black casting would not be broadly appealing and did not reflect the
cultural diversity of its target. They forced their view upon the creatives,
despite the fact that the core premise of the cultural expression was to
celebrate the very intimate shorthand slang that Charles and his friends
(all black) had created through their tight friendship over the years.
Anheuser-Bush managers insisted on a multicultural cast that approximated American ethnic diversity: one Latino, one Asian-American, one
Caucasian, and one African-American. Luckily for Anheuser-Busch, the
auditions were so hysterically bad that DDB was able to convince them
to ditch the idea. The embarrassment momentarily allowed DDB to
assert control. It handed over authority to Stone, who created a cultural
studio with his film mates and a few DDB creatives to transform the
initial film into a series of ads.

The campaign was a smash success for the Bud brand. But the hubris
of the Anheuser-Busch brand bureaucracy soon killed it. Rather
than recognize the centrality of Stone and his team and pay them to

continue, it instead treated Stone as just another content provider. Anheuser-Busch's model was to have accountants govern production costs with a very strict hand—it was one of the most tight-fisted clients in the business. And now Stone wanted a reasonable salary instead of the paltry sum he had been paid initially. Treating creative ideas as a commodity to be governed by procurement practices, it let Stone and his team go, and demanded that DDB come up with an equally effective replacement. DDB tried, but came up only with a series of off-strategy creative ideas—such as a Sopranos rip-off—that seemed deaf to the innovative aspects of "Whassup!" as a cultural expression. Anheuser-Busch had unknowingly thrown away much of the cultural value of Bud that "Whassup!" had earned for the brand.

Notes

1. We analyze Snapple's breakthrough cultural strategy in Chapter 2 of Douglas B. Holt, *How Brands Become Icons: The Principles of Cultural Branding* (Boston: Harvard Business School Press, 2004).
2. See ibid. for a complete analysis of the Volkswagen and Budweiser cultural innovations.

ABOUT THE AUTHORS

Douglas Holt is the L'Oréal Professor of Marketing at the University of Oxford, and Co-Principal of The Cultural Strategy Group. Previously he was a professor of marketing at the Harvard Business School. He is a leading expert on brand strategy, having established cultural branding as an important new strategy tool in his best-selling book *How Brands Become Icons: The Principles of Cultural Branding*. He has developed cultural strategies for a wide range of brands, including Coca-Cola, Microsoft, Ben & Jerry's, Sprite, Jack Daniel's, MINI, MasterCard, Fat Tire beer, Qdoba, Georgia Coffee, Planet Green, and Mike's Hard Lemonade, along with a number of non-profit organizations. He holds degrees from Stanford, the University of Chicago, and Northwestern, and is the editor of the *Journal of Consumer Culture*. He has been invited to give talks at universities and management seminars worldwide, including the Global Economic Forum in Davos. He lives in Salida, Colorado.

Douglas Cameron is Co-Principal of The Cultural Strategy Group, a consulting firm that specializes in helping managers, entrepreneurs, and activists develop cultural strategies. He has developed brand strategies and campaign ideas for a wide range of clients, including Ben & Jerry's, Clearblue, Coca-Cola, Fat Tire beer, FOX Sports, Freelancers Union, Fuse Music Television, Mike's Hard Lemonade, Sprite, and Svedka vodka. He co-founded and served as Chief Strategy Officer for Amalgamated, an influential non-traditional advertising agency known for developing cultural content across multiple media platforms. He began his career at Cliff Freeman & Partners, the most lauded creative shop of its time. He entered the world of marketing inadvertently: travelling the world as a bagpiper, he was invited by

David Ogilvy to perform at his French castle. Ogilvy insisted he take up advertising. He graduated from Dartmouth College, where he received the English department's top graduating honour. He lives in Boerum Hill, Brooklyn.

You can learn more about cultural strategy at **culturalstrategygroup. com**.

INDEX

Cooper, James Fenimore, Leatherstocking
tales, 51
Coors, association with Rocky Mountains,
224–5
"core proposition", 297
Corigliano, Mary, left Fuse to run Court TV,
263
Corona, 6
Corporation, The (film), a hit within anti-
globalization circle, 272
Cosmopolitan, 210
Coulter, Ann, 1
counter-culture, against bombs, Agent Orange
and DDT, 68, 82n8
Country Music Television, bough by MTV, 245
Coward, Noel, "Mad about the Boy", 328
craft beers, 225–9
aim to develop new ideology for, 229
craft breweries, craft skills of their brewers,
227–8
craft and cultural strategy, 199
Crate and Barrel(furniture retailer), 102
Critser, Greg, *Fat Land*, 136
Crockett, Davey, 51
Cronin, Jerry, 338–9, 352
crossing the cultural chasm, 65, 82n1, 130, 201,
242
Fat Tire Beer, 221, 242
requirements, 243, 244n6
Crunch, striptease classes, 212–13
crystalline fructose, not appreciably different
from HFCS, 145
CSDs, 138–9, 145, 148–9
cultural analysis, 196
apply cultural tactics?, 198–9
cull appropriate source material, 198
identify the social disruption that can
dislodge the orthodoxy, 197–8
map the category's cultural orthodoxy,
196–7
unearth the ideological opportunity, 198
cultural capital, 90–91, 99
inculcated in childhood, 92
Starbucks appeal to, 102
cultural capital cohort, 91–4

no time to devote to creative acts, 231–2
rise of (1980s), 89, 92–3
seeking fulfillment in creativity and, 230
seeking to emulate cultural elites, 109
sophisticated cultural expressions, 225
tastes continues to develop throughout
(1990s), 104
Whole Foods Market, 108
cultural capital trickle-down, 111
Starbucks and, 102–3
cultural capital trickle-down with design
codes, 147–8
cultural chasm, 23, 65, 82n1, 115, 116–18, 129, 221
crossing requires cultural innovation, 118
defined, 24
Fat Tire beer broke through, 221, 242
Patagonia broke through, 129–30, 221
cultural codes, shorthand for consumers, 175
cultural competition
four overlapping stages, 103
spans three elements of cultural expression,
176
cultural design, 189
functional value, 190–91
social value, 190
symbolic value, 190
cultural disruption, 12, 103
cultural elites, trickle-down design codes,
150
cultural expressions, 173–4
blue oceans, 173
conventional expressions of, 183
create "functional benefits", 179–82
cultural codes, 178–9
"emotional benefits", 176
ideology: artisanal-cosmopolitanism, 176–7
ideology, myth and cultural codes, 174–6
myth: accessible sophistication, 177–8
Nike and, 19
permeate society to construct meaningful
lives, 173–4
why mindshare and mousetraps ignore,
181–3
cultural expressions consist of ideology, myth
and cultural codes, 174–6

cultural innovation: mythologizing the
Lynchburg distillery, 56–8
cultural innovation, 2, 12–14
"creative" aspect of, 189
cultural capital trickle down, 85
delivers innovative cultural expression, 173
designing, 275–8
doing, 191
five key steps, 293–4
important for social enterprise, 115
Nike, 19
organizational models crucial to, 335
organizing for, 14–15, 113–14
Vitaminwater, 138–9
cultural innovation theory, 11–13, **12**, 111,
173, **190**
cultural strategy, 196
cultural innovations repurpose source
material, 186
brand assets, 188
media myths, 186–7
subcultures, 187
cultural jujitsu
challenger uses popularity of incumbent
against itself, 245, 263
fast-food firms on Starbucks, 110
cultural leadership, sustaining an innovation
through, 103
cultural orthodoxy: coffee a middle-class
staple, 85–8
Columbian coffee as artisanal-
Cosmopolitan precursor, 88–90
cultural Orthodoxy, **184**
feats of Star Athletes, 22–3
patriarchal medicine, 207–8
cultural research, 199, **200**, 246–7
cultural strategy
different approach from conventional
strategies, 199
Freelancers Union and, 278–9
new innovative discipline, 195
social innovation and, 265
technological innovation and, 202
tool for entrepreneurs into mass market,
221

cultural strategy model
applying, 13–14, **197**, 200–1
six-stage model, 196–8
apply cultural tactics, 198–9
craft the cultural strategy, 199
cull appropriate source material, 198
identify social disruption that can
dislodge the orthodoxy, 197–8
map category's orthodoxy, 196–7
unearth the ideological opportunity, 198
cultural studio, antidote to impoverished
capability, 284
cultural studio
community of practice, 331, 336n2
decision-making authority rests with, 334–6
initial learning in the embryonic, 338–9
kind of cultural underground, 330, 336
Levi's centered on iterative
experimentation, 332
provocative new gender ideology in London
Art World, 322
responsible for cultural innovation, 312
cultural studio cases, 355
Budweiser, 357–8
Puma, 356–7
Snapple, 355
Volkswagen, 355–6
cultural studios
iterative improvements, collaborative
improvization, 333
properties consistent, 336
cultural trickle-down model, 91
Culture Club, you wore a dress, 316
culture jamming
cultural form of resistance, 252
resonant subculture, rebuttal to MTV, 254
culture jams, generated national coverage,
263
Culture studio, decision-making rests with the
studio, 353–4
"culture wars", American liberal and
conservative views, 65–6, 82n2

DDB (Buds as agency), idea to Anheuser-
Busch, 357